MW00527304

296.439 T786 1999

JAN 00

Trees, earth, and Torah CHU
: a Tu b'Shvat
1999.

COLLECTION
OF THE
EDMUND J.
AND
LOUISE W. KAHN FUND

DALLAS PUBLIC LIBRARY

Trees, Earth, *and* Torah

A Tu B'Shvat Anthology

Humanities
010901
Dallas Public Library

Trees, Earth, and Torah

and

A Tu B'Shvat Anthology

edited by
Ari Elon
Naomi Mara Hyman
Arthur Waskow

The Jewish Publication Society
Philadelphia
1999 • 5760

Copyright © 1999 by Ari Elon, Naomi Mara Hyman, and Arthur Waskow

First edition. All rights reserved.

No part of this book may be reproduced or transmitted in any form or by any means, electronic or mechanical, including photocopy, recording, or any information storage or retrieval system, except for brief passages for review in connection with a critical review, without permission in writing from the publisher:
The Jewish Publication Society
2100 Arch Street
Philadelphia, PA 19103-1399

Cover design by Book Design Studio II
Interior design and composition by Book Design Studio II

Manufactured in the United States of America on recycled paper

99 00 01 02 03 04 05 06 07 08 10 9 8 7 6 5 4 3 2 1

Papercuts by Judith Hankin
Illustration of YHWH/Tree by Jackie Olenick

Editors' Note:
With few exceptions, the articles in this anthology are as they appeared in their original. As a result, there are variations in spelling and language style from piece to piece.

Library of Congress Cataloging-in-Publication Data

Trees, earth, and Torah : a Tu b'Shvat anthology / [edited by] Ari
    Elon, Naomi Mara Hyman, Arthur Waskow. — 1st ed.
        p.   cm.
    Includes bibliographical references and index.
    ISBN 0-8276-0665-6
    1. Tu b'Shvat. 2. Human ecology—Religious aspects—Judaism.
I. Elon, Ari. II. Hyman, Naomi M. III. Waskow, Arthur Ocean, 1933–.
BM695.T9T74   1999   99-11621
296.4'39—dc21   CIP

In Memory Of
Hazzan Chaim Lev Rothstein,
Rabbi Devora Bartnoff,
and
Rabbi David Wolfe-Blank

There is hope for a tree;
If it is cut down it will renew itself;
Its shoots will not cease.
If its roots are old in the earth,
And its stump dies in the ground,
At the scent of water it will bud.
And produce branches like a sapling.
JOB 14:7–9

Contents

Contents

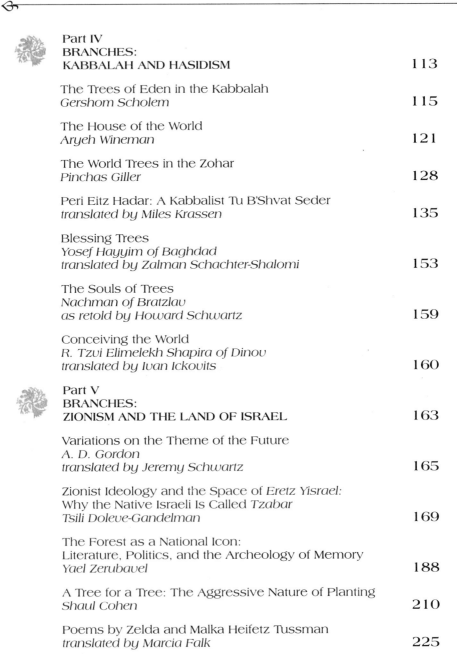

Contents

Acknowledging the Orchard Keepers

Trees, like this book, grow more fruitfully when many orchard keepers nourish them. The first and deepest of our thanks for orchard keeping must go to Ellen Frankel, our editor, who first sowed the seed that grew into this book, sowed it deep enough to withstand winters of depression and thunderstorms of obsession, and showed a forester's patience in tending to its slow and fitful growth.

Then to our spouses, friends, and teachers—Galit Elon, Bob Hyman, and Phyllis Berman—who had to weather those same seasons of our souls.

And to Rabbi Fred Dobb, whose intuition gave us the metaphor and structure for shaping the content of the book into the coherent pattern of a tree. Rabbi Dobb also undertook some extraordinary research into rabbinic and modern Jewish approaches to human-earth relationships, which will appear in another collection.

And to all those Jews who are committed to healing the relationship between *adam* and *adamah,* the earth and human earthlings, and whose example moved us to renew our commitment whenever we grew distracted. So to Judi Bari z"l, Ellen Bernstein, David Brooks, Jeffrey Dekro, Barak Gale, Rabbi Everett Gendler, Rabbi Arthur Green, De Herman, Rabbi Margaret Holub, Mark X. Jacobs, Rabbi Joanna Katz, Myriam Klotz, Rabbi Mordechai Liebling, John Ruskay, Rabbi David Saperstein, Rabbi Steve Shaw, David Shneyer, Naomi Steinberg, Rabbi Dan Swartz, Alon Tal, Mike Tabor, and Jonathan Wolf.

To our teachers: Rabbi Judith Abrams, Aryeh Ben Gurion z"l, Rabbi Abraham Joshua Heschel z"l, Rabbi Zalman Schachter-Shalomi, Esther Ticktin, Rabbi Max Ticktin, and each other.

&

To two of Ari Elon's students who undertook arduous tasks of translation from difficult Hebrew and brought into being admirable English: Joyce Galaski and Jeremy Schwartz. They, along with Toba Spitzer, Karen Landy, and Ken Hale, were members of a class at the Reconstructionist Rabbinical College that made itself into a wise and curious workshop on the meanings of Tu B'Shvat and helped work through some of the ideas that underlie this book.

Since the administrative support of ALEPH: Alliance for Jewish Renewal and The Shalom Center was crucial to the completion of this book, we owe special thanks to Susan Saxe, executive director of ALEPH during most of our work; to Miryam Levy, project director for The Shalom Center and researcher on this book itself during a crucial year; to Abigail Weinberg and Mike Gross of The Shalom Center staff; and to the Rita Poretsky Foundation, The Shefa Fund, the Alan B. Slifka Foundation, the Righteous Persons Foundation, the Gimprich Family Fund, the Nathan Cummings Foundation, Robert Schlossberg, and Viki Laura List, as well as hundreds of ALEPH members, for their support.

Finally, we owe thanks to three intertwined communities: the people of the Reconstructionist Rabbinical College; Elat Chayyim, the Jewish-renewal retreat center in the Hudson Valley near Accord, New York; and the bio-region/neighborhood of Mount Airy in Philadelphia, an extraordinary community of rivers, trees, and people from the overlapping Jewish-renewal, Reconstructionist, havurah, broadly progressive, interreligious, and eco-sensitive communities from which we draw sustenance even when we are not physically present.

Among its healers, singers, and teachers who have nourished our work were—still are—three who have died during its preparation: Hazzan Chaim Lev Rothstein, Rabbi Devora Bartnoff, and Rabbi David Wolfe-Blank. To them we have dedicated this book. May the sweetness of their songs and souls and the strength of their concern for earth and Torah fill us all with sweetness in our strength, as we sow the Jewish future among the forests of this fragile planet.

Ari Elon, Naomi Mara Hyman, and Arthur Waskow
April 30/Erev May Day, 1998
4 Iyyar 5758/Yom HaAtzma'ut LaYovel
Hod sheh b'Tiferet (Melodious Grace in
Compassionate Beauty), Day 19 in the Omer

Introduction to the Tree

More than any other Jewish festival, Tu B'Shvat is the celebration of Becoming. There is no halakhah, no legal structure, to define it. It springs wholly from the spiritual depth and growth of the Jewish people in relation with the One Who always beckons us to grow and in relation with the earth where all things grow.

For that very reason, we decided to shape this book in such a way as to reflect not only the growth and regrowth of a tree, but also the growth of a changing festival. Rabbi Fred Dobb, who assisted us by writing several major papers assessing the eco-teachings of the talmudic rabbis and twentieth-century sages, suggested that we might look at the whole process of Tu B'Shvat's development as itself a tree, rooted in biblical Judaism, carried upward in the massive trunk of the rabbinic tradition, then branching in the last 400 years into kabbalistic/hasidic Judaism, Zionism, and—most recently—what we call Eco-Judaism. (Some would say these three are not "branches" of Rabbinic Judaism, but three more slender new growths emerging like a banyan tree from where the trunk of Rabbinic Judaism has reentered the earth and rerooted itself.)

The celebration of Tu B'Shvat itself is the fruitful outcome of all this growth.

In the late Second Temple period Tu B'Shvat was part of the tithing calendar, which determined when offerings of food, including fruit, were brought to the Temple to celebrate the Source of all abundance and to recycle that abundance to the poor.

Then came centuries of rabbinic exile and estrangement from the earth. Although Tu B'Shvat as a festive day was hiding in some aspects of the Torah Tree, images and teachings of the Tree Itself flourished, and the tree-born teachings of *Bal Tashḥit,* Do Not Destroy, entwined themselves like a halakhic vine.

Then Jewish history took a new turn. Under the stimulus of various reconnections with the earth, Tu B'Shvat reemerged in astounding new shapes: in the sixteenth century, for mystics who went to live in Safed (Tzfat); in the nineteenth century, for socialists who sought to rebuild Zion; late in the twentieth century, for

Diaspora-dwellers who began trying to heal an endangered global biosphere.

From all these levels of the Jewish encounter with God and history have come the teachings and practices that we can draw upon today in celebrating Tu B'Shvat—a festival that is itself the fruit of the lovely Tree.

Finally, we see that the spirals of growth are not completed. The seeds of new possibility are present in teachers, groups, books, tapes, and other materials for further study and action that are listed in the "Seeds" section of the book.

The Editors

Trees, Earth, *and* Torah

A Tu B'Shvat Anthology

part I

The Living Tree: A Festival's Growth Through History

To describe the specific parts of the historical Tree of Tu B'Shvat—its roots in the Bible, its rabbinic trunk, and so on through branches to fruit and even to the seeds of its future—is to anatomize a tree: to describe its separate organs, severed one from another.

But a living tree has not only anatomy but also physiology. For the Tree of Tu B'Shvat, that physiology is its growth through history. What has been the life-juice, the sap, that moves through the tree, carrying new energy, calming one aspect while alerting another, moving its growth through time?

In the single essay of Part I, we address the process of the growth itself: What has brought Tu B'Shvat from its ancient roots to the seeds of its celebration in the next generation.

ROOTS IN HEAVEN
FRUITFULNESS OF US

Growing Tu B'Shvat:
The Life-Juice of the Tree of History

Arthur Waskow

Tu B'Shvat, the "New Year of the Tree," has itself grown like a tree. It has sometimes sprung to life in joyful abandon, sometimes suffered centuries of winter, and then sprung anew from what seems a barren trunk to flourish as a rich and fruitful festival, the delight of Jewish mystics and of those who love the earth.

First we may ask: What were the stages, the tree parts, of this growth? In each era, what was this day of Tu B'Shvat? What was the symbolism of trees entwined with it?

Then we ask: *How* did this happen? How did the history flow? Does the history itself hint at a flow beneath history, an unfolding of the Divine DNA from which the festival has grown? What has been the sap, the life-juice, flowing through the tree to make it grow from roots to trunk to branches, then to fruitfulness and seeds?

There have been three great periods of Tu B'Shvat:

- The Second Temple period, when the date concerned an agrarian people's earth connection through tithing of fruit;

- The long history of Rabbinic Judaism, during which the Jewish people were disconnected from any deep relationship with land, and Tu B'Shvat survived in its own wintry underground, barely observed or celebrated; and

- The period beginning in the sixteenth century with the settlement of kabbalists in the town of Tzfat (Safed), during which there have been several waves of reconnection of the Jewish people with the Land of Israel, with the earthy aspects of our planet, and with Tu B'Shvat.

The fifteenth day of the midwinter month of Shvat first explicitly appears as a special date of Jewish observance in a passage of the Mishnah. Although the Mishnah was not codified until approximately 200 C.E., after the destruction of the Temple and the shattering of the Jewish community of the Land of Israel, it purports to describe ongoing Jewish practice in the Second Temple period.

3

Says the Mishnah (Rosh Hashanah 1:1): "On the first of Shvat is the New Year for a tree, according to the words of the House of Shammai. The House of Hillel say, On its fifteenth day."

What do the Mishnah's two great schools of thought, that of Shammai and of Hillel, mean when they debate about the "new year" of a tree? They are concerned with tax law: how to divide the year for purposes of tithing.

Each year one-tenth of the increase of the earth—one-tenth of the fruit of a tree, one-tenth of the lambs of the flock, one-tenth of the new-sprouted barley—was brought to the Temple to be offered to God and given to the priests and the poor for eating. That tradition seems simple at first glance—but what is a "year"? Fruit from one year could not be used to tithe for another year.

So the Rabbis had to decide when a year begins and ends. Fruit that appeared after the "new year" day could not be used to pay the tithe for a crop of fruit that had appeared before that day, and vice versa.

The Rabbis debated. They agreed that the new year began deep in the winter, possibly half a year before the appearance of the fruit on which the tithe was to be taken. But would the first or the fifteenth of Shvat be used to distinguish the old crop of fruit from the new? Since Jewish months were lunar, the first day was the day of the new moon; the fifteenth, the day of the full moon. The decision, as it usually did, followed the teachings of the House of Hillel: the fifteenth of Shvat, the full moon of deepest, wettest winter, came to define the new year for tithing on a tree.

Before looking at the roots of this tax lawyer's argument or forward at the mystic fruit that grew from it, let us clear up the question of a name. (My life partner, Phyllis Berman, taught me this, and then with great delight I discovered that my coeditor Ari Elon shared the wisdom.) Since in Jewish practice the letters of the alphabet—really the *aleph-bet*—also stand for numerals, a date can be spelled out with letters. Since *yud* is the tenth letter, "Yud B'Shvat" is the tenth of Shvat, "Yud-Aleph B'Shvat" is the eleventh of Shvat, and so up to the fourteenth: "Yud-Dalet B'Shvat." But then a shift! For the next number would be "Yud-Heh B'Shvat," and yud-heh is also one of the names of God, pronounced "Yahh." The custom is never to speak this name except as an act of prayer.

Then what to do? The numeral 15 could also be expressed as the sum of 9 + 6. The ninth letter is *tet*, the sixth *vav*. Pronounced together, they make "Tu." So "Tu B'Shvat" became the most common name of the day when the hint of fruitfulness renews the cycle of the year.

Already we have a hint of a mystery. The Name of God is hidden and hinted at by a numerical trick. The fruitfulness of summer is hidden and hinted at by a date six months earlier, as far as possible from its full appearance: an invitation to mystics who are always searching for the Divine Presence just beneath the surface of the ordinary.

And perhaps an invitation to even bolder mystics: What would happen if we were to affirm out loud that at every full moon Yahh, the Breath of Life, is fully present? Would women who have a strong affinity with the lunar cycle feel more fully and publicly affirmed in their connection with God's Presence? Would the Messiah, hearing The Name called out and the light of the moon uplifted in its fullness, come more quickly?

These are questions for exploration on the night of Tu B'Shvat, perhaps. For now, we should note that six months from the full moon of deep winter comes Tu B'Av, the full moon of high summer. On that day in ancient Israel, women went to dance in the fields and to choose their husbands. The secret hint of fertility renewed that is at the heart of Tu B'Shvat becomes a public celebration.

Now let us go back to the tithing on fruit. Why does the Torah take such care with tithing? Let us examine a hypothesis, both historical and transhistorical.

Some time during the evolution of the Jewish people, the great agricultural revolution surged into its history. Human society became newly empowered to grow, to produce, to feed. This was not merely a sociological event: Through it, one of God's powers became more manifest in human hands.

Unshaped and unbounded, this new power could shatter the ancient, customary worlds of human practice. Given a shape of loving interconnection, however, it might grow a deeper sense of community, a broader sense of kinship, a higher sense of covenant with God.

5

For biblical Israel, then, the crucial way of bringing that aspect of God Who is the Creative Power of the universe into fruitful union with that aspect of God Who is the Loving Connection of the universe became the bringing together of the food that grew from all the different regions of the Land of Israel to a sacred center—the Holy Temple. If human beings in their relationship to earth *(adam and adamah)* suddenly had greater and more dangerous power, then the Temple offering was the context in which the love between *adam* and *adamah* must be expressed and heightened. Through these offerings, God became most constantly apparent, most fully One.

And for this people, fruit trees were a powerful, life-giving reality, like sheep and barley; so the imagery of fruit trees entered into the community's most powerful literature. For the first three years of its life, a fruit tree was in the state of *orlah,* "uncircumcision," from the same root as *arelah,* the uncircumcised foreskin of the penis. It was potentially fruitful but, out of respect for its divinely created potential, it was kept at rest for three years.

Then in the fourth year special offerings were brought to the Temple from the tree's fruit, and finally in the fifth year the regular tithe could begin and the fruit of the tree could be eaten.

Since the roots of Tu B'Shvat are in this tithing process, let us look more carefully at what tithing was.

First, who owed tithes? Landholders, orchard keepers, and nomadic owners of sheep and goats. Their slaves, servants, and employees did not, nor did their wives and children.

Why should they pay a tenth of the increase of their fields, trees, and meadows? Because they did not carry on economic enterprise in a vacuum. Part of their success came from the whole society and even beyond—from earth and rain and sunshine, from the Unity called God. So they owed part of their income to the greater reality.

Second, who was to represent their connection to God and the broader society by receiving tithes?

This was a difficult religious and political issue, and the answer, according to most modern scholars, changed during Israelite history—twice. The first change was a move from decentralized localism toward central power; the second, from top-down wealth and power toward social justice.

6

The earliest stratum of the Torah's provisions for tithing (Leviticus 27) directed that the tithe be turned over to the priests and the local shrines or, slightly later, the central shrine that had been placed at Shiloh. Tithes were used to pay for the upkeep of these religious centers and to support a loose and decentralized network of priests there, either directly as food for the priests or by selling them to buy supplies.

Then, as David consolidated the monarchy, the tithes became compulsory—a shift encoded in Numbers 18. They went to the Levites—a "national tribe" who lived in cities scattered throughout the kingdom. Scholars believe that these special cities possibly emerged or were assigned to the Levites during David's reign.

The new taxes made possible the glories of the Solomonic kingdom, with its large territory, its abundant economy, and its resplendent Temple. With these outward glories came the spiritual satisfactions of a sense of security, a sense that the God of Israel was able to protect the People of Israel, a sense that the earlier struggle and pain had been justified.

But the Bible also reports that the people began to suffer as overbearing wealth and power were channeled into erecting idols. While some felt the spiritual rewards of abundance, power, and comfort, others were feeling spiritually betrayed, as if to say: "Even the adherents of the God of Israel are acting like oppressive pharaohs!" For some, there was a spiritual crisis. Was the God of Israel the Celebrator of comfort and abundance, or the Protector of the afflicted and the desperate?

And so there emerged a wave of social and spiritual protest, spoken by those known as "the Prophets"—Amos, Hosea, Isaiah, and others. From this ferment came the writing or the public disclosure of the Book of Deuteronomy, which called for a second great change in the structure and purpose of tithing.

Deuteronomy requires that in every third year, the tithe be kept in every local settlement and used to protect the poor: the foreigner, the widow, and the orphan. Struggling to affirm the old pro-Levite rules at the same time as they transformed these rules, the authors of Deuteronomy repeated that this third-year tithe was also for the Levites but now they defined the Levites as landless and penniless, like the other poor who were to receive the tithe.

In order to strengthen this new approach to the tithe, Deuteronomy (26:12–14) requires that in every third year, after completing the tithe, each landholder declare before God:

> I have cleared out what is holy from the house, and I have given it to the Levite, the foreigner, the fatherless, and the widow, in accord with all the commands with which You commanded me. I have neither transgressed nor forgotten any of Your commandments. I have not eaten of it while in mourning, I have not cleared out any of it while I was in a taboo state, and I have not left any of it for the dead. I have heard the voice of YHWH my God. I have done just as You commanded me. Look down from your holy dwelling-place, from heaven, and bless Your people Israel and the earth You have given us, a land flowing with milk and honey, as You swore to our forebears.

The logic is clear:

Since from my house I have taken what is holy because it is due to the poor and have given it to them, look down from Your holy house and give us what is due to us, who without it would all be poor.

The great flow of abundance between the land and the people must be primed with the small flow of abundance between the landholder and the landless.

This Deuteronomic version of the tithe attempts to resolve the spiritual collision between a sense of God as giver of prosperity to the rich and a sense of God as protector of the poor, with a third choice: God as the One who provides prosperity to the people as a whole if the people will protect the poor.

Through this view of the tithe, Deuteronomy connects what we as moderns might call "environmental" and what we would call "political" or "economic" matters. The abundance that comes from rain, sun, and soil cannot be divorced from issues of wealth, poverty, and power. The spirituality of this book of Torah lies precisely in the assertion that these two spheres of life are intimately intertwined under God's governance.

Note that the Deuteronomic reformers did not throw out the earlier, traditional version of the tithe: Even while they gave it a new meaning and effect, they went out of their way to reaffirm its connection with the Levites. This is a characteristically Israelite, and then Jewish, way of dealing with change—even great upheavals. The wisdom of the past is not abandoned but rather reinterpreted, and in this way the identity and collective memory of the people are affirmed rather than violated.

So it was this sense of the tithe that lay beneath the Talmud's discussions of how God would pass a judge's sentence on the future of the trees and their abundance. At Tu B'Shvat, when the trees are most dormant, the tithe must be accounted. Almost four months later, at Shavuot, some trees have begun to bear fruit. Their first fruits are brought to the temple, and at that moment God passes judgment on how the people have acted by deciding how the fruit will grow in the coming year.

This whole pattern of Jewish life came to an end with the destruction of the Temple by the Roman Empire in 70 C.E. and the shattering of the Jewish community in the Land of Israel in 135, when a rebellion was crushed. Why this happened is an important part of the story of the evolution of Tu B'Shvat. The Roman conquest signaled that a great rush of new capabilities for control and domination had come into the world—capabilities a step beyond the agricultural revolution and beyond biblical Israel's resolution of the agricultural crisis. The new powers came not only in the shape of military force, but in new ways of organizing politics, economics, and science—controlling the earth as well as human societies. What might be seen as the Divine power for Doing, Making, and Controlling had entered human capabilities far more fully than ever before.

Such a great leap in Doing posed both great dangers and great opportunities to the societies of the Mediterranean Basin. They could be shattered, or they could make tiny enclaves of minimal survival in the old-time life-paths, or they could renew and transform their lives by absorbing some of the new teachings of Hellenistic civilization but rerooting them in the older wisdom. If they could do the latter, they could perhaps do once again, in a more flood-lit history, what their forebears had perhaps done long before when they faced the agricultural revolution: Balance the new energy of Doing with a new depth of Being, new levels of Making with new levels of Resting, new ability to control with new ability to commune.

Rabbinic Judaism, Christianity, and (later) Islam were precisely such efforts to create new forms of Being, Resting, and Communing that drew on biblical wisdom while digesting some aspects of Hellenistic-Roman civilization. For the Rabbis, one of the crucial aspects of this transformation was precisely the need to create forms of community that did not depend on living in a single land, shaping a longtime relationship with the earth. For them, offerings of the mouth through words of prayer and Torah study replaced offerings of the mouth through eating and celebrating food. The festivals were reconceived as moments of history and politics or of psychological rebirthing; understanding them as markers in the spiral of earth, moon, and sun became far fainter.

Tu B'Shvat, which had been so closely tied to growing trees and Temple tithing, became a casualty of this new life-path. It remained only a little more than a memory. No tithes were being taken, and the community had scattered into many lands. No longer was there a sense that the rain and sun and fruitfulness of a single land would be shaped by the actions of a single people.

So for hundreds of years this midwinter fiscal new year for fruit trees was viewed as a minor—indeed, minimal—holiday. Fasting and the saying of penitential prayers were prohibited, but the *Hallel* psalms of praise were not said as they were on the grand festivals.

Yet close to the severed stump of the minor festival, some tiny shoots still grew, in gentle celebration. In the Ashkenazic communities of Central and Eastern Europe, the custom arose of singing Psalm 104 and the fifteen Psalms of Ascent (Psalms 120–34), which may have been sung by the Levites as they ascended fifteen steps into the inner court of the Israelites at the Temple. Along with these fifteen psalms, fifteen different kinds of fruit were eaten— especially some from the Land of Israel. A strong association arose with carob or (in Yiddish) *bokser*—a tree mentioned as the chief food of the mystical rabbi Shimon bar Yoḥai during the years he hid from Roman soldiers in a cave. In addition to carob, the fruits specially favored were olives, dates, grapes, figs, and pomegranates—all specifically mentioned in the Torah as part of the goodness of the Land of Israel. The fifteen psalms and the fifteen fruits may be seen as simply celebrating the fifteenth of Shvat.

But they may have a deeper significance as well. Psalm 104 is a magnificent hymn to the Creator about the wonders of Creation. It celebrates the waters that God once allowed to flood the earth, but which now are constrained within the boundaries God sets—and come only as the rain that all life needs:

> *Trees of YHWH—filled and fulfilled;*
> *Cedars of Lebanon, which [God] planted,*
> *Where songbirds nest*
> *And the stork turns the fir trees into home. (16–17)*

The feeling that Tu B'Shvat is in some more than legal sense a new year, the moment of ascent from the depths of winter into new life may have kept its celebration alive after the tithing of fruits had long been abandoned.

While treekeeping, tithes on fruit, and Tu B'Shvat all languished, the rabbinic tradition began to enrich the symbolic meaning of trees. The Trees of Life and Knowledge in the Garden of Eden story, the Tree of Life to which Proverbs likens Holy Wisdom—these and other trees became powerful symbols in Jewish spirituality.

In addition to the spiritual symbolism, one biblical reference to trees took on halakhic-legal importance for the Rabbis. That was the Torah's command (Deut. 20:19–20) not to destroy trees in wartime. From these verses, the Rabbis deduced the general command of *Bal Tashhit* (Do Not Destroy), an entire ethic of protecting the natural world and the products of human labor. If even the trees of our enemies must be preserved, the Rabbis taught, all the more the earth and air and water when there is no war!

Nostalgia for the land seems to echo from the practices that kept Tu B'Shvat alive during this period. Then, after the expulsion of Jews from Spain in 1492, nostalgia became reality. A small but extraordinary community of Jews reappeared in the Land of Israel, settling in the tiny town of Tzfat in the hills above the Sea of Galilee. They were refugees from a shattered world that for centuries, under Muslim rule, had been a place of Jewish prosperity and learning.

The settlement in Tzfat was the harbinger of a new turn in the spiral of Jewish history. The expulsion of Jews from Spain, in the same year as the beginning of the Spanish Conquest of the Americas, betokened the first great triumph of the modern state—technologically adept, militarily powerful, politically and culturally unitary. Once again there was a great leap ahead in human power to use the Divine powers of Making, Doing, and Controlling.

Among the refugees in Tzfat, there began another great adventure—one that still continues—in imagining a new version of Judaism that could embody a deeper approach to Being, Resting, and Communing. That adventure began with enrichment of the mystical strand within Judaism—the Kabbalah—and with an enrichment of Tu B'Shvat. Whereas the rabbinic response to Hellenistic Doing had turned away from the earth, the kabbalists of Tzfat responded to the modern leap in Doing by turning back toward the earth. Perhaps they did so because they had indeed reconnected with the Land of Israel; perhaps because they dimly saw that modernity, already laying waste the Americas, might come to endanger the earth. Most important, they fused a new way of celebrating earth with a new way of celebrating God.

The kabbalistic refugees of Tzfat came with a mystical bent that, drawing perhaps on their own history of loss, addressed the universe as God's holy vessel—shattered. It was shattered in the very process of its emergence, by the intensity of the Divine energy that poured into creating it. This shattered vessel could be repaired, they said, through their own holy acts and words, focused on its reunification and the reunification of God's Own exiled Self.

This theology gave them a theory of history that not only explained the traumas of their own lives but that we can draw on as well to explain the traumas of the agricultural revolution, the Hellenistic-Roman conquest, the Holocaust, and the emergence of past and future renewals of Judaism and other traditions. If we draw on the Kabbalah of Isaac Luria of Tzfat, called the Ari (Lion), we can see the spiral of Doing and Being through history as the unfolding of Divine energies in a world that is itself, as the mystics have said, an aspect of the Divine.

In that world, what begins as a "thin film" *(reshimu)* of God evolves and unfolds and refolds and thickens to become the universe we know. The process of unfolding is God's way of reaching toward self-reflectiveness, toward becoming a universe that mirrors and reflects the Infinite God. The unfolding appears in evolution and in human history as the troubling spiral of Doing and Being, Doing and Being. Each is a step forward in God's unfolding: The jumps in greater ability to Do are dangerous but also sometimes bear enormous new potentials for both comfort and connection; the growth of new forms of community broaden and deepen love but can also frighten and confuse.

This spiral is the life-juice that grows the Tree of Tu B'Shvat from one form to another, from its biblical roots to its rabbinic trunk to its later branches and ultimately to fruit and seed. As it grows the tree of history, so it grows the celebration of that tree.

Perhaps most important, the kabbalists of Tzfat brought human action and the natural world into the center of the Divine unfolding. The flow of Divine abundance that had been interrupted in their own lives could be restored, they believed, by what they did.

All around them was that very Land of Israel that anciently had been judged in its fruitfulness by a God Who cared whether the poor were fed. Although the tithes could not begin again until the Temple stood once more, there was for them a vivid sense that a time of counting tithes was intimately connected with whether the land was fruitful. And all around them were those very trees on which the tithing had been done. During the 1,500 years of wandering, the spiritual symbolism of trees, the Tree, had been richly developed. So for them, trees were not only a physical manifestation of God's abundance but also an earthly shadow of a mystical reality: They saw God's own Self as the Tree of Life.

The kabbalists called it the "Tree of the *Sefirot*": a "Tree" with its roots in Heaven, carrying the great flow of Divine abundance, *shefa*, until its fruitfulness appeared in our perceptible reality; a "Tree" with fruits that here on earth are apparent in all the fruitfulness that we experience here; a "Tree" made up of the flowing emanations of the Ultimate Divine, emanations called *sefirot*, as they cascade into our lives. And though the Tree's roots are in heaven, the sun and rain that nurture them are the blessings of gratitude and the prayers for unifying the shattered Holy Name that human beings say with all their heart.

Thus a day of tithing trees for the sake of the earthly poor becomes a day for renewing the heavenly abundance of the One Great Tree. That is the great act of transformation that the kabbalists of Tzfat worked upon the older forms of Tu B'Shvat.

The result at Tzfat was the creation of a seder for the evening of Tu B'Shvat, where even more than fifteen varieties of nuts and fruit were eaten in four courses defined by four cups of wine.

We should note that this meal not only was the one ceremonial meal in all of Jewish practice that was defined as vegan/vegetarian —using no product of any animal—but it included only those fruits of the earth that required the death of not even a plant. The edible parts of many vegetables—carrots, potatoes, and others—come from the root or stalk or leafage of the plant, and so harvesting the food means killing the plant. Many other food plants die after one year's growth and harvesting. But nuts and fruits are exactly what trees toss out into the world, in far greater profusion than necessary to reproduce themselves and at no danger to their own lives.

The meal of Tu B'Shvat, then, was the diet of Eden, the Garden of Delight—the Garden of the Tree of Life. It was the meal in which human beings *(adam)* ceased to be at war with the earth *(adamah)*—the meal, therefore, of the days of Messiah.

The varieties of fruit and nuts were organized into four courses, each ending with a cup of wine. These courses represented the four letters of the Sacred Name and the Four Worlds of reality, as the kabbalists understood the process of God's creation:

- *Yud,* the tiny letter that is a marker for the Place that takes no space, symbol of the world closest to the Infinite God—*Atzilut,* the World of Being;

- *Heh,* the breathing sound that symbolizes *Beriyah,* the World of Knowing and Idea;

- *Vav,* the connective letter "and" that is the symbol for *Yetzirah,* the World of Forming, Connecting, Relating;

14

- *Heh* again, breathing forth *Asiyah*, the world of Doing—the world of our created universe.

Since the seed of the Tree—its tiny *Yud*—sits in the soil of Heaven and the Tree grows downward until *Asiyah* takes shape in our universe, the seder began at "the bottom"—at our fruitful level—and rose upward. The fruits and nuts were organized according to how they symbolized each world, expressed by the relationships between the hardness and softness of their skins and their innards. So the seder began with *Asiyah*, the "thickest," most palpable world, by eating fruits with thick, tough outer skins (pomegranates). Then, as the worlds grew more ethereal, the fruit grew softer. The second course *(Beriyah)* was fruit with soft skins and hard pits at their center (dates, olives, plums). The third course *(Yetzirah)* was fruit that was soft all the way through (figs, grapes). And for the fourth course there was no fruit at all—for *Atzilut*, Being, is utterly permeable, untouchable.

In each of the three tangible courses, the seder of Tzfat evidently sought to have ten different varieties of nuts and fruit, representing the Ten *Sefirot*, the ten emanations of God, that were present in each of the Four Worlds. In order to ascend the Tree from *heh* to *yud*, the kabbalists would ascend each Tree-within-the-Tree.

Saying blessings over these fruits would help to release the holy sparks of life-flow in them. Moreover, actually chewing the fruit would have an even more profound effect, since we have thirty-two teeth, and the word *Elohim*, God, appears thirty-two times in the biblical story of creation. Not by bread alone, says the Torah, "but by everything that comes forth from the mouth of God" do we live. What came forth from God's mouth? The entire universe, created through words God spoke. Therefore, for us to bring our "thirty-two" into conscious relation with these fruits of the Supernal Tree would reenact God's mouthing of creation.

Holy sparks of creation were imprisoned in the food. Those who joined in the seder would keep the life-flow of abundance going by returning these holy sparks to the Creator, to the Tree of Life, instead of hoarding the sparks on earth. Trapped on earth, the flow of God's abundance would be blocked, dammed up. Abundance that did not flow up the Tree to Heaven could not return to make abundance for our earth and us. By refusing food to our Creator, we would end up denying it to ourselves.

The four cups of wine that concluded each course of the Tu B'Shvat seder may have been modeled on the Four Cups of the Pesaḥ seder, but their form and meaning were quite different. For Tu B'Shvat, the first cup was white, the second was white with a drop of red, the third was half white and half red, and the last was red with a drop of white.

According to one interpretation, white represents the earth and its powers in quiescence; red, the earth in bloom. Thus the cups may have represented the shift in the yearly seasons from the paleness of winter through the awakening spring into blossoming summer and then the riotous color and fruitful fullness of fall, with a seed of white still hidden in it as the seed goes underground to sleep through winter.

Another view is that for these mystics, the cups represented the union of the masculine and feminine aspects of God: white represented the masculine semen and red the feminine blood with which they saw the universe begotten and birthed into being. Earthiness and sexuality suffused the kabbalists' sense of God's abundant *shefa*. These mystics did not flee the earth and earthiness; they sought it.

The new form of celebration made its way from Tzfat into the broader Jewish world, first by oral tradition and then by its inclusion in a compendium of practices for holy days called *Ḥemdat Yamim*, published in the seventeenth century. Early on, this handbook was reputed to have been written by adherents of the messianic claimant Shabbetai Zevi, and so it was shunned by many mainstream Jewish thinkers. But several of the chapters about specific festivals were so useful and attractive that they were published separately. Among these was the passage on the seder of the fifteenth of Shvat, called *Peri Eitz Hadar*—Fruit of the Lovely Tree—published in 1753. *Peri Eitz Hadar* encouraged and broadened the use of the seder, especially among Sephardic and Eastern Jews. (Among Ashkenazic Jews, even among Hasidim, the Tu B'Shvat seder remained unused, perhaps because they had been more deeply traumatized by the Shabbetai Zevi experience.)

The Festival of Trees took on another aspect late in the nineteenth century. The crisis of modernity was forcing European Jews to face another burst of nationalist energy, often directed, like the Spanish Expulsion, toward national cultural unity—and therefore hostile to the Jews. Some Jews responded with a modern Zionist nationalism of their own. Others focused on the alienation of the Jewish people from land and labor as a sickness to be cured by a cultural and practical Zionism, filled with spirit.

These "practical/cultural Zionists" focused not on achieving political statehood but on renewing the relationship between individual Jews, the Jewish people, and the very earth itself of the Land of Israel. Many who did not call themselves "religious" saw this relationship as the heart of a Jewish spirituality that had been damaged and distorted by millennia spent separated from the land—not only from its politics and history, but from its very soil and soul. So at the spiritual, emotional, and ideological levels, a concern for what grows or fails to grow in the Land of Israel was one strand in the weave of Zionism.

Alongside these concerns, the growing Jewish settlements in Palestine were discovering that planting trees was a practical act that had both political and biological-agricultural import. Tree planting, they said, restored the land, bringing with it a new ecological web of seeds and ground water, insects and small animals that made possible the sowing of crops. New clusters of trees also became a way of marking the new Jewish settlements, distinguishing them from previous Arab towns and villages.

Thus planting trees became both the practical means and the symbolic representation of planting Jewish communities in the Land of Israel. Perhaps in part influenced by Arbor Day, which was then current in America and which had been copied elsewhere in the world, the settlers began to have their children plant trees on the fifteenth of Shvat. In the Diaspora, under the auspices of the Jewish National Fund, the day become a day of focusing on collecting money to plant trees in the Land of Israel.

After Israeli independence, as Eastern and Sephardic Jews gathered alongside Ashkenazim in the State of Israel, the kabbalistic tradition of a Tu B'Shvat seder became known among Western Jews, just as the notion of tree planting for Tu B'Shvat became known to the Easterners. Then, probably through connections made by the Jewish National Fund and the rediscovery of Kabbalah through Jewish scholarship, Diaspora Jews in America began to learn about and experiment with a Tu B'Shvat seder. What was probably the first printed English-language Haggadah for a Tu B'Shvat seder, which focused on trees in Israel and had no mystical content except the pattern of eating fruits and nuts with cups of wine, was shaped by Seymour Hefter of the Jewish Community Center in Wilkes-Barre, Pennsylvania, in 1975.

Meanwhile, in the early 1970s the many-layered Jewish imagery of trees—biblical, kabbalistic, and Zionist—became especially important to a number of American Jews who were seeking to work in an explicitly Jewish and Torah-centered way to address some American or worldwide political and social issues. They saw their Jewish explorations as a response to modernity-run-amok. First as they faced the overwhelming fiery power of the United States in Vietnam, and then as they absorbed the dangers modern techno-industrialism were thrusting on the earth, they began to seek a Judaism that could draw on its premodern roots to create a postmodern spiritual community.

One such network of Jews focused on ending the Vietnam War. Most were young, but they included the venerable teacher Abraham Joshua Heschel. They had a special concern that U.S. government policy took as one of its tasks the destruction of Vietnamese forests—and it was felt especially striking to them that Torah requires that even if one decides to make war against a city, its trees must be protected (Deut. 20:19).

Out of this focus on deforestation as an especially vicious aspect of the war, they developed a Campaign for Trees and Life for Vietnam. They raised money for reforestation and reconstruction of devastated areas of Vietnam, and they planted symbolic trees of peace in such places as the lawn of the U.S. Capitol. Often these plantings were done on Tu B'Shvat, and the day became (to a rather small number of people) a focus of caring and working for peace.

Meanwhile, during the 1970s some American Jews were increasingly concerned that dangers to the earth had reached alarming levels. They joined in celebrating Earth Day as a time for public recommitment to protect the planet. These Jewish groups overlapped with those that had worked on Trees and Life for Vietnam. They took delight in the way the Rabbis had expanded the Torah's command not to destroy trees in wartime into the general command of *Bal Tashḥit* (Do Not Destroy).

For the new global environmentalists, the trees of the planet—especially great disappearing forests such as in the Amazon Basin—began to be seen as a crucial element in its health and its survival. What Zionists had said about trees in the Land of Israel, ecologists were saying about the forests of the world.

This connection brought together a new configuration in the history of Tu B'Shvat. Just as Tu B'Shvat had begun with the earthy questions of tithing and the regrowth of trees in wintertime and had become a cosmic moment in the mystics' calendar, so now again earth and spirit came together. For many of this new generation of Jews, forests and trees as biological and ecological realities became fused with the symbol of the Tree of Life and its flow of Divine abundance, *shefa*. So the day of celebrating the "new year of the tree" became the day to join together earth and Heaven:

- To join the celebration of living trees to the celebration of the Tree of Life;

- To join protection of the flow of abundance around the great round globe to affirmation of the Divine Flow from below to above, from above to below;

- To join a life-giving focus on reuniting the masculine and feminine in God to focus on renewing the potency of seed and fruit and their healing from poisons inflicted on them by human technological intervention;

- To join joy in eating without killing any creature to joy in living "by everything that comes forth from the mouth of God."

And so in the mid-1980s there appeared among American Jews a wave of new haggadot for Tu B'Shvat that joined the mystical and ecological perspectives, affirming indeed that they were the same perspective. Most of these haggadot drew on the pattern of the kabbalistic seder while giving it a midrashic turn in a new direction. In many of them, for example, the Four Worlds of the Kabbalah were fused with their symbolic referents—earth, water, air, and fire, all aspects of the planet's web of life, all in need of healing as aspects of the wounded physical body of this planet.

One of these new Tu B'Shvat haggadot, called *The Trees' Birthday* by Ellen Bernstein (1988), helped give birth to the first Jewish organization wholly devoted to healing the earth: Shomrei Adamah. Its success in stirring the hearts and minds of a new Jewish generation helped lead to a broader commitment among mainstream Jewish organizations in America to work through Jewish channels and with Jewish symbols to protect and heal the earth. By 1993 a number of mainstream Jewish groups had brought into existence the Coalition on the Environment and Jewish Life (COEJL). And by 1996 COEJL itself had defined Tu B'Shvat as a kind of Jewish Earth Day and was urging broad observance of the day as a time to act on behalf of the wounded earth.

This revivification of Tu B'Shvat as a day of "the trees and the Tree" comes in a dark moment of earth's history, when the web of life is for the first time endangered by one of its own species—the human race itself, its most intelligent and self-conscious species, the one most fully grown to bear the Image of God. There is a sense in which this dark moment fits with uncanny truth into the teaching of Tu B'Shvat itself, for Tu B'Shvat comes at precisely the most precarious moment in the cycle of nature. The darkness of Hanukkah may look more frightening to human eyes, but the actual danger to nonhuman life is greater when the cold has set in deeper. So deep winter, when trees and other vegetation must struggle to begin again, may be an especially appropriate moment to commit ourselves to renew the flow of nature's life in our own generation.

The ancient Jewish sensitivity to the tree as a symbol and metaphor of Torah (the Tree of Life) and God (the Tree of the *Sefirot)* is what stirred the kabbalists of Tzfat to involve themselves with Tu B'Shvat. We may extend their sensitivity by looking at the Most Holy Name of God as a calligraphic version of a tree in the cycle of its life: the *yud,* a tiny seed; the *heh,* a flowing, curving expanse of roots; the *vav,* a tall trunk; the *heh,* a flowing, curving expanse of branches. From the branches and their fruit comes the new seed, the new *yud.* The tree, like the *Yud-Heh-Vav-Heh,* always begins anew and can always say, as God said to Moses at the Burning Bush, that lowly tree: "Not only is my Name *Yud-Heh-Vav-Heh;* it is also, I am also, *Ehiyeh asher ehiyeh.* 'I Am Becoming What I Am Becoming.'"

part II

Roots: Biblical Judaism in the Land of Israel

The relationship of human beings to the earth—*adam* to *adamah*—is described by the Hebrew Scriptures as perhaps the central element in a sacred relationship to God. The story of an archetypal journey by an entire community to its God-intended land; stories of the fear and reality of God-intended exile from that land; the use of offerings of food from the earth as the crucial way of making connection with God; the institution of rhythms of restfulness for the land as well as for the human community— all these are ways of making the *adam/adamah* relationship holy. In a sense, the whole being of the people was an "Eco-Jewish" life practice and culture. In that culture, trees played a special role.

This anthology therefore, includes the key texts in this vein from the canonical scriptures of the People of Israel.

It also includes a powerful scholarly analysis of that culture's sense of its own relationship with trees—that culture seen in its own being, rather than as a precursor of later Judaisms or as a source of texts and teachings for later Judaisms.

Biblical Passages

This collection of passages from the Hebrew Bible addresses several aspects of *Trees, Earth, and Torah*. It includes material on tithing because that is where the tradition of Tu B'Shvat begins. It includes material on the Shmitah (sabbatical) Year and the Jubilee because the notion of Shabbat (Sabbath) for the earth seems crucial to the Bible's sense of the relationship between human beings, the earth, and God. It also includes passages about archetypal and sacred trees. One such passage—Deuteronomy 20:19–20—should be especially noted, since it is the source of rabbinic thought about protection of the earth in general, under the rubric of *Bal Tashḥit*—Do Not Destroy.

Tithing

Leviticus 19:23–25
23 When you enter the land and plant any tree for food, you shall regard its fruit as forbidden. Three years it shall be forbidden for you, not to be eaten. 24 In the fourth year all its fruit shall be set aside for jubilation before the Lord; 25 and only in the fifth year may you use its fruit—that its yield to you may be increased: I the Lord am your God.

Leviticus 27:30–33
30 All tithes from the land, whether seed from the ground or fruit from the tree, are the Lord's; they are holy to the Lord. 31 If a man wishes to redeem any of his tithes, he must add one fifth to them. 32 All tithes of the herd or flock—of all that passes under the shepherd's staff, every tenth one—shall be holy to the Lord. 33 He must not look out for good as against bad, or make substitution for it. If he does make substitution for it, then it and its substitute shall both be holy: it cannot be redeemed.

Numbers 18:21–26
21 And to the Levites I hereby give all the tithes in Israel as their share in return for the services that they perform, the services of the Tent of Meeting.

22 Henceforth, Israelites shall not trespass on the Tent of Meeting, and thus incur guilt and die: 23 Only Levites shall perform the services of the Tent of Meeting, others would incur guilt. It is a law for all time throughout the ages. But they shall have no territorial share among the Israelites; 24 for it is the tithes set aside by the Israelites as a gift to the Lord that I give to the Levites as their share. Therefore I have said concerning them: They shall have no territorial share among the Israelites.

25 The Lord spoke to Moses, saying: 26 Speak to the Levites and say to them: When you receive from the Israelites their tithes, which I have assigned to you as your share, you shall remove from them one-tenth of the tithe as a gift to the Lord.

Deuteronomy 26:12

12 When you have set aside in full the tenth part of your yield—in the third year, the year of the tithe—and have given it to the Levite, the stranger, the fatherless, and the widow, that they may eat their fill in your settlements . . .

Shabbat for the Earth

Leviticus 25:1–13, 23–24

1 The Lord spoke to Moses on Mount Sinai: 2 Speak to the Israelite people and say to them:

When you enter the land that I give you, the land shall observe a sabbath of the Lord. 3 Six years you may sow your field and six years you may prune your vineyard and gather in the yield. 4 But in the seventh year the land shall have a sabbath of complete rest, a sabbath of the Lord: You shall not sow your field or prune your vineyard. 5 You shall not reap the after-growth of your harvest or gather the grapes of your untrimmed vines; it shall be a year of complete rest for the land. 6 But you may eat whatever the land during its sabbath will produce—you, your male and female slaves, the hired and bound laborers who live with you, 7 and your cattle and the beasts in your land may eat all its yield.

8 You shall count off seven weeks of years—seven times seven years—so that the period of seven weeks of years gives you a total of forty-nine years. 9 Then you shall sound the horn loud; in the seventh month, on the tenth day of the month—the Day of Atonement—you shall have the horn sounded throughout your land **10** *and you shall hallow the fiftieth year. You shall proclaim release throughout the land for all its inhabitants. It shall be a jubilee for you: each of you shall return to his holding and each of you shall return to his family.* **11** *That fiftieth year shall be a jubilee for you: you shall not sow, neither shall you reap the aftergrowth or harvest the untrimmed vines,* **12** *for it is a jubilee. It shall be holy to you: you may only eat the growth direct from the field.* **13** *In this year of jubilee, each of you shall return to his holding.*

23 *But the land must not be sold beyond reclaim, for the land is Mine; you are but strangers resident with Me.* **24** *Throughout the land that you hold, you must provide for the redemption of the land.*

Leviticus 26:3–6, 11–16

3 *If you follow My laws and faithfully observe My commandments,* **4** *I will grant your rains in their season, so that the earth shall yield its produce and the trees of the field their fruit.* **5** *Your threshing shall over-take the vintage, and your vintage shall overtake the sowing; you shall eat your fill of bread and dwell securely in your land.*

6 *I will grant peace in the land, and you shall lie down untroubled by anyone; I will give the land respite from vicious beasts, and no sword shall cross your land.*

11 *I will establish My abode in your midst, and I will not spurn you.* **12** *I will be ever present in your midst: I will be your God, and you shall be My people.* **13** *I the Lord am your God who brought you out from the land of the Egyptians to be their slaves no more, who broke the bars of your yoke and made you walk erect.*

14 *But if you do not obey Me and do not observe all these commandments,* **15** *if you reject My laws and spurn My rules, so that you do not observe all My commandments and you break My covenant,* **16** *I in turn will do this to you: I will wreak misery upon you—consumption and fever, which cause the eyes to pine and the body to languish; you shall sow your seed to no purpose, for your enemies shall eat it.*

Leviticus 26:27, 32–35, 43–45

27 *But if, despite this, you disobey Me and remain hostile to Me, . . .* **32** *I will make the land desolate, so that your enemies who settle in it shall*

be appalled by it. **33** *And you I will scatter among the nations, and I will unsheath the sword against you. Your land shall become a desolation and your cities a ruin.*
34 *Then shall the land make up for its sabbath years throughout the time that it is desolate and you are in the land of your enemies; then shall the land rest and make up for its sabbath years.* **35** *Throughout the time that it is desolate, it shall observe the rest that it did not observe in your sabbath years while you were dwelling upon it.*

43 *For the land shall be forsaken of them, making up for its sabbath years by being desolate of them, while they atone for their iniquity; for the abundant reason that they rejected My rules and spurned My laws.* **44** *Yet, even then, when they are in the land of their enemies, I will not reject them or spurn them so as to destroy them, annulling My covenant with them: for I the Lord am their God.* **45** *I will remember in their favor the covenant with the ancients, whom I freed from the land of Egypt in the sight of the nations to be their God: I, the Lord.*

Deuteronomy 11:13–21
13 *If, then, you obey the commandments that I enjoin upon you this day, loving the Lord your God and serving Him with all your heart and soul,* **14** *I will grant the rain for your land in season, the early rain and the late. You shall gather in your new grain and wine and oil—* **15** *I will also provide grass in the fields for your cattle—and thus you shall eat your fill.* **16** *Take care not to be lured away to serve other gods and bow to them.* **17** *For the Lord's anger will flare up against you, and He will shut up the skies so that there will be no rain and the ground will not yield its produce; and you will soon perish from the good land that the Lord is assigning to you.*

18 *Therefore impress these my words upon your very heart: bind them as a sign on your hand and let them serve as a symbol on your forehead* **19** *and teach them to your children—reciting them when you stay at home and when you are away, when you lie down and when you get up;* **20** *and inscribe them on the doorposts of your house and on your gates—***21** *to the end that you and your children may endure, in the land that the Lord swore to your fathers to give to them, as long as there is a heaven over the earth.*

2 Chronicles 36:20–21
20 Those who survived the sword he exiled to Babylon, and they became his and his sons' servants till the rise of the Persian kingdom, 21 in fulfillment of the word of the Lord spoken by Jeremiah, until the land paid back its sabbaths; as long as it lay desolate it kept sabbath, till seventy years were completed.

Archetypal Sacred Trees

Genesis 2:8–9, 15–17
8 The Lord God planted a garden in Eden, in the east, and placed there the man whom He had formed. 9 And from the ground the Lord God caused to grow every tree that was pleasing to the sight and good for food, with the tree of life in the middle of the garden, and the tree of knowledge of good and bad.

15 The Lord God took the man and placed him in the garden of Eden, to till it and tend it. 16 And the Lord God commanded the man, saying, "Of every tree of the garden you are free to eat; 17 but as for the tree of knowledge of good and bad, you must not eat of it; for as soon as you eat of it, you shall die."

Genesis 3:1–8, 17–19, 22–24
1 Now the serpent was the shrewdest of all the wild beasts that the Lord God had made. He said to the woman, "Did God really say: You shall not eat of any tree of the garden?" 2 The woman replied to the serpent, "We may eat of the fruit of the other trees of the garden. 3 It is only about fruit of the tree in the middle of the garden that God said: You shall not eat of it or touch it, lest you die." 4 And the serpent said to the woman, "You are not going to die, 5 but God knows that as soon as you eat of it your eyes will be opened and you will be like divine beings who know good and bad." 6 When the woman saw that the tree was good for eating and a delight to the eyes, and that the tree was desirable as a source of wisdom, she took of its fruit and ate. She also gave some to her husband, and he ate. 7 Then the eyes of both of them were opened and they perceived that they were naked; and they sewed together fig leaves and made themselves loincloths.
8 They heard the sound of the Lord God moving about in the garden at the breezy time of day; and the man and his wife hid from the Lord God among the trees of the garden.

17 To Adam He said, "Because you did as your wife said and ate of the tree about which I commanded you, 'You shall not eat of it,'

Cursed be the ground because of you;
By toil shall you eat of it
All the days of your life:
18 Thorns and thistles shall it sprout for you.
But your food shall be the grasses of the field;
19 By the sweat of your brow
Shall you get bread to eat,
Until you return to the ground—
For from it you were taken.
For dust you are,
And to dust you shall return."

22 And the Lord God said, "Now that the man has become like one of us, knowing good and bad, what if he should stretch out his hand and take also from the tree of life and eat, and live forever!" 23 So the Lord God banished him from the garden of Eden, to till the soil from which he was taken. 24 He drove the man out, and stationed east of the garden of Eden the cherubim and the fiery ever-turning sword, to guard the way to the tree of life.

Genesis 18:1, 4, 8
1 The Lord appeared to him [Abraham] by the terebinths of Mamre; he was sitting at the entrance of the tent as the day grew hot,

4 Let a little water be brought; bathe your feet and recline under the tree.

8 He took curds and milk and the calf that had been prepared, and set these before them; and he waited on them under the tree as they ate.

Genesis 21:9–22:14
9 Sarah saw the son, whom Hagar the Egyptian had borne to Abraham, playing. 10 She said to Abraham, "Cast out that slavewoman and her son, for the son of that slave shall not share in the inheritance with my son Isaac." 11 The matter distressed Abraham greatly, for it concerned a son of his. 12 But God said to Abraham, "Do not be distressed over the boy or

your slave; whatever Sarah tells you, do as she says, for it is through Isaac that offspring shall be continued for you. **13** *As for the son of the slave-woman, I will make a nation of him, too, for he is your seed."*

14 *Early next morning Abraham took some bread and a skin of water, and gave them to Hagar. He placed them over her shoulder, together with the child, and sent her away. And she wandered about in the wilderness of Beer-sheba.* **15** *When the water was gone from the skin, she left the child under one of the bushes [= "trees"],* **16** *and went and sat down at a distance, a bowshot away; for she thought, "Let me not look on as the child dies." And sitting thus afar, she burst into tears.*

17 *God heard the cry of the boy, and an angel of God called to Hagar from heaven and said to her, "What troubles you, Hagar? Fear not, for God has heeded the cry of the boy where he is.* **18** *Come, lift up the boy and hold him by the hand, for I will make a great nation of him."* **19** *God opened her eyes and she saw a well of water. She went and filled the skin with water, and let the boy drink.* **20** *God was with the boy and he grew up; he dwelt in the wilderness and became a bowman.* **21** *He lived in the wilderness of Paran; and his mother got a wife for him from the land of Egypt.*

1 *Some time afterward, God put Abraham to the test. He said to him, "Abraham," and he answered, "Here I am."* **2** *And He said, "Take your son, your favored one, Isaac, whom you love, and go to the land of Moriah, and offer him there as a burnt offering on one of the heights which I will point out to you."* **3** *So early next morning, Abraham saddled his ass and took with him two of his servants and his son Isaac. He split the wood [= "tree"] for the burnt offering, and he set out for the place of which God had told him.* **4** *On the third day Abraham looked up and saw the place from afar.* **5** *Then Abraham said to his servants, "You stay here with the ass. The boy and I will go up there; we will worship and we will return to you."*

6 *Abraham took the wood [= "tree"] for the burnt offering and put it on his son Isaac. He himself took the firestone and the knife; and the two walked off together.* **7** *Then Isaac said to his father Abraham, "Father!" And he answered, "Yes, my son." And he said, "Here are the firestone and the wood; but where is the sheep for the burnt offering?"* **8** *And Abraham said, "God will see to the sheep for His burnt offering, my son." And the two of them walked on together.*

9 They arrived at the place of which God had told him. Abraham built an altar there; he laid out the wood; he bound his son Isaac; he laid him on the altar, on top of the wood. 10 And Abraham picked up the knife to slay his son. 11 Then an angel of the Lord called to him from heaven: "Abraham! Abraham!" And he answered, "Here I am." 12 And he said, "Do not raise your hand against the boy, or do anything to him. For now I know that you fear God, since you have not withheld your son, your favored one, from Me." 13 When Abraham looked up, his eye fell upon a ram, caught in the thicket by its horns. So Abraham went and took the ram and offered it up as a burnt offering in place of his son. 14 And Abraham named that site Adonai-yireh, whence the present saying, "On the mount of the Lord there is vision."

Genesis 35:8
8 Deborah, Rebekah's nurse, died, and was buried under the oak below Bethel; so it was named Allon-bacuth.

Exodus 15:25
25 So he [Moses] cried out to the Lord, and the Lord showed him a piece of wood [= "tree"]; he threw it into the water and the water became sweet.

Leviticus 23:40
40 On the first day you shall take the product of hadar trees, branches of palm trees, boughs of leafy trees, and willows of the brook, and you shall rejoice before the Lord your God seven days.

Deuteronomy 4:28
28 There you will serve man-made gods of wood and stone, that cannot see or hear or eat or smell.

Deuteronomy 12:2
2 You must destroy all the sites at which the nations you are to dispossess worshipped their gods, whether on lofty mountains and on hills or under any luxuriant tree.

Deuteronomy 16:21
21 You shall not set up a sacred post—any kind of pole beside the altar of the Lord your God that you may make—

Deuteronomy 19:4–6

4 —Now this is the case of the manslayer who may flee there and live: one who has killed another unwittingly, without having been his enemy in the past. 5 For instance, a man goes with his neighbor into a grove to cut wood; as his hand swings the ax to cut down a tree, the ax-head flies off the handle and strikes the other so that he dies. That man shall flee to one of these cities and live.—6 Otherwise, when the distance is great, the blood-avenger, pursuing the manslayer in hot anger, may overtake him and kill him; yet he did not incur the death penalty, since he had never been the other's enemy.

Deuteronomy 20:19–20

19 When in your war against a city you have to besiege it a long time in order to capture it, you must not destroy its trees, wielding the ax against them. You may eat of them, but you must not cut them down. Are trees of the field human to withdraw before you into the besieged city? 20 Only trees which you know do not yield food may be destroyed; you may cut them down for constructing siegeworks against the city that is waging war on you, until it has been reduced.

Joshua 10:26

26 After that, Joshua had them [five Amorite kings] put to death and impaled on five stakes [= "trees"], and they remained impaled on the stakes until evening.

Judges 9:6–15

6 All the citizens of Shechem and all Beth-millo convened, and they proclaimed Abimelech king at the terebinth of the pillar at Shechem. 7 When Jotham was informed, he went and stood on top of Mount Gerizim and called out to them in a loud voice, "Citizens of Shechem!" he cried, "Listen to me, that God may listen to you.
8 "Once the trees went to anoint a king over themselves. They said to the olive tree, 'Reign over us.' 9 But the olive tree replied, 'Have I, through whom God and men are honored, stopped yielding my rich oil, that I should go and wave above the trees?' 10 So the trees said to the fig tree, 'You come and reign over us.' 11 But the fig tree replied, 'Have I stopped yielding my sweetness, my delicious fruit, that I should go and wave above the trees?' 12 So the trees said to the vine, 'You come and reign over us.' 13 But the vine replied, 'Have I stopped yielding my new wine, which gladdens God

and men, that I should go and wave above the trees?' 14 Then all the trees said to the thornbush, 'You come and reign over us.' 15 And the thornbush said to the trees, 'If you are acting honorably in anointing me king over you, come and take shelter in my shade; but if not, may fire issue from the thornbush and consume the cedars of Lebanon!'"

2 Samuel 18:9–14

9 Absalom encountered some of David's followers. Absalom was riding on a mule, and as the mule passed under the tangled branches of a great terebinth, his hair got caught in the terebinth; he was held between heaven and earth as the mule under him kept going. 10 One of the men saw it and told Joab, "I have just seen Absalom hanging from a terebinth!" 11 Joab said to the man who told him, "You saw it! Why didn't you kill him then and there? I would have owed you ten shekels of silver and a belt." 12 But the man answered Joab, "Even if I had a thousand shekels of silver in my hands, I would not raise a hand against the king's son. For the king charged you and Abishai and Ittai in our hearing. 'Watch over my boy Absalom, for my sake.' 13 If I betrayed myself and nothing is hidden from the king—you would have stood aloof." 14 Joab replied, "Then I will not wait for you." He took three darts in his hand and drove them into Absalom's chest. [Absalom] was still alive in the thick growth of the terebinth,

2 Kings 6:4–6

4 and he [Elisha] accompanied them [his disciples]. So they went to the Jordan and cut timber. 5 As one of them was felling a trunk, the iron ax head fell into the water. And he cried aloud, "Alas, master, it was a borrowed one!" 6 "Where did it fall?" asked the man of God. He showed him the spot; and he cut off a stick and threw it in, and he made the ax head float.

Isaiah 10:33–11:9

*33 Lo! The Sovereign Lord of Hosts
Will hew off the tree-crowns with an ax:
The tall ones shall be felled,
The lofty ones cut down:
34 The thickets of the forest shall be hacked away with iron,
And the Lebanon trees shall fall in their majesty!*

1 But a shoot shall grow out of the stump of Jesse,
A twig shall sprout from his stock.
2 The spirit of the Lord shall alight upon him:
A spirit of wisdom and insight,
A spirit of counsel and valor,
A spirit of devotion and reverence for the Lord.
3 He shall sense the truth by his reverence for the Lord:
He shall not judge by what his eyes behold,
Nor decide by what his ears perceive.
4 Thus he shall judge the poor with equity
And decide with justice for the lowly of the land.
He shall strike down a land with the rod of his mouth
And slay the wicked with the breath of his lips.
5 Justice shall be the girdle of his loins,
And faithfulness the girdle of his waist.
6 The wolf shall dwell with the lamb,
The leopard lie down with the kid;
The calf, the beast of prey, and the fatling together,
With a little boy to herd them.
7 The cow and the bear shall graze,
Their young shall lie down together;
And the lion, like the ox, shall eat straw.
8 A babe shall play
Over a viper's hole,
And an infant pass his hand
Over an adder's den.
9 In all of My sacred mount
Nothing evil or vile shall be done;
for the land shall be filled with devotion to the Lord
As water covers the sea.

Isaiah 44:14–28
14 For his use he cuts down cedars;
He chooses plane trees and oaks.
He sets aside trees of the forest;
Or plants firs, and the rain makes them grow.
15 All this serves man for fuel:

He takes some to warm himself,
And he builds a fire and bakes bread.
He also makes a god of it and worships it,
Fashions an idol and bows down to it!
16 *Part of it he burns in a fire:*
On that part he roasts meat,
He eats the roast and is sated;
He also warms himself and cries, "Ah,
I am warm! I can feel the heat!"
17 *Of the rest he makes a god—his own carving!*
He bows down to it, worships it;
He prays to it and cries,
"Save me, for you are my god!"

18 *They have no wit or judgment:*
Their eyes are besmeared, and they see not;
Their minds, and they cannot think.
19 *They do not give thought,*
They lack the wit and judgment to say:
"Part of it I burned in a fire;
I also baked bread on the coals,
I roasted meat and ate it—
Should I make the rest an abhorrence?
Should I bow to a block of wood?"
20 *He pursues ashes!*
A deluded mind has led him astray,
And he cannot save himself;
He never says to himself,
"The thing in my hand is a fraud!"
21 *Remember these things, O Jacob,*
For you, O Israel, are My servant:
I fashioned you, you are My servant—
O Israel, never forget Me.
22 *I wipe away your sins like a cloud,*
Your transgressions like mist—
Come back to Me, for I redeem you.

23 *Shout, O heavens, for the Lord has acted;*
Shout aloud, O depths of the earth!
Shout for joy, O mountains,
O forests with all your trees!
For the Lord has redeemed Jacob,
Has glorified Himself through Israel.

24 *Thus said the Lord, your Redeemer,*
Who formed you in the womb:
It is I, the Lord, who made everything,
Who alone stretched out the heavens
And unaided spread out the earth;
25 *Who annul the omens of diviners,*
And make fools of the augurs;
Who turn sages back
And make nonsense of their knowledge;
26 *But confirm the word of My servant*
And fulfill the prediction of My messengers.
It is I who say of Jerusalem, "It shall be inhabited,"
And of the towns of Judah, "They shall be rebuilt;
And I will restore their ruined places."
27 *[I,] who said to the deep, "Be dry;*
I will dry up your floods,"
28 *Am the same who says of Cyrus, "He is My shepherd;*
He shall fulfill all My purposes!
He shall say of Jerusalem, 'She shall be rebuilt,'
And to the Temple: 'You shall be founded again.'"

Isaiah 55:12
12 *Yea, you shall leave in joy and be led home secure.*
Before you, mount and hill shall shout aloud,
And all the trees of the field shall clap their hands.

Isaiah 65:17–25
17 *For behold! I am creating*
A new heaven and a new earth;
The former things shall not be remembered,

They shall never come to mind.
18 Be glad, then, and rejoice forever
In what I am creating.
For I shall create Jerusalem as a joy,
And her people as a delight;
19 And I will rejoice in Jerusalem
And delight in her people.
Never again shall be heard there
The sounds of weeping and wailing.
20 No more shall there be an infant or graybeard
Who does not live out his days.
He who dies at a hundred years
Shall be reckoned a youth,
And he who fails to reach a hundred
Shall be reckoned accursed.
21 They shall build houses and dwell in them,
They shall plant vineyards and enjoy their fruit.
22 They shall not build for others to dwell in,
Or plant for others to enjoy.
For the days of My people shall be
As long as the days of a tree,
My chosen ones shall outlive
The work of their hands.
23 They shall not toil to no purpose;
They shall not bear children for terror,
But they shall be a people blessed by the Lord,
And their offspring shall remain with them.
24 Before they pray, I will answer;
While they are still speaking, I will respond.
25 The wolf and the lamb shall graze together,
And the lion shall eat straw like the ox,
And the serpent's food shall be earth.
In all My sacred mount
Nothing evil or vile shall be done
—said the Lord

Jeremiah 2:20–21

20 *For long ago you broke your yoke,*
Tore off your yoke-bands,
And said, "I will not work!"
On every high hill and under every verdant tree,
You recline as a whore.
21 *I planted you with noble vines,*
All with choicest seed;
Alas, I find you changed
Into a base, an alien vine!

Jeremiah 3:6, 13

6 *The Lord said to me in the days of King Josiah: Have you seen what Rebel Israel did, going to every high mountain and under every leafy tree, and whoring there?*

13 *Only recognize your sin; for you have transgressed against the Lord, and scattered your favors among strangers under every leafy tree, and you have not heeded Me—declares the Lord.*

Jeremiah 17:5–8

5 *Thus said the Lord:*
Cursed is he who trusts in man,
Who makes mere flesh his strength,
And turns his thoughts from the Lord.
6 *He shall be like a bush in the desert,*
Which does not sense the coming of good:
It is set in the scorched places of the wilderness,
In a barren land without inhabitant.
7 *Blessed is he who trusts in the Lord,*
Whose trust is the Lord alone.
8 *He shall be like a tree planted by waters,*
Sending forth its roots by a stream:
It does not sense the coming of heat,
Its leaves are ever fresh;
It has no care in a year of drought,
It does not cease to yield fruit.

Ezekiel 15:1–8

1 The word of the Lord came to me: 2 O mortal, how is the wood of the grapevine better than the wood of any branch to be found among the trees of the forest? 3 Can wood be taken from it for use in any work? Can one take a peg from it to hang any vessel on? 4 Now suppose it was thrown into the fire as fuel and the fire consumed its two ends and its middle was charred—is it good for any use? 5 Even when it was whole it could not be used for anything; how much less when fire has consumed it and it is charred! Can it still be used for anything?

6 Assuredly, thus said the Lord God: Like the wood of the grapevine among the trees of the forest, which I have designated to be fuel for fire, so will I treat the inhabitants of Jerusalem. 7 I will set My face against them; they escaped from fire, but fire shall consume them. When I set my face against them, you shall know that I am the Lord. 8 I will make the land a desolation, because they committed trespass—declares the Lord God.

Ezekiel 17:22–24

22 Thus said the Lord God: Then I in turn will take and set [in the ground a slip] from the lofty top of the cedar; I will pluck a tender twig from the tip of its crown, and I will plant it on a tall, towering mountain. 23 I will plant it in Israel's lofty highlands, and it shall bring forth boughs and produce branches and grow into a noble cedar. Every bird of every feather shall take shelter under it, shelter in the shade of its boughs. 24 Then shall all the trees of the field know that it is I the Lord who have abased the lofty tree and exalted the lowly tree, who have dried up the green tree and made the withered tree bud. I the Lord have spoken, and I will act.

Ezekiel 19:10–14

10 Your mother was like a vine in your blood,
Planted beside streams,
With luxuriant boughs and branches
Thanks to abundant waters.
11 And she had a mighty rod
Fit for a ruler's scepter.
It towered highest
among the leafy trees,
It was conspicuous by its height,

By the abundance of its boughs.
12 But plucked up in a fury,
She was hurled to the ground.
The east wind withered her branches,
They broke apart and dried up;
And her mighty rod was consumed by fire.
13 Now she is planted in the desert,
In ground that is arid and parched.
14 Fire has issued from her twig-laden branch
And has consumed her boughs,
She is left without a mighty rod,
A scepter to rule with.

Ezekiel 31

1 In the eleventh year, on the first day of the third month, the word of the Lord came to me: 2 O mortal, say to Pharaoh king of Egypt and his hordes:

Who was comparable to you in greatness?
3 Assyria was a cedar in Lebanon
With beautiful branches and shady thickets,
Of lofty stature, With its top among leafy trees.
4 Waters nourished it,
The deep made it grow tall,
Washing with its streams
The place where it was planted,
Making its channels well up
To all the trees of the field.
5 Therefore it exceeded in stature
All the trees of the field;
Its branches multiplied and its boughs grew long
Because of the abundant water
That welled up for it.
6 In its branches nested
All the birds of the sky;
All the beasts of the field
Bore their young under its boughs,
And in its shadow lived
All the great nations.

7 It was beautiful in its height,
In the length of its branches,
Because its stock stood
By abundant waters.
8 Cedars in the garden of God
Could not compare with it;
Cypresses could not match its boughs,
And plane trees could not vie with its branches;
No tree in the garden of God
Was its peer in beauty.
9 I made it beautiful
In the profusion of its branches;
And all the trees of Eden envied it
In the garden of God.

10 Assuredly, thus said the Lord God: Because it towered high in stature, and thrust its top up among the leafy trees, and it was arrogant in its height, 11 I delivered it into the hands of the mightiest of nations. They treated it as befitted its wickedness. I banished it. 12 Strangers, the most ruthless of nations, cut it down and abandoned it; its branches fell on the mountains and in every valley; its boughs were splintered in every watercourse of the earth; and all the peoples of the earth departed from its shade and abandoned it. 13 Upon its fallen trunk all the birds of the sky nest, and all the beasts of the field lodge among its boughs—14 so that no trees by water should exalt themselves in stature or set their tops among the leafy trees, and that no well-watered tree may reach up to them in height. For they are all consigned to death, to the lowest part of the nether world, together with human beings who descend into the Pit.

15 Thus said the Lord God: On the day it went down to Sheol, I closed the deep over it and covered it; I held back its streams, and the great waters were checked. I made Lebanon mourn deeply for it, and all the trees of the field languished on its account. 16 I made nations quake at the crash of its fall, when I cast it down to Sheol with those who descend into the Pit; and all the trees of Eden, the choicest and best of Lebanon, all that were well watered, were consoled in the lowest part of the netherworld. 17 They also descended with it into Sheol, to those slain by the sword, together with its supporters, they who had lived under its shadow among the nations.

18 [Now you know] who is comparable to you in glory and greatness among the trees of Eden. And you too shall be brought down with the trees of Eden to the lowest part of the netherworld; you shall lie among the uncircumcised and those slain by the sword. Such shall be [the fate of] Pharaoh and all his hordes—declares the Lord God.

Psalm 1:1–3

1 Happy is the man who has not followed the counsel of the wicked,
or taken the path of sinners,
or joined the company of the insolent;
2 rather, the teaching of the Lord is his delight,
and he studies that teaching day and night.
3 He is like a tree planted beside streams of water,
which yields its fruit in season,
whose foliage never fades,
and whatever it produces thrives.

Psalm 104

1 Bless the Lord, O my soul;
O Lord, my God, You are very great;
You are clothed in glory and majesty,
2 wrapped in a robe of light;
You spread the heavens like a tent cloth.
3 He sets the rafters of His lofts in the waters,
makes the clouds His chariot,
moves on the wings of the wind.
4 He makes the winds His messengers,
fiery flames His servants.
5 He established the earth on its foundations,
so that it shall never totter.
6 You made the deep cover it as a garment;
the waters stood above the mountains.
7 They fled at Your blast,
rushed away at the sound of Your thunder,
8 —mountains rising, valleys sinking—
to the place You established for them.

9 You set bounds they must not pass
so that they never again cover the earth.

10 You make springs gush forth in torrents;
they make their way between the hills,
11 giving drink to all the wild beasts;
the wild asses slake their thirst.
12 The birds of the sky dwell beside them
and sing among the foliage.
13 You water the mountains from Your lofts;
the earth is sated from the fruit of Your work.
14 You make the grass grow for the cattle,
and herbage for man's labor
that he may get food out of the earth—
15 wine that cheers the hearts of men
oil that makes the face shine,
and bread that sustains man's life.
16 The trees of the Lord drink their fill,
the cedars of Lebanon, His own planting,
17 where birds make their nests;
the stork has her home in the junipers.
18 The high mountains are for wild goats;
the crags are a refuge for rock-badgers.

19 He made the moon to mark the seasons;
the sun knows when to set.
20 You bring on darkness and it is night,
when all the beasts of the forests stir.
21 The lions roar for prey,
seeking their food from God.
22 When the sun rises, they come home
and couch in their dens.
23 Man then goes out to his work,
to his labor until the evening.

24 How many are the things You have made, O Lord;
You have made them all with wisdom;

the earth is full of Your creations.
25 *There is the sea, vast and wide,*
with its creatures beyond number,
living things, small and great.
26 *There go the ships,*
and Leviathan that You formed to sport with.
27 *All of them look to You*
to give them their food when it is due.
28 *Give it to them, they gather it up;*
open Your hand, they are well satisfied;
29 *hide Your face, they are terrified;*
take away their breath, they perish
and turn again into dust;
30 *send back Your breath, they are created,*
and You renew the face of the earth.

31 *May the glory of the Lord endure forever;*
may the Lord rejoice in His works!
32 *He looks at the earth and it trembles;*
He touches the mountains and they smoke.
33 *I will sing to the Lord as long as I live;*
all my life I will chant hymns to my God.
34 *May my prayer be pleasing to Him;*
I will rejoice in the Lord.
35 *May sinners disappear from the earth,*
and the wicked be no more.
Bless the Lord, O my soul.
Hallelujah.

Psalm 148
1 *Hallelujah.*
Praise the Lord from the heavens;
praise Him on high.
2 *Praise Him, all His angels,*
praise Him, all His hosts.
3 *Praise Him, sun and moon,*
praise Him, all bright stars.

4 *Praise Him, highest heavens,*
and you waters that are above the heavens.
5 *Let them praise the name of the Lord,*
for it was He who commanded that they be created.
6 *He made them endure forever,*
establishing an order that shall never change.
7 *Praise the Lord, O you who are on earth,*
all sea monsters and ocean depths,
8 *fire and hail, snow and smoke,*
storm wind that executes His command,
9 *all mountains and hills, all fruit trees and cedars,*
10 *all wild and tamed beasts, creeping things and winged birds,*
11 *all kings and peoples of the earth,*
all princes of the earth and its judges,
12 *youths and maidens alike,*
old and young together.
13 *Let them praise the name of the Lord,*
for His name, His alone, is sublime;
His splendor covers heaven and earth.
14 *He has exalted the horn of His people*
for the glory of all His faithful ones,
Israel, the people close to Him.
Hallelujah.

Proverbs 3:13–18

13 *Happy is the man who finds wisdom,*
The man who attains understanding.
14 *Her value in trade is better than silver,*
Her yield, greater than gold.
15 *She is more precious than rubies;*
All of your goods cannot equal her.
16 *In her right hand is length of days, In her left, riches*
and honor.
17 *Her ways are pleasant ways, And all her paths, peaceful.*
18 *She is a tree of life to those who grasp her,*
And whoever holds on to her is happy.

Proverbs 11:30
30 The fruit of the righteous is a tree of life;
A wise man captivates people.

Proverbs 13:12
12 Hope deferred sickens the heart,
But desire realized is a tree of life.

Proverbs 15:4
4 A healing tongue is a tree of life,
But a devious one makes for a broken spirit.

Job 14:7–9
7 There is hope for a tree;
If it is cut down it will renew itself;
Its shoots will not cease.
8 If its roots are old in the earth,
And its stump dies in the ground,
9 At the scent of water it will bud
And produce branches like a sapling.

Song of Songs 2:1–3
1 I am a rose of Sharon,
A lily of the valleys.
2 Like a lily among thorns,
So is my darling among the maidens.
3 Like an apple tree among trees of the forest,
So is my beloved among the youths.
I delight to sit in his shade,
And his fruit is sweet to my mouth.

Song of Songs 2:10-13
10 My beloved spoke thus to me,
"Arise, my darling;
My fair one, come away!
11 For now the winter is past,
The rains are over and gone.

12 The blossoms have appeared in the land,
The time of pruning has come;
The song of the turtle dove
Is heard in our land.
13 The green figs form on the fig tree,
The vines in blossom give off fragrance.
Arise, my darling;
My fair one, come away!"

Esther 9:13
13 "If it please Your Majesty," Esther replied, "let the Jews in Shushan be permitted to act tomorrow also as they did today; and let Haman's ten sons be impaled on the stake[="tree"]."

Daniel 4:7–14
7 "In the visions of my mind in bed
I saw a tree of great height in the midst of the earth;
8 The tree grew and became mighty;
Its top reached heaven,
9 And it was visible to the ends of the earth.
Its foliage was beautiful
And its fruit abundant;
There was food for all in it.
Beneath it the beasts of the field found shade,
And the birds of the sky dwelt on its branches;
All creatures fed on it.

10 In the vision of my mind in bed, I looked and saw a holy Watcher coming down from heaven. 11 He called loudly and said:

'Hew down the tree, lop off its branches,
Strip off its foliage, scatter its fruit.
Let the beasts of the field flee from beneath it
And the birds from its branches,
12 But leave the stump with its roots in the ground.
In fetters of iron and bronze
In the grass of the field,
Let him be drenched with the dew of heaven,

And share earth's verdure with the beasts.
13 Let his mind be altered from that of a man,
And let him be given the mind of a beast,
And let seven seasons pass over him.
14 This sentence is decreed by the Watchers;
This verdict is commanded by the Holy Ones
So that all creatures may know
That the Most High is sovereign over the realm of man.
And He gives it to whom He wishes
And He may set over it even the lowest of men.'"

Daniel 4:16–23

16 Then Daniel, called Belteshazzar, was perplexed for a while, and alarmed by his thoughts. The king addressed him, "Let the dream and its meaning not alarm you." Belteshazzar replied, "My lord, would that the dream were for your enemy and its meaning for your foe! 17 The tree that you saw grow and become mighty, whose top reached heaven, which was visible throughout the earth, 18 whose foliage was beautiful, whose fruit was so abundant that there was food for all in it, beneath which the beasts of the field dwelt, and in whose branches the birds of the sky lodged—19 it is you, O king, you who have grown and become mighty, whose greatness has grown to reach heaven, and whose dominion is to the end of the earth. 20 The holy Watcher whom the king saw descend from heaven and say,

Hew down the tree and destroy it,
But leave the stump with its roots in the ground.
In fetters of iron and bronze
In the grass of the field,
Let him be drenched with the dew of heaven,
And share the lot of the beasts of the field
Until seven seasons pass over him—

21 this is its meaning, O king; it is the decree of the Most High which has overtaken my lord the king. 22 You will be driven away from men and have your habitation with the beasts of the field. You will be fed grass like cattle, and be drenched with the dew of heaven; seven seasons will pass over you until you come to know that the Most High is sovereign over the realm of man, and He gives it to whom He wishes. 23 And the meaning of the command to leave the stump of the tree with its roots is that the kingdom will remain yours from the time you come to know that Heaven is sovereign.

2 Chronicles 2:7–8

7 *Send me cedars, cypress, and algum wood from the Lebanon, for I know that your servants are skilled at cutting the trees of Lebanon. My servants will work with yours* **8** *to provide me with a great stock of timber; for the House which I intend to build will be singularly great.*

 # Israel: The Orchard and Vineyard of God

*Howard Eilberg-Schwartz**

The priests . . . extend the metaphor of circumcision in an unprecedented way. They conceptualize the fruit that grows on immature fruit trees as its "foreskin" and the tree itself as "uncircumcised." [This] . . . is one example of how Israelites extended metaphors from the human and social domains to the domain of agriculture.

In this case, the relevant passage deals with a divine proscription against eating the young fruit of any tree grown in the land of Israel. "When you enter the land and plant any tree for food, you shall regard its fruit as its foreskin.[1] Three years it shall be uncircumcised for you, not to be eaten. In the fourth year all its fruit shall be set aside for jubilation before the Lord; and only in the fifth year may you use its fruit—that its yield to you may be increased: I the Lord am your God" (Lev. 19:23–25).

Most commentators understand the comparison between a male's foreskin and the fruit of young fruit trees to move in one direction only, from the domain of human circumcision to the domain of fruit trees. Consequently, they interpret this metaphor as a prohibition against using the fruit of juvenile trees.[2] "Anyone 'uncircumcised' was outside the holy community so produce not available to the community could be described this way."[3] "You

X 450380 80

shall regard its fruit as defective. The fruit tree in the first three years is to be regarded as a male infant during his first eight days, i.e., as unconsecrated."[4] Based on this understanding, many translations simply substitute "forbidden" for "uncircumcised."[5] But there is good reason to think that the metaphor between the male organ and fruit trees is grounded on other similarities as well. Of the dozens of other things that the priests declare forbidden, they apply the metaphors of "uncircumcised" and "foreskin" to none of them. Why then did they see a metaphoric relationship between this particular forbidden item and the male foreskin?

The answer emerges when one considers the physiology of fruit trees, and in particular the ones found in the land of Israel. During the early years of growth, fruit trees pass through a juvenile stage during which they generally do not flower and often produce little or no fruit. If the tree does bear a few fruit during this period, it is often defective. The juvenile period varies according to species. As a rule, however, the types of fruit trees growing in the land of Israel[6] do not bear fruit until the fourth year and beyond. Female date palms, for example, begin to bear dates at any age varying from four to twenty years, with an average of five from planting.[7] Olives may bear a fair crop in the sixth year.[8] Fig seedlings growing from their own roots take five to seven years to come into full bearing.[9] Pomegranates come into bearing in the fifth year and generally do not reach full maturity until the seventh.[10] Grape seedlings produce fruit in three to six years, and almond trees produce some flower buds in the fourth year and some fruit in the fifth.[11] Ancient sources confirm that ancient fruit trees produced fruit at approximately the same rates as those grown today. References in the Code of Hammurabi, for example, indicate that ancient Babylonians were able to rely on a respectable crop of dates in the fourth year.[12] The Tosefta (ca. 300 C.E.) defines a productive plantation as including vines that are five years old, fig trees six years old, and olive trees seven years old (B. *Sheb.* 1:3).

By equating a juvenile fruit tree with an uncircumcised Israelite male, this passage presupposes a symbolic association between circumcision and fertility. The infertile tree is "uncircumcised" just as a child, who is not yet rooted in the covenant, cannot bear fruit. Moreover, if a circumcised tree is one that yields a full harvest, the removal of a male's foreskin prepares him for a maximal yield. So the metaphor between fruit trees and the penis is not unidirectional. Fruit from juvenile fruit trees is proscribed like the male foreskin. By the same token, the uncircumcised male organ is like immature fruit trees in that it cannot produce fruit.

The extension of such metaphors to fruit trees might rest on another perceived similarity as well. Circumcising the male organ is analogous to pruning fruit trees. Both acts involve cutting away unwanted growth from a stem or trunk and the purpose of both cuttings is similar. Circumcision . . . is a symbolic cut that ensures human fertility. Similarly, pruning a fruit tree is crucial for maximizing its yield either by developing a good framework or maximizing the surface area for fruit production.

Unfortunately, biblical literature provides little information about the horticultural practices of ancient Israel. Nonetheless, it does indicate that Israelites pruned their grapevines and regarded that practice as crucial for the success of the vineyard (Lev. 25:1–5; Isa. 5–6). Since biblical writers classified the grapevine as a kind of tree (Judg. 9:13; Joel 1:12, 2:22; Ezek. 15:2, 6), we know that Israelites regularly pruned at least one kind of fruit "tree" in order to maximize its yield.

There is no direct evidence that the priestly writer saw an analogy between circumcision and pruning. But the priestly work does make an explicit comparison between pruning and the act of cutting another part of the body, namely the hair. During the Sabbatical year, Israelites are instructed not to carry out any horticultural activity, including the pruning of grapevines. These untrimmed vines the priests call "your nazirites" *(nezireka)* or the "nazirites" of the fields *(nezireha)* (Lev. 25:5, 11). . . . This use of the term "nazirite" is secondary. Its primary referent is an Israelite who has consecrated himself to God by vowing not to eat grape products or cut his hair (Num. 6:2–5). The extension of the term "nazirite" to untrimmed vines rests on a metaphoric association between an unpruned vineyard (which is being dedicated to God) and a man who has untrimmed hair (because he has consecrated himself to God). Here, then, is an incontrovertible instance where the priests recognize an analogy between not cutting part of the human body (i.e., the hair) and not pruning grapevines. The existence of this metaphor does not prove that the priests also saw an analogy between pruning and circumcision. But it does make that interpretation more plausible.

It may also be the case that the link between circumcision and pruning is presupposed in the notion that juvenile fruit trees are "uncircumcised" (Lev. 19:23).

Now there is a certain ambiguity in this expression. Does it imply, as some commentators suggest, that the fruit is not cut during the first three years of the tree's growth? That the tree is "uncircumcised" because its fruit is not cut off like the foreskin of an uncircumcised male organ? By this reading, the tree's circumcision is its ceremonial stripping in the fourth year when the fruit harvest is dedicated to God.[13] There are, however, reasons to doubt this interpretation. To begin with, this passage only states that the fruit is the foreskin and that it cannot be eaten. It does not say that the fruit must remain on the tree. Furthermore, if the cutting of the fruit in the fourth year is the symbolic circumcision of the tree, then the foreskin of the tree is being offered to God. But in the priestly practice of human circumcision, the foreskin is not offered to God (see Genesis 17).

An alternative interpretation is thus called for. Calling the fruit "foreskin" might suggest that it should be cut off, just as the male foreskin is cut off. This interpretation would presuppose good horticultural practice, for pruning immature fruit trees is important for maximizing their yield in maturity. "For the first year or several years . . . fruit production is neither expected nor desired. The maturing of fruit and to a certain extent even the formation of fruit buds and potential fruiting wood might tax the energies of the plant so that increase in size would be checked seriously."[14] The greater the size of the tree, the greater the surface area for the production of fruit. In the case of palms, "The grower must not let his young palms bear too many dates, particularly if he wants them to produce offshoots (for future fruiting) at the same time. In most cases, a palm may be allowed to bear its first two bunches of fruit in its fourth year, and three or four bunches in each of the next two years. If even a full grown palm is allowed to bear its limit in any year it is likely to bear less the following season."[15] Fig trees, for their part, require severe pruning as young trees in order to build up a good framework, which is crucial for maximizing subsequent yield (Lev. 19:25).[16] By calling immature fruit "foreskin" and by forbidding the consumption of such fruit, the passage discourages farmers from attempting to maximize a tree's yield before it is sufficiently mature. Moreover, it may even encourage farmers to cut away the fruit of their young trees ("the foreskin"), just as they are expected to cut away the foreskin of their newborn son.

The expectation that farmers harvest their trees in the fourth year and beyond (Lev. 19:24–25) is consistent with the aim of increasing the yield. Allowing a tree to bear a full crop in these years does not tax its growth. That maximizing the yield is the central motivation behind these rules is confirmed by the exhortation that one should observe these rules "so that its yield to you may be increased" (19:25). This probably means, as many commentators point out, that God will increase the yield when the divine laws concerning fruit trees are obeyed. But that theological meaning may well presuppose good horticultural practice. When a farmer discourages a tree's yield during its juvenile period, God will see to it that the tree bears a large number of fruit.

To summarize this line of argument, the symbolic equation of an uncircumcised male and a young fruit tree rests on two, and possibly three, associations. The fruit of a juvenile tree is proscribed like the foreskin of the male organ. Furthermore, a male who is uncircumcised and not part of the covenantal community is infertile like an immature fruit tree. Finally, this symbolic equation may draw part of its plausibility from an analogy between circumcision and pruning. Cutting away the foreskin is like pruning a fruit tree. Both acts of cutting remove unwanted excess and both increase the desired yield. One might say that when Israelites circumcise their male children, they are pruning the fruit trees of God.

As the above analysis indicates, the themes of procreation and fertility are central to the priestly conception of circumcision, even though priests circumcised their male children eight days after birth. This enables us to account for the otherwise "uncanny coincidence" that ancient Israelite priests and twentieth-century African tribes, separated in time and space, both make an association between circumcision and fruit trees . . . Wood from fruit trees is frequently employed in African circumcision ceremonies to ensure the fertility of the novice and the strength of his organ.

The association between fruit trees and circumcision is based on two intersecting metaphors, each of which is found in diverse cultural contexts. The first is the metaphoric association between fruit, on the one hand, and human sexuality and genitalia, on the other . . .

Trees, for their part, frequently serve as metaphors for the male organ . . . Given the association in diverse cultures between fruit and human sexuality, on the one hand, and between trees and the male organ, on the other, it is not surprising that fruit trees become symbolically connected with circumcision rites in contexts that are geographically and temporally remote from one another . . .

Other Readers, Similar Conclusions

Since my analysis of Israelite circumcision has relied heavily on ethnographic literature, it is worthwhile pointing out that my interpretations dovetail in some interesting ways with the insights of ancient interpreters: Philo, a first-century Egyptian Jew, who attempted to reconcile Platonism and biblical religion, and the early rabbis (200–600), an elite group of Jewish interpreters who undertook an extensive reinterpretation of the faith and practices of ancient Israel.

. . . Philo drew attention to the similarity between pruning and circumcision:

Why does one circumcise (both) the home-born and the purchased (child) . . . as for the deeper meaning, the home-born characters are those which are moved by nature, while the purchased ones are those who are able to improve through reason and teaching. There is need for both of these to be purified and trimmed like plants, both those which are natural and genuine, and those which are able to bear fruit constantly; for well-grown (plants) produce many superfluous (fruits) because of their fertility, which it is useful to cut off. But those who are taught by teachers shave off their ignorance.[17]

Philo's understanding of circumcision as signifying the shaving off of ignorance finds no support in Israelite writings. However, for our purposes it is significant that Philo saw an analogy between

55

pruning fruit trees and circumcising the male organ. Both acts remove unnecessary excess.

Like Philo, the rabbis also saw circumcision as fundamentally linked to issues of procreation. This connection becomes evident when the rabbis consider how Abraham knew he was supposed to circumcise the penis and not some other organ. After all, God instructs Abraham to circumcise "the flesh of his foreskin." How did Abraham know that God intended him to circumcise the sexual organ and not the foreskin of his heart or ears? "Rav Huna said in Bar Kappara's name: Abraham made the following analogy (gezerah shavah). Scripture uses the word 'foreskin' in reference to a tree (Lev. 19:23) and in reference to man (Gen. 17:11). Just as foreskin of trees refers to the place where it yields fruit, foreskin of man must refer to the place where he produces fruit" (Gen. Rab. 46:4; see also Lev. Rab. 25:6; and B. Shabbat 108a). Another sage disagrees and suggests that the covenantal language itself signaled that God had in mind the foreskin of the penis. " 'And I will make My covenant between Me and thee, and will multiply thee exceedingly' (Gen. 17:2). This means 'I will put my covenant between me and you, in the place that is fruitful and multiplies'" (Lev. Rab. 25:6). Like Philo, the rabbis also saw an analogy between circumcision and horticultural practices. Explaining the significance of Abraham's circumcision occurring at a "ripe" old age, "R. Simeon b. Lakish said, '[God said], I will set up a cinnamon tree in the world: just as the cinnamon tree yields fruit as long as you manure and hoe [around] it, so too in the case of Abraham, [he will be fruitful] even when his blood runs sluggishly and his passions and desire has ceased'" (Gen. Rab. 46:2). The rabbis do not equate pruning and circumcision. But they do see an analogy between the work required to maximize the yield of a cinnamon tree and circumcision which enables Abraham to produce fruit at a very old age.

These interpretations do not have the status of "native exegesis" when it comes to understanding what circumcision meant to priests who lived at least five centuries earlier. They derive from the distinctive points of view of their authors. These same authors, moreover, offer other interpretations of circumcision that find no substantiation in Israelite literature. Nonetheless, these interpretations show that the symbolic exegesis performed above is not simply an idiosyncratic reading possible only from the vantage point of symbolic anthropology. Other readers, reading from other points of view, arrived at similar conclusions. These interpretations also show that the connection between circumcision and horticultural practices made sense to those who lived in cultures in which agriculture played a central role. The rabbis were alive to this understanding of circumcision because they also relied on agricultural metaphors to conceptualize human sexuality. To provide one example among many, the rabbis compare the stages in a girl's sexual maturation to the ripening of a fig. During childhood, she is like an unripe fig; during puberty, she is like a ripening fig; when she becomes a woman, she is like a fully ripened fig (M. *Nid.* 5:7).[18]

Israel, the Orchard and Vineyard of God

My claim that fruit trees serve as metaphors for male organs in the priestly writings gains further plausibility when one realizes that this association represents an elaboration of other metaphors already operative in Israelite thought. Before the priestly source was produced, the analogy between fruit trees and Israel as a religious community was already deeply engrained in the religious imagination of Israel. Time and again, Israelite writers depict God's relation to Israel in terms of metaphors related to the cultivation of orchards and vineyards. It would take dozens of pages to reproduce all the passages in which such metaphors appear. As the following representative examples make clear, such metaphors cut across the entire tradition, whether surveyed by genre or chronologically. They appear in early and late prophetic literature, in writings of the Deuteronomist, and in wisdom literature. Such metaphors provide the basis for several chapter-long parables in prophetic literature (Isa. 5; Jer. 24; Ezek. 17, 31), Ps. (80:9–16), and the deuteronomic narratives (Jud. 9:10ff). They appear in sources composed before and after the rise and fall of the Assyrian empire as well as in literature composed before, during, and immediately following the Babylonian exile.

If such metaphors are not limited to a particular genre or historical period, they are concentrated in passages that deal with a limited repertoire of themes. These themes typically involve the various stages in the unfolding relationship between Israel, as a collective entity, and God. For example, writers compare the early phase of this developing relationship, which is frequently conceived of as idyllic, to a farmer who lovingly plants an orchard or vineyard (e.g., Jer. 2:21, 11:16; Ps. 44:3, 80:9–12). "Let me sing," writes Isaiah, "for my beloved. A song of my lover about his vineyard. My beloved [i.e., God] had a vineyard [i.e., Israel] on a fruitful hill. He broke the ground, cleared it of stones, and planted it with choice vine. He built a watchtower inside it. He even hewed a wine press in it, for he hoped it would yield grapes" (Isa. 5:1–2). According to Hosea, God experienced the first encounter with Israel as pleasing as "grapes in the wilderness" and considered the patriarchs "as first figs to ripen on a fig tree" (Hos. 9:10).

The relationship, however, did not bear fruit in the way that God anticipated. God hoped the vineyard "would yield grapes. Instead, it yielded wild grapes" (Isa. 5:2) and turned into an alien vine (Jer. 2:21). Consequently, God withheld the care formerly lavished on Israel. "Now I am going to tell you what I will do to My vineyard: I will remove its hedge. I will break down its wall, that it may be trampled. And I will make it a desolation; it shall not be pruned or hoed" (Isa. 5:5–6). By breaching the wall, God enabled every passerby to eat the fruit of the vineyard (Ps. 80:9–16), and out of anger, God even set fire to the vineyard (Ezek. 15:6; Ps. 80:17). When God's punishment is completed, Israel will be desolate like the olive tree when the vintage is over (Isa. 24:13) or an olive tree to which God has set fire (Jer. 11:16). After Israel's punishment "only the gleanings shall be left . . . as when one beats an olive tree. Two berries or three on the topmost branch, four or five on the boughs of the crown" (Isa. 17:6). God will "uproot" Israel from the land (Jer. 1:10; 18:7; 31:28) and discard Israel like a farmer discards bad figs (Jer. 24).

Although God makes Israel undergo terrible sufferings in the form of military defeats and exile, there still remains hope that the relationship between God and Israel will be restored to its former vitality. At that time God will plant Israel once again firmly on its soil. "I will restore my people Israel. They shall plant vineyards and drink their wine. They shall till their gardens and eat their fruits. And I will plant them on their soil, nevermore to be uprooted from the soil I have given them" (Amos 9:14–15).

At this time, God will be to Israel like the dew, and Israel will blossom like the vine and be as beautiful as the olive tree (Hos. 14:6–8). "See a time is coming when I will sow the house of Israel and the house of Judah with seed of men and seed of cattle, and just as I was watchful over them to uproot and to pull down . . . so I will be watchful over them to build and to plant" (Jer. 31:27–28). "And your people, all of them righteous, shall possess the land for all time. They are the shoot that I planted" (Isa. 60:21, see also 61:3; Ezek. 34:26).

The restoration is sometimes compared to the way that a tree destroyed by fire or storm has the capacity to regenerate itself. "And the survivors of the house of Judah that have escaped shall renew its trunk below and produce fruit above" (Isa. 37:31). A shoot will grow out of the stump of Jesse (Isa. 11:1; Zech. 6:12–3) and God will raise up a branch of David's line (Jer. 23:5, 33:15). Alternatively, Israel is like a shoot cut from a tree which is replanted (Isa. 60:21).

From these examples, it is easy to see why orchards and vineyards served as popular metaphors for describing the relationship between God and Israel. Israelite writers saw an analogy between Israel dwelling securely on its land and fruit trees growing productively under the care of the farmer. Israel's insecurity is compared to an orchard or vineyard that is either unprotected or destroyed by its planter.

Israelite writers also draw on the domain of horticulture to conceptualize the relationship between God and individual Israelites. These metaphors are concentrated in but not limited to the Psalms. For example, one who studies the teaching of the Lord "is like a tree planted beside streams of water that yields its fruit in season whose foliage never fades and whatever it produces thrives" (Ps. 1:3). In contrast to the wicked, "I am a thriving olive tree in God's house. I trust in the faithfulness of God forever and ever" (Ps. 52:10). "The righteous bloom like a date-palm. They thrive like the cedar in Lebanon, planted in the house of the Lord. They flourish in the courts of our God, in old age they still produce fruit" (Ps. 92:13–14).

According to Jeremiah, a person who places trust in the Lord is like "a tree planted by waters, sending forth its roots by a stream. . . . It has not a care in year of drought, it does not cease to yield fruit" (Jer. 17:8). When Jeremiah's enemies plot his downfall, the prophet conceptualizes their scheme as an attempt to uproot him. "I did not realize it was against me they fashioned their plots. 'Let us destroy the tree in full sap, let us cut him off from the land of the living'"(Jer. 11:19).[19] Exasperated by the flourishing of the wicked, Jeremiah accuses God of injustice: "Why are the workers of treachery at ease? You have planted them, and they have taken root. They spread, they even bear fruit" (Jer. 12:1–2). By contrast, Eliphaz, one of Job's interlocutors, believes that a wicked man "will wither before his time, his boughs never having flourished. He will drop his unripe grapes like a vine. He will shed his blossoms like an olive tree . . . their womb has produced deceit" (Job 15:32–35).

Fruit trees also serve as metaphors for the domestic unit. "Our sons are like saplings well tended in their youth; Our daughters are like corner stones trimmed to give shape to a palace" (Ps. 144:12). "Your wife shall be like a fruitful vine within your house; your sons like olive saplings around your table" (Ps. 128:3).

Human Fruitfulness

Given the frequent comparison between the prosperity of Israel and the thriving of an orchard or vineyard, it is not surprising that some Israelite writers associate the harvest of fruit trees with human progeny. Just as a farmer who cares for an orchard sees its fruit ripen and enjoys its harvest, so Israelites who are securely rooted on their land will produce children and see them grow to maturity. The symbolic connection between agricultural and human yields is given linguistic and literary expression in Israelite writings. In Hebrew, as in English, a single term (zera) is applied to agricultural and human "seed." The Hebrew stem that means "be fruitful" (peru) derives from the same stem as the word for "fruit" (peri). Firstborn children are referred to as a person's first yield (Ps. 105:36). Children are called "fruit of the womb" (Gen. 30:2; Deut. 28:4, 18). In addition, we have seen how the terms "twig," "shoot," "stump," and "branch" are used in reference to descendants from the house of David (Isa. 11:1; Jer. 23:5, 33:15; Zech. 6:12–13). One writer even applies the term "son" *(ben)* to describe the stem of the tree, Israel, that God metaphorically plants on the land. The domains of human reproduction and horticultural yield are each structured to a significant extent in terms drawn from the corresponding domain.[20]

Numerous biblical passages treat the fate of Israelite fruit trees and children as parallel themes. According to Jeremiah, God said to the exiled community in Babylonia, "Build houses and live in them, plant gardens and eat their fruit, take wives and beget sons and daughters . . . multiply there do not decrease" (Jer. 29:5–6). The Psalmist declares that the faithful "plant vineyards that yield a fruitful harvest. God blesses them and they increase greatly" (Ps. 107:37–38). The post-exilic writer of Isaiah 65 extends the metaphor still further; drawing an analogy between enjoying the fruit of one's harvest and experiencing the joy of seeing one's children grow to maturity. At the time of restoration, Israelites "shall plant vineyards and enjoy their fruit. They shall not build for others to dwell in, or plant for others to enjoy. For the days of My people shall be as long as the days of a tree . . . They shall not bear children in vain. But they shall be a people blessed by the Lord and their offspring shall remain with them" (Isa. 65:21–23).

The association between a plentiful yield from fruit trees and the thriving of human children was more than just metaphoric. War, one of the conditions that undermined the productivity of orchards and vineyards, also threatened families. War took men from the home and from the farm, and consequently, neither Israelite women nor fruit trees would receive the attention required to bear fruit. The Deuteronomist thus instructs army officials to make the following declaration before an army departs for war: "Is there anyone who has planted a vineyard but has never harvested it? Let him go back to his home, lest he die in battle and another initiate it. Is there anyone who has paid the bride-price for a wife, but who has not yet taken her? Let him go back to his home, lest he die in battle and another man take her" (Deut. 20:6–7). In addition to taking men away from the home, invading armies extirpated Israel's or-

chards and children. During times of war, people would see neither the fruit of their trees nor the fruit of their wombs reach maturity. "They will devour your harvest and food, they will devour
your sons and daughters, herds and flocks, vines and fig trees"
(Jer. 5:17).

"Though you plant vineyards and till them, you shall have no
wine to drink or store, for the worm shall devour them. Although
you have olive trees throughout your territory, you shall have no
oil for anointment, for your olives shall drop off. Though you beget
sons and daughters, they shall not remain with you, for they shall
go into captivity." The cricket shall take over all the trees and produce of your land (Deut. 28:40–42).

In the above passages, the themes of harvesting a fruit tree and
the ripening of fruit are treated as analogous to the harvesting of a
woman and the maturing of one's children. That is why these
themes are so often set in parallel.

Other passages make the connection between the fertility of fruit
trees and humans still more explicit. One psalmist, we recall, likens
a "good wife" to a fruitful vine that produces much fruit (Ps.
128:3). A post-exilic writer invokes the image of a withered tree to
describe an infertile man. "Let not the eunuch say, 'I am a withered tree,' for thus said the Lord, 'As regards eunuchs who keep
My sabbaths, who have chosen what I desire and hold fast to My
covenant, I will give them . . . a monument and a name better than
sons or daughters'" (Isa. 56:3–5). In concluding the argument of
this section, it is perhaps interesting to note that the analogy between fruit and children continues to capture the imagination of
those living in the land of Israel. The authors of *The Fruits of the Holy
Land*[21] dedicate the book "in humble thankfulness and overwhelming pride to the heroic fighters of Israel's Eternal City, June
1967; For are they not the finest fruit of Israel?"

As the preceding discussion makes evident, the association between fruit and fruit trees, on the one hand, and human sexuality
and fertility, on the other, was widely familiar in ancient Israel. If
Israel repudiated the fertility cults of its neighbors as histories of Israelite religion so often suggest, it did not do so because the theme
of human fertility represented an abomination. Human fecundity

constituted a central preoccupation in Israel's understanding of God's covenantal obligations. Like other peoples, Israelites regarded fruit and fruit trees as appropriate symbols of that theme. In turn, fruit and fruit trees became connected to the idea of covenant.

There are several grounds for assuming that the priests who wrote during or shortly after the exile were familiar with the metaphoric equation of Israel and fruit trees. The large number of such comparisons in diverse sources suggests that this theme was not limited to any particular religious circle. More specifically, the extensive use of such metaphors by the prophet Ezekiel, who was also a priest, shows that such metaphors were considered persuasive in priestly circles. (Ezek. 15:6, 17:1–24, 34:26ff, 37:16–19). Finally, since the metaphoric association between Israelites and fruit trees was popular among writers describing the exile and restoration, it is reasonable to assume that the priests, who may also have written during the same period of time, were conversant with it.

We now see that the priestly analogy between a juvenile fruit tree and an uncircumcised male member builds directly on those metaphors already circulating in Israelite religious culture. Before the priests gave literary expression to their conception of circumcision, Israelite writers had already invoked the images of fruitful orchards and vineyards to express the covenantal promise. If Israel trusted in God, God would plant Israel on the land. The act of planting trees already symbolized God's covenant with Israel. "I will restore my people Israel. . . . And I will plant them on their soil, nevermore to be uprooted from the soil I have given them" (Amos 9:14–15). "I will make an everlasting covenant with them that I will not turn away from them and that I will treat them graciously. . . . I will delight in treating them graciously, and I will plant them in this land faithfully, with all My heart and soul" (Jer. 32:40–41). "I will grant them a covenant of friendship . . . The trees of the field shall yield their fruit and the land shall yield its produce. [My people] shall continue secure on its own soil . . . I shall establish for them a planting of renown" (Ezek. 34:25–29). Since the priests also considered circumcision a sign of the covenant, it is not surprising that they saw an analogy between the male organ and fruit trees. After all, both served as symbols of Israel's faith.

63

Given the recurrence of this symbolic complex, one must also probe the significance of what might otherwise appear to be trivial and incidental elements of Israelite narratives. Turning to the narratives themselves, one does indeed find instances where an association between fruit, trees, and fertility seems to be presupposed. These associations need not have been conscious. . . . Writers often have the feeling that the addition or subtraction of an element to a story makes the narrative "work," even if they are not always able to explain this sense of fit. But the sense that one element works better in the narrative than another may be rooted in a set of cultural associations of which the author is not aware. This is all the more true of Israelite narratives, which probably underwent a period of oral transmission.

The association between human fertility and agricultural produce, for example, seems to underlie the Jahwist's story about Adam and Eve. According to the Jahwist, the first humans became aware of their nakedness only after eating from the fruit of a tree in the garden. In response to that awareness they sewed together fig leaves to cover their loins (Gen. 3:6–7). The first mention of sexual intercourse comes after Adam and Eve have eaten fruit. According to the Jahwist, moreover, God metes out parallel punishments for disobeying the divine command against eating fruit from the Tree of Knowledge. Women will have severe pain during childbirth and men will bring forth agricultural yield with the greatest of toil. The male labor in harvesting the crop, therefore, is set parallel to the female labor of bearing children (Gen. 3:16–19). The Jahwist is also the one who gives the name Tamar (date palm) to Judah's daughter-in-law.

Like a date palm, Tamar turns out to be fertile and thus produces twins (Gen. 38:27). The Tamar of the Deuteronomic narrative does not seem to have any associations with fertility (2 Sam. 13). The Jahwist is also responsible for the story about mandrakes to open her womb (Gen. 30:14–16). Finally, this is the writer who describes Jacob's method of ensuring the fertility of the speckled and spotted goats and the dark colored sheep of Laban's flock. Jacob peels white stripes in poplar and almond shoots and sets these up in the watering troughs of the goats, particularly when the sturdier animals were mating (Gen. 30:31–43). Here, the tree branch is supposed to influence the reproductive behavior of animals. This narrative intersects in suggestive ways with the priestly association between fruit trees and pruning on the one hand and the male organ and circumcision on the other.

Given these associations in the Jahwist strand between fruit, fruit trees, and human sexuality, one may even be tempted to see a parallelism between this writer's idea that Eve was created from Adam's rib and the method of propagating fruit trees by taking a cutting. If this seems improbable, recall the many instances cited above in which Israelite writers poetically compared the birth of human progeny with the planting of shoots taken from a mature tree. These observations can be offered only tentatively. But given the recurring use of fruit and fruit trees as metaphor for various aspects of the human experience, they do have some measure of plausibility.

part III

The Trunk:
Rabbinic Judaism

As Hellenistic civilization with all its political, economic, ecological, philosophic, and military impact swept over the Mediterranean basin, earth-based biblical Judaism was shattered. The Jewish people were severed not only from their traditional land, but from the characteristic way of connecting with God that had grown up in their earth-based culture. Offerings of food from the land and long periods of rhythmic respectful rest with and for the land no longer offered a coherent connection with God. The religious leaders who became "the Rabbis" focused instead on words of prayer and Torah study as the medium of encounter with God.

Without a land of its own, without authority to share in governing the lands where it was scattered—in short, with no earth-place to be responsible for governing—the Jewish people muted, though they never erased, their concern with the rhythms of the earth. Even though the Mishnah encoded such earth-focused times as the Fifteenth of Shvat, the date was almost obliterated as a time for observance or celebration, while other earth-born festivals were reinterpreted as anniversaries of historical transformation.

When the rabbinic tradition did address issues of human behavior toward the earth, it drew especially on the imagery and law of trees that had been set forth in Deuteronomy. Indeed, the Rabbis drew much of their law about the environment from the Deuter- onomic command to refrain from destroying the fruit trees of an enemy. How to apply this teaching—how to balance the calls of economic need and ecological protection, the calls of sacred words and holy earth—was always a question in rabbinic thought. This section presents some texts of rabbinic teaching as well as some contemporary studies of the various rabbinic tugs and dances about trees and the earth.

Mishnah and Gemara on Tu B'Shvat
(Chapter 1 Mishnah 1)

There are four New Years. On the first of Nisan is the New Year for
Kings and for Festivals; on the first of Elul is the New Year for the
tithe of animals—R. Eliezer and R. Shimon say, On the first of
Tishrei—on the first of Tishrei is the New Year for the years, for
Sabbatical Years, for Jubilee Years, for planting and for vegetables;
and on the first of Shvat is the New Year for Trees, according to the
view of the School of Shammai, but the School of Hillel say, On the
fifteenth thereof.

Our Rabbis taught: If the fruit of a tree blossoms before the fifteenth of Shvat, it is tithed for the outgoing year; if after the fifteenth
of Shvat, it is tithed for the incoming year (B. *Rosh HaShanah* 15b).[1]

Midrash from *The Book of Legends,*
Sefer Aggadah

Hayim Nachman Bialik and Yehoshua Ravnitsky

"No one to converse with (*siaḥ*, "tree") in the field" (Gen. 2:5). All
trees converse *(mesiḥim)*,[1] as it were, with one another. Indeed, one
may add, all trees converse with mortals; all trees—created, as trees
were, to provide fellowship for mortals (Gen. Rab. 13:2).[2]

At the sight of comely beings and beautiful trees, one should say,
"Blessed be He who has created beautiful creatures" (Tosefta
Berakhot 6:4).[3]

R. Abbahu taught: What is the proof that the Holy One admires
men of high stature? The verse "I destroyed the Amorite . . . whose
height was like the height of the cedars" (Amos 2:9) (B. *Bekhorot*
45b).[4]

69

It is told of R. Ishmael and R. Akiva that, while they were walking through the streets of Jerusalem accompanied by a certain man, a sick person confronted them and said, "Masters, tell me, how shall I be healed?" They replied, "Take such-and-such, and you will be healed." The man accompanying the sages asked them, "Who smote him with sickness?" They replied, "The Holy One." The man: "And you bring yourselves into a matter that does not concern you? God smote, and you would heal?" The sages: "What is your work?" The man: "I am a tiller of the soil. You see the sickle in my hand." The sages: "Who created the vineyard?" The man: "The Holy One." The sages: "Then why do you bring yourself into a matter that does not concern you? God created it, and you eat the fruit from it!" The man: "Don't you see the sickle in my hand? If I did not go out and plow the vineyard, prune it, compost it, and weed it, it would have yielded nothing." The sages: "You are the biggest fool in the world! Have you not heard the verse 'As for man, his days are as grass' (Ps. 103:15)? A tree, if it is not composted, weeded, and [the area around it] plowed, will not grow; and even if it does grow, if not given water to drink, it will die—will not live. So, too, the human body is a tree, a healing potion is the compost, and a physician is the tiller of the soil" (M. *Sam.* 4).[5]

R. Huna said: All creatures seek their mate. R. Ammi said: Even cedars seek their mate. You can see this for yourself. For in Babylon there had been no cedars.[6] And when Nebuchadnezzar came here [to the land of Israel], he uprooted cedars from here and planted them in Babylon. It was of their rejoicing that Scripture said to Nebuchadnezzar, "Even pines rejoice at thy downfall, and [it goes without saying] the cedars of Lebanon" (Isa. 14:8) (*Lam. Rab.* 1:4, Section 30).[6]

R. Tanhuma said: It happened that a female palm that stood in Hammetan yielded no fruit. A scion of a male palm was grafted onto it, but it still yielded no fruit. A palm grower who passed by saw it and said, "She gazes upon a palm at Jericho and has a desire for it." When they went and got a scion of that palm and grafted it onto the female, she yielded fruit right away (*Gen. Rab.* 41:1 and *Num. Rab.* 3:1).[7]

70

When a tree that bears fruit is cut down, its moan goes from one end of the world to the other, yet no sound is heard (*Pirke de-R. Eliezer* 34).[8]

"Shemonah Esrei for the New Year of the Trees": A Medieval Amidah for Tu B'Shvat

Joyce Galaski

In the year 882 C.E. a new synagogue was built in Old Cairo, also known as Fostat. An attic room in the synagogue was designated as a *geniza,* a storeroom for old religious books and documents, which were placed in it over the course of several centuries. A superstition developed that it was bad luck to remove anything from this *geniza,* and so its contents remained virtually untouched for hundreds of years.

In 1896, when the scholar Solomon Schechter persuaded the leaders of the synagogue to let him look at the *geniza,* he found a treasure house of early books and documents, many of them crumbling from age. Among the many *piyyutim,* or liturgical poems, found in the *geniza* was one entitled "*Shemonah Esrei le-Rosh HaShanah la-ilan*" ("Eighteen Benedictions for the New Year of the Trees"). It is thought to have been written by Rabbi Yehuda Halevi b. Rabbi Hillel, a poet who was unknown until the discovery of several of his works among the *geniza* manuscripts.[1]

Scholars believe that he lived in Israel in the tenth or eleventh century.[2] (He has no connection to the famous poet and philosopher Yehuda Halevi, who lived in Spain a few generations after him.)

Since it has been widely believed that there was no ritual or liturgy for Tu B'Shvat before the seventeenth century, when the kabbalists of Tzfat created the Tu B'Shvat seder, this "*Shemonah Esrei* for the New Year of the Trees" comes as a surprise. It is actu-

71

ally one of two *piyyutim* for Tu B'Shvat by the same author that were found in the Cairo *geniza*. They raise the interesting possibility that there may have been other liturgy for Tu B'Shvat written in Israel in the early Middle Ages which became lost, as these poems nearly did.

This poem is a *kerovah*, a *piyyut* connected to the *Amidah* prayer. It has eighteen stanzas, one for each of the eighteen[3] sections of the *Amidah*, and the last line of each stanza is the *hatimah*, or concluding blessing, for that section of the *Amidah*. Like many *piyyutim*, this poem has an interesting and complex structure. It is written in alphabetical acrostic; the first, second, and fourth lines of each stanza all rhyme and all begin with the same letter of the alphabet: *alef* for the first verse, *bet* for the second, and so on.

Since there are twenty-two letters in the Hebrew alphabet and only eighteen benedictions in the Shemonah Esrei, the last stanza contains a line, or half-line, beginning with each of the last five letters of the alphabet. The third line of every stanza is preceded by the words, *"be-Rosh Shanah La-ilan"* ("On the New Year of the Trees").[4] The fifth line of every stanza is a biblical verse which begins with the word *ki* ("for") and which has some connection to the blessing of the *Amidah* that concludes that stanza. In addition, the second line of each stanza begins with the name of a tree or plant that grows in the land of Israel—walnut, cypress, grape, etc.— or with a more general word related to trees or plants, such as orchard, vineyard, or blossom.[5]

One of the most striking things about the poem is the way the author combines these images of trees and plants with the themes and blessings of the *Amidah*.

In translating the poem, I have tried to illustrate the alphabetical acrostic form in the first three stanzas of the English, using the letters *a*, *b*, and *g* to correspond to the Hebrew letters *alef*, *bet*, and *gimmel*. However, I have not maintained this form in the rest of the translation. (I felt that doing so would require too great a sacrifice of meaning to form.) While I have tried to stay fairly close to the meaning of the Hebrew text, I have sometimes changed words either to make the translation flow better or, in a few places, to make its meaning more comprehensible to the English-speaking reader.[6]

SHEMONAH ESREI FOR THE NEW YEAR OF THE TREES

Awesome rains of salvation send down upon my people,
As the walnut tree blossoms for my beloved ones.
On the New Year of the Trees
Awaken the strength of my faithful ones,
For Adonai is sun and shield.[7]
Blessed are You, Adonai, Abraham's shield.

Brilliant light will He shine for His followers,
Brightly will He make the cypress shine for His redeemed ones.
On the New Year of the Trees
Bless with the rains of revival the land of the living,
For the one who finds Me finds life.
Blessed are You, Adonai, Who revives the dead.

Great, praised, and exalted above all gods,
Grape wine from the vineyard of God.
On the New Year of the Trees
Give overflowing joy to those who say, "None is like God,"
For great in your midst is the Holy One of Israel.
Blessed are You, Adonai, the holy God.

Build Your Temple for Your chosen one,
The chestnut tree rises to its height.
On the New Year of the Trees
Interpret for us Your Torah,
For Adonai gives wisdom.
Blessed are You, Adonai, Who grants understanding.

Adorn the one who gazes from the peak of Amanah,[8]
Let the myrtle flower for the believer.
On the New Year of the Trees
Take back the seed of Jacob[9]
For I will turn the captivity of the land as of old.
Blessed are You, Adonai, Who desires our return.

Grant prosperity to Your people,
May the rose sparkle and never fade.

On the New Year of the Trees
Testify that You have forgiven Your people,
For I will pardon the remnant of Israel.
Blessed are You, Adonai, gracious and forgiving God.

Brightness will shine on Jacob's country,
There will the leafy olive rule.
On the New Year of the Trees
May we be told,
For God has redeemed Jacob.
Blessed are You, Adonai, Redeemer of Israel.

Give freedom and redemption to Your people,
The carob will make sweet its blessing to praise You.
On the New Year of the Trees
O Living One, heal the nation that calls on You,
For I will bring healing to you.
Blessed are You, Adonai, Who heals the sick among His people
  Israel.

You, Who make the land rejoice, purify
And bless with rain this most desired of lands.
On the New Year of the Trees
Send rains of blessing to the land,
For those He blesses shall inherit the land. *And grant dew*
  and rain for blessing.
Blessed are You, Adonai, Who blesses the years.

Hasten salvation for Your waiting people,
Lovely will be the harvest of their fruits.
On the New Year of the Trees
May You call for the gathering of the exiles,
For I will redeem them and they shall keep increasing.
Blessed are You, Adonai, Who gathers in the exiles of Your
  people Israel.

As has been proclaimed in our words,
May the vineyard yield us its fruits.

On the New Year of the Trees
May the weight of justice tip our scales,
For Adonai is our judge.
Blessed are You, Adonai, King Who loves justice.

Proclaim salvation to Your servant,
Like the almond tree whose fragrance lasts but twenty-one days,
On the New Year of the Trees
May the heretics who betrayed Him be destroyed,
For the wicked will perish.
Blessed are You, Adonai, Who destroys enemies and humbles the
*   arrogant.*

From the time He destroyed His Temple,
Like myrrh from the earth He removed His dwelling place,
On the New Year of the Trees
He will be a fortress to the people close to Him,
For the islands wait for me.
Blessed are You, Adonai, support and stronghold of the righteous.

Images of joy and loveliness,
Visions of nard and saffron will we see.
On the New Year of the Trees
We will proclaim: "The city will be rebuilt on its ruins,"
For Adonai builds Zion.
Blessed are You, Adonai, Who builds Jerusalem.

Clear the path for my children,
Let blossoms multiply for my delight.
On the New Year of the Trees
Listen to our pleas,
For Adonai listens to the needy.
Blessed are You, Adonai, Who listens to prayer.

Arrange the sacrifices for His Temple,
Bearing offerings of willows will the people ascend.
On the New Year of the Trees
May He receive His people's gift,

For Adonai delights in His people.
Blessed are You, Adonai, Who restores His presence to Zion.

His fruits will He give to gladden us,
Produce of orchards and of the land.
On the New Year of the Trees
Your redeemed ones will praise You day and night,
For pleasant and lovely is Your praise.
Blessed are You, Adonai, Whose Name is good and to Whom all
   thanks are due.

With the fruits of trees will we be blessed,
Gourd and pomegranate will blossom for this people.
On the New Year of the Trees,
May sycamore and wild fig grow tall,
Proclaim: "For true peace will I give you in this place."
Blessed are You, Adonai, the One Who makes peace.

Commentary

Images of God's power and love as manifested through nature flow through this poem, interweaving with the traditional blessings of the *Amidah* and, at times, adding new dimensions to our understanding of them. The poem opens with the line *Eider nizlei yesha tazil la-hamonai* (literally: "Power of the rains of salvation rain down upon my multitudes"). Tu B'Shvat comes in the midst of the winter rains in Israel and there can be heavy rainstorms at this time of year. Thus, in the opening line, the poet evokes the sense of awe at God's power that one can feel watching the rain pour down from the skies. However, this is not simply rain, but *nizlei yesha*, "rains of salvation." There is a double meaning here; in Israel, lack of rain can mean drought and starvation, so the powerful rains of winter are in fact "rains of salvation" for the land and for the people. But the meaning is also symbolic; the poem is filled with the poet's messianic hopes for the restoration of the land to the people of Israel and the flowering of both the land and the people. In praying for the "rains of salvation," the poet is praying for God to send salvation to the people with the sudden power of a winter rainstorm.

Although it comes during the winter rains, Tu B'Shvat is also the time of the flowering of the first trees in Israel. The image of the blossoming walnut tree in the second line of the poem is very different from the imagery of the first line. It is an image of beauty, of grace and tenderness. The God who sends powerful rainstorms also sends flowers for the people He loves.

This first stanza of the poem takes the place of the first paragraph of the *Amidah*; both end with the blessing *Barukh Atah Adonai, magen Avraham*, "Blessed are You, Adonai, Abraham's shield." Both evoke images of God's power and of God's love and protectiveness, which come together in the image of the shield. But while the first paragraph of the traditional *Amidah* stresses our relationship to God as the God of our ancestors, the poem, which is filled with nature imagery, does not even mention ancestors except in the final blessing.

The contrast between the second stanza of the poem and the second paragraph of the traditional *Amidah* is equally striking. The second paragraph of the *Amidah* praises God as *me-ḥayei ha-meitim*, "the One who gives life to the dead."

This blessing has usually been associated with the doctrine of the resurrection of the dead. However, the author of the poem gives it a completely different interpretation. In the fourth line of this stanza, he writes *Bareikh be-gishmei teḥiyah le-eretz ha-ḥayyim*, "Bless with the rains of revival the land of the living." Thus he is associating *te-ḥiyat ha-meitim*, "giving life to the dead," with the "rains of revival" which give new life to the land after the winter. His focus is not on life after death, but on *eretz ha-ḥayyim*, "the land of the living." The meaning of *me-ḥayei ha-meitim* is also expanded by the biblical verse in this stanza: *Ki motzi matza ḥayyim*, "For the one who finds Me finds life." This is a quotation from Prov. 8:35, where it is the voice of Wisdom speaking. But in the context of the poem, it seems to refer not only to finding wisdom, but to finding God. The juxtaposition of the fourth line of the stanza and this biblical verse with the blessing *me-ḥayei ha-meitim* make the poem function as a kind of midrash on this section of the *Amidah*. They add the dimensions of the revival of the earth, and of the spiritual revival of one who finds God, to the idea of "reviving the dead."

77

The poet's hopes for the restoration of Zion are also a central theme of the poem, as his prayer for the flowering of the land blends together with his prayer for the return and restoration of his people. While one might expect this theme associated with the blessings of the *Amidah* that speak of the ingathering of the exiles or the building of Jerusalem, its role in the fifth stanza of the poem is particularly interesting. This stanza concludes with the blessing *"Barukh atah Adonai ha-rotzeh be-teshuvah"* which is usually translated "Blessed are You, Adonai, Who desires repentance." However, *teshuvah* means "return" as well as repentance, and I have translated the blessing as "Who desires our return," since this is clearly its meaning in the poem. The biblical verse in the fifth line of the stanza is *Ki ashiv et shvut ha-aretz ke-varishonah,* "For I will turn the captivity of the land as of old." Thus *teshuvah* in this context takes the meaning of "turning the captivity of the land" or liberating the land from foreign domination and returning it to the people of Israel. The fourth line of this stanza, "take back the seed of Jacob," can be interpreted as either asking God to take back Israel as His people or asking God to bring the people of Israel back to their land. Both the fourth and fifth lines set a context which transforms the meaning of the blessing in the last line, "Blessed are you . . . Who desires our return," from one which speaks of repentance to one which speaks of the return to Zion.

The themes of the return to Zion and the flowering of the land are interwoven throughout many of the stanzas of the poem. They come together in the last stanzas in a vision of the people redeemed and the land restored. The tone of the poem is hopeful, and at times even exultant, with its images of flowers, abundant harvests, vines blossoming, and trees growing tall. The poet's prayer to God to take back His people and restore them to their land is often more exuberant than pleading. The image with which the poet leaves us, in the last stanza, calls to mind some of the prophecies of Isaiah—it is a vision of a flowering land, its people blessed with plenty and with peace.

Translator's Comments

This poem is written in very difficult medieval Hebrew, making it problematic for even a native Hebrew-speaker to comprehend. It is filled with allusions to biblical and rabbinic text so obscure that even a scholar will miss many of them. The language of the Hebrew sometimes flows well but sometimes seems awkward and stilted. Why then did I find myself falling in love with it as I struggled to translate it?

One reason is that I found myself fascinated, and often moved, by the way the poet weaves together imagery about trees and nature with verses from the Bible and blessings from the *Amidah*. It not only gave me a new understanding of Tu B'Shvat; it gave me a new understanding of blessings of the *Amidah* which I have recited hundreds of times.

There was also something about the history of the poem that moved me. It was probably recited on Tu B'Shvat in a synagogue or synagogues somewhere in Israel in the tenth or eleventh century. It then found its way to the *geniza* of the synagogue in Old Cairo, where it was buried under dusty piles of books and documents for almost one thousand years. While it was discovered by scholars nearly a century ago and was published in Hebrew a few decades ago, I don't know if it has actually been used in prayer since the eleventh century.

I am planning to use this *"Shemonah Esrei* for the New Year of the Trees" in a service for Tu B'Shvat this year. There is something about praying from a text that has been lost for nearly one thousand years that I find very moving. I suddenly find myself spiritually connected to a religious poet of the tenth or eleventh century whose works were almost all lost, and to the members of his congregation whose memories have disappeared from the face of the earth . . . *Barukh Atah Adonai, me-ḥayei ha-meitim,* Blessed are You, God, who gives life to those who have died.

רבי יהודה הלוי ברבי הלל[*]

שְׁמוֹנֶה-עֶשְׂרֵה לְרֹאשׁ הַשָּׁנָה לָאִילָן

אֶדֶר נִזְלֵי יֶשַׁע תַּזִּיל לַהֲמוֹנִי,
אֱגוֹז יַפְרִיחַ לְמַעֲדָנִי,
אַמֵּץ אֱמוּנִי :
כִּי שֶׁמֶשׁ וּמָגֵן יְיָ (תהלים פ"ד, יב)

בָּרוּךְ אַתָּה יְיָ מָגֵן אַבְרָהָם.

בְּרֹאשׁ שָׁנָה לָאִילָן

בְּהִלּוֹ נֵרוֹ יָאִיר לַנְּחוּיִּים,
בְּרֹאשׁ בָּהִיק יַזְהִיר לְפְדוּיִים,
בֶּרֶךְ בְּגִשְׁמֵי תְחִיָּה לְאֶרֶץ הַחַיִּים :
כִּי מֹצְאַי מָצָא חַיִּים (משלי ח', לה).

בָּרוּךְ אַתָּה יְיָ מְחַיֵּה הַמֵּתִים.

בְּרֹאשׁ שָׁנָה לָאִילָן

גָּדוֹל וּמְהֻלָּל וְרָם עַל כָּל אֵל,
גֶּפֶן הַמְשׁוּלָה כֶּרֶם אֵל,
גֶּבֶר שָׂשׂוֹן בְּאוֹמְרִי אֵין כָּאֵל :
כִּי גָדוֹל בְּקִרְבֵּךְ קְדוֹשׁ יִשְׂרָאֵל (ישעיה י"ב, ו).

בָּרוּךְ אַתָּה יְיָ הָאֵל הַקָּדוֹשׁ.

בְּרֹאשׁ שָׁנָה לָאִילָן

דְּבִיר תִּבָּנֶה לְמִסַּיְּמָהּ,
דְּלֵב יַאֲרִיךְ בְּקוֹמָהּ,
דְּרֹשׁ לָנוּ מַחְכִּימָהּ :
כִּי יְיָ יִתֵּן חָכְמָה (משלי ב', ו).

בָּרוּךְ אַתָּה יְיָ חוֹנֵן הַדָּעַת.

בְּרֹאשׁ שָׁנָה לָאִילָן

הַדַּר שָׂרָה מֵרֹאשׁ אֲמָנָה,
הֲדַס יַפְרִיחַ לְמַאֲמִינָה,
תְּשׁוֹבֵב לְמִי מָנָה :
כִּי אָשִׁיב אֶת שְׁבוּת הָאָרֶץ כְּבָרִאשֹׁנָה (ירמיהו ל"ג, יא).

בָּרוּךְ אַתָּה יְיָ הָרוֹצֶה בִּתְשׁוּבָה.

בְּרֹאשׁ שָׁנָה לָאִילָן

וְעַמָּךְ לְטוֹבָה תַּתְאִיר,
וְרַד יַזְהִיר וְאֵל יַכְאִיר,
וְעַד סְלִיחָה לְעַם זוּ לְהַבְאִיר :
כִּי אֶסְלַח לַאֲשֶׁר אַשְׁאִיר (ירמיה נ', כ).

בְּרֹאשׁ שָׁנָה לָאִילָן

---

[*] משורר ארצישראלי לא ידוע, לא מאוחר משנת אלף לספירה.

80

זֹהַר יַזְהִיר מְקוֹם יַעֲקֹב,
זַיִת רַעֲנָן הַמָּשׁוּל בְּיַעֲקֹב,
זֹאת יֵאָמֵר לְיַעֲקֹב,
כִּי פָדָה יְיָ אֶת יַעֲקֹב (ירמיה ל״א, י).

בָּרוּךְ אַתָּה יְיָ גּוֹאֵל יִשְׂרָאֵל.

בְּרֹאשׁ שָׁנָה לָאִילָן

חַפֵּשׂ פְּדוּת לִקְהָלֶךָ
חָרוּב יַמְתִּיק וּבְרָכָה בּוֹ לְהַלֶּלֶךָ,
חַי תְּרַפֵּא גּוֹי מְיַחֲלֶךָ :
כִּי אַעֲלֶה אֲרֻכָה לָךְ (ירמיה ל׳, יז).

בָּרוּךְ אַתָּה יְיָ רוֹפֵא חוֹלֵי עַמּוֹ יִשְׂרָאֵל.

בְּרֹאשׁ שָׁנָה לָאִילָן

טַהֵר מָשׂוֹשׂ כָּל הָאָרֶץ,
טִיף בְּרָכָה לִקְרוּאֵי חֵפֶץ אֶרֶץ,
טַכֵּס לְהַגְשִׁים בְּרָכָה לָאָרֶץ :
כִּי מְבֹרָכָיו יִירְשׁוּ אָרֶץ (תהלים ל״ז, כב).

(וְתֵן טַל וּמָטָר לִבְרָכָה. בָּרוּךְ אַתָּה יְיָ מְבָרֵךְ הַשָּׁנִים.

בְּרֹאשׁ שָׁנָה לָאִילָן

יָהּ חִישׁ יֵשַׁע לְעַמְּךָ אֲשֶׁר קִוּוֹ
יְבוּלִים בְּפָרִים יָנוּב,
יֵאָמֵר לֶאֱסֹף נְדוּחִים אֲשֶׁר יִקָּווּ :
כִּי פְדִיתִים וְרָבוּ כְּמוֹ רָבוּ (זכריה י, ח).

בָּרוּךְ אַתָּה יְיָ מְקַבֵּץ נִדְחֵי עַמּוֹ יִשְׂרָאֵל

בְּרֹאשׁ שָׁנָה לָאִילָן

כְּהַשְׁמִיעַ בְּמִילֵינוּ,
כֶּרֶם יִתֵּן פִּרְיוֹ לָנוּ,
יַכְרִיעַ צֶדֶק מֹאזְנֵינוּ :
כִּי יְיָ שֹׁפְטֵנוּ (ישעיה ל״ג, כב).

בָּרוּךְ אַתָּה יְיָ מֶלֶךְ אוֹהֵב צְדָקָה וּמִשְׁפָּט.

בְּרֹאשׁ שָׁנָה לָאִילָן

לְהַשְׁמִיעַ יֵשַׁע לְעַבְדּוֹ,
לוֹז לְעֶשְׂרִים וְאֶחָד יִגָּמֵר נִרְדּוֹ,
לְאַבֵּד נֶצָרִים וּמִינִים אֲשֶׁר בּוֹ בָּגְדוּ :
כִּי רְשָׁעִים יֹאבֵדוּ (תהלים ל״ז, כ).

בָּרוּךְ אַתָּה יְיָ שׁוֹבֵר אוֹיְבִים וּמַכְנִיעַ זֵדִים.

בְּרֹאשׁ שָׁנָה לָאִילָן

מֵעֵת חֶרֶב בֵּית אָבוֹ,
מוֹר מֵאֶרֶץ הָעֲדָה יָשׁוּבוֹ
מָעוֹז יְהִי לְעַם קְרוֹבוֹ :
כִּי לִי אִיִּים יְקַוּוּ (ישעיה ס׳, ט).

בָּרוּךְ אַתָּה יְיָ מִשְׁעָן וּמִבְטָח לַצַּדִּיקִים.

בְּרֹאשׁ שָׁנָה לָאִילָן

נְעַם שָׂשׂוֹן בְּהִגָּיוֹן
נֵרְדְּ וְכַרְכֹּם נָחַז בְּחֶזְיוֹן,
נִבְנְתָה הָעִיר עַל תִּלָּה נַשְׁמִיעַ בְּרִצְיוֹן :
כִּי בָנָה יְיָ צִיּוֹן (תהלים קי"ב, יז).

בְּרָאשׁ שָׁנָה לָאִילָן

בָּרוּךְ אַתָּה יְיָ בּוֹנֵה יְרוּשָׁלַיִם. אֶת צֶמַח דָּוִד עַבְדְּךָ וכד'

סֹלּוּ סֹלּוּ הַמְסִלָּה לְבָנַי,
סָמְדָר יַרְבֶּה לְעַדָּנַי,
סֻכּוֹת שִׂיחַ חֻנָּנַי :
כִּי שֹׁמֵעַ אֶל אֶבְיוֹנִים יְיָ (תהלים ס"ט, לד).

בְּרָאשׁ שָׁנָה לָאִילָן

בָּרוּךְ אַתָּה יְיָ שׁוֹמֵעַ תְּפִלָּה.

עֶרְךְ קׇרְבָּן אוּלְמוֹ,
עָרְבָה מִנְחָה לָשֵׂאת עִם בְּהִתְרוֹמְמוֹ :
עוֹלַת שַׁי יְקַבֵּל מֵעַמּוֹ
כִּי רוֹצֶה יְיָ בְּעַמּוֹ (תהלים קמ"ט, ד).

בְּרָאשׁ שָׁנָה לָאִילָן

בָּרוּךְ אַתָּה יְיָ הַמַּחֲזִיר שְׁכִינָתוֹ לְצִיּוֹן. מוֹדִים אֲנַחְנוּ לָךְ וכד'

פִּרְיוֹ יִתֵּן לְשַׂמְּחֵנוּ בְּגִילָה,
פַּרְדֵּס עִם צֶמַח אֶרֶץ וִיבוּלָהּ,
פְּדוּיֶיךָ מְהַלְּלִים יוֹמָם וָלַיְלָה :
כִּי נָעִים נָאוָה תְהִלָּה (תהלים קמ"ז, א).

בְּרָאשׁ שָׁנָה לָאִילָן

בָּרוּךְ אַתָּה יְיָ הַטּוֹב שִׁמְךָ וּלְךָ נָאֶה לְהוֹדוֹת.

צִמְחֵי אִילָנוֹת בִּבְרָכָה נֶחֱזֶה,
קִקָּיוֹן רֹאשׁ יוֹם. רִמּוֹן צִיץ לְעַם זֶה,
שְׁקֵמִים וְשִׁירוֹק יִגְבַּהּ כָּנָה :
תַּשְׁמִיעֵנוּ כִּי שָׁלוֹם אֱמֶת אָתֵּן לָכֶם בַּמָּקוֹם הַזֶּה (ירמיה י"ד, יג).

בְּרָאשׁ שָׁנָה לָאִילָן

בָּרוּךְ אַתָּה יְיָ עוֹשֵׂה הַשָּׁלוֹם.

(ע"פ "לקט שירים ופיוטים", כפי שהעתיק ר' מנחם זולאי מכת"י אוקספורד 2737/B)

אדר נזלי ישע – גבורת גשמי ישע. בהילו נרו יאיר לנחויים – באורו יאיר לעם שנחאה אותו (ע"פ שמות ט"ו, יג). בהיק –
מנחיק ("נבחין בתורה" – תרגום שיר השירים ז, ג). המשולה כרם אל – ישראל שנמשלו לכרם ד' צבאות (ישעיהו ה', ז). דביר
תבנה למסויימה – בית המקדש תבנה לאומה המסוימה. דולב ("ערמונים – דולבי" – ירושלמי כתובות פרק ז', הלכה
ט). מחכימה – התורה. שרה מראש אמנה – מביטה מראש ההר אמנה (שיר השירים ד', ח). למי מנה – לעם שעליו נאמר "מי
מנה עפר יעקב" (במדבר כ"ג, י). לטובה תתאיר – תעשהו טוב תואר. ואולי – תותירהו לטובה עי"ד הכתוב (דברים כ"ח, יא) "ואל
יכאיר – אל יהא מכוער. סליחה להבאיר – לומר פיוט ליל ג' של שבועות: "אנכי" – ראש לדיברות הבאיר). זית
רענן המשיל ביעקב – ע"פי ירמיהו י"א, טז. חפש פדות – (בשין שמאלית) בקש גאולה או (בשין ימנית) תן חופש ופדות, עי"ד
שדרשו "אחפש את ירושלים בנרות" – אשחרר (פסיקתא). טיף – גשם. לקרואי חפץ ארץ – על דרך הכתוב (מלאכי ג', יב). טכס
– תקן. יגון – יחיו נאים. במלינו – במלים שלנו. ואולי יש לקרוא "בחלינו", עי"ד "יהיי שלום בחילך"! יכריע צדק מאזנינו –
רמז לראש השנה, בו יישקל גורל העץ במאזנים. יגמור נרדו – יבשיל פירותיו, כמו שאמרו: הלוז הזה משחוא מוציא ניצו ועד שהוא
גומר את פירותיו (תענית כ"ז, עמ' ב). בית איבו – בית מקדשו (יערן). נצרים – נכרים, נוצרים. ושושיו: אחד בשבת לא היו מתענים מפני
הנוצרים (תענית כ"ז, ד; ירושלמי תענית, ד', הלכה ח). בעם יום – כ"א יום (ירושלמי תענית, ד', הלכה ח). נצרים – נכרים, נוצרים. טכס
– תקן. יגון – יחיו נאים. במלינו – במלים שלנו. מור מארץ העדה יישובו – מעת הבושם מור (ישראל) עקר מושבו
מן הארץ. בריציון – ברצון. לעדוני – למעודנים שלי. סכות – להקשיב. אולמו – היכלו, מקדשו. ערבה מנחה – מנחת ערבה
לשאת כשהים עולה לרגל בחג הסוכות. המשרר ראש נגד עיניו את הפסוק וערבה מנחת מנחה ד' (מלאכי ג', ד). קיקיון ראש יום – אולי
יש לקרוא: "ראש יונה"? (יונה ד', ו). שירוק – מין עץ לא ידוע, ואולי יש לקרוא "שורק" – גפן מובחרת או ייתכן שלפנינו צורה
עברית מ"סרקא" הארמית – תאינת-בר, המקבילה לשקמה (משל סרכא דאקים תאניתא – שיר השירים רבה א', ו).

Is the Tree Human?

Eilon Schwartz

The Talmudic law *bal tashchit* ("do not destroy") is the most predominant Jewish precept cited in contemporary Jewish writings on
the environment. This article gives an extensive survey of the roots
and different interpretations of the precept from within the tradition.

The precept of *bal tashchit* has its roots in the Biblical command not
to destroy fruit-bearing trees while laying siege to a warring city.
The Rabbis expanded this injunction into the general precept of *bal
tashchit*, a ban on any wanton destruction. Such a precept was interpreted in different ways, along a continuum whose poles I have
described as the minimalist and maximalist position. In the minimalist
position, interpreters limit the application of *bal tashchit* to only those
situations in which destruction of natural resources and property
cannot be justified in terms of its economic or aesthetic worth to
the Jewish community. In the maximalist position, interpreters expand the application of *bal tashchit* to any situation in which nature
and property are destroyed for something other than human needs.

The last part of this article compares and contrasts the substance
and style of the discussion of *bal tashchit* from within the Jewish tradition with the contemporary discussion of environmental ethics.

No single Jewish concept is quoted more often in demonstrating
Judaism's environmental credentials than the Rabbinic[1] concept of
bal tashchit ("do not destroy"). It appears in virtually all of the literature that discusses Jewish attitudes toward the environmental crisis. Yet rarely are more than a few sentences given to actually
explaining its history and its meaning. Such a superficial approach
has been relatively widespread in contemporary environmental
ethics and its relation to traditional cultures. Advocates of a particular culture bring prooftexts to show that the culture is part of the
solution; critics use it to show that the culture is part of the problem. Both approaches do little service to investigating a different
cultural perspective from our own, one which is based on different
philosophical assumptions debated in a different cultural language.[2]

In keeping with Clifford Geertz's call for thick anthropological descriptions of culture, I have chosen to analyze *bal tashchit* as it unfolds throughout Jewish legal, or *halachic*,[3] history. Only by entering the classical world of Jewish texts is it possible to transcend apologetics and get a glimpse of a traditional cultural perspective on its own terms. In the process, I believe we will gain a richer understanding of the *content* and the *context* of Jewish cultural views of the natural world.

Bal Tashchit

Historically, Jews have been considered "a people of the book" on the basis of the role texts have played in Jewish life. From the Bible, followed by the *Mishnah* and the *Gemara*, which together make up the Talmud, continuing through medieval commentaries on these texts, and including compilations of questions posed to Rabbis with their answers on the practical application of these ancient texts to new situations, Judaism has developed an elaborate interpretive tradition, rooted in the Bible and extending into modern times. Traditional texts, beginning with the Bible, are the core texts for subsequent *halachic* decisions.

Bal tashchit is based on a relatively small collection of sources.[4] The original basis for it is Biblical, although it is expanded by the Rabbis far beyond the original context of the Bible. *Bal tashchit* is considered to have its roots as *halachah de-oraita*, a law "of the Bible," but to consist largely of prohibitions *de-rabbanan*, "of the Rabbis." In order, then, to understand the *halachic* precept, it is necessary to explore both its Biblical roots and its Rabbinic interpretation.

The origin of the principle of *bal tashchit* is in the attempt to explicate one specific Biblical passage from Deuteronomy which is describing what constitutes proper behavior during time of war. I include two translations of the original Hebrew, in order to emphasize the difficulty in understanding the Hebrew verses, and the interpretative possibilities which emerge from the ambiguity of the text itself.

The Biblical Source

When in your war against a city you have to besiege it a long time in order to capture it, you must not destroy its trees, wielding the ax against them. You may eat of them, but you must not cut them down. Are trees of the field human to withdraw before you under siege? Only trees that you know do not yield food may be destroyed; you may cut them down for constructing siegeworks against the city that is waging war on you, until it has been reduced.

Deut. 20:19–20, New Jewish Publication Society Translation

When thou shalt besiege a city a long time, in making war against it to take it, thou shalt not destroy the trees thereof by forcing an ax against them: for thou mayest eat of them, and thou shalt not cut them down for the tree of the field is man's life to employ them in the siege. Only the trees which thou knowest that they be not trees for food, thou shalt destroy and cut them down; and thou shalt build bulwarks against the city that maketh war with thee, until it be subdued.

Deut. 20:19–20, King James Bible Translation

The passage deals with the proper ethical behavior with regard to trees during wartime. Fruit-bearing trees should not be chopped down while a city is under siege. Only non-fruit-bearing trees may be chopped down. The reason behind such a prohibition seems to be cryptically supplied by the verse itself. In the King James translation we read "for the tree of the field is man's life," implying some causal relationship between the human being and trees, such that cutting down the tree is, in effect, damaging the human being as well. Yet the JPS translation offers a different interpretation of the verse: "Are trees of the field human to withdraw before you under siege?" It translates the verse as a question rather than a statement. It implies a rhetorical question which denies a relationship between human beings and trees: trees are not human beings and therefore should not be victims of their disputes.

The discrepancy among the translations echoes medieval commentators' varying interpretations of the verse. The JPS translation seems to be agreeing with Rashi's[5] interpretation of the verse. Rashi

accentuates the categorical distance between the human being and
the tree to create a rationale for why the tree should not be cut:

> The word *ki* is used here in the sense of "perhaps; should . . .":
> Should the tree of the field be considered to be (like) a human
> being, able to run away from you into the besieged town, to
> suffer there the agonies of thirst and hunger, like the towns-
> people—if not, why then destroy it?
>
> Rashi's commentary on Deut. 20:19

Rashi's interpretation of the verse is based on his understanding
of the Hebrew word *ki* as being interrogative, turning our text into
a rhetorical question. Is the tree of the field to be part of the same
(moral) world as the human being? No. The tree of the field is not
the target of the siege; the people of the town are. One has no
moral right to destroy the trees because of a dispute among human
beings. The trees must not be destroyed because of human disputes.

Rashi in effect has argued for an environmental ethic which
views (fruit) trees as having existence independent of human
wants and needs. In spite of its strong anthropomorphic language,
Rashi's position gives ethical consideration to the trees, although it
is still not clear why that should be so. The case is accentuated by
the setting of the verse itself. In wartime, when human life is so
endangered that values are often eclipsed altogether, it is difficult to
maintain an ethical outlook on any issue, how much the more so
with regard to nature.

Indeed, some commentators were aware of, and concerned by,
the radically nonanthropocentric nature of such a juxtaposition in
which strategic considerations during war, considerations which
might save human life, seem to be overruled by consideration for
the trees' welfare. Samuel ben Meir [Ramban] (1085–1144), for
example, understands the word *ki* as "unless" and therefore interprets the verse as a prohibition against chopping down the fruit tree
unless the enemy is using the trees as camouflage ["unless the
human being is as a tree of the field"], in which case it may be removed.[6] Nahmanides [Ramban] (1194–1270) argues that if chopping trees is necessitated by the conquest, then it is obviously
permissible to remove any and all trees.[7] Rashi's interpretation re-
sists such an anthropocentric reading.

86

Yet Rashi seems to have taken the verse out of context. For if we accept Rashi's interpretation "is the human being a tree of the field?" how are we to understand the very next verse, in which permission is given by God to cut down non-fruit-bearing trees? What is the distinction between fruit-bearing and non-fruit-bearing trees that protects one and not the other? Rashi's interpretation does not offer a means for distinguishing. Indeed, the text asks whether a human being is the tree of the field, whereas Rashi asks whether a tree of the field is like a human being. Rashi's reversal of the syntax of the sentence helps to support his interpretation but is not supported by the original phrasing of the verse.

Ibn Ezra's (1089–1164) interpretation, later echoed by the King James version, attacks Rashi's position on both grammatical and logical grounds and offers an alternative possibility:

> In my opinion . . . this is the correct meaning: that from (the trees) you get food, therefore don't cut them down, "for man is the tree of the field," that is—our lives as human beings depend on trees.
>
> Ibn Ezra's commentary on Deut. 20:19

Human responsibility for the tree is based on human dependence upon the tree. Trees are a source of food, and thus cutting them down reduces one's food supply for after the siege.

Ramban goes on to suggest that such an act is a sign of loss of faith, for the trees are being cut down to help in the siege. The soldiers, not believing that God will lead them to victory, destroy their own future food supply, fearful that the day of victory will never come.[8]

Ibn Ezra's explanation makes sense in the context of the verse. Fruit trees are not to be chopped down, for their importance as food for human beings is clear. Non-fruit-bearing trees, on the other hand, have no immediate importance for the human being, and therefore it is permissible to chop them down. The prooftext "because the human being is a tree of the field" shows us our link to the natural world, and how our abuses of nature can result in abuse of ourselves.

The Rabbinic Understanding
and Expansion of the Text

The Rabbinic discussion of the text, and the Rabbis' extrapolation of
it into the *halachic* precept of *bal tashchit*, although terse, expands
the text in myriad and often conflicting directions. Let us begin
with the primary prooftext in the Talmud for *bal tashchit*. It is an
expansion on the *mishnaic* text which states:

> He who cuts down his own plants, though not acting lawfully,
> is exempt, yet were others to [do it], they would be liable.
>
> *Baba Kamma* 8:6[9]

Here it is clearly stated that cutting down plants is acting unlawfully, presumably because of *bal tashchit*. One who cuts down another's plants is monetarily liable. One who cuts one's own plants,
while not liable, is also a transgressor. In other words, it is not
merely a question of destroying another person's property. Even
destroying what appears to be one's own property is forbidden, although seeking monetary penalty or compensation is inapplicable.

The Talmud then proceeds to define what is permitted to be cut
down and what is forbidden:

> Rav said: A palm tree producing even one *kab* of fruit may not
> be cut down. An objection was raised [from the following]:
> What quantity should be on an olive tree so that it should not
> be permitted to cut it down? A quarter of a *kab*.—Olives are
> different as they are more important. R. Hanina said: Shibḥath
> my son did not pass away except for having cut down a fig tree
> before its time. Rabina, however, said: If its value [for other
> purposes] exceeds that for fruit, it is permitted [to cut it down].
> It was also taught to the same effect: "Only the trees which you
> know" (Deut. 20:20) implies even fruit-bearing trees; "That
> they are not trees for food" (Deut. 20:20) means a wild tree.
> But since we ultimately include all things, why then was it
> stated, "that they are not trees for food"? To give priority to a
> wild tree over one bearing edible fruits. As you might say that
> this is so even where the value [for other purposes] exceeds
> that for fruits, it says "only."
>
> *Baba Kamma* 91b–92a

The Talmudic passage here defines the worth of the tree in terms of its produce. A palm tree may be allowed to be cut down when it is producing less than one *kab* [2.197 litre] of fruit; an olive tree, which is deemed more important, presumably for economic reasons, can be cut down only when it is producing less than a quarter *kab*. Although such amounts might be an evaluation of the point at which a tree is still fulfilling its purpose in the world, it is just as likely that it is an evaluation of the point at which the tree is still economically valuable, as hinted at by viewing olives as "more important." Rabina then, offers a general rule of thumb: one may cut down a fruit tree whenever the value of the tree cut down is worth more than its production of fruit. The Talmud then interprets our original Biblical passage in the spirit of its economic reading of the law. "Trees for food" are not simply fruit-producing tree. They are trees which are producing enough fruit to be economically worthwhile. So, not only may non-fruit-producing trees be chopped down, but fruit-producing trees which are not economically productive are ultimately part of the same category.

As is stated in the *Mishnah*, one who chops down another's tree unlawfully is to be fined. One who chops down one's own trees, "although not acting lawfully, is exempt." In our text, Rabbi Hanina makes a curious aside when he states that his son died because of having cut down a fig tree before its time, even though it was allowed since its economic worth cut down was greater than its worth as a fruit-producing tree. Death as divine punishment for cutting down the tree, even though it is permitted by the *halachah*, certainly demands that we relate to *bal tashchit* as something far more substantial than simply respecting the economic value of fruit-producing trees for human society. It is a mysterious theme that reappears often in the *halachic* literature. For example, the same story is related in another Talmudic passage:

> Raba, son of Rabbi Hanan, had some date trees adjoining a vineyard of Rabbi Joseph, and birds used to roost on the date trees [of Raba] and fly down and damage the vines [of Rabbi Joseph]. So Rabbi Joseph told [Raba:], "Go cut them!" [Raba said:] "But I have kept them four cubits away." [Rabbi Joseph said:] "This applies only to other trees, but for vines we require

more." [Raba said:] "But does not our *Mishnah* say 'this applies to all other trees'? [Rabbi Joseph said:] "This is so where there are other trees or vines on both sides, but where there are trees on one side and vines on the other a greater space is required." Said Raba, "I will not cut them down because Rav has said that it is forbidden to cut down a date tree which bears a *kab* of dates, and Rabbi Hanina has said, 'My son Shikḥath only died because he cut down a date tree before it's time.' You, sir, can cut them down if you like."

Baba Batra 26a[10]

Here, the date trees of Raba are the nesting ground for birds which are damaging the vineyards of Rabbi Joseph. The trees must be uprooted, for they are not planted the proper distance from the vineyard of Rabbi Joseph. Nevertheless, Raba refuses to uproot the trees, *even though it is* halachically *required*, because they are still producing the minimum *kab* of fruit, and Rabbi Hanina's son died for uprooting a date tree before its time. Raba does, however, allow Rabbi Joseph to dare to remove the trees. I will consider the fear around chopping a tree before its time more fully later. For now, it should be noted that chopping a tree down "before its time" should not be taken lightly.

So far we have examined two Talmudic passages regarding *bal tashchit*. Although one deals with the responsibility of one property owner to his neighbor, and the other deals with responsibility independent of others, they both understand the meaning of the *halachah* in similar ways. Both deal solely with fruit trees. As is recalled from the original Biblical prooftext, it is allowed to chop down non-fruit-bearing trees. Only fruit-bearing trees are forbidden. In the two Talmudic passages the Rabbis limit the prohibition and, in the process, offer an interpretation of the reasoning behind *bal tashchit*. No tree is to be destroyed as long as it is economically worthwhile. However, if the value of the tree is greater for having been cut down (Rabina's dictum), or if the tree is causing damage to the value of another's property (Rabbi Joseph's complaint), then it is permitted to be chopped down. The tree's worth, and in general the worth of nature, is ultimately evaluated in terms of its economic worth to humans. Notice that the destruction of the bird's nesting place is of no moral concern in the text. Yet, although the cutting down of the tree is permitted, it appears to be nevertheless problematic. The death of Rabbi Hanina's son offers a disturbing addendum to the otherwise utilitarian interpretation.

So far, I have considered a rather narrow understanding of *bal tashchit*, focusing solely on its implications for duties and obligations concerning fruit-producing trees. The Rabbis however, did not understand *bal tashchit* as a precept solely concerned with fruit trees, but rather as a far-reaching principle which defines our responsibilities and obligations to the Created world.

The initial discussion as to whether one is prohibited from cutting down trees takes place in a larger Talmudic discussion as to whether one may harm oneself. The *mishnaic* text which the Talmud then elaborates parallels the previously quoted *Mishnah*. They are here quoted together, in context:

> . . . Where one injures oneself, though forbidden, he is exempt, yet were others to injure him, they would be liable. He who cuts down his own plants [*koreit*], though not acting lawfully, is exempt, yet were others to [do it], they would be liable.
>
> *Baba Kamma* 8:6

Once again, there is a distinction between damage inflicted by another party and damage inflicted by oneself. Here, one who injures another person is clearly liable. One who injures oneself, although liable, is not punishable in civil courts. But what is the connection between damage to plants and injury to persons? The link is explicated in the Talmudic discussion:

Tannaim[11] differed on this point, for there is one view maintaining that a man may not injure himself and there is another maintaining that a man may injure himself. But who is the *Tanna* maintaining that a man may not injure himself? . . . He might be the *Tanna* of the following teaching:

> Garments may be rent for a dead person as this is not necessarily done to imitate the ways of the Amorites. R. Eleazar said: I heard that he who rends [his garments] too much for a dead person transgresses the command *bal tashchit*, and it seems that this should be the more so in the case of injuring his own body. But garments might perhaps be different, as the loss is irretrievable, for R. Johanan used to call garments 'my honourers,' and R. Hisda whenever he had to walk between thorns and thistles used to lift up his garments saying that whereas for

91

the body [if injured] nature will produce a healing, for garments [if torn] nature could bring up no cure.

Baba Kamma 91b

The Talmudic text seeks to understand how some of the *Tannaim* came to the conclusion that it was forbidden to injure oneself. The Talmud quotes a *baraita* which holds that one may rip one's clothing in memory of the dead. Rabbi Eliezer then asserts that ripping clothing too much transgresses *bal tashchit*. And, if ripping clothing is a transgression of *bal tashchit*, how much the more so is "ripping," or injuring, one's body? Therefore, injury to one's own body must be forbidden according to *bal tashchit*. Still, the Talmud points out, there is a distinction between garments and the body: ripping a garment can be irretrievable, whereas the body may heal. Indeed, Rabbi Hisda, when walking through scrub brush, used to lift up his garments, preventing them from ripping, while allowing his body to be cut and bruised, knowing that it would heal. So, injury to one's body is not prevented by *bal tashchit*, although the ripping of clothing is.

Such a conclusion, that is, that *bal tashchit* does not apply to the human being, is contradicted in another Talmudic passage:

> Reb Judah said in Samuel's name: We may make a fire for a lying-in woman on the Sabbath [in the winter]. Now it was understood from him, only for a lying-in woman, but not for an invalid; only in winter, but not in summer. But that is not so; there is no difference between a lying-in woman and any [other] invalid, and summer and winter are alike. [This follows] since it was stated, R. Hiyya b. Abin said in Samuel's name: If one lets blood and catches a chill, a fire is made for him even on the Tammuz [summer] solstice. *A teak chair was broken up for Samuel; a table of juniper-wood was broken up for Rav Judah. A footstool was broken up for Rabbah, whereupon Abaye said to Rabbah, "But you are infringing on* bal tashchit." "Bal tashchit *in respect of my own body is more important to me," he retorted.*

> *Shabbat* 129a

Here *bal tashchit* is used in reference to the breaking of furniture for warming an ill person on the Sabbath, and, of course, in reference to human health. Notice, it has already been decided that one may disregard rules of the Sabbath in order to take care of the ill. The question now is whether the needs of the individual human being override the rules of *bal tashchit*, in this case, a prohibition on destroying furniture. If we interpret *bal tashchit* in utilitarian terms, that is, the economic worth of something to human beings, then there should be no question. The health of the human being obviously takes precedence over the furniture's existence. Indeed, Rabbah argues just that. But the very presence of the question suggests that the answer is not taken for granted. There is a tension between an interpretation which evaluates all worth in terms of its use to human beings, and one which sees worth independent of human wants and even needs.

But what is the connection between the Biblical prohibition on cutting down fruit trees and the expanding Rabbinic definition, which, as we have so far seen, includes clothing, furniture, and even human beings? Maimonides [Rambam] (1135–1204) argues that the Rabbinic prohibition of *bal tashchit* includes the destruction of household goods, the demolishing of buildings, the stopping of a spring, and the destruction of articles of food as well.[12] At first glance, the expanding definition seems to dilute the discussion of human beings' obligations to the natural world. Comparing a tree to a piece of furniture seems to turn both into the works of human beings. Yet, the addition of the bodily health of human beings into the category of *bal tashchit* refocuses our interpretation. The world of creation includes the creation of the natural world and the world which humans have created from God's Creation. There should be no needless destruction of any of the creation.

The central point, then, is how one is to evaluate "needless," or "wanton," destruction. As we have seen, there is some tension as to whether it is to be evaluated according to the effective use of human beings, or whether there is an inherent value which exists apart from human use, which must be balanced alongside human wants and needs.

Although the dominant interpretation seems to be a utilitarian one, there is evidence of a different interpretation.

Conspicuous Consumption

R. Hisda also said: When one can eat barley bread but eats wheaten bread he violates *bal tashchit*. R. Papa said: When one

93

can drink beer but drinks wine, he violates *bal tashchit*. But this is incorrect: *Bal tashchit*, as applied to one's own person, stands higher.

Shabbat 140b

How is one to evaluate what is permissible, and what is excessive, consumption? In this short piece, the Rabbinic debate is presented clearly. Rabbi Hisda states that when one can eat barley bread, a poor man's bread, and instead chooses to eat wheaten bread, a more expensive bread, it is a violation of *bal tashchit*. In the same manner, Rabbi Papa claims that if one can drink beer, a poor man's beverage, and instead drinks wine, a more expensive drink, it is a violation of *bal tashchit*. One must provide for human needs. However, one is not permitted to consume beyond what is necessary to live. To do so would be *bal tashchit*—wanton destruction.

Such a view clearly has ascetic overtones. The link between *bal tashchit* and living a simple life certainly suggests that link between demanding less and not cutting down trees. However, motivation for a simple life has often come from social considerations as well. Excessive consumption means that one is using one's wealth on oneself, often flaunting one's wealth, at the expense of helping out those who are less fortunate. A Talmudic passage emphasizes the point:

At first the carrying out of the dead was harder for [the dead's] relatives than his death, so that they left him and ran away, until Rabban Gamaliel came and adopted a simple style and they carried him out in garments of linen, and all the people followed his example and carried out [the dead] in garments of linen. Said Rabbi Papa: And now it is the general practice [to carry out the dead] even in rough cloth worth [only] a *zuz*.

Ketubot 8b

Although the text makes no mention of *bal tashchit*, later commentators will use it as a prooftext in applying *bal tashchit* to excessive consumption. Rambam, for example, links the two in his discussion of the laws of mourning.[13] Here, the norm for burial had become so cost prohibitive, that the poor would abandon their dead, unable to afford such an expense. Rabbi Gamaliel successfully changed the practice from an excessive one to a modest one, which evolved into virtually an ascetic one. It is clear here that the motivation for simplicity is social.

94

Yet, for all that can be said for simplicity, the text is blunt as to which perspective wins out in the Talmudic argument: "but this is incorrect. *Bal tashchit*, as applied to one's own person stands higher." The statement is quite powerful. It is considered *bal tashchit not to* drink the wine or eat the wheaten bread. Human comfort and enjoyment are to take precedence. Not according them priority would be to limit human pleasure in the world, which would be a form of destruction—destruction of human pleasure. Although there is a tradition of abstinence in Judaism, it is generally frowned upon. Human beings are to enjoy the bounty of Creation. Although two traditions are clearly present, the one which places humans as the evaluator of worth is plainly dominant.

Maimonides canonizes this dominant tradition, leaving out the minority view. In three short *halachot* in his *Mishnah Torah* he summarizes the Talmudic extrapolation of the Biblical text.[14] There is no tension in Maimonides' summary. Wanton destruction is clearly defined as the cutting down of fruit trees when there is no economic justification for its removal. Although the Rabbinic expansion of the text is presented, in fact the summary limits the text. Only when something is clearly of benefit, and its destruction does not bring about demonstrably more benefit, will its destruction be considered *bal tashchit*. Anytime there will be economic gain from its use, its destruction is justifiable.

The Responsa Literature

Two positions, then, can be seen emerging from the Rabbinic discussion on *bal tashchit*. The first, which is clearly the dominant position, I describe as the minimalist position. It seeks to limit *bal tashchit* as much as possible to only those situations which are clearly proscribed by the Biblical injunction in Deuteronomy. Although seemingly expanding *bal tashchit* to encompass human creation and not simply nature, it in fact creates a clear hierarchy in which human utilitarian needs always override any inherent value of the created object. In contrast, the maximalist position does expand *bal tashchit* as a counterweight to human desires. Human needs define usage, although the definition of what constitutes human need is far from clear. Consumption should be limited to what is necessary, and the inherent value of the creation stands as a countermeasure to human usage.

The many interpretations offered in the literature on the human responsibility to the natural world thus cited leaves much latitude for the application of the concept of *bal tashchit* in Jewish law. An anthropocentric reading of the traditions would lead to a minimalist application of the principle, with human considerations always determining the conduct towards nature. However, a reading of the tradition which gives a degree of inherent worth to the natural world independent of human use would demand a much more complex negotiation between human wants and needs and nature, leading to what I call a maximalist application of the principle. The *halachic* process enabled each *posek*—each *halachic* authority—to offer his own interpretation of the concept through his own reading of the meaning of *bal tashchit* as it is expressed in the texts of Biblical and Rabbinic literature and interpreted by later generations. Not surprisingly, different *poskim*[15] chose to understand the *halachah* in the different ways suggested by the interpretations already cited.

The Minimalist Tradition

One of the main *halachic* questions, once having accepted the idea of *bal tashchit* as relating to wanton destruction, is in what situations is it to be overridden. The *Tosefot*, for example, commenting on a Talmudic passage, argue that *bal tashchit* is overridden by the obligation to honor royalty.[16] In *Sefer HaChasidim* it is argued that rewriting a page of Torah only so that it looks better also overrides the *mitzvah* of *bal tashchit*.[17] Ovadiah Yosef (b.1920) claims that the fulfillment of a *mitzvah*, such as the breaking of the glass as part of the wedding ceremony, overrides *bal tashchit*.[18] He, like *Sefer HaChasidim*, also argues that *bal tashchit* is overridden in order to show honor to a *mitzvah*, such as by buying a newer, fancier mezuzah.[19]

It is also permissible to destroy property and even plants for educational reasons. Relying on a Talmudic passage which allows one to rip clothing or break pottery in order to demonstrate anger as an educational tool (although it is forbidden to do such acts out of anger)[20], Abraham Isaac Kook (1865–1935) argues that one is allowed to destroy when one is teaching that something is forbidden, so that two trees which are forbidden to be planted together under the laws of *kilayim* may be planted together and then uprooted to teach that such a planting is forbidden. The trees are deliberately planted and then uprooted to teach the *halachah*.[21]

Maimonides is asked whether a tree may be cut down which is in danger of falling and damaging a mosque which lies underneath. Here, it is a question as to whether *bal tashchit* applies when social relations between Jews and Moslems might be jeopardized by not removing the tree. Maimonides, in keeping with his radically minimalist position, answers that it is permitted to cut the tree down not only when there is damage inflicted, but also when there is the potential for damage.[22] Elsewhere, Maimonides allows for the removal of a tree which threatens to break off in a storm and injure those walking past in the adjacent public area.

Judah Rosannes (1657–1727) holds that the prohibition is only on the chopping down of the entire tree, and there is therefore no problem with *bal tashchit* when chopping down branches from the tree.[23] Baruch Wiesel gives permission in his *Makor Baruch* (1755) to destroy an older house and build a newer one.[24]

Indeed, the anthropocentric view of *bal tashchit*, which sees nature as having been created for the use of human beings, is a central theme in the literature. Naphtali Zvi Berlin (1817–1893) states emphatically that the very purpose of a tree and its fruit is for it to be cut down for the use of human beings.[25] In his commentary on the Deuteronomy verse, Yaakov Tzvi from Kalenburg (d. 1865) states:

> It is not virtuous to use anything in a manner different from that which it has been created . . . also a tree, which was aimed in its creation to produce fruit as food for human beings to sustain them, it is forbidden to do anything to them which would harm human beings . . .[26]

Jonah ben Abraham Gerondi (1200–1263) holds that the body of a human being is to be considered part of the world of creation, hence part of that which *bal tashchit* is to be applied. One has no right to cause it harm.[27] Menahem Azariah Da Fano (1548–1620) states that, although in general one should choose to be stringent with oneself, when it comes to financial losses to oneself, one is

97

forbidden to be severe in order not to transgress *bal tashchit*.[28] Here we see once again the theme of human needs as a concern of *bal tashchit*, which takes precedence over other needs. Ephraim Weinberger argues that any deprivation to the body's health is a transgression of *bal tashchit*:

> Even if he doesn't allow himself to eat foods that are good for his health and strengthen his body, although they are expensive, he transgresses the prohibition. Any abuse of bodily health in general is a transgression of *bal tashchit*.[29]

In a *responsa* about animal experimentation, Jacob Reischer states that even when there is only the possibility of medical or economic benefit, *bal tashchit* applied to human beings always takes precedence.[30] In the *Shulhan Arukh of the Rav*, in the laws of *bal tashchit*, revealingly printed under "laws pertaining to the protection of the body and the spirit and laws of *bal tashchit*," Shneur Zalman of Lyady (1745–1813) states: ". . . and also those that destroy anything that it is destined for human beings to enjoy transgress *bal tashchit*."[31]

The application of *bal tashchit* to the human being expresses the minimalist position quite well: although *bal tashchit* demands that nothing be wasted, this applies first and foremost to the human being. Although some have understood *bal tashchit* as applying to the preclusion of human *needs*, the most minimalist understanding maintains that preventing human *pleasure* by preventing human use of the world is an act of *bal tashchit*. The seemingly expansionist position which extends the precept of *bal tashchit* to all things, only to be circumvented by any human desire as the ultimate form of *bal tashchit*, is presented quite forcefully in both respects in *Sefer HaChinuch*:

> The root reason for the precept is known (evident): for it is in order to train our spirits to love what is good and beneficial and to cling to it; and as a result, good fortune will cling to us, and we will move well away from every evil thing and from every matter of destructiveness. This is the way of the kindly men of piety and the conscientiously observant; they love peace and are happy at the good fortune of people, and bring them near the Torah. They will not destroy even a mustard seed in the world, and they are distressed at every ruination and spoilage that they see; and if they are able to do any rescuing, they will save anything from destruction, with all their power.

... Among the laws of the precept, there is what the Sages of blessed memory said: that the Torah did not forbid chopping down fruit trees if any useful benefit will be found in the matter: for instance, if the monetary value of a certain tree is high, and this person wanted to sell it, or to remove a detriment by chopping them down—for instance, if this was harming other trees that were better than it, or because it was causing damage in the fields of others. In all these circumstances, or anything similar, it is permissible.[32]

According to Zevi Ashkenazi (1660–1718), continuing the position alluded to by *Sefer HaChinuch*, the purpose of *bal tashchit* is not to prevent destruction so much as to teach human beings sensitivity.[33] Nature has no inherent value apart from its use by human beings.

The Maximalist Tradition

Jacob Reischer is asked whether one may uproot trees from his garden which obstruct the view from his neighbor's house windows. Reischer rules that the trees are to be removed, but not before one searches for another solution such as the replanting of the trees in an alternative location.[34]

Jair Hayyim Bacharach (1638–1702) is asked whether one can remove a fruit tree whose branches obscure the view from one's own window. Note that here permission is being asked to remove a tree which is a nuisance to oneself, as opposed to one which is a nuisance to one's neighbor. Bacharach makes two important points. The first is that since the nuisance can be dealt with through the pruning of the branches of the tree, which is not forbidden by *bal tashchit*, it is not permitted to chop the tree down. The second is that chopping down a tree is to be allowed for essential needs, but not for luxuries. . . . Rashba permitted the expansion of a house. Bacharach relies on this *responsum* to argue that, while there the chopping down of the tree was for an essential need, here it is not and therefore, based on the precedent of Rashba, it is not to be permitted.[35] Jacob Ettlinger is asked whether one may chop down elderly trees in order to build a home on the only piece of property

99

which the individual is allowed to buy in town. Without having a home, he may not get a license to marry. Ettlinger allows for the trees to be chopped down, although he also points out that everything must be done to find an alternative, and that such permission is granted because not to do so would prevent the man from marrying. Although permission is granted, the tenor is one of limiting the exceptions to *bal tashchit* rather than extending them.[36]

Similarly, Moses Sofer gives permission to uproot a vineyard which is losing money, and to use the land for field crops instead. Nevertheless, he states that, although usually it is forbidden to uproot the vineyard, this particular time, since the economic loss is so great, permission is given.[37] Ovadiah Yosef also gives permission to chop down a fruit-bearing tree, in this example to expand one's home, while limiting the exceptions. Yosef allows the expansion of the house in this case in order to allow room for a family which has been blessed with many children. However, he asserts that it is forbidden to chop down the trees if one is expanding one's home for luxury, or for landscaping or general beautification. Once again, a distinction is made between perceived needs and wants.[38]

Citing the danger involved in chopping down trees, Pinhas Hai Anu (1693–1765) refuses to give permission to cut down a fig tree in order to build a storage shed.[39] Yaakov ben Shmuel from Tzoyemer (end of seventeenth century) simply states that it is forbidden to chop down trees in order to build a home.[40] Interestingly, the same Naphtali Zevi Judah Berlin who stated that the purpose of a tree is to be cut down for the use of human beings gives the most maximalist of the interpretations of *bal tashchit*. Asked whether a tree can be removed to build a home, he answers no. Berlin claims that one may cut down a tree only in cases explicitly spelled out by the Talmud: either when it damages other trees, in which case one tree has no precedence over another, or when it damages another's field.[41]

Berlin points out that there is a distinction between the chopping down of a tree and other transgressions of *bal tashchit* in that only the chopping down of a tree is punishable by flogging. Berlin also mentions the Talmudic notion of there being danger involved in the chopping down of trees from the story of Rabbi Hanina's son as reason to be particularly cautious.

The vast majority of examples from the literature with regard to the cutting down of trees refer explicitly to fruit trees or do not mention the kind of tree being discussed. The original distinction between fruit-producing trees and non-fruit-producing trees seems to be maintained. The *Tosefot*, however, commenting on a passage from the Talmud that "one who cuts down good trees will never see blessing in their lives" state: "One who cuts down even a non-fruit producing tree." In other words, although not strictly forbidden, such an action will prevent the doer from being blessed in his life's deeds.[42] Although Greenwald (twentieth century) in his *responsum* makes a distinction between non-fruit-producing trees which have a use as trees for human beings, for example in providing shade, beauty, or even a pleasant aroma, and trees which have use only as firewood and should therefore be used for that purpose, the application of *bal tashchit* to non-fruit-producing trees is a direct rejection of Maimonides's holding that *bal tashchit* does not apply to them.[43]

In the discussion of conspicuous consumption, which as an issue is directly linked to the maximalist position, two *responsa* are of interest. In the first, Joseph Karo (1488–1575) warns against the wasting of public moneys on extravagances.[44] In the second, the first chief Ashkenazic Rabbi of Israel, Abraham Yitzhak HaCohen Kook, is asked whether there is any prohibition in the Torah to the improvement of the military cemetery. Kook answers that, while it is certainly a *mitzvah* to fix up the cemetery so that it is in honorable condition, it would be considered a violation of *bal tashchit* to invest large amounts of money in order that it be lavish.[45]

Finally, two different *responsa* apply *bal tashchit* to "ownerless property," which includes wild animals and vegetation, and abandoned property.[46] Such a view is in keeping with the idea that there is no such thing as ownerless property, since in fact, all the world is ultimately the property of God: "Because the earth is Mine."[47] It is a theocentric utilitarianism. As such, in the Sabbatical year, although all land becomes ownerless temporarily, that is, returned to God, its original owner, nevertheless *bal tashchit* continues to apply.

Although it is clear that even in those sources which have been attributed to a maximalist position there is a strong sense of a hierarchy in which human needs override other considerations, nevertheless in the maximalist position there are other considerations which need to be weighed against the human. In all cases, human *needs* outweigh other considerations. However there is a debate which takes place as to what defines needs. In addition, there seems to be a distinction made between trees, particularly fruit-bearing trees, and other properties.

The *halachic* principle of *bal tashchit* has been open to different, often contradictory interpretations. From its beginning, tension existed with regard to how to understand the prohibition: whether such a prohibition was to define the world in terms of human use, or whether such a prohibition demanded an evaluation of use that took into account more than human wants.

Discussion

I would like to briefly point to some of the conclusions which can be divided into those having to do with the *content* of the discussion, and those having to do with the *context* of the discussion—the cultural language of the debate.

With regard to the *content*, several points can be made:

1. It is quite obvious from the survey of the literature that there is no one Jewish approach to *bal tashchit* and its application, but rather multiple approaches which are debated from within the tradition. In general, any claim to *the* Jewish view on an ethical situation should be held as suspect.
2. The discussion in many ways is remarkably similar to our contemporary discussion. Here, too, we see two poles on the continuum. The minimalist position has human needs and wants having precedence over the rest of the Creation; the maximalist position has human wants counterbalanced with the legitimate claims of the natural world. The tradition documents a debate between the two positions which has continued since Rabbinic times.
3. The minimalist position is without question far more dominant within the tradition. This too, parallels the contemporary debate. Those voices which question a utilitarian approach to the natural world are in the minority.

4. There is no hint in the maximal position of a holistic environmental ethic. This should not be particularly surprising in that the holistic environmental position is based on the science of ecology and the concept of species, and on the assumption that human culture is a small part of the larger ecosystem. Premodern Aristotelian science, which is the scientific tradition within which *bal tashchit* developed, saw nature as static and species as eternal. *Bal tashchit* was applied on the level of the individual.

5. There is also no hint in the *halachic* tradition of *bal tashchit* of the Romantic idea of reconnecting humans to their natural selves. At least within the *halachic* discussion of *bal tashchit*, respect for nature in no way is connected to a desire to reconnect human culture with its natural, and truer, antecedents. I believe that the absence of such a tendency reveals a strong preference in Jewish ethical philosophy to see morality as transcendent of the natural world, and not immanent within it. The pagan-Jewish debate in many significant ways is connected to a debate about whether morality is defined by "what is"—a materialist, sociobiological perspective—or whether it is to be defined by "what should be"—an idealistic model of moral philosophy. Although natural metaphors and images are present in the Jewish textual tradition,[48] particularly in the Bible, nature is primarily not considered to be a pristine state of the world, but a temporal reality which needs to be redeemed.

With regard to the *context*, any comparison of the contemporary discussion on environmental ethics and the traditional Jewish perspective will be limited. We can only understand another cultural perspective through the prism of our own cultural categories, and therefore any attempt to enter another cultural perspective can only be partial.[49] Only those parts of the tradition which can be explicated in contemporary terms can be translated into a contemporary context. The other parts can only be rumored. What I have so far considered is that part of the traditional discussion which appears to translate relatively easily into the contemporary cultural language and thus be easily compared. The *content*, therefore, seems to be similar only when understood as emerging from a similar cultural context. However, the Jewish discussion is in many ways a discussion that is different in kind from the contemporary discussion and that defies a simple comparison. It is working from a cultural *context* with very different assumptions. A comparison of the two languages of discourse can help locate some of the different cultural assumptions and can teach us about the outlooks of both traditional Jewish and contemporary culture. It helps us to glimpse at that which is incapable of being translated into contemporary categories.

1. Although primarily presented here as a moral discussion, the discussion of the *halachot* often seems legalistic to the modern ear, without regard to any ethical question. Although the discussion at times seems focused on the moral relationship to nature, with the Biblical and Rabbinic texts used as prooftexts for the ethical position, at other times the discussion seems to be internally focused, allowing the texts to develop apart from any moral discussion. In short, the discussion of *bal tashchit* hints at a different type of moral discourse, neither utilitarian nor rights-based, anthropocentric or biocentric.

2. The legal assumptions of the *halachic* tradition also sound strange to the modern individual. Much of the contemporary environmental discourse concerns the concept of rights. It has been pointed out by some legal historians that such an idea seems foreign to the traditional Jewish *halachic* tradition. Rather than focusing on rights, the tradition focuses on duties. Calling the *halachic* system a system based on duties, rather than rights, is also a partial translation of traditional categories, but it suggests the underlying assumption from which the *halachic* system works. The *halachah* extends beyond that which is forbidden, and rather legislates normative behavior.[50]

3. The strikingly particularistic nature of the *halachic* discussion is also suggestive in terms of the demands of an environmental ethic. The *halachic* discussion continually focuses on a particular incident about a particular animal or a particular tree in a particular place. The discussion then no longer revolves around the theoretical question of the human relationship to the natural world, but rather the trade-offs between human and other interests in particular situations. Although certain general principles are clearly established from the particular discussion, it is

the unique situation which forms the basis of the discussion. The amount of deliberation which is invested in whether a tree may be cut down when one is building a home can be understood as an important statement as to the inherent worth of the tree, as well as testimony to the inherent worth of deliberation within Jewish *halachic* culture.

4. The particular nature of Jewish *halachic* discussion is connected to the centrality of community as a defining category. Mary Midgley points out in the debate around contemporary environmental ethics that traditional societies lived in "mixed communities" which allowed human sympathies to transcend the species boundary.[51] Callicott extends the concept of "mixed community" to the biotic community as well.[52] The *halachic* discussions around *bal tashchit* are testimony to a functioning mixed community. The species barrier is clearly transcended as discussion includes concern for the community's trees (and even more centrally, animals[53]) in the deliberation. And as Callicott suggests, such a model has various concentric circles of interest, from the most immediate connection of family, but extending out in lesser degrees beyond the species, to animals and eventually the biotic community. It is a morality based on relationships which emerge from particular communities in particular places. Such a dynamic of morality rooted in relationships—between human beings, humans and God, humans and animals, humans and nature—will lead to a very different kind of moral discourse.

The above discussion has been deliberately meant to echo a larger argument in ethics between rights-based ethics and the communitarian critique of the limits of such an approach. It should be noted, however, that communitarian positions on the environment nevertheless remain within an anthropocentric view of community which does not transcend the species barrier.[54] A religious culture which can see the Creation as having value independent of its utilitarian worth to human beings will philosophically find it much easier to view the Creation as having inherent worth.[55] Whether that potential can be realized is one of the major challenges facing the Jewish environmental community today.

Contemporary environmental ethics has a rich and complex discourse to describe contemporary society's relationships with the natural world. Yet, we have compromised such rigorous research when treating other cultural perspectives. This caricatures traditional cultures and allows us no significant insights into other perspectives. If looking at other cultural perspectives is to be a meaningful stepping-stone in the rethinking of our own perspectives, we must recognize the limitations of cultural translation while at the same time attempting to describe the culture from within its own cultural language. Only then will we be able to peek into a truly other cultural world and glimpse at a different way of seeing. The investigation of *bal tashchit* is offered as both an insight into a Jewish perspective, and a glance as to what nature looks like through different cultural eyes.

Thou Shalt Not Destroy

Norman Lamm

The Biblical norm which most directly addresses itself to the ecological situation is that known as *bal tashhit,* "thou shalt not destroy." The passage reads:

> When thou shalt besiege a city a long time, in making war against it to take it, thou shalt not destroy the trees thereof by wielding an ax against them; for thou mayest eat of them but thou shalt not cut them down; for is the tree of the field man that it should be besieged of thee? Only the trees of which thou knowest that they are not trees for food, them thou mayest destroy and cut down that thou mayest build bulwarks against the city that maketh war with thee until it fall.

> Deut. 20:19–20

These two verses are not altogether clear and admit of a variety of interpretations; we shall return to them shortly in elaborating the Halakhah of *bal tashhit*. But this much is obvious: that the Torah forbids wanton destruction. Vandalism against nature entails the violation of a Biblical prohibition. According to one medieval authority, the purpose of the commandment is to train man to love the good by abstaining from all destructiveness. "For this is the way of the pious . . . those who love peace, are happy when they can do good to others and bring them close to Torah and will not cause even a grain of mustard to be lost from the world . . ."[1] A more modern author provides a somewhat more metaphysical explanation: the fruit tree was created to prolong man's life and this purpose may therefore not be subverted by using the tree to make war and destroy life.[2] Those few cases in Scriptural history in which this norm was violated are special cases. Thus when Hezekiah stopped all the fountains in Jerusalem in the war against Sennacherib (II Chronicles 32:2–4, 30), which Sifre regards, as a violation of the Biblical commandment equal to chopping down a fruit tree, he was taken to task for it by the Talmudic Sages (B. Pesaḥim 56a).[3] In another incident Elisha counseled such a scorched earth policy (II Kings 3:17–20); Maimonides considered this a temporary suspension of the law for emergency purposes *(horaat shaah)* a tactic permitted to a prophet but an act which is not normative.[4]

The Talmudic and midrashic traditions continue this implicit assumption of man's obligation to, and responsibility for, nature's integrity: Nothing that the Lord created in the world was superfluous or in vain (B. Shabbat 77b); hence all must be sustained. An aggadah, often repeated in the literature, says that God created the world by looking into the Torah as an architect into a blue print. Creation, the Rabbis were saying, is contingent upon the Torah—or, the survival of the world depends upon human acceptance of moral responsibility.

The Halakhic Perspective

Let us now return to the commandment of *bal tashhit* to see how the Biblical passage is interpreted in the halakhic tradition. At first blush it would seem that the Biblical prohibition covers only acts of vandalism performed during wartime. The Halakhah, however, considers the law to cover all situations, in peacetime as well as in war;[5] apparently the Bible merely formulated the principle in terms of a situation in which such vandalism is most likely to occur and in a most blatant fashion. Indeed while Maimonides forbids the destruction of fruit trees for use in warfare,[6] other authorities such as Rashi[7] and Nahmanides[8] specifically exempt the use of fruit trees for such purposes as bulwarks from the prohibition; what the Torah proscribed is not the use of trees to win in a battle, which may often be a matter of life and death, but the wanton devastation of embattled areas so as to render them useless to the enemy should he win, e.g., a "scorched earth" policy.[9]

The specific mention in the Biblical passage of destroying by wielding an ax is not taken by the Halakhah as the exclusive means of destruction. Any form of despoliation is forbidden by Biblical law, even diverting the irrigation without which the tree will wither and die (Sifre to Deuteronomy 20:19).[10] Again it was assumed that the Torah was enunciating a general principle in the form of a specific and extreme case.

Similarly, the mention of "fruit trees" was expanded to include almost everything else: "And not only trees but whoever breaks vessels, tears clothing, wrecks that which is built up, stops fountains, or wastes food in a destructive manner transgresses the commandment of *bal tashhit* ('thou shalt not destroy'), but his punishment is only flogging by rabbinic edict."[11] Likewise is it forbidden to kill an animal needlessly or to offer exposed water (presumed to be polluted or poisoned) to livestock (See Hullin 7b; Tosefta Baba Kama 115b).[12]

In order to understand the relevance of the Halakhah on *bal tashhit* to the problem of ecology, it is important to test certain underlying assumptions of the halakhic conception. First, then, it should be pointed out that there is present no indication of any fetishistic attitude, any worship of natural objects for and of themselves. This is obvious from the passage just cited, wherein other objects, including artifacts, are covered in the prohibition. Furthermore, non-fruit-bearing trees are exempt from the law of *bal tashhit*, as are fruit trees that have aged and whose crop is not worth the value of the trees as lumber (Baba Kama 91b).[13] Also, fruit trees of inferior quality growing amidst and damaging to those that are better and more expensive, may be up rooted (Bava Kama 92a).[14]

What must be determined is whether the Halakhah here is concerned only with commercial values, perhaps based upon an economy of scarcity, and possibly, even more exclusively, on property rights; or whether there are other considerations beyond the pecuniary that, although they are formulated in characteristic halakhic fashion *sui generis* and without reference to any external values, nevertheless may point indirectly to ecological concerns.

It is at once obvious that commercial values do play a central role in the law. Thus the fruit tree may be destroyed if the value of the crop is less than its value as lumber as mentioned above or if the place of the tree is needed to build a house thereon.[15] Such permission is not granted according to the later authorities for reasons of esthetics or convenience, such as landscaping.[16] However, the economic interest is not overriding, it must yield to considerations of health so that in case of illness and when no other means are available to obtain heat, fruit trees may be cut down and used for firewood (Shabbat 140b).[17] Even when the criterion is a commercial one, it is clear that it is the waste of an object of economic values per se that the Halakhah considers unlawful; it is not concerned with property rights nor does it seek, in these instances, to protect private property. Thus in a complicated case concerning a Levirate marriage, the Mishnah counsels one to act so that he does not needlessly disqualify the woman from later marrying a priest (*Yevamot* 44a). The Gemara quotes R. Joseph, who avers that Rabbi, redactor of the Mishnah, thereby intended a broader principle which R. Joseph phrases as "One should not spill water out of his pool at a time when others need it," that is, one should never spoil an object or an opportunity even where the gain or loss refers completely to another individual and not to himself.[18] We previously quoted the author of the *Hinnukh,* who explains all of *bal tashhit* as teaching the ideal of social utility of the world rather than of purely private economic interest: the pious will not suffer the loss of a single seed "in the world" whereas the wicked rejoice at the destruction of the world."[19] In his summary of the laws included in the rubric of *bal tashhit,* the author mentions that

109

it certainly is proper to cut down a fruit tree if it causes damage to the fields of others.[20]

A most cogent point is made in this respect by the late R. Abraham Isaiah Karelitz, of blessed memory, author of *Hazon Ish*. Maimonides, codifying the law of the Sifre,[21] decides that *bal tashhit* includes the prohibition to divert an irrigation ditch which waters a fruit tree. What, however, if the tree were watered manually by filling a pail with water and carrying it to the tree: is the passive failure to do so considered a breach of *bal tashchit*? *Hazon Ish* decides that it is not in violation of the law, because all sources indicate that the commandment of *bal tashchit* is directed not at the owner of the tree or object, but at all Israelites. Were the law addressed to individual proprietors, one could then demand of them that they continue to irrigate their trees in any manner necessary and the failure to do so would constitute a transgression. However, the law is addressed to all Israel, and hence it is negative in nature, prohibiting an outright act of vandalism such as diverting a stream from a tree but not making it incumbent upon one actively to sustain every tree.[22] What we may derive from this is that the prohibition is not essentially a financial law dealing with property *(mammon)*, but religious or ritual law *(issur)* which happens to deal with the avoidance of vandalism against objects of economic worth. As such, *bal tashhit* is based on a religio-moral principle that is far broader than a prudential commercial rule per se, and its wider applications may well be said to include ecological considerations.

Support for this interpretation may be found in the decision codified by R. Shneour Zalman of Ladi, applying the law of *bal tashhit* even to ownerless property *(hefker)*. His reasoning is that if the Torah disallowed needless destruction of property of an enemy in war time, it certainly forbids destruction of ownerless property.[23] Here again we find that we are dealing with a religio-moral injunction concerning economic value (not property), rather than an economic law which has religious sanction.

That this is so may be seen, too, from the special seriousness with which the Talmud approaches the subject, and from aggadic and quasi-halakhic sources dealing with it. Thus, the Talmud relates that R. Hanina attributed the untimely death of his son to the latter's cutting down a fruit tree prematurely *(Baba Kama* 92b). The

110

Rabbis hesitated to pay a social call to a dying scholar who, for medicinal purposes, kept a goat in his house in order to drink its milk; the goat despoils the grazing land and hence is to be banished from such pastures (*Baba Kama* 89a). The Tabernacle was built of acacia wood (Exod. 25) to teach man that if he wishes to build a house for himself he should not despoil fruit trees for this purpose (*Exod. Rab.* 35). Even though one is halakhically permitted to destroy a fruit tree if he wishes to build his home on its place,[24] nevertheless he should refrain from doing so.[25]

part **IV**

Branches:
Kabbalah and Hasidism

Through much of the history of Rabbinic Judaism, a mystical strand of Jewish thought—sometimes at the intellectual and spiritual heart of the tradition, often at its institutional periphery—has danced with the Hidden Presence of God in the world—sometimes, the hidden presence of God in the earth itself.

For example, in Kabbalistic thought for centuries, trees that are mentioned in two passages of Tanakh have held special intensity of meaning. One passage—the story of *Gan Eden*, the Garden of Delight—gave enormous importance to the Tree/s of Eden (one or two?—precisely the question that the Kabbalists thought crucial). In the other passage, Proverbs equates the "tree of life" with Wisdom—perhaps with Torah, perhaps with an aspect of Divinity Itself.

Indeed, the Kabbalists came to imagine the emanations of God (called the *Sefirot*) connected in an organic pattern that they called a tree. Yet early Kabbalists rarely connected these images with earthly trees.

The Kabbalah received new energy in the wake of the expulsion of Jews from Spain in 1492, and during the sixteenth century an extraordinary grouping of creative Kabbalists resettled in the tiny town of Tzfat (Safed) in the Galilee region of the Land of Israel—actually within the Land, close to its rhythms.

113

So the mystical sense of God's Presence became charged with the earthiness of living close to the land. The Tzfat community created new forms of celebration that viewed the land and the rhythms of nature in new ways.

Midnight became a special time of Heavenly Opening. Sunset on the eve of Shabbat became a time of singing on the hilltops. And earthly trees became intertwined with the image and symbol of the One Tree, God's Own Self, the Tree that has its roots in Heaven and its fruitfulness on earth.

From these mystics emerged the notion of a seder for the Fifteenth of Shvat, celebrating the rebirth of trees. Their seder was built around fruits and nuts and cups of wine of different colors, which became for them edible symbols of the mystical Four Worlds as well as invocations of God's Holy *shefa*, all of life's abundance.

In this section of the anthology, we present some of the crucial documents of the Kabbalah—the mystical thought that lies beneath and that calls forth much of the form through which we celebrate Tu B'Shvat today. And we include as well some of the Hasidic hymns to the closeness of God in the world of grass and trees that inherited and enriched these Kabbalistic images.

The Trees of Eden in the Kabbalah

*Gershom Scholem**

In their endeavor to develop the crisis of tradition out of the concepts of the tradition itself, the Sabbatians [followers of Shabbetai Tzvi, a Messianic claimant of the seventeenth ceutury] were able to refer back to symbols of the earlier Kabbalistic literature whose implicit antinomianism had for more than three hundred years hardly aroused any attention, let alone protests. But now, in the excitement of the Messianic uprising and in the hands of the Sabbatians, these symbols showed their explosive power in shattering the tradition.

There are, above all, three typological descriptions which recur here again and again, and which originate in the most recent layer of the *Zohar.* In these sections, especially in the "Faithful Shepherd" *(Ra'ya Mehemna),* and in the *Tikkune Zohar,* an extensive commentary to the first chapters of Genesis composed as an independent volume, these typological figures are used at many points and are varied in the most diverse ways. [One of these is] the figure of the two trees of Paradise, the Tree of Life and the Tree of the Knowledge of Good and Evil.

What do the two trees in Paradise represent? Already in biblical metaphor wisdom, identified by Jewish tradition with Torah, is designated as Tree of Life (Prov. 3:18); thus opens the whole realm of typology. The trees in Paradise are not merely physical trees; beyond this they point to a state of things which they represent symbolically.[1]

In the opinion of the Jewish mystics both trees are in essence one. They grow out into two directions from a common trunk. Genesis tells us that the Tree of Life stood in the center of Paradise, but it does not indicate the exact position of the Tree of Knowledge. The Kabbalists took this to mean that it had no special place of its own but sprouted together with the Tree of Life out of the common matrix of the divine world. The two trees are different aspects of the Torah, which have their common origin in revelation.

The Tree of Life represents that aspect which has hitherto been unrealizable because, due to the sin of Adam, it remained virtually

115

hidden and inaccessible, and we do not know the taste of its fruits. The law which is concealed in the life of this tree is that of a creative force manifesting itself in infinite harmonies, a force which knows no limitations or boundaries. The paradisaic life under this law never came into being. The sin of Adam was that he isolated the Tree of Life from the Tree of Knowledge, to which he directed his desire.

Once the unity of the two trees in men's lives were destroyed, there began the dominion of the Tree of Knowledge. No longer did unitary gushing, unrestrained life prevail, but the duality of good and evil in which the Torah appears in this aspect of revelation. Since the expulsion from Paradise, in the exile in which we all now find ourselves, we can no longer apperceive the world as a unified whole. The Tree of the Knowledge of Good and Evil under whose law the world now stands corresponds to a condition of this world in which distinctions must be made before the unity of life can be regained: the distinctions between good and evil, commandment and prohibition, holy and profane, pure and impure.

For the author of those sections of the *Zohar* the two trees were not only, as they were for the other Kabbalists, symbols of the *sefirot*, of the manifestations of God in Creation, of which the Tree of Knowledge represented the tenth and last *sefirah*, but beyond this they were models for two possible forms of life in the light of revelation. Of course at the present only the one is tangible and capable of fulfillment. Precisely out of those very distinctions and limitations, man is to restore the lost form and the violated image of the divine in himself and thus bring the Tree of Knowledge, with which he is mystically associated, to its full development.

This Torah of the Tree of Knowledge is, however, nothing other than the world of tradition which represents the law of the unredeemed world since the expulsion from Paradise. Only the redemption, breaking the dominion of exile, puts an end to the order of the Tree of Knowledge and restores the utopian order of the Tree of Life, in which the heart of life beats unconcealed and the isolation in which everything now finds itself is overcome. Thus the inner logic of this conception of the dominion of the Tree of the Knowledge of Good and Evil as the legitimate form of revelation in an unredeemed world had to regard the redemption itself as a return home to Paradise, where all things will again be in their true place.

116

Although it is not a matter of a physical return to a geographical Paradise, it is in any case life in a state of the world which corresponds to that of Paradise or in which Paradise, for its part, expands into the world. The Torah of the Messianic age will then be that of the Tree of Life, which no longer knows anything of all those separations and limitations. This Torah is still revelation and, in Kabbalistic terms, an evolution of the divine name; but it has nothing further to do with the form under which we have known it until now. It is a utopian Torah for a utopian state of the world. The Sabbatians saw in such a vision no contradiction to acknowledging the forms of the tradition, that is, those of historical Judaism, for the period of exile. Without question this thinking of the Jewish Messianic heretics is structurally connected closely to that of the spiritualistic sects in Christianity. It was not, however, influenced by them in its specific historical appearance and formulation, which remained entirely Jewish.

According to the conception of the Sabbatians, who here again followed the intimations of these same sections of the *Zohar,* such a state of redemption, of liberation from exile, was achieved at the time of the revelation on Sinai. It is not surprising that when this typological thinking was applied to the exodus from Egypt—the very archetype of exile—revelation should seem the opportunity of redemption. But Israel, which was to receive this revelation, was not equal to the opportunity and it lapsed into worship of the golden calf.

Thereupon the Torah under the aspect of the Tree of Life, which would have made up the content of the revelation, reverted to its hidden state, and the tradition, the Oral Torah which encompassed the real revelation like a husk enclosing a kernel, began its dominion under the aspect of the Tree of Knowledge; only in this form could it be realized in history.

At this point the figure of the two trees in Paradise is brought into relation with that of the two pairs of tablets of the law. The first tablets, which were given to Moses before the people lapsed into the heathen cult of the golden calf, were the laws for a redeemed world and represented a revelation of the Tree of Life. They were the law of freedom. To this the spiritualistic exegesis of the *Tikkune Zohar* applied the famous passage of the Mishnah regarding these first tablets of which the Torah says (Exod. 32:16): "And the tablets were God's work, and the writing was God's writing, incised, *harut,* upon the tablets." The word *harut,* however, can also be read as *herut,* which means freedom.[2]

While the talmudic exegesis still understood this reading to mean that it was precisely the study of the Torah which lent true freedom, a freedom under the law, the mystical interpretation of the *Zohar* saw it as the freedom of the redemption expressed through the Torah on the first set of tablets. This idea is taken up and stressed by both Nathan of Gaza and Cardozo. No one has yet read the Torah of the Tree of Life which was inscribed on the first tablets. Israel was entrusted only with that second set of tablets, and they render the Torah as it is read under the dominion of the Tree of Knowledge and Differentiation, which is also called the Tree of Death.[3]

But with the redemption the first tablets will again be raised up; they will be a Torah in which the restoration of the state of Paradise is associated with a utopia that as yet has never been, that as yet has never been capable of realization. In this exegesis of the *Zohar* we can already notice the unconcern with a passage of the Torah such as Exod. 34:1, which says explicitly that the second set of tablets contained the same words as the first. It did not matter. The parallel between the trees in the primeval history of man and the tablets in the story of the revelation was simply too seductive for the radicals of mysticism.

The third typology is that which saw a parallel between the course of world history and the history of the Creation. A day for God, according to one interpretation of a verse in Psalms, is a thousand years. Thus the six thousand years of world history correspond to the six workdays leading up to the great cosmic Sabbath, to redemption on the seventh day of the universe. Like a good Jewish exegete, Cardozo argues—even though he carries this exegesis over into heresy—that other laws hold on the Sabbath than on a workday. The activities of the workday are to a large extent prohibited on the Sabbath and other activities take their place. Whoever performs the actions of a workday on the Sabbath violates the law. But on the cosmic Sabbath the Tree of Life reigns, and not the Tree of Knowledge. "Thus there clearly follows from all of this that, with the onset of the order of the Tree of Life on the great cosmic Sabbath, not only shall we no longer need to observe the order of the six weekdays, which corresponds to the mode of life prescribed in the six orders of the Mishnah. But beyond this, everyone who wants to serve God as he does now [i.e., by the traditional way of life] will in those days [of the Messiah] be called a desecrator of the Sabbath and a destroyer of the plantings [i.e., a downright heretic]."[4]

The Mishnah is the first codification of the oral Torah, and the six orders into which it is divided by subject constitute the framework of *halakhic* Judaism. The author of the above-mentioned parts of the *Zohar* indulged abundantly in remarks regarding the inferiority of the Mishnah; he opposes it to the mystical order of life of the Kabbalah and to the Messianic abrogation of those aspects of the Torah which it contains. Cardozo, who was very much attracted by these seditious passages, in his above-mentioned formulation simply drew the consequences. He presents us with the palpable intrusion of implicit antinomianism into the world of tradition. What was commandment becomes downright prohibition. And from here it was only a short step to a further consequence, of which we have yet to speak: acts prohibited now become not only permissible but are even considered holy.

However Cardozo, who remained loyal to the tradition in his personal observance, established a safeguard within these channels of thought which put off any explicit antinomianism, at least for a transitional period. As long as the Messiah has not returned from his mission into those realms where Cardozo does not dare to follow him, believing that they can be entered only by the Messiah—he decisively rejected mystical apostasy for anyone other than the Messiah himself—so long does the tradition retain its undiminished validity.

The restoration of the true figure of man, Adam, is not complete as long as the Redeemer himself remains in the world of the "husks," of the powers of the "other side," where he gathers up the holy sparks. With his return, which corresponds to the New Testament conception of the parousia, the law of the renewed world—the Torah of the Tree of Life—will come into effect. Thus the world of the tradition is liable to collapse at any time, and for the Sabbatians the reasons for this collapse have been given long

119

before it actually takes place. According to the immanent logic of their conceptions, its crisis cannot be averted.

The real Adam is restored in the figure of the Messiah and now begins his career in a renewed world which stands under the law of freedom. In the writings of the Sabbatians hidden conflicts come to light on this issue and are expressed, for example, in the differences between the positions of Cardozo and Nathan of Gaza. The Messiah could be conceived as one who has completely mastered the Tree of Knowledge and its Torah, and from this experience, which is that of the Jew in exile as well as that of suffering mankind, pushes forward into the new realms of the Tree of Life. He could appear as the heir of the millennia who thereby gives the redemption a plenitude which it might have never had if Adam had not succumbed to temptation.

For according to the Lurianic Kabbalah the first opportunity for redemption presented itself to Adam on the day of his creation. Had Adam decided otherwise on the proposition of the serpent, the redemption of all worlds would already have begun then and the first Sabbath would also have been the last—the final cosmic Sabbath. But whether the Adam who would never have tasted the fruit of the Tree of Knowledge would have been richer than the one who went through this experience could remain doubtful.

In fact we find, especially in the writings of Nathan of Gaza, a very different conception of the Messiah which stands in opposition to this one. According to Nathan's view, the soul of the Messiah was from the first and since the beginning of the world inextricably bound up with the Tree of Life and was never subjected to the law of the Tree of Knowledge. Thus he always stood beyond good and evil, commandment and prohibition, because he never left the state of Paradise. Only from our perspective do his actions often seem reprehensible, illicit, and scandalous, when in truth they conform to the laws of his origin.[5]

The House of the World

Aryeh Wineman

The classic structure of existence is constructed, threatened, and will ultimately be perfected as the defiling, threatening force is utterly removed.

"But Jacob journeyed on to Succoth, and built a house for himself and made stalls for his cattle; that is why the place was called Succoth" (Gen. 33:17).

Beginning his interpretation of this verse, Rabbi Ḥiyya referred to another verse: "Unless the Lord build the house, its builders labor in vain; unless the Lord watches over the city, the watchman keeps vigil in vain" (Ps. 127:1). He commented,

> Come and note: At the moment that the first stirring to create a universe arose in the divine will, He brought forth from the spark of darkness[1] a mist which then glowed in the midst of the darkness. The light remained above even as it descended below, glistening in a hundred different paths—some hardly detectable and others expansive—bringing the House of the World into being.

> This House is situated at the very center of all that is. How many entrances and chambers it has! It is surrounded everywhere by concealed, holy places where the birds of the heavens build nests, each according to its own kind. From its midst there emerges a single large and mighty Tree, with thick branches and fruit, having abundant sustenance in it for all. That Tree ascends upward to the very clouds of the heavens, until it disappears from view among three mountains, and then comes into view both climbing higher and also descending. The House, nourished and watered by the Tree, conceals numerous celestial and unknown treasures. In this way that House was constructed and beautified. The Tree is visible during the daylight hours but at night is hidden from view, while the House, in contrast, is seen at night and is hidden from view during the day.

> At the hour that darkness sets in, the House appears, its doorways all firmly closed in all directions. At once numerous spirits fly about in the air, seeking to enter and ascend within it, curious as to what it contains. They join with the birds, acquiring their knowledge and flying about and observing, until the

darkness, now attached to the House, is awakened and sends forth a single flame and strikes with mighty hammers, opening the doors and cleaving the rocks. That flame then flares both up and down, striking the world, and voices are awakened both above and below.

After connecting with air emerging from amidst the pillar of clouds of the inner altar and spreading out in all four directions, a herald immediately ascends and calls out. A million hosts stand to the left and a myriad of myriads[2] to the right, while the herald stands in his place, calling out forcefully. Then, so many there are who chant and worship! Two doors open, one to the south, the other to the north. The House ascends and stands, linking the two sides as song is chanted and words of praise ascend. Whoever then enters does so as in a whisper, and the House glistens with six exceedingly bright lights, illumining all directions. Streams of balsam flowing from there, watering all the wild beasts and the birds, as it is written, "[You make springs gust forth in torrents; they make their way between the hills] giving drink to all the wild beasts; the wild asses slake their thirst. The birds of the sky dwell beside them and sing among the foliage" (Psalms 104:10–12), and song continues until daybreak.

Then when dawn appears, the stars and the constellations of the heavens and all their hosts chant songs of praise, as is written, "[Who set its cornerstone] when the morning stars sang together and all the divine beings shouted for joy?" (Job 38:6–7). And note, "Unless the Lord builds the house, its builders labor in vain; unless the Lord watches over the city, the watchman keeps vigil in vain" (Ps. 127:1). This refers to the sublime King who is constantly engaged in constructing and perfecting that House. When? Whenever proper terrestrial worship and devotions ascend from below.

"Unless the Lord watches over the city [the watchman keeps vigil in vain]" (Ps. 127:1). To what time does this refer? To the hour that the darkness of evening sets in, when armed camps wander about through the world; the doors are closed and guarded from all sides to prevent any uncircumcised and unclean one from approaching, as it is stated, "[Awake, awake, O Zion! Clothe yourself in splendor; Put on your robes of majesty, Jerusalem, holy city!] For the uncircumcised and the unclean shall never enter you again" (Isa. 52:1)—those whom, in the future, the Holy One, blessed be He, will remove from the world! Who, then, is the uncircumcised and who is the

unclean one [to whom the verse refers]? Actually, they are one
and the same, the very one who enticed [Adam and Eve] and
whom they followed to cause death for all[3] and who continues to defile this House until that time when the Holy One,
blessed be He, will expel him from the world.

And so it is, that "unless the Lord watches over the city, the
watchman keeps vigil in vain" (Ps. 127: 1).

Commentary

The hours of dawn and dusk, the alternation and marvel of light
and darkness, was a source of fascination in Zoharic literature. The
hour of dawn is painted in word images: "The person rising early to
set out on a journey is told to look up, at a certain moment, to the
eastern sky where, at daybreak, he will see something resembling
letters appearing in movement, formed by sparks of the very letters of the alphabet with which God created the world."

That same fascination is also evident in our passage, a descriptive account that extends between the foci of dawn and of
darkness.

Light and darkness, however, serve as a symbolic language in the
hands of the Zoharic author, who reveals his highly poetic tenden-
cies in this passage. In the light of some basic kabbalistic symbols,
this account can be understood as one that relates, with intricate
allusion, the story of the formation of the world of the *Sefirot* including the Shekhinah, the conflict that threatens to endanger the
Shekhinah, and the resolution of that conflict by the removal of
the threat itself.

Both tree and house in the account serve as symbols of *sefirot*:
the tree is *Tiferet*, the house, *Malkhut* (the Shekhinah), representing respectively masculine and feminine aspects of the divine. The
very beginning of all movement and of creation and formation appears in the glowing mist, the divine urge to break out of its state of
absolute concealment and boundlessness. The house, formed
through *Tiferet*, attracts threatening forces that endanger it—the
forces of impurity, the antithesis of holiness. Counteracting these
forces is the worship of the divine, which effects union between

123

Tiferet and *Malkhut,* and with that divine union all the seven lower *sefirot* glisten. *Tiferet* guards the Shekhinah, and ultimately the threatening forces of the *Sitra ahra*—which also bring death in the world—are removed and annihilated.

Some questions may already have arisen in the reader's mind: How does the author proceed from the biblical verse about Jacob and his construction projects to this story which reflects cosmic proportions comprising the Zoharic reading of the same verse? And, can this passage be properly defined as a "story"?

Approaching the first question, it is important to grasp the Zoharic author's tendency to read any and every verse in a biblical text as an allusion to a deeper meaning. This meaning generally concerns the history of the higher supernal world, the creation of this world, and the drama and interaction between the two. Hence a verse from the biblical account of the life of Jacob, a verse speaking of the patriarch's constructing dwellings for his family and his animals, is here grasped as referring ultimately to the construction of the Shekhinah within the configuration of sefirot in the World of Emanation. The description comprising the Zoharic interpretation of Gen. 33:17 suggests the intricate processes and modes of divine being coming into existence through emanation. The link confirming the presumed cosmic meaning of the verse from Genesis is located in the verse from Psalms (127:1), which is read as implying that any house that is built is actually built by God. If so, then in its ultimate and esoteric level the verse is grasped as speaking of an act of construction on the part of divine powers within the higher world.

A single word in the biblical verse provides a crucial key in the Zoharic interpretation of that verse. The occurrence of the word *sukkot* (thatched booths) in the verse in Genesis is immediately associated with the festival of Sukkot (Booths) and with the commandment to dwell in such booths during the days of that festival along with the mystic significance of the festival and the festival booth. An entire array of associations reverberate from the word which, a non-kabbalist might assume, is employed quite innocently in a verse from the Torah relating to the work activities of Jacob. Zoharic interpretation understands the seven-day Sukkot festival as symbolizing the Seven Primordial Days that created the world, namely the seven lower *sefirot*. Those seven *sefirot* (lower than *Binah*) are experienced on the seven days of the Sukkot festival.[4] These symbolic associations transform a prosaic statement in the Torah into a poetic statement of cosmic processes.

Let us turn to the second question raised concerning this passage; namely, is it a story? The Zohar's exegesis on Gen. 33:17 is, on the surface, a highly lyrical description of what is essentially recurrent. The passage includes a description of day and night, of evening twilight and the emergence of dawn—daily recurrent happenings. As such, however, the passage lacks the ingredient of time and would not follow any kind of narrative pattern.

Though the passage seems to describe what is recurrent in nature, the time factor is nevertheless present at two distinct points: the opening and the ending of the account. In its opening, the description turns to the initial divine thought or impulse to bring a world into being, to create the world of the *sefirot* that would then serve as the inner structure of all being; thus the opening of the passage depicts the beginning point of all time. The passage concludes—again beyond the realm of the recurrent—at the endpoint of the drama of both human and cosmic history, characterized by the removal of the forces threatening the Shekhinah, the cessation of all threat to the integrity and structure of the World of Emanation, and the banishment of death from the world. Together, the beginning and the end of the passage establish a time frame that transforms the stuff of basically recurrent description into a narrative in which threat is permanently overcome and a state of wholeness is restored. The descriptive account is inscribed upon a canvas extending from the beginning point of time to its culmination and, in this sense, most clearly exemplifies what is encyclopedic in character. It encompasses the larger drama of existence that includes, even if by implication alone, the total *human* story.

The reader has probably noted the highly archetypal nature of this narrative. Its key images are distinctly cross-cultural, and it is precisely the presence of such images—it might be felt—which contributes a sense of literary power to the passage.

In numerous cultures, both the tree and the house serve as images of the universe.

While the tree in this passage refers specifically to the *sefirah Tiferet,* the tree image has different meanings in various religious traditions. It often suggests the regeneration of the universe and is also associated with the center of the universe.[5] Heinrich Zimmer refers to the "inexhaustible life-strength" that the tree represents to human awareness;[6] in contrast with the finite human life span, the tree appears, to human eyes, never to grow old or to die.[7] In the words of the biblical prophet, "For the days of My people shall be as long as the days of a tree" (Isa. 65:22). In this connection the tree-image suggests the infinite life of the universe and serves as a symbol of immortality.[8]

The tree came to suggest an axis connecting the various worlds, its roots, trunk, and branches with their foliage serving as images of the netherworld, the earth, and the celestial worlds, respectively.[9] Not only birds but the heavenly bodies were thought to connect with the foliage of the cosmic tree.[10] And as an image of seemingly never-ending life, the tree became a symbol not only of immortality—the tree or fruit or sap of life—but of the divine as well; various trees were actually regarded as divine in nature.[11] Some early peoples perceived the universe as a tree encompassing the earth and the heavens,[12] and regarded the lights of the heavens as the fruit of the "Tree of Heaven."[13] Goblet concludes his account of the cross-cultural nature of the tree image with the suggestion that viewing the universe in the form of a tree constitutes a very natural way of thinking in traditional societies.[14]

The archetypal symbol of the tree probably came to the Zohar most directly from *Sefer habahir,* the earliest known kabbalistic text that antedates and certainly influenced the Zohar. In that text, the divine powers, situated in a hierarchy one layer above the other, are represented by the tree image![15] In a parable found elsewhere in *Sefer habahir,*[16] a king seeks to plant a tree in his garden, and not finding a spring of water there, he first digs for a source of living water. Finding it he opens a well and then plants the tree, which is constantly nourished by the well he has dug.[17] God asserts that He planted a tree so that all would find delight in it.[18] On the cosmological nature of the tree described, an interesting passage in *Sefer habahir* speaks of the tree's twelve diagonal boundaries, suggesting the spatial and nonspatial dimensions of the cosmos that spread out to infinity. In addition, souls are situated along the tree just like birds sitting in its branches.[19]

The Zoharic author states that "the Tree of Life [identified with *Tiferet*] pours forth life unceasingly into the universe" (1:131a), a life, however, that in the present state is limited due to the impact of the impure powers sometimes likened to the bark of the Tree of Emanation.[20] In another passage (Zohar 2:64b),[21] the branches of the Tree of the Holy One are said to be surrounded by twelve boundaries comprising the boundaries of the world. The tree's seventy branches are said to represent the pagan nations, whereas the people of Israel, we read, are situated in the very body of the tree.[22]

The particular description of the tree in our Zoharic passage conveys a distinct sense of mystery as the tree rises above the rocks, climbing to a lofty region quite beyond human grasp and comprehension. Beyond its reference to the Zoharic world-picture and its symbolism, that soaring of the tree to the region of the very highest *sefirot* also connotes a freedom from the limitations associated with what is earthly in nature. . . .

Still another pattern from the world of ancient myth is overheard in this Zoharic passage and redefined in the idiom of the Zohar: creation is depicted as a contest between the deity who wills to create, to construct a universe, and an antagonistic force opposed to creation and structure themselves. In this passage from the Zohar, the hostile and defiling force is the *Sitra ahra*, which emerges as a consequence of the complexities of divine emanation and of human sin; that demonic reality is manifest in the threatening spirits and armed camps described in the account. It is the *Sitra ahra* that brings death into an existence which would otherwise be un-marred by death. The House is secure only when the *Sitra ahra* is vanquished, and it is God who will ultimately remove the *Sitra ahra* from the world.

It is then that the true nature of the Tree as boundless life—the nuance so central to the cosmic tree as archetype—will be realized in a world without death.

A more precise treatment, both of the narrative art and of the meanings of this highly lyrical, symbolic, and archetypal passage, must consider the relationships between this account and its textual context. The text surrounding the story contains a number of motifs and themes that either echo in this account or parallel it. These come together to create a texture in which the story of the House of the World is fully integrated, placed within a landscape appropriate to its own rhythms and motifs and thematics.

The World Trees in the Zohar

*Pinchas Giller**

It is common for mystics to experience the Divine in the forces and laws of the phenomenal world. The mystic's soul dissolves into union with this World, so that space and time are transcended. Often a sense of innocence, as premoral as infancy, accompanies this feeling that William James called "pantheistic, optimistic, anti-naturalistic . . . in harmony with otherworldly states of mind."[1] All things are perceived as one, and the very world seems to be alive. This desire to be at one with the sacredness of the phenomenal World comprises the joyous beatific heart of nature mysticism.

In pursuing this sensibility, the Jewish mystical tradition, or *Kabbalah,* had a divided heart. There was much in classical Judaism that denied the world of present reality. God, as defined by Maimonides and other medieval Jewish philosophers,[2] was wholly outside of the World and could never be perceived or described. In the philosophical tradition, God's nature is more apparent in the myriad things that God clearly is *not,* rather than what God is. Nature was ultimately secular and mundane, so that a sense of oneness with the phenomenal world was not seen as ultimately profound. This idea was best encapsulated by a sage of the Mishnah in the second century C.E., who stated that "the one who interrupts his study, saying, 'how beautiful is this tree,' truly forfeits his soul" (*Pirkey Avot* 3:9).

And yet, kabbalists felt the impulses of the nature mystic. The laws and rituals of classical Jewish tradition encouraged a contemplative sensibility which promoted a strong sense of one's being in the phenomenal world. Yet kabbalists also perceived the natural world through the prism of the sacred texts, the rich literary heritage of the Bible and Talmud. Purely kabbalistic works such as the *Bahir* and the Zohar interpreted the vocabulary of these texts symbolically. Nature could be perceived directly, and through descriptions in the sacred works. Hence, the tree blossoming in medieval Provence or Gerona was not more real to the mystic than the cedar of Lebanon described in Psalms 92, or the young saplings of Lev. 19:23–25. Moreover, their portrayal in the sacred texts is their most authentic dimension, particularly their significance in Jewish law *(halakhah)*. So it is that the fruits delineated in Deut. 8:8, the date, fig, grape, pomegranate and olives, were given special benedictions by the Rabbis of the Talmud. Classical Judaism regarded them with an extra measure of significance because they were the fruits of the land of Israel and were central to the imagery of the Bible, and also because the *halakhah* had defined them as important.

It was the contribution of classical Kabbalah to see the images of the present world as *symbols* of the Divine, so that aspects of nature also symbolize the ways in which God interacts with the World. Classical Kabbalah—the mystical tradition of the Zohar, the Tzfat renaissance and Hasidism—portrays a mythic universe in which the phenomenal world and the sacred texts are equally significant as signposts to supernal realities. The Zohar, the central kabbalistic work, sees the flow of the Divine into present reality as happening in a series of stages. These stages are a universal aspect of human spirituality. The neo-Platonists and other Western mystics of late antiquity called them *hypostases,* Tantric mysticism called them *chakras* and the kabbalists called them *sefirot.*

God's Divinity flows into the world through the medium of the ten *sefirot,* stages in the passage from the ineffable, unquantifiable aspects of Divinity to the mundanity of present reality. Each *sefirah* represents a particular aspect of God. The *sefirot* are also the instruments through which the prosaic and the transcendent interact. Recurring images in the central texts of Judaism are interpreted as referring to various *sefirot.* In kabbalistic spirituality, meditation and contemplation of the nature of reality are combined with mystical reading of the sacred texts in order to illustrate the distinction be-

129

tween the sublime unity of God and the disorder and multiplicity of created world. At best, the phenomenal world points to transcendent realities, causing the author of the influential Kabbalistic work *Ḥemdat Yamim to* exclaim "these are all analogies for the situation in the transcendent world! The lower worlds are but a shadow of the upper."[3]

The relationship of the *sefirot* reflects the tensions arising from the unity of and separation between the creator and the created. The Zohar calls this esoteric tradition, which explains the union of the upper and lower worlds, the "Secret of Unity" *(Sod ha-Yiḥud)*. Trees, then, certainly exist in present reality. They are also symbols of the interplay of elements in the hidden recesses of Divinity.

Such mysticism would tend to draw one out of the natural world into a contemplation of the wholly transcendent. Kabbalah's symbolic aspect, however, drew kabbalists back into the natural world. Classical Jewish spirituality is participatory; every prohibition, ritual and benediction brings the individual into discourse with the real nature of the created world. For example, the palm, myrtle, willow and citron that are brought to the Temple for the Sukkot festival symbolize the flow of the Divine into present reality.[4] Each one of them symbolizes a different *sefirah*. Hence the person holding the four species, waving them in six directions and shaking them at certain point in the *Hallel* prayers, experiences and responds to the state of the upper world through the medium of the natural world. Moreover, the mystic creates a state of unification with the transcendent. This performance and observance of the precepts of the law, as a response to the esoteric dimension of existence, is called *theurgy*. This need to sanctify nature lent itself to the ritual of the Kabbalists, particularly in the Tu B'Shvat seder described in the compelling seventeenth-century work *Ḥemdat Yamim*. For kabbalists in the period following the Tzfat renaissance and the Sabbatian heresy, Tu B'Shvat was the occasion for *tikkun*, or mystical repair.[5]

The Zohar portrays the earth as a model for the structure of the true, transcendent world. Every living thing refers to an esoteric quality. Therefore, trees and herbs have mystical significance and esoteric power.[6] The Zohar displays an almost childlike sense of wonder at the paradox of a tree's existence. Like everything else in the phenomenal world, trees represent aspects of the Divine. In fact, the ten *sefirot* are most often portrayed in a linear model, representing the trunk of a tree with its roots in heaven and its boughs and branches extending into present reality. Different kinds of trees may reflect the emphases of different *sefirot*. Agriculture, therefore, has an esoteric dimension that involves balancing the various energies inherent in the plants being cultivated.[7]

Fruit trees are most important, in the Zohar's hierarchy, for they play the central role in the story of the Edenic fall from grace. Fruit trees invoke the *sefirah Tiferet*, the great central column through which existence flows, as if through the trunk of a tree.[8] *Tiferet* is made up of six *sefirot*, which then unify with the *sefirah* which is called *Malkhut* or *Shekhinah*. The seven parts of the tree—roots, bark, wood, branches, leaves, flowers, and fruit—allude to the interaction of these seven *sefirot*.[9]

Fruit are also invoked as an image of fecundity and fertility. This fecundity might be literal, as when the "fruit tree" is used to symbolize the sage's marital relationship.[10] Fruit are also used to indicate spiritual fecundity, the expansion of the world of teaching. The sage is compared to a tree, in which the students of the academy, "the masters of the Mishnah . . . nest in the trees like fledglings."[11] Similarly, the *tzaddik,* or religious saint, and his community are symbolized as a tree with spreading branches and strong roots.[12]

With some exceptions (the willow and the hyssop shrub), the non-fruit-bearing trees have their origin in the more prosaic, divided realm of *Malkhut. Malkhut* is the *sefirah* through which transcendent realities enter the prosaic, mundane and ambivalent world of present reality. In the classical diagrams of the *sefirot,* it sits at the bottom of the sefirotic tree. The juncture of *Malkhut* and *Tiferet* is the *sefirah Yesod,* the realm of sexuality, the juncture of the two World Trees.[13]

Trees in the mundane world represent the interaction and interplay of the Divine *sefirot*. The tree also serves as a metaphor for the structure of the whole universe. Many cultures have conceived the image of the World Tree, whose roots lie in one dimension, while its trunk and branches probe another.[14] Jewish lore certainly contains similar imagery, for the World Trees, the Tree of Life *(Eitz*

Hayyim) and the Tree of Knowledge of Good and Evil *(Eitz ha-Da'at Tov ve-Ra),* originate in Judaism's creation tradition.

The World Trees originate in the literal reality of the creation account. In the Zohar's world view, narrative images of the Bible, such as the Flood, the Garden of Eden and the parting of the Red Sea, exist not only in the past, but also in the present and future. The flood still rages, and the chaos of the social order and the political world is only one sign of its power. Similarly, the Garden of Eden exists as a destination for the righteous upon their deaths. This paradise of the afterlife is, among other things, portrayed as a garden of fruit trees beneath which "all the waters of creation gather and separate."[15] Hence the World Trees really exist. In fact, they are the source of all phenomenal reality. Their existence, however, is expressed in terms of the *sefirot.*

These World Trees are agents of two aspects of Divinity.[16] The Tree of Life begins from the transformative feminine womb of the *sefirah Binah.* It extends into the realm of *Tiferet,* the group of *sefirot* that represent the qualities of dimensionality and spirituality.[17] The Tree grows upside down, out of transcendent reality into present reality, with its roots in *Binah* and its branches extending into the prosaic erotic juncture of *Yesod* and *Malkhut.*

The Tree of Life represents the union of the six intermediate *sefirot.* It is an idealized realm of unity, untroubled by the divisions that afflict the lowest *sefirah Malkhut.*[18] Although its union of the six intermediate *sefirot* gives it a multifaceted nature, these facets are subsumed into its essential unity. It is also the metaphor for the Torah, as it extends out of the transcendent into the tangible. Mythic images and symbols of primordiality, such as Adam, symbolize the functions of the Tree of Life. The immolations and offerings of Temple Service also symbolize this tree's ascent from the corporeal into the incorporeal realm.[19]

If the upper *sefirot* are a realm of harmony and unity, the lowest *sefirah, Malkhut* represents the division and discord of present existence, the realm of the secular and mundane.[20] The Tree of Knowledge represents this divided, dualistic realm. It "suckles from both sides, and knows them as one knows both the sweet and the bitter . . . half sweet, from the right side, and half bitter, from the left side."[21] Its positive dimension is its association with the *Shekhinah*, the Kabbalah's archetype of the idealized feminine Divinity. Therefore, the Tree of Knowledge is symbolized by Eve. Its male aspect is represented by the demiurgic angel *Metatron*.[22]

The Tree of Knowledge also has a negative aspect. It is, after all, the Tree of Knowledge of Good *and* Evil, potentially a tree of death that God will pluck up and plant in the underworld at the end of time! It is ambiguous, encompassing many opposites: good and evil, bitter and sweet, truth and falsehood, pure and impure.[23] It encompasses images of mixture and lack of refinement, like silver mixed with dross, the illicit mixing of crop seed, the mixture of wool and linen in a garment, and the mixed multitude (*erev rav*) of the Exodus account.[24] Yet it is also an abundantly giving tree, for its fruit is the very roiling, unruly multiplicity of existence.[25]

The attempt to bridge the gap between the two World Trees is the path of enlightenment. Seeing the World Trees as anything other than contiguous constitutes the heresy of Gnosticism. If the Tree of Life did not grow into the Tree of Knowledge, it would be as if God had withdrawn from the world and no longer influenced it directly. To deny God's existence in the world in this way would be, in the language of the Talmud, "cutting the shoots" (*kitzutz ba-netiyot*). In the imagery of the World Trees, this cutting of the shoots is a literal image, for the heretic has broken the contiguity of the two trees.[26]

One potential hazard in properly understanding the relationship of the World Trees derives from the distinction between the mystical understanding of the Torah and the Law as it is observed. The Tree of Knowledge represents the rituals and practices of present existence, the domain of what Judaism calls the Oral Torah *(Torah she-be-ktav)*. Its divided, ambivalent nature represents the dialectics of the law and its minutiae, the obsession with detail and practice which characterizes Rabbinic Judaism.[27] The Tree of Life reflects the deeper, more consistent secrets of kabbalistic wisdom. This distinction between the outward manifestation of Judaism in the Law and its sublime inner consistency originates at the theophany at Sinai. The first tablets that Moses received at Sinai came from the Tree of Life. After the incident of the golden calf, the second tablets, which included Judaism's exoteric practices, were given from the realm of the Tree of Knowledge.[28] In fact, those whose minds are engrossed in the Torah overcome this division, for though they might be physically in the realm of the Tree of Knowledge, their consciousness has ascended to the Tree of Life.[29]

Mediating and bridging the distinction between the two World Trees is the job of the enlightened mystic. The *tzaddik* is therefore intrinsic to this mythos, for the *tzaddik* lives at the junction of the World Trees.[30] Like saints and thaumaturges of many religious traditions, the *tzaddik* keeps one foot, as it were, in the realm of the Tree of Knowledge and one foot in the wholly spiritual realm of the Tree of Life. Therefore, in the Zohar's exegesis of (Gen. 1:12) "Every fruit tree making fruit whose seed is on the whole land . . .," the term "fruit tree" represents *Tiferet,* while the phrase "making fruit" represents the eroticism of the *sefirah Yesod.* This *sefirah* is also symbolized by the *tzaddik,* "whose seed is on the whole land," and the *Shekhinah* "in whom all seeds are combined."[31] The union of the mundane and the transcendent in the life of the *tzaddik* is symbolized, as is common in Kabbalah, in terms of an erotic metaphor.

The instrument of this task is the Zohar itself. The Zohar sees itself as a medium for uniting the outward form of Judaism as it is practiced with its inner abstraction. In fact, the gap between exoteric Judaism and its inner spirituality parallels the distinction between the World Trees. The enlightened students of the Zohar are like angels, going back and forth between two worlds. The Zohar is the vehicle for the sage's integration of the values of each of the World Trees.

This shifting reality lies at the center of the Zohar's world. The inner and outer, the transcendent and the mundane, are unified as one. One may look outside at the natural world, but its effect is always to draw one back to the Law, to the sacred text, to the underlying drama of the *sefirot* and their hidden interactions, to the struggle of good to extricate itself from evil. The World Trees are symbols of the evolution of consciousness. For the kabbalist, the challenge is to envision one unified World, from the sacred and the profane, from the natural and the transcendent. That is the task of "the enlightened [who] understand the shining of the higher mother, the realm of *Binah,* the Tree of Life . . . for in the future Israel will taste from the Tree of Life that is this book, the *Zohar.*"[32]

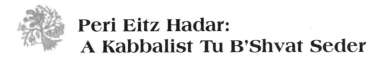

Peri Eitz Hadar:
A Kabbalist Tu B'Shvat Seder

translated by Miles Krassen

Introduction

The notion of a Tu B'Shevat seder, that is, a ritual involving the eating of specific fruit, drinking wine, and studying or reciting specific selections from the sacred literature of Judaism, does not seem to have been known before the late seventeenth century. Until the sixteenth century, most kabbalists were more concerned with providing mystical bases that would strengthen the motivation for observing the laws and traditions of classical Judaism, than with creating new rituals. At that point, the kabbalists of Tzfat did create some new rituals, most notably the *Kabbalat Shabbat* service. The kabbalistic Tu B'Shevat seder seems to have been created sometime later, in the wake of kabbalistic creativity in sixteenth-century Tzfat.

The text of the seder, which has come to be known as *Peri Eitz Hadar*, is essentially the same as the section on Tu B'Shevat which appears in the Sabbatian influenced anthology of kabbalistic customs, *Ḥemdat Yamim* (Izmir, 1731–1732).[1]

However, it is not yet possible to determine when the text was actually composed or who its author may have been. The *Ḥemdat Yamim* was, itself, primarily a reworking of materials copied from various kabbalistic sources, some of which, at least, date back to the final decades of the seventeenth century.[2] From internal references in the text, it is clear that the chapter on Tu B'Shevat did not originally follow the chapter that precedes it in *Ḥemdat Yamim*.[3] It seems probable, therefore, that the compiler of the *Ḥemdat Yamim* copied the Tu B'Shevat seder from one of these earlier sources. At any rate, the text has been printed separately many times as a pamphlet entitled *Peri Eitz Hadar*, since its first edition in Venice, 1728.[4]

Both the text of *Peri Eitz Hadar* and the seder that it contains seem to have been popular only among the Sefardic communities of the East. No mention of the text or its customs is to be found in the classic Ḥasidic literature of Eastern Europe.[5] This may be due to the fact that *Ḥemdat Yamim* was condemned as a heretical Sabbatian text by Jacob Emden, who attributed it to the Sabbatian theologian, Nathan of Gaza. Emden's influence, it seems, did not extend beyond the Ashkenazic community. In the East, the *Peri Eitz Hadar* continued to be reprinted until the present day. It now appears that as a result of the unique historical conditions that have resulted from the establishment of the State of Israel, the Tu B'Shevat seder, *Peri Eitz Hadar*, is finally gaining acceptance among certain elements in the contemporary Ashkenazic communities as well. This is due, in part, to the unprecedented proximity of diverse Jewish communities in Jerusalem, which is resulting in a period of mutual influencing. Sefardic Torah scholars study in Ashkenazic yeshivot and sages of Baghdad and Morocco have become experts in the writings of Hasidic masters. At the same time, Ashkenazic kabbalists have increasingly come under the influence of works composed or popularized among the Sefardic communities. It may be added that under these favorable conditions kabbalistic works of all types and periods are appearing in print with ever greater frequency.

Formally, *Peri Eitz Hadar* contains four basic sections. After an introduction that explains the basis for the Tu B'Shevat seder, there is a prayer to be said before the actual seder begins. This is followed by a description of the order of the fruit to be eaten and the way wine should be blended in each of the four cups.[6] However, the bulk of the seder consists of selections from the Bible, early rabbinic texts, and the Zoharic literature. In fact, the greatest portion of this material is taken from the Zohar.

As a result, the *Peri Eitz Hadar* is essentially a kabbalistic work, meant to be read and applied by a reader thoroughly schooled in the outlook of the Kabbalah, particularly as it developed in the School of Isaac Luria. This fact renders the text, even in translation, virtually incomprehensible for a modern reader. This is due to several factors. First, the text does not explain the rather complex basic principles of Kabbalah as they developed since the late twelfth century. In particular, the text assumes that its reader is familiar and comfortable with the kabbalistic classic, *Sefer ha-Zohar*, an esoteric work characterized by obscure allusions and highly symbolic language.[7] In addition the author's outlook involves certain fundamental notions about nature, the cosmos, and the spiritual role that human beings are meant to play, which may be unfamiliar and even strange to a contemporary reader. Such notions, moreover, are not defended or justified, but are implicit in the author's and the intended reader's worldview.

The Tu B'Shevat seder celebrates an important moment in the yearly cycle of nature, the appearance of fruit on trees. In the Land of Israel, this stage occurs during mid-winter. In order to understand how the *Peri Eitz Hadar* approaches this celebration, it is necessary to gain some understanding of how the kabbalists viewed nature. In general, the kabbalistic view shared many traits that were typical of other pre-modern cosmological systems, which tended to regard nature as in some sense sacred. This approach to nature is in marked contrast to those that have become typical of the modern period.[8] For the kabbalist, nature is neither a source to be exploited for utilitarian benefits, nor a sentimental vestige of the past to be romanticized by poets and naturalists. It is rather an ultimate link in a chain of divine manifestation that directly emerges from the divine source of life.

Implicit here is a notion of sacred cosmology, which is not limited to material existence. The kabbalists' faith involves a hierarchy of worlds that are ontologically higher than the material world. These worlds are populated by angels and spiritual forces that span the ontological regions that separate humanity and the material world from God. Moreover, the forces in these worlds serve as conduits and sources for the divine energy that becomes manifest in nature and in Creation in general.

Although each world is characterized by an increasing degree of opacity that veils its divine root, all worlds share a common underlying structure. Thus contemplation of any world can lead to knowledge of the structure of the ultimate theosophical realm. This realm is the world of the ten *sefirot*, which is composed of the ten divine qualities and aspects that constitute the inner life of God, insofar as it is accessible to human imagining. This principle is no less true of nature. Indeed, nature (along with the human body) is, in a sense, the most available arena of divine revelation, since the higher worlds are not apparent to the senses. As such, nature may serve as a mirror in which all of the mysteries of the concealed Godhead are reflected.

This fundamentally sacred view of nature renders it comparable to the Torah itself. For the kabbalist, the Torah is not merely an account of the sacred history of Israel and its divinely mandated laws. It is a primary manifestation of divine revelation. All of the secrets and mysteries of the cosmos and the inner workings of the Godhead are somehow contained within it. However, it is a cipher, which only yields its concealed meanings to those who hold the keys of divine gnosis, the kabbalists, who through contemplation and mystical experience have gained access to the symbol system that opens the Torah's deeper levels of meaning. For the kabbalist, nature parallels the Torah. The very same secrets that are concealed within the quintessential sacred text may be learned through directly contemplating aspects of nature. The structure of different kinds of fruit, the growing patterns of trees, the habits of birds, indeed all natural phenomena are, in essence, aspects of a divine epiphany that proclaims the truth of God's existence.

However, here it should be added that the kabbalist's position is not identical to that of medieval religious philosophers, like Maimonides, who also viewed nature as a source for knowledge of God. In their view, the knowledge of the wondrous construction of nature and its laws led to an appreciation for its Creator. Here, knowledge of God is theosophical. It regards nature as a symbolic representation of the hidden divine realm and not merely as an immaculately designed product of divine engineering.

We have thus far been considering nature as source for divine knowledge. There is another aspect of the kabbalist's view of nature that is equally fundamental. This is related to the question of humanity's relation to nature.

The kabbalistic cosmos in its present state, especially according to the School of Isaac Luria, is dualistic. Evil as well as good is present in some sense and to some degree in each of the worlds that exist below the world of divine emanation itself. Indeed, the way in which evil is present in each world is symbolized in the seder by the classification of fruits, according to the location of their shells, skin, or rind. Thus the presence of evil in our material world is also a reflection of conditions in the higher worlds, which themselves reflect the state of things in the theosophical realm. There, however, evil by definition cannot exist, although its roots, or potential for existence, are located in the highest ontological levels of divinity.[9] Nevertheless, while evil is external to the divine realm of holiness itself, it is located in proximity to its tenth *sefirah*, *Malkhut*. Thus, as long as evil has not been entirely vanquished, it has the capacity to threaten the tenth *sefirah* and to separate Her[10] from the higher *sefirot*. The ascendancy of evil above is reflected by various conditions in the material world that are characterized by injustice. In terms of the sacred history of Judaism, the disruption of the divine realm is represented by Israel's exile among the nations, which symbolizes the absence of God's Kingdom on earth.

The duality of good and evil is also symbolically present within nature. Sources of life, such as food, represent the powers of holiness. That which may not be eaten symbolizes the external evil forces.[11] The edible portion of wheat, for example, symbolizes the tenth *sefirah*, while chaff represents the external forces. The edible portion of fruit is associated with forces of holiness, while its shell represents the forces of evil. Here we should note that the symbolism compels us to recognize that the "external forces" have an important role to play. They are not evil in an absolute sense. Indeed, the examples from nature teach us that when the cosmos is in a harmonious state, the "external forces" perform the positive function of acting as guardians that protect the more vulnerable manifestations of holiness.[12]

However, it is obvious that nature alone is not sufficient for maintaining a harmonious state. Just as evil may assail the tenth *sefirah* above, those aspects of nature that should protect its life-giving elements can, under certain conditions, overrun them. As a result, the forces of holiness in nature can be cut off from the sources of life that sustain them, just as *Malkhut* can be separated from the higher *sefirot*.

If, then, neither the divine realm nor nature can be counted on to maintain a state of cosmic harmony, what factor remains which might act to fulfill this function? For the kabbalist, the answer is humanity. Indeed, according to kabbalistic exegesis, the separation of the tenth *sefirah* was first caused by the sin of Adam. Symbolically, through eating the fruit in direct violation of the divine command, Adam separated the forces of holiness in nature from their divine source, thus empowering the external forces. As a result, the

Edenic state of harmony was broken and humanity and nature became adversaries. Thus, from the kabbalistic point of view, the sin of Adam testifies to the awesome power that humanity possesses. It is humanity that is primarily responsible for the state of nature and the cosmos.

If the first human misused his power to disrupt the Edenic state of harmony, the kabbalists believe that same power may still be used positively in order to reestablish and maintain the fragile cosmic balance. It is important to understand how, from the kabbalistic point of view, this power may be exercised. First, we should recall that Adam's sin consisted in separating an aspect of nature from its divine source. From this we may infer that a positive exercise of the human power to affect the cosmos involves connecting it, or more correctly, maintaining its connection, to the forces above. To a certain extent, this is directly accomplished by observing those laws concerning nature that are explicitly mandated by the Torah and interpreted and elaborated upon by the rabbinic authorities. However, while the kabbalist believes implicitly in the cosmic efficacy of such divine commandments, he also believes that their effectiveness depends fundamentally on a deeper, essentially human quality, intentionality.

The kabbalist not only fulfills the obligations of Jewish law, but transforms them into theurgic acts by having their specific cosmic effects in mind at the time that he performs them. Thus in fulfilling a specific commandment, he has in mind a precise effect, which he believes will occur in the upper worlds as a result of his action and intention. This intention is called the *kavvanah* of the commandment. Knowledge of these *kavvanot* constitutes one of the most important areas of kabbalistic concern.[13]

Knowledge and practice of the *kavvanot* has important ramifications in the realm of nature. Indeed, nature's well-being, from the kabbalistic point of view, is largely dependent on the *kavvanot* of commandments that pertain to nature, such as blessings said over food. The *kavvanot* that accompany the fulfillment of these commandments are meant to ensure that divine energy, or *shefa*, will be drawn down from its ultimate source of life in the divine realm, through the intermediate channels that deliver it to the realm of nature. Failure to perform this sacred role of guardianship impairs the functioning of this concealed process and threatens the ability of the guardian angels to replenish nature.

The School of Isaac Luria places emphasis on two additional concepts that are relevant to our text. According to this school, kabbalists are not only concerned with taking responsibility for the ongoing process of maintaining cosmic harmony. The cosmos has suffered serious structural damage in a catastrophic process of creation. Thus a long historical process of rectification, or *tikkun*, is required in order to restore the cosmos to its proper state. As a result of the catastrophe, sparks of divine light fell from their allotted places in the upper worlds and became embedded and concealed in the lower orders. A primary responsibility, according to kabbalists of the Lurianic School, is the retrieval of these sparks, which must be elevated through performing the commandments and studying Torah with *kavvanah*.[14]

However, the catastrophic effect was not limited to the lights of the world of emanation. As a result of Adam's sin, a parallel shattering occurred within the unity of the human soul. Sparks from the collective soul became separated and fell. Consequently, the sacred history of Israel was interpreted by Lurianic kabbalists as a complex process of transmigration. In order to return to a state of perfection, the various elements of Adam's original soul had to gradually restore themselves through penitential acts, performed over the course of a series of lives. However, this process was further impeded by human sin. As a result, some of the soul-sparks fell to lower levels of existence and became sources of vitality for non-human aspects of creation, such as plants and animals. Thus the sacred act of eating food took on an additional kabbalistic significance, since it was believed that fallen soul-sparks, awaiting redemption, were present in food.[15] This belief added an additional significance to the Tu B'Shevat seder, with its emphasis on eating and blessing fruit. While the Lurianic theory of transmigration may strike modern sensibilities as strange, it may be well to observe that this theory serves to connect humanity to nature in a fundamentally spiritual way. Every aspect of nature, whether animal, vegetable, or mineral, may potentially contain sparks of holiness that are essential for the completion and redemption of a person's soul and those of his or her relatives.

Because of the kabbalistic perspective, Tu B'Shevat takes on a significance that goes beyond a simple celebration of an important stage in the cycle of nature. For one thing, the symbol of the cosmic tree is so central to kabbalistic thinking that any dramatic change affecting trees in the material world must be seen as a reflection of a cosmic event of the greatest importance. Thus Tu B'Shevat represents not only the New Year's Day for trees in this world, but even more importantly, for the kabbalist, the time when the cosmic tree becomes fecund. Since nature and all of creation is directly dependent on the spiritual bounty that is received from the cosmic tree, the kabbalistic perspective of the *Peri Eitz Hadar* considerably magnifies the importance of Tu B'Shevat. Indeed, one may say that the day becomes associated with a cosmic myth of divine potency and fertility. Thus the introduction to the *Peri Eitz Hadar* indicates that the central focus of the *tikkun* is the ninth *sefirah*, *Yesod*, which represents the divine phallus, or male generative principle within God.[16] An emphasis is placed on contemplating the relationship between *Yesod* and *Malkhut*, the female principle, which "bears fruit" as a result of being impregnated by *Yesod*.

The mythological perspective is complemented by a theurgic practice. As is often the case, kabbalistic practice involves numerical correspondences between words, or *gematria*. In this case, the letters of the Hebrew word for tree, *ilan*, have the same value as the sum of the letters that spell two divine Names, *YHVH* and *ADoNaY*. This indicates that the New Year's Day for the *ilan* involves the union of the two Names. Moreover, in kabbalistic tradition, these two Names represent the male and female divine principles. When the letters of these two Names are combined to form *YAHDVNHY*, they become an object on which a kabbalist can meditate in order to bring about the actual union of the corresponding *sefirot*. This meditation is appropriate for Tu B'Shevat.

As a result of the association of the *tikkun* of Tu B'Shevat with divine potency, an additional motive is discussed in the introduction to the *Peri Eitz Hadar*. It is assumed that the harmony of the relationship between *Yesod* and *Malkhut* is adversely affected by human sexual improprieties. Thus Tu B'Shevat, with its emphasis on rectifying the *sefirah*, *Yesod*, becomes an occasion for correcting, or atoning for, the damage that was done to *Yesod* by improper sexual behavior. This introduces another mythic and magical element, the tendency to view nature's bounty as related to, and even dependent upon, human sexuality. However, this motive is addressed through the theurgic, contemplative focus on *Yesod* and devotionally, through adopting an attitude of atonement. The pietistic element, which seems to conflict to a certain extent with the otherwise celebratory character of the *seder*, may be a compensation for the fact that Tu B'Shevat occurs during a penitential period. This period, called *Shovavim*, is otherwise characterized by fasting and penitential acts.[17] The weeks of *Shovavim* are explicitly connected in *Ḥemdat Yamim* with correction of "damage to the [sign of the] covenant," i.e., male ejaculation in halakhically unacceptable circumstances (*shikhvat zera le-batalah*).

It is important to note the chain of associated symbols here that must be connected. Tu B'Shevat is associated with trees. The cosmic tree is nourished by the *sefirah*, *Yesod*. *Yesod* is identified with the divine phallus. The functioning of the divine phallus which impregnates *Malkhut* (the Tree of the Knowledge of Good and Evil) is affected by male sexuality. The time of year during which Tu B'Shevat occurs is appropriate for atoning for male sexual misdeeds.

To sum up, the Tu B'Shevat seder, which is presented in *Peri Eitz Hadar*, essentially views Tu B'Shevat as part of a penitential season when atonement can be made for male sexual impropriety. As such the seder is a kabbalistic *tikkun* for the *sefirah*, *Yesod*. As a result of this *tikkun*, the fertility of the cosmic tree is enhanced. This ultimately results in nature's receiving the vitality required in order to bring forth its bounty. The *tikkun*, involves three types of activity: blessing fruit, eating fruit, and meditating on the kabbalistic symbolism of the fruit. This latter activity primarily involves the contemplative study of selections from the Zoharic literature.

Peri Eitz Hadar

Although the Fifteenth of Shevat occurs during the "days of the *Shovavim*,"[18] it is not a fast day, since it is the New Year's Day for the fruit of the tree. Through the *tikkun* that is performed on this day with fruit, the *sefirah*, "*Tzaddik*, Life of the Worlds," is aroused.[19]

143

This mystery is mentioned in the Zohar, *Bereshit*,[20] "on the third day, the earth made fruit from the potency of that [supernal] *Tzaddik*. As it is written, '*And God said, let the earth bring forth . . . fruit trees that produce fruit . . .*'[21] '*Fruit trees* ' refers to '*the tree of the knowledge of good and evil*' that bears fruit.[22] '*That produce fruit*' alludes to *Tzaddik*, the foundation of the world. . . .*"[23]

It is a good custom for the faithful[24] to eat many fruits on this day and to celebrate them with words of praise, just as I have instructed my companions. Even though this custom is not mentioned in the Lurianic writings, it is nevertheless a wondrous *tikkun*,[25] on both exoteric and esoteric levels.[26]

For in the Palestinian Talmud, *Asarah Yuhasin*, ch. 10,[27] the following appears. "'*Listen, humble ones, and rejoice*'[28] R. Hizkiyah R. Kohen said in the name of Rav, 'In the future a person will have to account for everything that his eyes saw and he did not eat. R. Elazar was concerned about this teaching and used to save poor man's gleanings. He would eat them, each one at its time.'"[29] The reason is that whoever enjoys produce in this world without pronouncing a blessing is called a robber.[30] For by means of the blessing, one draws down *shefa*. The angel who is assigned to that fruit [which was eaten] is filled by the *shefa* so that a second fruit can replace the first. Thus one who enjoys the fruit without blessing it is a robber. For through eating an aspect of creation [without blessing it], he eliminated the spiritual element that it contained. [Thus he] prevented that divine power from being manifest in the world, when he should have drawn down a blessing from above. As a result, the angel's power is annulled, since it no longer possesses the *shefa* [that it needs in order to replenish the fruit]. That is why the person is called a robber.

He also said that it is as if he robbed from his father and mother.[31] For through the *kavvanah*[32] of the blessing recited when eating fruit, a person who eats rectifies the sparks of his own soul as well as the sparks that pertain to the souls of his parents. This is the esoteric meaning of, "*I will make him disgorge what he has swallowed,*"[33] which is related to [the secret of the verse], "*the riches he swallowed, he vomits, [God empties it out of his stomach].*"[34] So if one enjoys the fruit without a blessing, it is as if he robbed his parents of the divine sparks that pertain to their souls.[35] "*He is a comrade of the Destroyer.*"[36] For the

Destroyer's only intention is to rob the divine sparks and to absorb them [in the realm of evil] and to [prevent them from] returning to [their source] in holiness. That is the esoteric meaning of *"for a person does not live on bread alone, but on all that goes forth from the mouth of the Lord."*[37] This alludes to the secret of the blessing, which retrieves [the sparks] from impurity to holiness.[38] It is brought about through the *"mouth of the Lord,"* i.e., by means of the chewing of the thirty-two teeth which correspond to the thirty-two times that *Elohim* is mentioned in the Story of Creation,[39] as we have explained at length in the previous section concerning the *tikkun* of the meal.[40]

The punishments [for these transgressions] also apply to someone who sees species of fine fruit and allows them to dry up and go bad without eating them. [By not eating them], he prevented the angels of the fruit from receiving [their share of] divine goodness. Since he did not say a blessing over the fruit, the angel's power is annulled and it is bereft of the *shefa* that depends on the blessing. He also robs his parents. For since he did not eat the fruit, he also neglected to eat the sparks that pertain to their souls, as has been explained. Accordingly, R. Eleazar used to save poor man's gleanings of all kinds of new fruit to eat. [For he wanted] to increase blessings and perform the *tikkun* immediately, so as not to miss the [opportunity for fulfilling] the *mitzvot*.

In order to effect this *tikkun*, it is fitting for us to eat all kinds of fruit on this very day and to bless them with this intention. For a *mitzvah* is best when performed at the proper time.

According to the Zohar, "R. Yehudah said, why is it written, *'even this God made corresponding to that?'*[41] God made the earth to correspond to the firmament. Everything [below] alludes to what is above. For when R. Abba would see a certain tree whose fruit would change into a bird that flew from it, he would weep and say, 'if human beings only knew to what this alludes. . . .' As R. Yose said, these trees from which wisdom can be learned,[42] such as the carob, palm, pistachio, and the like were all borne in one chariot.[43] All those [trees] that bear fruit, except the apple tree, allude to one supernal mystery. . . . And all the small ones, except for the hyssop, are the offspring of one mother. In heaven, powerful intermediaries are placed over each of the earth's plants, and each has its own mystery, just as above."[44]

145

From this you can understand that although the blessed Creator rules over the earth and everything has an angel assigned to it, nevertheless of greatest importance is the fact that everything is connected to the supernal attributes.[45] As they said there in the Zohar: "why is it written, *'I went down to my walnut garden'?*[46] He said to him, come and see. This is the garden that went forth from Eden and it is the *Shekhinah*.[47] 'Walnut' refers to the Holy Chariot,[48] the four tributaries that spread out from the garden like a nut . . ."[49] From this we can infer that herbs can be distinguished by the pre-eminence of their divine roots above.

R. Hayyim Vital explained that there are thirty kinds of fruit trees. Ten [have their divine roots] in the World of Creation, corresponding to the ten *sefirot* of that world. Since their roots are far removed from *tuma'ah*[50] and close to the purely divine World of Emanation, they have no shell, either within or without.[51] They may be eaten as they are.[52] They include the following: grapes, figs, apples, citrons, lemons, pears, quince, strawberries, sorbs , and carob.

There are ten types of fruit [whose roots are] in the World of Formation. Esoterically, they correspond to the ten *sefirot* of Formation, which are intermediate, between the World of Creation and the World of Making. They are neither as close to the forces of evil as [the *sefirot*] of the World of Making nor as distant as the [*sefirot*] of the World of Creation. Consequently, the seed kernels within the fruit are not eaten, since they are not soft like the seeds within the fruit that correspond to the World of Creation. They include: olives, dates, cherries, jujubes, persimmons, plums, apricots, hackberries, lotus fruit, *uzerar.*[53]

There are ten other kinds of fruit [whose roots are] in the World of Making, corresponding to the ten *sefirot* [of that world]. Consequently, we eat what is within and discard what is without. For the fruit's shell is a barrier between it and the World of Delights,[54] so that it will not take on the impurity [of the evil forces].[55] This is the esoteric meaning of the evil urge and 'the *kelippah*' cleave to the *nefesh*.[56] The following correspond to *sefirot* of the World of Making: pomegranates, walnuts, almonds, pistachio, chestnuts, hazelnuts, acorns, coconut, pine nuts, peanuts.

Now the ten kinds of fruit [that represent the World] of Creation have been purified of everything that relates to the forces of evil *(pesolet)*[57] and are left completely good. But a barren tree [represents] the opposite. It corresponds to pure evil, containing nothing but the *kelippah*.[58] Just as the ten kinds of fruit [that correspond to the World] of Formation have an edible exterior and a hard interior, the kernel within, so it is with the *kelippah*.[59] When a fallen holy spark is great, the *kelippah* is not able to contain all of that light within itself. So [the *kelippah*] enters within the holiness and surrounds it.

The ten kinds of fruit [that correspond to] the World of Making have a soft interior surrounded by a hard shell. This is like the *kelippah*, when it takes a holy spark within itself, in order to be enlivened by it. It surrounds the spark just as a shell encompasses the fruit. Consequently, we learn that there is no physical thing here below that does not correspond to something above. *"For one is protected by another on a higher level, and both of these by still higher ones."*[60] As things are below, so they are above. For there would be no shadow if there were no one to cast it.

My father perceived the esoteric wisdom [alluded to by the] wording of the Mishnah, which says, "New Year's Day for fruit of the tree," rather than "for fruit of the trees." The [sages of the Mishnah] were alluding to the Holy Tree, the Tree of Life,[61] as Isaac Luria's disciples explained. For tree *(ilan)* has the same numerical value as the holy name, *YAHDVNHY*,[62] as they wrote in their explanation of the following passage from the Zohar, *Aḥarei Mot*. "That great and mighty tree [which contains nourishment for all is called the Tree of Life], the tree that planted its roots in these living ones."[63] Also, the Lurianic writings state that when the word tree *(ilan)* is spelled out fully, its numerical value is the same as twelve permutations of the name *YHVH*.[64] Thus [tree] alludes to *Tiferet*, the Tree of Life, which contains twelve permutations of *YHVH*, as stated in Zohar, *Beshalaḥ*, "twelve [supernal, engraved] regions ascended [in the scale], in the great and powerful holy Tree."[65] Also see the passage, *"'And they came to Elim and there were twelve springs of water there and seventy date palms . . .'*[66] and the Holy Tree grew strong in twelve regions . . ."[67]

The meaning is that the fifteenth of Shevat is the New Year's Day for tithing the fruit of trees. For most of the year's rain has already fallen. The sap has begun to ascend through the trees, and fruit begin to take form on the trees from this time. Similarly, in the di-

147

vine realm, it is the New Year's Day for the fruit of the supernal tree which bestows its holy abundance on its fruit, the [upper worlds]. From them the *shefa* descends until it reaches the trees in our world below and the powers that oversee them.

"And establish for us, the work of our hands."[68] Through the special power of this *tikkun*, performed on this very day, through the power of the blessings and contemplation of the mystery of the fruit's divine roots, an effect will be produced in their structure and character above. Moreover the person performing the *tikkun* can also be affected. For through the beauty of this *tikkun*, he can correct what he distorted *(me'uvat lo yukhal litkon)*[69] in damaging the [sign of the] covenant through inchastity.[70] By virtue of performing this *tikkun* for the fruit tree, he will heal his part[71] in the flawing of *Tzaddik* who makes fruit.[72] There is the added benefit of the penitential period, mentioned above.[73] Thus a *tikkun* for the flaw of the covenant is performed. . . .

My teacher used to say that one should intend through eating the fruit to correct the sin that Adam committed with the fruit of the tree. Even though our intention is directed toward this end all the days of the year, a *mitzvah* is best when observed at its proper time, and this day is the beginning for fruit of the tree. Moreover, as we have frequently stated, speech has the power to arouse the *sefirot* and to cause them to shine more wondrously with a very great light that sheds abundance, favor, blessing, and benefit throughout all the worlds. Consequently, before eating each fruit, it is proper to meditate on the mystery of its divine root, as found in the Zohar and, in some cases, in the *tikkunim*, in order to arouse their roots above. But, first of all, read the following selections.

> Torah: Gen. 1:9–13; Deut. 8:1–10; Lev. 26:3–13.
> Prophets: Ezek. 17:22–24; 34:22–31; 36:27–36; 47:1–12; Joel 2:18–27.
> Writings: Ps. 72; 147; 148; 65; 126.
> Zohar: vol. 1, 33a; vol. 3, 86a; 270b.

After this say the following prayer:

Please, God, who makes, forms, creates, and emanates supernal worlds and created their likeness on the earth below, according to their supernal form and character. "*All of them You made with wis-dom,*"[74] supernal [forms] above and lower [forms] below, to join together the tent so as to be one. You caused trees and grass to grow from the earth, according to the structure and character of [the forms] above, so that human beings might gain wisdom and understanding through them, and thus grasp the hidden [forms]. You appointed your holy angels over them as agents to oversee their growing. And you caused *shefa* and the power of your supernal qualities to flow upon them.

"*The fruit yielded a harvest,*"[75] every "*fruit tree producing fruit according to its kind.*"[76]

"*The earth is sated from the fruit of Your work,*"[77] so one may "*eat of its fruit and be sated by its bounty.*"[78] From [the fruit], every living soul is enlivened through the spiritual power that is in them, [which is] the fruit of the mouth of your holy angels who guard its fruit.

"*From me your fruit is found,*"[79] the reward of children.

"*Its fruit is food and its leaves a source of healing.*"[80] So on this day, the beginning of Your deeds concerning [the trees'] budding and renewal, "*a person will earn with its fruit . . . ,*"[81] "*producing fruit after its kind.*"[82] For so the days of budding will be full for the fruit of the supernal tree, "*the tree of life which is in the midst of the garden*"[83] and it makes fruit above.

May it be Your will O Lord our God and God of our ancestors, that through the sacred power of our eating fruit, which we are now eating and blessing, while reflecting on the secret of their supernal roots upon which they depend, that *shefa*, favor, blessing, and bounty be bestowed upon them. May the angels appointed over them also be filled by the powerful *shefa* of their glory, may it return and cause them to grow a second time, from the beginning of the year and until its end, for bounty and blessing, for good life and peace.

And fulfill for us the word which you promised us through Malachi, Your seer, "*And I will banish the devourer from among you and he will not destroy the fruit of your earth and the vine of your field will not miscarry, says the Lord of Hosts.*"[84] Look down from your sacred dwelling place in heaven and bless us this year with bounty and blessing.

"You will make him a source of blessings forever, you will cause him to rejoice in the joy of Your countenance."[85] *"And the earth will bestow its harvest and the tree of the field will yield its fruit."*[86]

The blessing of goodness will come upon them, that its fruits will be blessed within us. Whether one eats a lot or a little, the health of his body will also be blessed. *"There YHVH commanded blessing, eternal life."*[87]

And may the splendid power of the blessings [said] while eating the fruit illuminate the source of blessings, *Tzaddik*, the Life of the Worlds, and let the rainbow appear, proudly rejoicing in its colors. From there, may *shefa*, favor, and compassion be bestowed upon us, to pardon and forgive the iniquities and misdeeds that we committed and sinned. We violated the covenant and damaged the fruit of *Tzaddik*, the Life of the Worlds, and caused the rains of its beneficence to be withheld, so that all the sources [of *shefa*] were harmed. Now let everything return to its original might *"and let His bow remain taut."*[88] *"For You, YHVH , bless the Tzaddik, favor crowns him like a shield."*[89]

And may all the holy sparks which were dispersed by us or by our ancestors and [also] through the sin that Adam committed with the fruit of the tree now return to be included in the splendid power of the Tree of Life. May all evil be removed from them through the power of Your great name which emerges from the verse, *"the power that he swallows, he vomits out."*[90]

And may everything return to its original might and not be rejected. For only You, *YHVH* , restore the dispersed of Israel. Therefore, swiftly cause the offshoot of Your servant David to flower and raise up its might through Your salvation. And the hand of *YHVH* is upon the whole world in its entirety.

"Instead of a briar, a cypress will arise, instead of the nettle, a myrtle will arise. And it will be a testimony for YHVH and an everlasting sign which will never be effaced."[91]

"Let abundant grain be in the land to the mountain top, let its fruit tremble like [the cedars of] Lebanon and may the inhabitants of cities sprout like the land's grass."[92]

"Then the trees of the forest will rejoice"[93] and the tree of the field lift its branch and bear fruit daily.

"And you shall take from the first of the fruit of the earth"[94] to bring first fruits before the altar of *YHVH* in praise and thanksgiving to *YHVH,* our God, and [it shall result in] great good for the house of Israel.

"The arid desert will be glad and the wilderness will rejoice and blossom like a rose, it shall greatly flower and also rejoice and be glad. The glory of Lebanon will be given to it, the splendor of Carmel and Sharon. They will see the Glory of YHVH, the splendor of our God."[95]

May it occur swiftly, in our days, *amen.*

Act for the sake of Your Name. Act for the sake of Your loving kindness. Act for the sake of Your right hand. Act for the sake of Your Torah.

May the words of my mouth and the meditations of my heart find favor before You, *YHVH,* my rock and my redeemer.

"May the favor of the Lord, our God, be upon us . . ."[96]

Now, after offering this prayer, one's word can prosper through the ritual *tikkun* of fruit according to the following seder.

Wheat: Make from it some kind of pastry or dessert and reflect on Zohar, vol. 3, 188b. Then everyone should say the blessing, *"borei minei mezonot."*

Olive: Reflect on Zohar, vol. 3, 247a and also on the *Ra'aya Mehemna* there. Then one of those present should say the blessing, *"borei peri ha-eitz."* The *kavvanah* is simply *YHVH.*

Dates: Reflect on Zohar, vol. 3, 17a. Afterwards, one of those present who did not already eat from the previously blessed fruit says the blessing with the *kavvanah, YHHV.*[97] Similarly, one person who has yet to partake says the blessing for each of the remaining fruits.

Grapes: Reflect on Zohar, vol. 1, 192a and vol. 3, 127. Then one says the blessing for the grapes, *"borei peri ha-gafen,"* with the *kavvanah, YVHH.* Then everyone drinks a cup of entirely white wine with the *kavvanah* of the Name of 72.[98]

Figs: Reflect on Mishnah, *Ma'asarot,* chapter 2. The *kavvanah* is *HVHY.*[99]

Pomegranate: Reflect on *Tikkunei Zohar,* beginning of *tikkun* 24. The *kavvanah* is *HVYH.*

Citron: Reflect on Zohar, vol. 2, 120b. The *kavvanah* is *HHYV.*

Apple: Reflect on Zohar, vol. 3, 74a and 286b. The *kavvanah* is *VHYH*. Here everyone should drink a cup of wine that is mostly white with a little red in it. Their *kavvanah* is the Name of 63.[100]

Walnut: Reflect on Zohar, vol. 2, 15b. The *kavvanah* is *VHHY*.

Chestnuts, Almonds or Hazelnuts: Reflect on Zohar, vol. 1, 161b, Secrets of the Torah. The *kavvanah* is *VYHH*.

Carobs: Reflect on Zohar, vol. 3, 216b, *Ra'aya Mehemna*. The *kavvanah* is *HHVY*.

Pears: Reflect on the first mishnah of *Berakhot*, chapter 6.[101] Also reflect on the fourth mishnah in *Kale's*, chapter 1. The *kavvanah* is *HYHV*. Everyone should now drink a cup of wine that is half white and half red. The *kavvanah* is the Name of 45.[102]

Medlar:[103] Reflect on the second mishnah of *Berakhot*, chapter 6 and the first mishnah of *Demai*, chapter 1. The *kavvanah* is *HYVH*.

Quince: Reflect on the third mishnah of *Berakhot*, chapter 6 and the third mishnah of *Ma'aserot*, chapter 1. The *kavvanah* is *AHVH*.

Hackberry: Reflect on the fourth and fifth mishnayot of *Berakhot*, chapter 6. The *kavvanah* is the name of 72.

Jujube: Reflect on the sixth mishnah of *Berakhot*, chapter 6. The *kavannah* is *YAHDVNHY*.

Pistachio: Reflect on the seventh mishnah of *Berakhot*, chapter 6. The *kavvanah* is *AHVH*.

Cherry: Reflect on the eighth mishnah of *Berakhot*, chapter 6. The *kavvanah* is the Name of 52.[104]

Nishpolas: Reflect on the first mishnah of *Berakhot*, chapter 7. The *kavvanah* is *EL*.

Lupine: Finish all of chapter 7 in Mishnah, *Berakhot*.

Afterwards, everyone should drink a cup of red wine with a little bit of white wine in it. The *kavvanah* is the Name of 52.

Wherever all thirty of the fruits mentioned above, whose roots are in the worlds of Creation, Formation, and Making, can be found, it is a *mitzvah* to obtain them. For whoever does much is surely worthy of praise. However, wherever they are not all available, there should be no less than twelve types of fruit, corresponding to the fruit of the supernal tree, the Tree of Life. It is established as a Holy Tree in twelve directions, the secret of the twelve permutations of the Name, *YHVH*. For each of these the *kavvanah* should be one of the twelve permutations, according to the order mentioned above . . . .

Blessing Trees

Rabbi Yosef Hayyim of Baghdad
translated by Zalman Schachter-Shalomi

Blessed are You YAH, our God, Majesty of Earth.
You made the world so that nothing lacks in her
And You created good creatures and good trees for people
  to enjoy!

This blessing is to be recited in the month of Nisan when the trees are budding. Kabbalists felt that that was a special time to participate in the rescue of wandering spirits, incarnated in lower life forms. Looking at the buds and blossoms, one can become aware of their presence, like Rabbi Yitzhak Luria, who took his students out into nature to teach them there. On one such occasion, upon raising his eyes, he saw all the trees peopled with countless spirits, and he asked them, "What is your lot here?" They replied, "We did not repent during our lifetime. We have heard about you, that you can heal and mend us." And he promised to help them. The disciples saw him in conversation, but they were not aware of with whom he conversed. Later they asked him about it, and he replied, "If you had been able to, you would have been shocked to see the crowds of spirits." He then urged them to intend in the prayer *"ha-me'ir la-aretz"* [The One who enlightens the world] to think of all those alive in bodies at this time, and in the words "ve-ladarim aleha b'raḥamim" [and to those who dwell therein, with compassion] to think of the discarnate holy souls in search of their restoration. When a person passing by offers a blessing of delight in the blossoming of nature they are reclaimed to holiness.

Then recite, as follows:

> *Merciful Parent—*
> *Act for the sake of Your sacred Torah,*
> *Act for the sake of Your holy Names written explicitly or*
>   *hinted at,*
> *Act for the sake of Abraham, Isaac, Jacob, Moses, Aaron, Joseph*
>   *and David,*
> *Act for the sake of Miriam, Leah, Hannah, Rebeccah, Sarah,*
>   *Tamar and Rachel,*
> *And be kind, merciful, caring, nurturing and protecting*
> *To all the* Nefesh-*life forces,* Ruaḥ-*spirits and* Neshamah-*souls*
> *That did not manage to reach their resting place;*
> *And on the life forces, spirits and souls reincarnated [enwheeled]*
>   *in minerals, plants and animals,*
> *Those that cannot speak and humans that can.*
> *And You, YAH, insuring the good of thousands of generations,*
> *In Your endless beneficence, let flow to them*
> *Abundant nurture, light and life.*
> *Give them, please, the strength, the help and the means to be*
>   *made whole.*
> *By Your inner light help them complete their clearing, their*
>   Tikkun, *swiftly.*
> *Save them from all pain, obstruction and malice.*
> *Allow affirming Beings to encourage them*
> *and to place them in a good light.*
> *This kindness is Your way,*
> *Offering free Grace to each one when born.*
> Ana B'ko'akh—*Source of Mercy. . . .*
> *And an other formulation of the Holy Name of 42 (6 x 7)*
> *Oh, that the beautiful Presence*
> *in endless compassion*
> *shed Light all radiant!*
> *Oh, that Your Will, God Most Exalted*
> *in sound and inflection encoded,*
> *manifest in us!*
> *Oh, that the mating most total and sacred*
> *in infinite greatness*
> *attain to the crowning!*

We sprang from the Light-drop
of the womb of the Tzaddik,
to grow to completion.
We entreat in this prayer the hope of our people,
that the blissful fulfillment
send us its blessing.
Oh, that the mating most holy, most sacred
be roused to its peak-point
as all power is sweetened!
May the root of the Tzaddik, *the way of the Sacred*
find its completion
right here and right now!
Through Time and Space
Your glory shines
majestic One.

Sermon on the Blessing
over the Trees in Nissan

A free and partial (nontechnical) translation:

The AR"I taught:

"It is worth that you know that those who are reincarnated in the lower life forms—that is, minerals, *mute ones* that are inanimate; *growers*, plants; *living movers*, animals—as distinct from *talkers*, human life forms—cannot just any time they wish be raised to be mended. The time for them to be raised is as follows: Know! One who is incarnated into an inanimate being and has been sentenced to a specific term of years—then when the time has arrived when they can be raised to the level of plant life it has to happen during the four median months: Av, Elul, Tishrei and Heshvan. If the term of the sentence expires in those months they can ascend. If not they must tarry until the next year when these months arrive. The time of ascending from vegetation to animal life forms is Nisan, Iyyar, Sivan and Tammuz. The time for the ascent of animal incarnates to human form is Kislev, Tevet, Shvat and Adar.

"So the rabbis hinted at that in the Talmud (*B. Berakhot* 32) 'One who encounters a black bull in Nisan days ought to flee from him and climb to the roof' for Satan dances between his horns. This all means that the black bull signifying severe decrees is more likely to incarnate the spirit [of a malicious person] than any other animal—therefore one ought to flee from him. This is not so with other beasts. And because the time to ascend from vegetation to animal incarnation is from Nisan on—therefore the warning pertains to Nisan when the malicious reincarnate might rise from the vegetable feed and enter [the bull]. If the violence did not manifest in Nisan one need not fear, for the incarnate has settled in the new existence" (end of quote of the AR"I).

Thus the months in which the mute ones, the growers and the living movers can be raised are **A**v, **N**isan and **K**islev, spelling the acronym AN"K. Thus you will grasp the hidden meaning of "Behold Yah is standing on a wall of AN"K" for it is in these months that the Blessed One assists and helps these wandering spirits to become purified and to rise. They get their start during the months Av-Nisan-Kislev.

This accords with the three patriarchs—for Abraham said "I am but dust and ashes" referring to the mutes, earth and dust, and this ascent to plant life begins in Av (meaning "father"—Abraham). And in the merit of Isaac—raised like a sheep onto the altar, the ascent from living mover to human is slated for the month of Kislev. This is "God will show him my son as the sheep"—that through my son Isaac the rise from animal to human will be accomplished. And Jacob, who is compared to a plant, "Israel will flourish and blossom" begins the rise of the plant to the animal level. . . .

Hence the blessing for the trees is slated for Nisan in order to assist the raising of the plant world which begins in that month. Then by making the blessing and the secret contained in it, those who do so may succeed and raise the spirits two rungs at once, from plant directly to the human level, and thus will not require to be wandering through the realm of animals. So in studying Torah in connection with the blessing they will merit to raise the [wandering spirits] and to repair/heal them.

Therefore Hasidim and people of [healing] action make every effort to recite this blessing, in the presence of a minyan of ten so that after the recital they might chant Torah verses and proclaim the Kaddish. All this is that the study and Kaddish might assist in the purging and raising of the souls which are in the plants. . . .

. . . In this we must offer praise to the Master of it all who has empowered us to do the work of "sorting." And although there are certain months which are set for this in which the mineral becomes plant and others in which the plant becomes animal and still others in which the animals become raised to the level of human—it is also given to us to raise them in a more abrupt way.

For a human studying Torah who walks on the road can in this way raise the sparks and souls in the mineral all at once to the human level as the kabbalists, basing themselves on the Talmud, have said. And David sang "Blessed are those who walk in wholeness on the path"—in the Torah of HVYH. And, so too "Who can count the *dust* of Jacob?" meaning the pearls of the holy sparks released from the dust-mineral.

In the same manner as we raise the sparks in animals and vegetables in proper eating with a blessing, so too we trust that we shall raise the sparks in the blossoming trees all at once to the human level since in a Torah way we walked out of the city thus raising the sparks from dust—in this way one Mitzvah entrains to the next. . . .

. . . Nisan is neither hot summer nor cold winter. It is a royal time. It behooves a king to be neither arrogant nor extremely humble. Arrogant he won't care to govern the plain people, too humble he won't be able to impose his commands. We ought to be humble to an extreme but a king ought not to be too humble nor too proud. The median path is best.

. . . There was a king, he was proud, outright arrogant for he thought that only in this way could he maintain his status in relation to those governed. In his pride he paid no attention to the welfare of his people and country, causing much harm in his neglect. The king's beloved friend and advisor urged him to take a walk with him through his fragrantly blooming garden. Walking along with the king on a side path, they came by a composting fertilizer heap from which the gardeners took the loam. The king walked on and missing his companion he turned and found him standing near the dung. The king asked him why he chose to stand there in the stench. The vizier said, "Sire, the dung heap is talking to me and I attend to its words." The king asked what it was saying and the vizier replied, "Why did you avoid me? Don't you realize that once I too was but sweet and fragrant fruit? You ate me, digested me, excreted me, and made me stink; and now you avoid me!?" The king suddenly realized what the vizier was trying to tell him. All that was tasty and fragrant becomes spoiled in contact with humans. How could we be so arrogant. He became so humble that it was not so good for he could not govern well. So the vizier took him to the garden again, and stopping at the dung heap he now reported that the compost said "Why do you avoid me? It is true that I stink but if not for me there would not grow the fragrance and the sweet taste of the fruit." Thus did the king learn how to be humble on the inside and dignified on the outside.

. . . So Nisan [and Tishrei] is a good time to do the sorting. Thus are the sparks redeemed, when we are neither depressed and say who are we to raise sparks? nor so arrogant to think that we have done no wrong and never caused any sparks to be exiled . . .

. . . Having been redeemed from Egypt in Nisan and redeemed many exiled sparks along with us, this is an excellent time for this holy work. One is assisted by the energy in this season concerning which it is written: "They went out [of Egypt] with great possessions," spiritual possession that is.

. . . Therefore a person shall intently and with enthusiasm recite the *berakhah* which is for the Tikkun of the souls incarnated in the herbs and trees at that time and intercede for them. This happened once to the AR"I z"l; he went out into the field to meditate and study some Torah. Raising his eyes, he saw in the branches of the trees countless spirits. Asking them what they were doing there, they replied, "We died without Teshuvah. We heard though that it is in the power of the AR"I to give us Tikkun." He promised that he would do so. His disciples, seeing that he was in dialogue with ones they could not see, asked him and he said, "If you had been given permission to see this, you would have been amazed at the multitudes of spirits." So he asked them to intend that in the passage from the words "You who shine light brightly on the Earth" to "those who dwell on her with compassion" that "shine brightly on Earth" refer to all who are alive and the words "dwelling with

158

compassion" refer to the displaced holy souls who will receive their Tikkun through good-hearted people who will make a *berakhah* on them. This is why this blessing was prescribed as a Tikkun.

. . . the Zohar also speaks of this: There are certain days in the year, the days of Nisan and Tishrei, in which the souls swarm through the world . . .

. . . thus the blessing saying, "good creatures and good trees." Good creatures refers to the spirits that cleave to the blossoms of the trees awaiting our blessings to be raised.

. . . Also keep this in mind seeing the trees in bloom; they are full of sap and fragrance but then later in the winter they will wilt and fall and be dry . . . take a moral lesson from this how things are impermanent.

The Souls of Trees

Nachman of Bratzlav
as retold by Howard Schwartz

Reb Nachman was once traveling with his Hasidim by carriage, and as it grew dark they came to an inn, where they spent the night. During the night Reb Nachman began to cry out loudly in his sleep, waking everyone up in the inn, all of whom came running to see what happened.

When he awoke, the first thing Reb Nachman did was to take out a book he had brought with him. Then he closed his eyes and opened the book and pointed to a passage. And there it was written "Cutting down a tree before its time is like killing a soul."

Then Reb Nachman asked the innkeeper if the walls of that inn had been built out of saplings cut down before their time. The innkeeper admitted that this was true, but how did the rabbi know?

Reb Nachman said: "All night I dreamed I was surrounded by the bodies of those who had been murdered. I was very frightened. Now I know that it was the souls of the trees that cried out to me."

Conceiving the World

R. Tzvi Elimelekh Shapira of Dinov
(in B'nei Yissakhar)
translated by Ivan Ickovits

We learn from tradition that the daughters of Israel would go out in a circle on Yom Kippur [and on Tu B'Av, the fifteenth of Av] and the men who did not have mates would go out and look for a mate. . . . [Why on Yom Kippur? Because] on Yom Kippur God seeks out Israel in joy and gives her the Second Tablets, binding Himself to her forever. Hence, Yom Kippur is a day designated for marital union. . . .

[Why on Tu B'Av?]

The Talmud states: Forty days before the formation of the embryo the heavens declare that this soul will be wed to this soul. Forty days before the twenty-fifth of Elul (the day of creation according to R. Eliezer) is Tu B'Av (the fifteenth of Av). Thus, it was on the Tu B'Av before creation that Israel became a thought in the divine Mind and Israel was first destined to receive the Torah (the Second Tablets) on Yom Kippur.[1] This is the reason that the tribes were permitted to intermarry on that day and the day was designated for marital union.

This is also the case with Tu B'Shvat. Tu B'Shvat is forty days before the twenty-fifth of Nisan, which is the day of creation according to R. Yehoshua. We already know that the human being is likened to a tree.

Therefore, even though we don't hold that Nisan is the month of creation, we designate Tu B'Shvat as the New Year for the Trees in that the first blossom is the embryonic stage of what will blossom into fruit and flower and fill the world with beauty.

R. Hayyim Elazar Shapira of Munkatcz
(commenting on the passage above)
from Sha'ar Yissakhar,
translated by Ivan Ickovits

The *B'nei Yissakhar* cites the tradition that we pray for a beautiful *etrog* on Tu B'Shvat. We also know from *Hazal* that "the way of man is

160

to pursue a woman." Man *(ish)* is the numerical value of Shvat and a woman is likened to an *etrog*. We know this from the fact that of the four species, only the *etrog* is referred to in a feminine gender. Hence, the way of *ish* (Shvat) is to pursue a woman *(etrog)*.

The union of the masculine and feminine forces in creation begins on Tu B'Shvat in that it is forty days before creation (according to R. Yehoshua), where the notion of union arises. This initial spark of passion (on Tu B'Shvat) culminates on Passover, when the union of the male with the female takes place in all its fullness (as is known from the meditations of the AR"I *z"l*). Tu B'Shvat begins the initial ascent to Passover.

When R. Eliezer states that the world was created in Tishrei and R. Yehoshua holds on Nisan it may be that R. Yehoshua is referring not to creation itself but to its final purpose. [This can be understood] If we adopt Rashi's alternative comment on Gen. 1:1 [reading *be-reishit* instead of the usual *bereshit*] that "For the sake of *reishit*" the world was created. "Who is called *reishit?*—Israel is called *reishit*." Hence, while R. Eliezer speaks of creation, R. Yehoshua alludes to its purpose. As is the case in any birth, the heavenly decree of the newborn's destiny is proclaimed forty days prior. The destiny of birth is marital union in that it is this union which serves to perpetuate creation itself. Therefore, Tu B'Shvat is the moment of the divine proclamation of the birth of Israel *(reishit)* which happens on Pesaḥ and culminates with the crossing of the Red Sea, traveling through the divine birth canal into freedom.

The celebration of this proclamation should reflect the celebration of birth itself. Hence, we have a Tu B'Shvat seder to embody the Pesaḥ seder we will celebrate two months later. The circle of the seder attests to the cyclical nature of the creation cycle; the celebration of *reishit*, of Israel's divine mission, of the ascent to freedom. Tu B'Shvat, like Tu B'Av is a celebration of love, joy and union.

part V

Branches: Zionism and the Land of Israel

Late in the nineteenth century, among European Jews there arose a movement that not only demanded an end to the scattering of the Jewish people through the world, but also criticized the entire philosophical, institutional, psychological, and religious framework of rabbinic Judaism as a way of defining the people. Some of the Zionist critics focused chiefly on achieving political self-determination for the Jewish people; others focused on renewing the relationship between the Jewish people and the earth, its own earthiness as well as its land.

So a certain kind of eco-psychological consciousness, sometimes romantic and sometimes practical, helped give shape and energy to Zionism and to the communities that newly settled in the Land of Israel. These earthy strands of reconnection with the land, "redemption" and reforestation of the land, were woven along with the political strands of claiming turf and making economic and ecological decisions into the fabric that became the State of Israel.

This section of the anthology begins with a passage from A. D. Gordon, one of the guiding lights and heroes of the land-oriented energy of the Zionist movement. His work was one of the crucial bridges from hasidic spirituality to the spirituality-of-earth that

163

infused some elements of Zionism. From there we move to cultural histories of the tree-planting movement and the revival of Tu B'Shvat as a day for Zionist reforestation, and finally to the way in which competitive tree planting became a microcosm of the conflict between Zionism and Palestinian nationalism.

Variations on the Theme
of the Future

A. D. Gordon
translated by Jeremy Schwartz

And it shall come to pass,
O child of Adam,
when you return to Nature,
on that day you shall open your eyes,
and you shall peer directly
into Nature's eyes
and there you shall see
your own image.
You shall know that you have returned to yourself,
for in hiding from Nature,
you hid from yourself.
And furthermore, you shall see,
that from upon you,
from upon your hands and feet,
from upon your body and soul,
fragments are peeling and falling,
crumbling and falling.
Heavy fragments,
hard,
oppressive;
you straighten yourself,
you stand up tall,
you grow.
And you will know that these are the shards of your shell,
    your kelippah,
in which you had constricted yourself
in your bewilderment,
and out of which you have finally grown.
And you will recognize on that day:
nothing had been according to your measure,
you must renew everything:
your food and your drink,

your dress and your home,
the character of your work and the way that you learn
—everything . . .

And on that day, with all the power of your heart, you will sense the pressure with which the walls of the houses in the city—and even in the village—press upon your soul, and you will sense the slightest barrier which stands between your Self and the Boundless Space of the World, between your Self and the Boundless Life of the World. And so, when you build a house, you will not set your heart on the multiplication of its rooms and closets but you will set your entire heart on this: that there be nothing in it that separates from Boundless Space, from Boundless Life, for when you sit in your house, when you lie down and when you rise up, at every moment and every hour, your entire being will be in the midst of that Space, in the midst of that Life. And thus also will you build houses of Torah and wisdom, also houses of labor and work, setting a space between one house and another—a large space, so that no house will rob or conceal from another its place in this world. You will learn Torah from the mouth of Nature, the Torah of building and fashioning, and you will learn to do as it does in all that you build and in all that you fashion.

On that day you will know and take to heart, O child of Adam, that you had been wandering aimlessly until you returned to this point. For you didn't know life. Even after you stopped eating from the pre-made, you still didn't recognize the Nature of life; you didn't stop living from the pre-made, whether made by you or by others. A different life, a life not from the pre-made, a life in the midst of the making of life, in the midst of the fashioning of life: this you didn't know. And so your life was torn into two tatters: one very small tatter of life and one very large tatter of non-life—of labor, of trouble, and of bother. "Shabbat"—and "pre-Shabbat." And you didn't think, it didn't occur to you, that there is no life in living from the pre-made, if there is not life in the act of making; doesn't Nature also live in the midst of creating life, in the midst of fashioning life? And so, all your days, you were a seeker of life, a pursuer of life—and not alive. Your life was dangling before you: either in the past or in the future; present you didn't know. When you saw that your own life

166

was small and poor, you craved to annex to yourself the lives of others. So you would rob, plunder, and extort as much as possible from whomever and whatever you thought to have life. You sucked, you drank, you drained your comrades' blood, if they didn't succeed in sucking your blood. To you, the life of a parasite became the sign of greatness, strength and splendor; wealth the sign of happiness, the rule of one human over another the sign of strength and glory. You didn't sense, you didn't perceive, that the pre-made life which you swallowed became a rot in your bones. And even your prophets, who arose to repair your world and renew your life, prophesied falsehood and emptiness. They added nothing at all to the teaching, "Those who took the trouble to prepare before Shabbat will enter the Shabbat and eat." They only taught you to put a bit in your mouth and in the mouth of those eating with you from the communal plate, a bit with which to prevent yourself and the others from eating more than your share, more than you prepared "before Shabbat." But you, child of Adam, do you not desire life also "before Shabbat," and at every time and every hour, at every single instant? What good is the bit in your mouth to you?

And it shall come to pass on that day, O child of Adam, that you shall receive a new spirit, you shall feel a new feeling, a new hunger—not a hunger for bread, nor a thirst for money, but for labor. You will find delight in every labor and in every deed that you do, like the delight you find in eating and drinking. On that day, you will take care to make your labor pleasurable and appealing, like you now take care to make your food appealing, and like you now take care to increase the fruit of your labor—money. You will know to work your fill every day, no more and no less. Most of all, though, you will take care to do all your labor and all your deeds in the midst of Nature, in the midst of the Boundless Space of the World. That is how you will do your work in the field and that is how you will do your work in the house, for that is how you will build your house.

And it shall come to pass when you work at your labor, that the spacious expanse of the universe will seem to be your work-place, and you and Nature the workers. The two of you will be of one heart and of one spirit. You will say on that day: Nature is beautiful on its surface, but it is seven times more beautiful in the spirit of its life, in its labor. And when you stop for a moment to straighten your

167

back, and to take a breath, you will breathe in not only air, but you will feel that you are breathing in something more, something subtle which you can't identify, but which will make your emotions and your thoughts bear fruit, which will add life and light to your spirit. Indeed, you will have moments as if your entire being were melting into the Infinite. Then you will stand in speechless silence. Not only speech, but even song, even thought, will seem to you a desecration of that which is holy. You will grasp the hidden truth of silence and its holiness. You will experience something which cannot be expressed except by labor. So you will labor powerfully, with strength and joy. And you will hear a divine voice issuing forth from your labor and saying, "Work, children of Adam, all of you, work!" Then you will know and internalize, that in labor there is a reservoir of spirit, such that you can see only its outer edge, but its entirety can only be seen with many eyes, that look at it from all sides. . . . And following the divine voice, Nature answers, "Amen! Work, children of Adam! Let your labor not be belittled in your eyes. You shall complete that which I have left lacking in order that I, myself, should complete that which you lack. . . ."

On that day, the fruit of your labor, child of Adam, will be: life. For there will be life within your labor. Not a single moment of your life will be wasted. Even on a day of calamity, when afflictions come upon you, your afflictions will be significant, deep, holy. Or on a day of darkness, when you stumble a moment and sin, you will have within you enough strength, enough grandeur, to bear the sin, and enough hell-fire with which to be refined. You will know the pain that pours out a supreme, holy spirit upon you, and supreme love for all that live and suffer, and you will know nothing of the profane, you will know nothing of the petty, you will know nothing of vacuous living.

On that day, child of Adam, you shall lift your eyes round about, you shall lift your eyes upward, and you will see the earth and all that exists therein, and you will see the heavens with all their legions, with all the incomprehensible, endless numbers of worlds that are there, and lo, all of them, all of them are near to your Self, all of them bring You blessing. Then you will grasp the eternity that inhabits the moment. Then you will know how great is your wealth, how great the blessing, that life carries to you. Then you will know, and say in your heart: How poor, how wretched is life appropriated from others, rule over others, light gotten from others! On that day you will love all that exists, you will love the children of Adam, you will even love yourself—for your heart will be filled with love. You will believe in yourself, you will believe in humankind, you will believe in all that one has to believe—for you will be entirely filled with life.

Your emotions and thoughts, your spirit, will be like the swelling stream—ever new, ever your own. You will also feel your entire self, and behold, you are ever new, ever your own. Thus will you seem to yourself and thus will you seem to your comrades—for your source will be blessed.

On that day, human will no longer be a burden to human, which the bearer bears for an hour—and becomes weary. For there will be sufficient space for every person, and sufficient distance between one person and another, that one will not fall to another, but will ever and always draw the other near.

On that day, child of Adam, you will know Nature, for your eyes and all your senses will be sufficiently clear, your heart sufficiently open, your mind sufficiently deep. On that day, the light of your wisdom and your science will no longer be a cold and terrible light, but it will be a living light, flowing abundantly from all of the worlds.

On that day, child of Adam, you will know how to live with Nature, for *it will be your will* to know. . . .

Zionist Ideology and the Space of *Eretz Yisrael*: Why the Native Israeli Is Called *Tzabar*

Tsili Doleve-Gandelman

In contemporary Hebrew the term *tzabar*, or cactus, has come to mean a child born in *Eretz Yisrael* at the time of the *Yishuv* or thereafter. Popular etymology sees it as an affectionate nickname appropriate to the native Israeli, who appears to be rough and prickly on the outside, but warm and kindhearted. In this paper it will be shown that the notion of *tzabar* acts as a symbolic "shifter" or passage-operating agent between history and nature, and that this is the basis of its symbolic efficacy.

The Jewish, Hebrew-speaking child, by virtue of his being called a *tzabar*, may be viewed as a linguistic shifter. The child is both an index pointing to an existential relationship with its land of birth in which he/she is "rooted," and a symbol (*tzabar* also belongs to the specific code of Zionist ideology). Similarly, the *tzabar* child is a shifter between time and space—or, in other words, between history and the actual land of the Jewish people. Here, history means symbols, myth, and a code-ruled relatedness; land, in its concreteness, means contact as well as an existential relatedness and an existential pointing. It is primarily through the concept of *tzabar* that Zionist ideology, growing out of Jewish history, was symbolically inscribed in the space of *Eretz Yisrael*.

Unraveling this web of meaning requires the consideration of several topics: (1) the conceptual connection between Zionism and Zion (*Eretz Yisrael*) as a circumscribed space; (2) the role of the Jewish National Fund or the *Keren Kayemet le-Yisrael* (KKL) in the concrete realization of this connection; and (3) the function of the preschool system in its symbolic implementation and the part played by the KKL within this preschool system.

The connection between Zionist ideology, the Jewish people, and the land of Israel was accomplished constitutionally as well as symbolically by the KKL. At the time of the *Yishuv*, the existing autonomous system of education was one of the main channels for the transmission of Zionist ideology. Although this paper relates exclusively to the preschool system, involving children from three to six years of age, the symbolic function of the *tzabar* is not limited only to this age category. However, it is during the kindergarten years that the ceremonies and rituals expressing the ultimate values of the ideology under examination are the most frequent. Thus, the links between the Hebrew kindergarten in *Eretz Yisrael* and Zionist ideology can be best observed at this level. It is also at this level that the functioning of the KKL, as the embodiment of the connection of the people with the land with the nature of *Eretz Yisrael*, can best be described.

This study thus attempts to demonstrate that the *tzabar* acts as a symbolic shifter from history to nature, from linear time to cyclical time (that is, nature time). In order to illustrate this, symbolic events, such as the birthday ceremony, shall be referred to: first, as it was performed in the kindergarten (a ritual which to some extent was appropriated by the KKL); and second, as it was performed under the aegis of the KKL as the birthday ceremony of that organization. Also dealt with will be a second metaphorical use of the ceremony (the actual birthday of the child being the only celebration which is nonmetaphorical)—the so-called birthday of the almond tree—the harbinger of spring. It is the symbolic network of relationships between all of these elements which will eventually support the view of the *tzabar* as an agent shifting history into nature.

The Beginnings of Zionism and the Links with the Land

Among all the organs of the Zionist movement, it was the KKL that put into concrete form the connection between this ideology and *Eretz Yisrael*. Its function was the purchasing and amelioration of the land in Zion, that is, the region in the Ottoman Empire known as Palestine and Syria and, later, under the British Mandate, as Palestine.

It was explicitly stated that the land was to remain in public ownership, as formulated during the fifth Zionist Congress (1901) which created the KKL: "The KKL shall be the eternal possession of the Jewish people." The KKL was the Zionist version of an agrarian reform (though, in this particular case the reform preceded the purchasing of the land). It was important to centralize the purchasing of land in order to minimize speculation in a region that was in its first phase of settlement and development.

Though the idea of the KKL was a revolutionary one, it shared several reference points with Jewish tradition. Hermann Shapira, who first proposed the idea of the KKL, based his conception on the biblical institution of the jubilee year as it is expressed in Lev. 25:33: "The land shall not be sold for ever." The very name "*Keren*

Kayemet le-Yisrael" is also part of Jewish tradition, since it is derived from the talmudic dictum about good deeds: "The fruit of which a man enjoys in this world, while the capital abides *[keren kayemet]* for him in the world to come" (M. *Peah 1, 11*). The good deed, the financing of the KKL, was to be drawn from a wide strata of the Jewish people. The KKL created a worldwide organization for fundraising by means of special stamps, inscriptions in a Golden Book *(Sefer ha-Zahav)*, contributions for the planting of trees and reforestation and, above all, via the blue box.

At the beginning of the century, this tin box, designed like a charity box, was in more than one hundred thousand Jewish homes. The KKL was felt to be the property of the entire Jewish people. For all its revolutionary character, the blue box was, nevertheless, the successor of other tin boxes with charity purposes.

The originality of the KKL is, on the one hand, its concretization of the goal of Zionism, that is, the *redemption of the land* and its dialectical counterpart, the *redemption of the people*. On the other hand, it maintained points of reference derived from Jewish tradition. In a sense, it united the temporal depth (the Jewish tradition) with the spatial extension (the worldwide distribution) of the Jewish people. These two aspects of the KKL made it the dominant symbol of Zionist ideology, especially within the educational system. The KKL was not a mere purchaser of land but also the permanent creator and generator of symbols aimed at proclaiming the rights of the Jews to *Eretz Yisrael*—a right which was based on an historic pact but which now derived its meaning from the concept of the redemption of the land.

J. Weitz,[1] who was the KKL official in charge of the afforestation, and one of its chief ideologues, wrote in the first volume of *Shorashim* (Roots), the journal of teachers employed by the KKL in *Eretz Yisrael*:

> The forest was the glory of Nature. . . . In the days of yore, Israel had been covered with forests. . . . Yet, in the course of our Exile it was continually the object of conquest, wars and depredation for conquering peoples who succeeded in denuding her and left her deserted and naked, arid and sterile as she today appears under our gaze. . . . And when the sons of Israel returned to their land at the beginning of the *Hibbat Tzion*

movement and they saw there were no longer trees in the land, they began to plant anew as though from the very beginning *(mi-bereshit).*

The establishment of a connection with the land for redemption of the Jewish people was not the exclusive idea of the KKL. It was also present in a variety of ideological trends, such as the idea of the productivization of the Jewish people and the socialist ideas as interpreted and propagated by the labor movement in *Eretz Yisrael (enu'at ha-avodah).* Above all, it was A. D. Gordon, influenced by Tolstoyan ideas and the Russian *Narodniki,* who gave the cosmic dimension to working the land of *Eretz Yisrael.* Gordon insisted that the only means of redemption for the Jewish people was through the creation of a new intimate link with nature.

Hebrew Preschool Education and the Zionist Vision in *Eretz Yisrael*

The beginnings of the Hebrew kindergarten and its development are inseparable from the history and the struggles of the Zionist movement. The new educational tradition was, in fact, the result of permanent interaction between various pedagogical doctrines of European and American derivation, on the one hand, and the ideological objectives of a society in the process of self-constitution, on the other. These objectives were the creation of a new form of existence, of a new cultural tradition. In this context, the kindergarten teachers saw the integration of the newly acquired professional doctrines with the wider objectives set by society as their chief task. The more remarkable among them were members of the Second Aliyah.

The society of the *Yishuv,* with its futuristic orientation, was naturally interested in the young generation. The autonomous Jewish network of schools, which grew rapidly under the British Mandate,[2] is witness to this attitude. The young generation was seen as the carrier of changes within the family during the school and preschool years, and also as young adults-to-be. It was the child who embodied the message of a new culture via a new language which was to

173

be introduced into the home. Thus, through the educational system, the sociocultural vision, which was the heritage of the elite, was to be transmitted to the new generation, and to their parents. Hence, the paramount importance of creating and acquiring dominant symbols and values for this educational system.

The Creation of the New Zionist Cultural Tradition in the Kindergarten

The educational system, and especially the kindergarten, translated the abstract ideology of Zionism into symbols, ceremonies, and festivals necessary for the child's social identity and the perpetuation of an engagement in a society which, until 1948, was founded on a basis of volunteer work.

The Zionist movement was born out of the negation of the Diaspora, which, to a great extent, meant the negation of religious practice. But secularization was problematic. The absence of the festivals, which were no longer celebrated within the home, created a void which was felt deeply by the educators, since these traditions were an integral part of their youth in the Jewish shtetls of Eastern Europe. Beyond this nostalgia, the void was intolerable in a society that was intensely ideological and militant. This point is highlighted in the professional journals of the educators.

For instance, the kindergarten teacher N. Shargadovska wrote in *Netiveinu:*[3]

> Owing to the void which was felt by the sons of immigrants torn from their familiar environment, special importance must be granted to the preparation of the Holy Days. Everything must be done to ensure the celebration of the Shabbat or the festivals, for each holiday is not only an historical remembrance but must be related to the resurrection of our people on our land.

Traditional Jewish Holy Days, and especially festivals that lent themselves to transformation and reinterpretation, were part and parcel of the new tradition which was being constituted in *Eretz Yisrael* by the Zionist movement. This process of reinterpretation had a double effect. The elements within the tradition were silenced and the links between the people and its land, preserved and symbolized (precisely) through religion, were now emphasized. The connecting link between the Jews and the land was the key to the redemption of the uprooted Jew. In the words of the teacher Ts. Katinka:[4]

> It is through the festival that love for the heroes of his nation, for his people and his land, is born in the heart of the child and made strong—by festivals such as Hanukkah and Pesaḥ. The child is brought into proximity with nature and is taught to give expression to the relation existing between the Jew and Nature. This relation existed yesterday as it exists today. The classic example is Tu B'Shvat.

The Function of the KKL in the Kindergarten

The *Keren Kayemet le-Yisrael* was a central element in the new culture being created in the kindergarten. This was due, first of all, to its role as the purchaser of the land of *Eretz Yisrael*. The KKL defined the practical conditions for the revival of Zion; it concretized its symbolism into reality. Moreover, as mentioned, the KKL possessed a double dimension: it had, on the one hand, the spatial extent of the whole Diaspora and, on the other hand, the temporal depth which belonged to the Jewish tradition. The KKL had become the main symbol of the redemption of Israel, and as such, it constantly generated more specific symbols which became widely used within the educational system.

This function of the KKL as a generator of symbols became institutionalized in 1927 through the initiative of the teachers who created the "Committee of Teachers for the KKL" *(mo'etset ha-morim lerna'an KKL)*. At first, the so-called work for the KKL was intended for children of ten years and over but eventually came to be generalized at the kindergarten level, where it was found to be especially successful. The function of the work for the KKL in the educational system was conceived by Ussishkin, the president of KKL, in the following manner:

The work done at school revolves around the idea of the redemption of the fatherland and its people. . . . Essentially, the work

175

accomplished by the child is intended to accustom him to live the national reality, and to inculcate in him the idea that he has duties to his people and his land. . . . The role of the school is, above all, to breed the feeling of the sanctity of a unique task in the heart of the child: the one and only task with which our generation has been entrusted: redemption.

An examination in detail of the writings of the kindergarten teachers themselves reveals a profusion of articles confirming the basic function of the KKL as a generator of the child's social identity, exalting the rootedness in *Eretz Yisrael* as the land of birth *(le-eretz huledet)*. The land of Israel is "fatherland" in the sense of the "land in which one is born" *(le-eretz moledet)*. These children are fortunate to see around them, from the very moment of their birth, landscapes that belong to their own land. These words reflect the popular poem by the Hebrew poet Tchernichovsky:[5]

> *Man is nothing but a piece of the soil of a small land* (eretz).
> *Man is nothing but the form of the landscape of his native land.*

Similarly, nature walks, even if short, were part of the kindergarten routine even in urban environments. Changes in the seasons (and in the flora and fauna which accompanied these) were all themes for lessons and discussions. Wild flowers gathered in the fields during the outings were put in vases in the corner of the class reserved for the KKL.[6] The KKL corner *(pinat Keren Kayemet le-Yisrael)* was a set corner in all kindergartens. It also included the blue box and the national flag, which existed long before the creation of the State of Israel. The corner was decorated with green plants and there were books and pictures showing communities and localities in the *Yishuv*, which the teacher changed occasionally. The children would often come to look at these pictures.

In order to strengthen the link between the child and the land, the kindergarten possessed a real garden, which was cultivated by the teacher and children. The professional journals of the kindergarten teachers featured many articles devoted to gardening activity, which was considered to be an important educational theme, and was also associated with the KKL. For instance, during the Shavuot festival, at the beginning of summer, first fruits *(bikkurim)* picked from the garden were symbolically offered to the KKL, as had been done in the days of the Jerusalem Temple. Even in every-day life, every fruit gathered by the children from the garden was, first of all, exhibited in the KKL corner.

The blue box was part of all the ceremonies performed in the kindergarten. Every Friday, during the Kabbalat Shabbat ceremony, as with the celebration of other festivals not directly linked with the KKL, the children would put symbolic contributions into the blue box.

S. Fayens-Glick, a kindergarten inspector, provides an insight into how the teachers themselves saw the presentation of the KKL in their nursery schools:

> The very fact of having made the KKL the base of kindergarten education implies a further extension of the idea it represents and its transformation into a symbol; a symbol—as Bialik said—of all the great and profound values of the Hebrew people: that is to say, on the material plane, a symbol of the tie with the land which is "mother of all life," and on the spiritual plane: a bond with the great tradition of our people. . . . The symbolic way toward the idea of the KKL passes, in the education of the child, through the contributions and presents which are offered to the KKL.

The Birthday Ceremony in the Kindergarten and the KKL

As the medium of Zionist education, the KKL was the creator of specific symbols. Kindergarten teachers, and those responsible for their creation, were well aware of the function of these symbols, centered around the concept of redemption, namely, the concrete redemption of the land and through it, of the people. However, this is only the explicit level. It would seem that there is another metaphorical level, which is implicit or hidden. Here the special relationship between the kindergarten child and the land and nature of *Eretz Yisrael* takes on its full meaning. In this metaphorical relationship, the child born in *Eretz Yisrael* (the *tzabar*) can be said to be functioning as a symbolic shifter, that is, as an operator of passage. This shifting, and the passage achieved, is from the time axis, emphasizing history (Jewish ritual has been described by Heschel as "architecture in time"[7]), to the space axis, stressing land and nature, namely the specific nature of *Eretz Yisrael*.

From the data on the functioning of the KKL within the preschool system, it appears that this shifting action can best be observed in two types of ceremonies performed in the kindergarten. The first, nonmetaphorical ceremony is the birthday celebration of individual children. The second type is metaphorical: it includes the so-called birthday of the KKL, and the birthday of the almond tree celebrated during the Tu B'Shvat festival, also known as "the New Year of the Trees." A detailed description of certain aspects of these ceremonies will bring to the fore the shifter character of the child.

As the birthday ceremony was not part of the Jewish tradition, it was like an empty vessel with a potential to express the new ideology—much more so than other festivals in the kindergarten which, despite all the changes made to adjust them to the new Zionist spirit, remained essentially traditional.

Thus, the birthday ceremony of the child was to a large extent appropriated by the KKL. There was another reason for this. A birthday is generally part of an individual calendar, it is in many ways a celebration of the notion of "person" in its specific sense of autonomy and individuality.[8] In this engaged society (as Zionist society was at its beginnings), autonomy and individuality appeared problematic, if not dangerous.[9] Therefore, the very acceptance of the glorification of the person necessitated the intervention of the KKL as a mediator.

The Birthday Ceremony of the Child

During the birthday ceremony the KKL was present in two ways: first, through its contribution box, and second, through the greeting card sent to the child.

The blue box was set on the ceremonial table with the other objects used during the ceremony.[10] During the celebration when the child had become the focus of attention of the whole gathering, he inserted into the box a number of coins corresponding to his age. As Fayens-Glick expressed it:

The symbolic way toward the idea of the KKL passes through the contributions and presents offered to the KKL during the child's birthday, when he has become the focus of attention, and all eyes are staring at him while he lets fall, one by one, his handful of coins corresponding to his age into the box of the KKL. How many invisible threads are weaving an invisible network between his soul and the box? How many rays are emanating from it and caress his soul? How deep is this experience? When the child grows older and understands the link which exists between the tilling of the soil and the redemption of the land, the symbol, and the thing it symbolizes, will be fused together to express one single idea: the man who resurrects his land and brings about its redemption also resurrects his own self and achieves his own redemption.[11]

When the child received the *berakhot,* the verbal blessings of his peers and the customary small gifts, the KKL joined in through the intermediary of a birthday card in the form of a calendar.

This picture card consists of a blessing that is surrounded by twelve squares bearing the Hebrew names of the months, so that the whole card looks like a Hebrew calendar. In each square, two elements of the nature of the designated months are represented as part of the flora and fauna of *Eretz Yisrael.* The fauna belong to primeval nature in the sense that they represent nondomesticated animals, mainly birds. The represented flora, too, are wild flora. The only two elements representing cultivated plants are the pomegranate and the vine, characteristic of the Israel of biblical times, and they are represented in the squares of the summer months, when wild flowers are rare.

Thus, most of the elements belong to wild nature. Similarly, the background of their representation is wild: the sea, a barren land, or the sky. Yet, the separation between each square is a frieze of cypresses, trees which signal field limits or borders in Mediterranean lands. This surrounding area is constituted by time, which is represented both by a cultural aspect of twelve months and by a natural aspect, which is cyclical and belongs to wild primeval nature.

Culture and nature are woven into the picture. Even in the central part showing cultivated fields and distant villages, one observes nature in its primeval sense: wild flowers, two enormous trees, flights of birds passing through the sky.

179

It is in this wild part of the central landscape that four parts of a printed text are found—read from right to left, as in Hebrew writing. The first and second parts describe the child, or rather, since they are written in the first person singular, it is the child himself who presents his person. Then there follows a poem by Bialik, the national poet:

> *Here is the benediction*
> *which Hayyim Naḥman Bialik*
> *sends the children of Israel:*
> *Let God multiply you from ten thousand to*
> *ten thousand*
> *like the plants in the fields*
> *and the wild flowers.*
> *May you be the joy of your parents*
> *and the glory of your land of birth* (eretz moledet)
> *Amen and again amen.*

In the fourth part, the KKL addresses the child directly, as if in its own voice: "The KKL sends you its blessing for your birthday." The blessing itself is written on what looks like a scroll of parchment carried by a dove with an olive branch in its beak.

In summary, the KKL is represented in three aspects: as an institution, it is the box that unites the whole Jewish people; as the nature and culture of *Eretz Yisrael*, it is the "agri"-culture of the land, but the land also produces wild nature. The land is both *Eretz Yisrael* and *eretz moledet,* that is, the fatherland. In a song written by the poet Nathan Alterman, sung during the birthday, the fatherland is as exceptional and unique as is the birthday among the other days of the year. A refrain of the song reads thus:[12]

> *Among all the days of the year*
> *One only is the day of birth (*yom huledet*)*
> *Among all the lands in the world*
> *One only is the fatherland (*moledet*)*

Thus, through the *huledet/moledet* rhyming, there takes place an assimilation between the child and the land.

The Birthday Ceremony of the KKL

There are several words in Hebrew to designate anniversary. Yet it is the term *yom huledet* (birthday) which is always used when the anniversary is that of the KKL. In that sense, the phrase has already been metaphorically transposed. Thus, the professional journal of the kindergarten teacher often speaks of the birthday of the KKL.

In fact, the metaphorical usage of birthday, extended to the KKL, is also celebrated in the kindergarten. One finds documentation concerning two categories of such birthday celebrations. The first is more intimate and takes place in the kindergarten, while the second is a central and more public celebration. The first will be referred to only briefly, but the second will be the subject of a longer and more detailed description.[13]

The intimate ceremony of the KKL birthday continued to be performed in the kindergarten even after the creation of the State of Israel. The kindergarten teacher, Zbodanski-Rodanski, tells about a celebration which took place the year before the establishment of the state:

> It consisted of a theatrical performance reproducing the establishment and settlement of eleven kibbutzim, in the Negev desert. In this celebration, the KKL was presented mainly in its cultural aspect and emphasis was laid on the men who redeemed the earth from its desolate state and transformed the desert landscape and the primeval nature into culture. The second part of the ceremony concerned the blue box. Here, elements overtly taken from the birthday of the child came into play. Birthday songs were sung, contributions in coins were made, as in the case of the birthday of the child, but here the number of coins was not associated with the number of years of the KKL.

However, the large public celebration which took place in the KKL house in Tel Aviv, was not continued after the creation of the state.

The following is a very detailed description of this festival written by T. Katsiri,[14] a kindergarten teacher:

> As they reach the threshold, the children start singing a song which celebrates the redemption of the land and of the people, thanks to the KKL and its blue box. . . .
>
> In two corners of the hall are exhibitions of the fruits of the land, a present from Tnuva. The children enter the hall and the

181

ceremony begins. First, there is a blessing from the KKL. In their turn, the children answer by a blessing:

Let the KKL buy a lot of land.
Let a lot of Jews come and settle in Eretz Yisrael.
Let the children come to Israel and let them not be killed over there. . . .
Shalom, shalom *and blessings.*

Each class presents a box full of coins and its presents for the KKL. Even the land offers its own blessings in the form of its crops. The cauliflower and the cabbage, the beet-root and the tomato, the carrot and the radish thank the KKL for their redemption from the arid earth and its transformation into fertile soil.

The KKL answers the blessing of the children with another; a small box, a gift for the doll-house of each class, is offered together with a present from the earth, a banana for each child. . . . The feast ends with the hymn "Hatikvah."

Here again, as during the individual birthday of the child, a veritable duet of blessings between the KKL and the child took place. The blessings were copied from the kindergarten celebration as was the central placement of the blue box during the festivities. Yet, unlike the anniversary of the individual child, the ceremony did not mark linear time, which is the time marked by birthdays. The age of the KKL was never mentioned.

The KKL was presented as the institution which creates the link between the Jewish people and the land. It is the KKL that made the land fertile and brought her redemption. Thus, symbolically, by way of this circularity, a certain identification between KKL and land occurs—the latter fertilized by the former. Consequently, the KKL gives each child a gift from the land, usually a fruit.

This relationship between the land and the KKL is to be found in other texts which celebrate the interchangeability between mother and land. For instance, in one issue of *Hed ha-Gan*,[15] this "Song for the KKL" by A. Glazer is found:

I made for myself a small garden
Mother gave me a spade
But when I shall be grown up
Who shall give me the land?
Know this:
There is a good mother

> *who cares for you*
> *She is my mother*
> *and thine:*
> *It is the KKL*
> *On the map there are dots*
> *and empty spaces*
> *The dots are villages.*
> *How can they be multiplied?*
> *If you do not know how*
> *Make a gift*
> *to the KKL.*
> *Thus by thy hand*
> *thou hast drawn*
> *on the arid land*
> *a new village.*

As in the birthday ceremony, the KKL is described as intimately related to the land while, at the same time, being separate from it. It is both "my" and "thy" mother. The interdependence between the child and the metaphorical mother, the KKL, is repeatedly emphasized. The link is even more bilateral since the KKL relies on the child's contribution to his box in order to achieve their common aim.

Despite the identification of the KKL with the land, in which it is primarily "mother" through the medium of the birthday, the KKL also presents itself as a child. There is, however, an important difference: the child's birthday (or his age) is inscribed in linear time, while the KKL birthday never relates to its age or to the number of years. The KKL is thus predominantly mother but simultaneously child.

The Birthday Story of the Almond Tree

The second metaphorical birthday which has been observed is the so-called birthday of the almond tree, the tree which is the harbinger of spring. First among the trees with deciduous leaves, the almond tree grows a flowery bloom in springtime. Even more remarkable is the fact that it grows blossoms before its leaves appear.

183

In the tradition created in the *Eretz Yisrael* kindergarten, the celebration of the almond tree is associated with Tu B'Shvat, a quasi-festival belonging to the religious tradition marking the new year of the trees. . . . This Tu B'Shvat festival, completely reinterpreted and controlled by the KKL, became not only the feast of the trees but also the celebration of *afforestation*.

Although the almond tree does not actually belong to the seven species which characterize *Eretz Yisrael*,[16] it used to grow in Israel in biblical times.[17] At the turn of the present century, almond trees were extensively cultivated in *Eretz Yisrael*. Yet, later on, almost all were destroyed by pest. The almond trees exist in two species; the cultivated one producing sweet almonds, and the wild species in the mountains, with its white blossoms and bitter fruit. During the British Mandate, the almond tree was mostly represented by the wild species, that is, the natural, noncultivated type.

In the course of time, the perception of the almond tree and its presentation in the kindergarten underwent an interesting transformation, which is very apparent in the work of L. Kipnis,[18] a foremost creator of Hebrew children's stories in *Eretz Yisrael*. The almond tree first appears in his work as an adult religious Jew. In a well-known story published in 1919 to 1920, and entitled "Happy New Year," one reads that "the almond trees prayed to God that He should preserve them from the bad winds . . . and all the prayers were metamorphosed into blossoms." The dominant metaphor is clearly the image of the religious Jew praying during the holidays of the Jewish New Year and Yom Kippur. It is during the New Year season that the destiny of people is decided. It is also a time of forgiveness or absolution, a sign of which is the white clothes religious Jews put on—just as the almond tree puts on its white blossoms.

As time went by, Kipnis changed his symbols. The image of the tree as an adult "Judaized" entity (in the traditional religious meaning of the term), existing in linear time, disappeared. It was replaced by a child almond tree denoting the cosmic elements in nature and announcing the spring revival. As such it came to be inscribed in a time that was preeminently cyclical. However, this was not a radical substitution, and the old model survives as a faded watermark behind the new one.

In 1930, Kipnis published a text entitled "The Almond-Tree Birthday" in the journal *Gilyonot*:

> Once upon a time, in the orchard surrounding the house, there was a young almond tree. Even before the end of summer the tree lost all its leaves and remained "naked." She [the author uses the feminine form *shekedia*, and not *shaked*, to designate the tree] felt cold and was very sad. And it so happened that on a cold winter day a light spring breeze visited the garden; it blew upon the trees and murmured its secret to them: "Tomorrow is the birthday of the almond tree." And immediately, the trees started shaking their branches and whispered to one another:

> "Tomorrow is the birthday of the almond tree!" A bird and a bee also heard the news and propagated it among their friends! . . . and even little Noam drew near the tree and shouted: "Tomorrow is Tu B'Shvat: Tomorrow is your birthday: Tomorrow I shall have all my friends come to offer you their birthday blessings." Yet the almond tree, while listening to all these speeches . . . only thought to herself: "Tomorrow is my birthday, many people will come to see me—and I am stark naked; How can I receive them?" She brooded and brooded all day and all night. All the other trees went to sleep but she could not sleep.

> But lo: in the middle of the night the Queen of trees appeared to her. "Good evening almond tree: Why are you so worried and do not sleep?" The almond tree answered: "How can I sleep and not worry? Tomorrow is my birthday, a lot of people will come to see me and here I am stark naked." The Queen caressed her and said: "Do not worry at all before the rise of the day you will receive a marvelous birthday robe." "Really?" asked the tree. "Yes, yes," the Queen answered. "All almond trees, whoever they be, receive a white robe for their birthday. And now go to sleep so you can be rested and gay in the morning." And the Queen caressed the almond tree until it went to sleep. And when it was asleep, she gave her kisses on her branches. And at every spot which her lips kissed sprung a delicate white, rosy blossom. . . .

> In the morning, when the almond tree woke up she could hardly recognize herself; she was completely dressed up in magnificent white blossoms. And all the surrounding trees gazed at her and started blessing her. One shouted "Good morning!" Another one said: "Happy New Year!" And all exclaimed: "What a beautiful dress!" ("Let your dress bear you luck.") Many birds alighted

185

on her branches and started singing the birthday song. Similarly, the bees came and sang. And Noam came with his friends; they made a circle around the tree and sang to her: "Happy New Year almond tree! Happy New Year!"

This story was subsequently rewritten by Goytin[19] with musical accompaniment, and published in *Hed ha-Gan*. In this latter version the last lines emphasize the resurrection of spring: "All the guests shout: Good day! Good day! Long live thy new dress, almond tree! How beautiful is thy white dress. Thou art the harbinger of springs and for this, beautiful tree, receive our thanks and blessings."

In the two versions, it has been seen that the almond tree is unmistakably represented as a child. The Queen caresses her into sleep and she receives, as a feasted child does, a new and beautiful dress. Yet there is a difference in the identification: the child is inscribed in the linear time of history, whereas the almond tree is inscribed in cyclical time; her birthday is placed under the aegis of the spring revival. The anxiety of the almond tree relates to its annual capacity for self-reproduction. In a way, it can be said that its yearly blossoming annihilates linear time and substitutes cyclical time for it.

At the same time, if the almond tree is mostly perceived as a child, it is also perceived as a mother: it produces blossoms which in their turn shall produce fruit. Observe the parallelism with the KKL, which is now a mother, and now a child.

The Kindergarten Child as a Symbolic Shifter

A series of identifications have been seen: the almond tree is identified with the child, but he, in his turn, is identified with the world of plants. This has already been seen in the blessing sent by the KKL to the kindergarten for each child's birthday. Those kindergarten children are not any children: they were born in *Eretz Yisrael* and, by virtue of this fact, are interchangeable with its nature. The children born in the land of Israel are nicknamed *tzabarim* (pl.), that is, the fruit of the cactus. This cactus grows in *Eretz Yisrael* either as a wild plant or as a semicultivated one, just as the almond tree.

Thus, the child is identified with an herb of the field, with a wild flower, and, finally, with the *tzabar* fruit, while the KKL is related to the earth, to the land, that is, to the mother. The birthday is both a celebration and the commemoration of a separation: the birth, the separation from the mother, which introduces linear time, that is, the historical person, or, in other words, the age of the child. Yet, in the metaphorical context of the birthday, it is also the nonseparation from the mother, a nonseparation rooted in cyclical time. This is the parallelism of the nonseparation between an almond tree-*tzabar*-child and earth-mother-KKL, which operates a change on linear time, bringing it back to a cyclical dimension, that of the spring renaissance. Within this context cyclical time also indicates the spring renaissance of the people of Israel coming back to its land, a process most concretely expressed in the *tzabar*. The *tzabar* is an integral part of the land and, rooted in its soil, cannot be separated from it. It is the children who, since a new group of them appears year after year, embody the miracle of the spring renaissance. The child, the *tzabar*, has been taken away from the linear current of history and implanted in nature.

With the realization of the meaning of the Holocaust during World War II, and the necessity of creating a state for the survivors, and with the subsequent creation of the State of Israel, the ideology of the *Yishuv* underwent a change. It reinscribed itself symbolically into linear time, that is, historical time, the time of Jewish history. Yet, this description clearly demonstrates that the *tzabar* was conceived as a creature which cannot be separated from the soil, from the land, and, by virtue of this character, became a shifter which could symbolically transform historical, linear time into spatial, cyclical time.

The *Eretz Yisrael* born child acts as a temporal shifter converting time into space: the space of the Land of Israel.

It is interesting to observe that the KKL has been the generator of a number of rituals. This is because it is a symbol of continuity—be it fictitious continuity—between a people and its land. It is precisely because of the semi-fictitious character of this continuity that the KKL has always been obliged to create and recreate the image of nonseparation between a people and its land through the connection it made between children and the wild nature of the land. Therein lies its symbolic function and symbolic efficacy.

Thus, there is a perpetual interplay between the individual and the collective, between linear time and cyclical time, in a person's life, representing both the time of history and the time of a people's renaissance—an interplay which is not arbitrary, but is part of the symbolic work of ideology.

The objective of this study has been to show the striving of a society intending to go back into the flux of history. It actually did so, not through the upholding of traditional religious practice (this was the time-honored role of the Diaspora), but through the creation of shifting interchangeability between *tzabar* and land.

With the realization of the meaning of the Holocaust and the subsequent creation of the State of Israel, the ideology of the *Yishuv* underwent a change and reinscribed itself symbolically into the linear time of Jewish History. Consequently, the KKL, which continued to function as an organization, and also as a locus for symbolic creation, even after the creation of the State, lost its hidden symbolic function and therefore its symbolic efficacy. It was the hidden symbolic functioning that had permitted the *tzabar* to operate as a shifter between history and space. Its loss explains the very sharp reduction in the activities of the KKL within the preschool and the educational system in general.

As for the *tzabar* which, as has been seen, was primarily a symbol and an index (actually a shifter between symbol and index), it currently appears as the third mode of signification in the Peircian trilogy: as an icon. The term *tzabar* now evokes only the iconic image of the cactus fruit, as a psychological portrait of the native Israeli personality.

The Forest as a National Icon: Literature, Politics, and the Archeology of Memory

Yael Zerubavel*

The admiration of trees as symbolizing the beauty, purity, and magnitude of nature is a familiar theme in Romantic literature. In the emergent Hebrew culture of the pre-state Jewish society in Palestine, trees carried an even greater symbolic value: they became an icon of national revival, symbolizing the Zionist success in "striking roots" in the ancient homeland. Children were often named after trees and children's literature described young trees as children.[1] The depiction of the Jewish nation as a tree provided a powerful visual representation of historical processes that were at the core of Zionist consciousness. The image of a chopped tree with a new branch sprouting from its side was used as the emblem of *La No'ar,* a highly popular book series for young adults: the chopped tree symbolized the curtailed Jewish national life during centuries of life in exile, while the new branch represented the beginning of national renewal, a symbolic analogue to the Hebrew youth themselves. This tree image was later modified in a poster issued by the Zionist Federation, reversing the relation between death and renewal. The poster shows a tall tree with an abundance of green leaves, and only one dead branch is sticking out on its side. The statement inscribed below this transformed image reinforces its message: "Branches of our people are chopped down and fall off, but the tree is alive and well. Give your hand to our national renewal. Be a member of the Zionist Federation."

For the Zionist settlers, trees were more than a visual or a literary metaphor. The act of planting a tree was seen as a necessary ritual of connecting to the land. "The tree is the lifeline of nature, of mother-earth . . . ," writes a Zionist forester. "Those who have never planted a tree cannot feel the earth, and therefore will never know what homeland means."[2] The Jewish National Fund [JNF], the Zionist agency entrusted with the mission of purchasing land and promoting the Jewish settlement of Palestine, regarded tree planting as a sacred activity that would lead to the redemption of the land" *[ge'ulat ha-aretz].*[3] Hebrew educational institutions supported the JNF agenda and socialized children to give weekly donations to the JNF blue box, teaching them (in the words of a famous Hebrew song) that every penny counts and contributes to the redemption of the land. The annual festival of *Tu B'Shvat* provided an excellent temporal locus for teaching about trees and the JNF's mission of afforestation.[4] Tree planting emerges as a central patriotic ritual of this holiday in the secular national Hebrew culture.

In many frontier cultures, the colonization of wilderness implies deforestation. But for the Zionist settlers, planting trees was a means of reintroducing nature—like the Hebrew nation—into its native landscape. Zionist memory portrayed the land as covered with forests during antiquity and as turned into a "wasteland" [she-mama] or a "desert" [midbar] during centuries of Jewish exile. The "redemption of the land" was thus seen by the Jews who returned to the land of their forefathers as its liberation from a state of desolation.[5] Afforestation became an important colonizing tool supporting Zionist memory as well as Zionist ideology of developing the land and settling in it.[6]

Cultural symbolism and practical considerations contributed also to the emergence of another important function of forests as living memorials for the dead. The naming of a forest after an individual person or a group clearly draws on the importance of memory and the commemoration of the dead in Jewish tradition.[7] But this custom is also an effective tool for promoting JNF's fundraising campaign for its afforestation efforts. As monuments, the forests establish a symbolic continuity between the past and the future and accentuate the particular national bent of Zionist collective memory.[8] Named after major historical figures,[9] forests have become landmarks of Zionist historiography. Moreover, the establishment of forests as living memorials for soldiers who died during Israel's wars, or for communities of Jews who perished in the Holocaust, demonstrates the tendency to represent their deaths within the Zionist master commemorative narrative, highlighting their contribution to national renewal.[10]

This interpretive framework is visually displayed in the poster announcing the establishment of the "Forest of Martyred Children" who died during the Holocaust where the growing trees symbolically replace the fading images of the dead children. This symbolism was even more explicitly articulated to the Israeli children who participated in the tree-planting ceremony for the "Forest of Martyred Children." The representative of the JNF's teachers association is quoted as having told them: "Remember, children, that you do not plant trees, but people."[11] The depiction of an Israeli settlement in the background serves to tie the forest-memorial to the meaning of the forest as an icon of national survival. The forest thus has a double redemptive meaning: it redeems the memory of the dead from the pitfall of oblivion, and it redeems the land from the afflictions it suffered during centuries of Jewish exile.

The prototypical Zionist pioneering narrative focuses on the determined Zionist settler to highlight his struggle to colonize land and nature against all odds. The literature describing the settlement efforts shows how the Jewish settler overcomes the painful history of exile, the great desolation of the land of the forefathers, and the Arabs' hostility toward the Jews. The portrayal of the individual settler's trials and triumphs thus stand for the success of the nation as a whole; the story of a particular settlement serves as a microcosm representing the larger Jewish settlement in Palestine—i.e., the *yishuv*.[12] This literature carried the burden of contributing to national goals by providing valid documentation of nation-building efforts, a mission that often came at the expense of its literary value.[13]

Yet one of the most popular "settlement novels" of the Zionist pioneering period, Eliezer Smolly's *The Founders [Anshei be-Reishit]*, published in 1933,[14] offers a somewhat different representation of the settlement process. The story follows the challenges of a Jewish guard who settles in a forest which he is hired to protect. The story ends when a fire set by Arabs causes a massive destruction of the forests and the guard's farm. The fire thus appears to have undermined the guard's official mission to protect the trees and his hard-won achievements as a seeder. In 1963, A. B. Yehoshua wrote a novella entitled *Facing the Forests [Mul ha-Ye'arot]*[15] which revolves around a similar theme: a Jew, who is assigned the job of a guard of a large national forest, fails in his mission when the forest is set on fire by an Arab and is destroyed.

The Founders enjoyed vast popularity among the Hebrew youth and was well received by critics as an important achievement. The novel became an immediate "classic." Smolly was awarded literary prizes for his work, including the most prestigious Israel Prize for Literature.[16] *Facing the Forests* was among the works that established Yehoshua's status as an outstanding representative of a new generation of Hebrew writers whose literary talents were praised by such harsh critics of contemporary Israeli literature as Baruch Kurtzweil.[17] Although the novella also triggered negative reviews for political as well as literary issues,[18] it has continued to attract literary attention, and Yehoshua, who was recently awarded the Israel Prize for Literature, is now one of Israel's best known writers.

In light of the symbolism of the forests, the status of these works within the Israeli literary canon raises the inevitable questions: How are we to understand the literary focus on the deliberate destruction of national forests? How are we to interpret the meaning of burning trees in a culture that glorifies tree planting and celebrates their growth as a testimony of national redemption?

Jewish Guards Facing National Forests

The two works on which this essay focuses, *The Founders* and *Facing the Forests*, were written thirty years apart, yet the thematic resemblance between them is remarkable.[19] Both focus on the Jewish guards' experiences in national forests located far from any Jewish settlement. For both protagonists, this assignment follows a period of wandering and is designed to provide them with a much-needed opportunity to redirect their lives. The guards' insular lives among the trees is interrupted by brief encounters with Jewish visitors and superficial ties with local Arabs. Both works end with subversive acts by Arabs who see themselves entitled to the land now owned by the Jews and therefore set the forests on fire as an act of revenge.

In spite of the unusual thematic affinity between these two works, the differences between them supersede and indeed subvert this resemblance. Smolly's novel is inspired by the historical figure of Alexander Zeid, one of the founders of the prestigious HaShomer organization, who settled with his family as the guard of the JNF's forests in Sheik Abreik in 1926.[20] Smolly recreated the Zeid family story as a fictional narrative, yet his novel clearly draws on the historical reality of the times and is imbued with the views and values of the socialist-Zionist settlers of the Second *Aliyah*. Smolly writes in the preface to his novel that it developed from stories he had told his students as a school teacher and he explicitly acknowledges his didactic motivation in composing this work.[21] In contrast, Yehoshua's story is a highly allegorical and provocative text written for adult readers, and its focus on a controversial political issue was in many respects ahead of Israeli public discourse at the time.

The guards clearly play a pivotal role in the two works discussed here, and their characters are critical for understanding the meaning of their forest experience.[22] In spite of the structural similarity in their situation—the entrance to the forest symbolizes the hopes for a turning point in their lives—the guards differ in their approach to this change. Hermoni, Smolly's protagonist, is internally motivated to make a fundamental change in his life. He is a veteran guard who had roamed the country for twenty-five years doing his work, "being constantly on the move from place to place, and so his life seemed almost to have slipped by without this dream having been fulfilled"(7). Hermoni is portrayed as the prototypical embodiment of *ha-shomer*, the guard of the Second *Aliyah*: highly individualistic, ideologically committed, strong-willed, courageous, and hard-working.

In contrast, Yehoshua's protagonist is portrayed as a weak, unstable, passive person, who consistently shrinks from undertaking any responsibility—a home, a family, or a job—and neglects his studies. A counter-image of the Second *Aliyah* guard, he lacks commitment, willpower, morals, and even passion. The student accepts the position of a guard thoughtlessly, if not reluctantly. His friends are the ones who find out about this position and who determine what research topic he should pursue. Yehoshua refers to the student's role in the forest as *tzofei* [observer], thus emphasizing his passive character. Yet the use of the term *tzofei* (which also implies a prophet) is highly ironic: the student who wears thick glasses is marked by his blurred vision, both literally and figuratively. Yehoshua also accentuates the sense of alienation and aimlessness that pervades his protagonist's life by leaving him and the other characters nameless. The use of generic references in *Facing the Forests* stands in marked contrast to the names chosen by Smolly for the Hermoni family, which express the major precepts of Socialist Zionism: connection to land [*Hermoni*], hope [*Tikva*], labor [*Avoda*], and strength and courage [*Eitan* and *Oz*].

Upon reaching their new posts, both men are overcome by surprise at the sight of the large forested areas. "Hermoni, who had grown up in the forests of Russia, felt a thrill run through him—in the twenty-five years of wandering through this country, he had

193

never seen a forest like it . . . " (22). Similarly, when the student's friends tell him of the availability of a position as a fire watcher, he responds: "Forests . . . What forests? Since when do we have forests in this country?" (204). But when he reaches the site, he is surprised to discover five hills covered with pine trees, and this view "strikes him with awe" (208).

This is how the narrator of *The Founders* describes the forest: "It was an ancient forest of oaks, carobs, and birches, with glades of lush, green grass—perfect for grazing sheep and cattle" (8); "[it was] a forest of sturdy, upright oaks, spreading their thick, leafy boughs, and stretching away without, numbers on all sides. Old, red carob trees abounded, laden with fruit, and on the floor of the forest grew bracken and bushes of all sorts, so profusely that they often barred their paths" (22). Hermoni is moved by the unexpected lushness of the site where he plans to settle down and build a farm. For an Eastern European pioneer like him, the sight of a forest is a moving reminder of the landscape he left behind, even if it is different in its growth and its scope.[23] Although Smolly's description of an indigenous forest is grounded in the historical reality of the Sheik Abreik region, it is possible that the description of the lushness of the forest is also influenced by his own vivid images of the Eastern European forests of his childhood.[24] Yet the antiquity and the lushness of the forest described in *The Founders* inevitably introduces tension within the vision of settlement. Given that the Zionist mission was commonly conceived as "making the desert bloom," what is Smolly's vision of settlement within the context of an old forest? The resolution of this tension is articulated by Hermoni: "This is the kind of life we'll make for ourselves. . . . We'll turn these barren valleys into gardens of Eden. They'll be covered with corn and barley, oats and hay, and we'll plant vineyards and orchards on the hillsides in place of these thorns and thistles" (20). At another point he tells his family: "If the soil in these hills is good enough to grow such fine forest trees, it will be good for fruit trees too. We'll plant figs and vines here in the winter, and turn these barren hills into a Garden of Eden" (Heb. 17, modified trans.). Despite his excitement over the lushness of the forest, Hermoni redefines the terrain within the framework of his vision as "barren valleys" [*amakim shomemim*] and "barren hills" [*geva'ot kerhot*]. It thus appears that the conceptual opposition between wilderness and settlement reshapes the natural landscape according to these socially constructed categories. As a symbolic landscape, the forest is now defined not only as wilderness but also as a desert. This view is later affirmed by other Jewish settlers who visit the Hermoni family.[25]

It is interesting to note that, within the framework of his vision, even when Hermoni acknowledges the existence of trees within the immediate landscape, he redefines them as "barren" [atzei serak], ignoring the existence of fruit trees such as carobs and figs in the ancient forest. Indeed, the ambiguous position of the fig tree in this novel demonstrates the power of cultural categories in creating symbolic landscapes. Even though the family gathers the delicious fruit and eats it with pleasure (20), Hermoni includes the fig among the trees he plans to plant in his future Garden of Eden, as if they did not already exist in that environment. Within this framework, the farm and the forest stand in opposition to each other as the embodiment of Culture and Nature, and the settlement process implies the imposition of social boundaries and a new social order on the world of nature.[26] This point is further illustrated by the borrowing of the first word in the biblical story of Creation [be-reshit; i.e., "in the beginning"] in the Hebrew title of the novel (Anshei be-Reishit). The act of establishing a single settlement in the Land of Israel thus mirrors God's act of creating the world. In this instance, however, the people take charge of their own fate, assuming the right and the responsibility to create order out of chaos and become the guardians of this new order.[27]

Natural Bonds, National Alliances: Jews, Arabs, and the Forests

In both *The Founders* and *Facing the Forests,* the relations between the Jewish guard and the forest are subject to changes when other elements are introduced into the story. Although Smolly portrays the settlement as a struggle against the wilderness in which it is being built, their relation is modified when others enter the scene: the forest and the farm are then grouped together as "home terri-

195

tory" while others are portrayed as outsiders and potential or real invaders. Indeed, as the chapter headings indicate, the progress of the settlement process is constructed by the successive difficulties that the Hermoni family encounters in the forest. The novel is thus punctuated by descriptions of recurrent invasions of the farm and the forest, alternating between the forces of nature (thunderstorm, wild animals, insects, etc.) and the Arabs.

During the first phases of settlement, the Arabs are divided into two groups. The more favorable one consists of the local shepherds with whom Hermoni develops friendly relationships, letting them use the spring water and the grazing land for free. The other group was primarily perceived as hostile to Hermoni and the forest—Abu Naomi, a Syrian Arab who took control of the forest before Hermoni's arrival and who levied taxes from others for its use, and the charcoal burners, whom Hermoni expels because they carelessly and greedily destroy the forest trees. Although the terms "Arab" and "Bedouin" are sometimes used interchangeably, the latter appears to have more favorable connotations and is more closely associated with the shepherds. Hermoni feels an affinity with the Bedouin, and they display admiration for him and appreciate his role as the protector of nature. In contrast, the coal burners are identified as Arab farmers who were brought to the forest from afar and have no qualms about destroying it.

To understand Hermoni's dual perception of the Arabs along these lines, it is important to point out how his identity is portrayed in the novel. Born and reared in Russia as a typical exilic Jewish child,[28] he appears a transformed person following his twenty-five years of experience in Palestine. Since the beginning of the narrative, Hermoni relates to himself as a "Jewish Bedouin," and this definition is reaffirmed by his friends and by the narrator. Hermoni clearly feels more comfortable in nature and among the Arab shepherds than with Jewish city-dwellers or bureaucrats, and his own children appear to be more knowledgeable about Arab than Jewish customs. . . .

Hermoni's initial position toward the Bedouin he encounters in the forest thus stems from his own identification with them. "It may be difficult for you to understand," he explains to his friend Galili, "but I couldn't part from my horse and my rifle, from a life of danger, to settle down as a property owner. Here I can combine the two. . . . Perhaps that forest will tie me down at last, me, the eternal Bedouin" (59, modified trans./Heb. 51). He also chooses to adopt the Arabic place name and call his farm *Ein Ro'im*; namely, the Shepherds' Spring. Indeed, in portraying *shomer* [guard] as a "Jewish Bedouin" Eliezer Smolly reflects a predominant view of that period that saw the Bedouin as an available local model of the native for the Zionist settlers.[29]

As the settlement continues to develop, tensions mount among the shepherds about the use of the land for cattle. Moreover, with the rise of the national conflict throughout the country, the position of the shepherds vis-à-vis the farm further shifts toward other Arabs, who are hostile to the Jewish settlement. At the end, the novel constructs the Jews and the forest as one group and portrays all the Arabs as their common enemy. Abu Naomi and the other Arabs, on the other hand, are portrayed from the beginning as the enemy who attempt to bring destruction to both the forest and the farm. When Hermoni first enters the forest, he is shocked to see "branches [that] were cut off trees leaving scars, heaps of black ash, mutilation of bushes and twigs." Pained by the sight of the injured trees, Hermoni remarks: "That is how our neighbors care for the treasure in their midst! . . . that's how they respect the few trees left in the country!" (23). As the protector of trees, the guard thus positions himself against the Arabs. The forest becomes his home territory, while the destructive Arabs are portrayed as outsiders and invaders who finally destroy it. The positioning of the Arabs against both the forests and the Jews receives its most dramatic expression in the fire that threatens the survival of both.

The fire destroys both the forest and the farm. The destruction is the final proof of the natural alliance between the ancient forest and the Zionist settlers: the survival of the trees, the Jewish guard, and the Zionist settlement are thus interlinked as they face the Arabs who wished to obliterate them all.

In *Facing the Forests*, the Jewish guard's psychological and physical distance from the forest is paralleled by an initial attitude of indifference toward the Arab worker whose tongue was cut off. ("The Arab turned out to be old and mute. His tongue was cut out during the war. By one of them or one of us? Does it matter?" [21]). In

197

contrast to the guard's aloof position vis-a-vis the forest, the Arab man and his daughter are described as an integral part of the environment in which they live. When they enter the forest, the guard can no longer distinguish them among the trees; and they suddenly emerge out of the forest as if they were born out of its womb (219). Moreover, their description as dirty, smelly, and with no power of speech portrays them as animal-like, thus part of the world of nature. Whereas *The Founders* portrays the Jewish guard and the forest within one and the same category and the Arabs as confronting both, *Facing the Forests* inverts this classification: the forest and the Arabs are seen as part of nature, and the Jewish guard remains the civilized outsider to their world. Yet, as is the case with the earlier novel, the initial alliance within the triad of the forest, the Jewish guard, and the Arabs is bound to transform as the story unfolds.

The guard's growing intimacy with his immediate environment appears to suggest a linear progression with the possibility of a forest fire, and an intense curiosity about the ruins of an Arab village within the forest begins to take control of the student's experience and redirect the plot. . . .

When the student learns about an Arab village that used to be on that site, his curiosity leads him to an active search for its remains. In sharp contrast to the passivity that characterized his earlier attitude toward his formal studies, he now becomes utterly absorbed in this "research project" and sees its outcome—a map of the entire forest region—as his true legacy for the future. The new information about the destroyed Arab village also provokes his interest in communicating with the mute Arab and serves as a turning point in their relations. . . .

The initial alliance between the forest and the Arab on the one hand and the Jewish guard on the other hand changes as a new alliance is formed between the Jewish guard and the Arab against the forest. "Together, in silence, they return to the forest, their empire, theirs alone" (227). The Arab and his girl now cling to him desperately until gradually the three appear "like a family" (230). The student awaits the fire with growing anticipation and hope, and he smilingly welcomes the first "long, graceful flame.". . .

The appearance of an alliance between the Jewish guard and the Arab is short-lived. Although the Arab carries out their shared

vision, the student prefers to see himself, not as an active participant, but a spectator only, referring to the fire as a "midnight show"
(230). The morning after, when the police investigation leads to
the suspicion of arson, and after they question him for several
hours, the student breaks down and points out the Arab as the suspect. The police arrest the Arab and take him away, and returns
the student, whose time in the forest is up, back to the city (235).
The student who betrayed the forest now betrays the Arab and the
tacit understanding between them prior to the Arab's action.

The two literary works thus present a fundamental difference in
the guards' attitude toward the forests, the Arabs, and the fire.
Whereas Hermoni relates to the fire as an instrument of evil that
ruins his dream, the student feels that the fire was the fulfillment of
a dream that is now "turning from a vision into a fact" (231).
Whereas Hermoni is devastated by the sight of destruction, the student reacts with indifference. His detachment from this scene of
death is further accentuated by its contrast to the reaction of the
old man in charge of the forests, who seems to be "near collapse
with fury and pain" (233). The guard's casual response to the hurt-
ing old man—observing that the trees must be insured and therefore the fire will not affect the old man's budget—is highly
inappropriate within the context of Zionist ideology. It deliberately
ignores the significance of the forests as a national icon that would
render the fire a national disaster far exceeding its financial cost.

Forests, Monuments,
and National Redemption

Given the Hebrew culture's glorification of the tree as a symbol of
national renewal, how are we to interpret the destruction of forests
as a literary theme? A further examination of the role of the forest
as a site of national memory may help shed light on this issue and
illuminate the changing representation of the forest in these two
literary works.

The difference in the description of the forests in the two works
examined here is highly significant. Whereas Smolly describes a
forest of ancient trees that the JNF acquired, Yehoshua alludes to

new pine forests it planted. The two forests therefore serve as two different national monuments: The ancient forest of *The Founders* functions as a symbolic bridge between antiquity and the present. By settling in the forest Hermoni literally reconnects with the roots of the ancient Jewish past and his home becomes a symbolic representation of the Zionist revival. This symbolism is affirmed by the use of a common literary trope—the unearthing of relics of an ancient settlement while in the process of building a Zionist settlement.[30] The Hermoni family discovers a large piece of marble with engravings that are without doubt Jewish: a menorah, a shofar, grapes, and pomegranates (17). The forest thus reveals a monument of historical continuity of Jewish settlement of Palestine.

Interestingly enough, the settlement process also leads to the discovery of other relics from different pasts associated with that land. The comparison between these various monuments of the past helps construct the meaning of the forest as a national icon. While preparing a new field, Hermoni discovers a "wonderful treasure of ancient Arab manure" (57/Heb. 50, modified trans.). In contrast to the refined ruins of the ancient Jewish civilization, then, the Arab "antiquities" are part of nature and a degraded material at that. Hermoni nonetheless considers this finding of great value and he immediately puts it to use as a fertilizer for his fields. When a Christian relic is found—an ancient sword with a cross on it which they believe to have belonged to the crusaders—Hermoni gives it to the children for play (69). Unlike the Jewish stones, it appears to have no sentimental or sacred value, and, unlike the manure, it has no functional value for the farm. The last treasure buried in the soil is a can full of golden coins which Hermoni uses to pay for his house. His friends justify this use by pointing out that this use demonstrates poetic justice: "The people to whom those coins belonged destroyed the country, and it's only right that you should help to rebuild it with the same money" (119). The original Hebrew text is far more telling than this English translation allows: *"shalom yeshalem ha-mavir et ha-be'era"* (Heb. 101), which literally means that the one who sets a fire will have to pay for the damage. Though it appears in this context as a proverbial statement, it foreshadows the fate of Hermoni's house, which is later destroyed by the fire, and the hope for revenge.

The portrayal of the forest as a site of national memories in *The Founders* draws on the historical reality of using national tensions between the Jews and the Arabs, but Smolly clearly portrays it from the Zionist settlers' perspective. Smolly elaborates the scope of the Arabs' attack on Zeid's farm in 1929 to further dramatize Hermoni's determination to begin from the beginning.[31] He depicts the Arabs' disregard for the trees as a means of foreshadowing their disregard for Jewish lives.[32] Coinciding with the killing of Jews by Arabs in Jerusalem and Hebron, the attack on the farm and the forest highlights the connecting tissue between the forest, the local settlement *(Ein Ro'im),* and the larger Settlement [the *yishuv*]. *The Founders* thus constructs the burned forest as a monument of the destructiveness of the Arabs, who victimize the land in order to undermine the Jewish settlement. In this respect, the novel extends the memory of the burned forest beyond the scope of the event, identifying it with other attempts to destroy the Jews that likewise failed.[33] While the Jews are portrayed as directing their energies toward protecting the past and constructing the future, the Arabs are associated with invasion, vandalism, and death, causing the destruction of both the ancient forest and of the new Zionist settlement.

For Hermoni, whose earlier vision was to create his "Garden of Eden" in the ancient forest, the fire means the destruction of this budding dream. The novel, however, introduces a deliberate inversion of the biblical story on the Garden of Eden: unlike the first family who were expelled from the Garden, the first Zionist family who settled in the forest remained in its place in spite of the Arabs' attempts to expel them. Their heroism stems from their attachment to the place, and serves as proof of the bond between the Jew and the land. Conversely, the desertion of a settlement might have appeared subversive to the Zionist pioneering narrative, since it indicates the weakening of one's ideological commitment and readiness for patriotic sacrifice.[34] Indeed, the very conclusion of *The Founders* redefines the significance of the Arabs' act by establishing the fire as a limited setback within a continuing historical process of Jewish resettlement. . . .

Faced with the burned forest and his burned crops, the Jewish settler finds solace in the possibility of planting new trees and plowing new fields. As the title of the novel indicates, Smolly puts the

Zionist settler at the center of his work's universe. The settler is both the subject and the object of the settlement process; he re-shapes his own identity as he revives his nation and its roots in the land. Because he, and not the forest, is at the center of the settle-ment process, the destruction of the forest does not imply a dead end. The settler has the power to "begin from the beginning" and ultimately renew both the forest and the nation.

Clearly, Eliezer Smolly—a committed Zionist writer and teacher—wanted to end the novel with a dramatic display of the settler's unshaken commitment to the settlement ideal, for the ben-efit of his students and other Hebrew youth. Drawing on the trope of the "first furrow" of the pioneering period, and the biblical allu-sions to a new beginning, the novel thus ends with the message of renewal. Hermoni's last words become his legacy to his son Eitan and the young readers of this novel: Never give up the struggle in the face of hardships, and when you suffer a setback, go back to the beginning, and start over. . . .

The comparative analysis of *The Founders* and *Facing the Forests* re-veals fundamental changes in the literary representation of the re-lations between settlement and nature, the past and the future, Palestinian Arabs and Jews. Written in the early 1930s, *The Founders* constructs these relations according to the national ideology that was predominant during the early pioneering period. *Facing the Forests* challenges these conceptions by presenting a more complex and ambiguous reality of the post-Independence era. Marking an emergent trend in Israeli literature in the 1960s, it is one of the early literary works that express the younger generation's reluctance or lack of ability to shape its life according to the idealistic concerns of the founders' generation or to accept them as given.[35] In *Facing the Forests*, Yehoshua deliberately creates symbolic inversions of a typ-ical pioneering narrative. Whereas *The Founders* presents the ideol-ogy of the early settlement period of Israeli society, with its belief that individual and collective redemption go hand in hand, *Facing the Forests* challenges this premise. In fact, as the story develops, it ap-pears that the alienated guard may find his personal redemption in supporting the cause of the Arab village and the liberation of its memory. If this were the case, one could have argued that Yehoshua

202

created an anti-Zionist narrative that demonstrates the tension between individual and collective redemption. But Yehoshua does not push this idea to its extreme by letting his protagonist develop a genuine commitment to the Palestinian cause. In fact, the first indications of the student's secret desire for a fire in the forest are revealed before he learns about the ruined Arab village. References to "lunatic hope" (the Arab's; 227), a mind "that is slipping, becoming crazed" (the guard's; 228/Heb. 113, modified trans.), associate a growing state of mental imbalance with the flames that finally burst out "as if in madness" (231, modified trans./Heb. 118). The guard's interest in the fire, then, does not stem from the awakening of a dormant political conscience. Rather, he uses the political cause as a way of allowing room for his destructive urge and justifying his encouragement of the Arab. Consequently, his immediate euphoric response to the fire dissipates the following day, as does his short-lived support of the Arab.[36]

The conclusion of the story reveals that the forest experience fails to produce an inherent transformation within the guard and the destruction of the forest does not bring about a sense of fulfillment. Marked by his blurred vision and feeble character, the student proceeds through a complex act of multiple betrayals on both individual and collective levels. He betrays his "true friends" by sleeping with their wives, his responsibilities as a guard, the ideology that elevates forests as a cherished national treasure, and the entire Jewish people whose donations support the afforestation projects. At the end, he also betrays what could have been a personal search for redemption, as well as the Arab who carried out his own fantasy of seeing the forest burning. Unlike Hermoni, he is portrayed as a passive and self-destructive person who suffers from lack of moral integrity. Unlike the admired settler of the Second *Aliyah* who remains loyal to his cause, the pathetic guard of later years invokes neither respect nor sympathy on the part of the reader. . . .

Whereas the potentially circular ending of *The Founders* is subordinated to the linear thrust of the Zionist master narrative, *Facing the Forests* ends in a circular motion, locked within the constraints of the present. The linear temporal ordering of the plot is thus subverted by a full return to an aimless circularity.[37] The story's resistance to closure is clearly manifested by its conclusion with an open question. When the student appears at their doorsteps, his former friends greet him dismissively: "What it is now?" *[nu, ma yesh?]* (Heb. 122/236, modified trans.). This rhetorical question leaves the reader with no satisfactory account for the student's course of action or grounds to believe that the future holds the promise of resolution.

The passive and alienated Jewish guard never achieves a personal redemption, but the Arab emerges as the doer whose eyes reveal a true sense of fulfillment. We suspect that the Arab, though imprisoned, has achieved his personal liberation through his act of revenge. But Yehoshua does not allow the Arab to have an independent voice or presence beyond his relation to the Jewish guard, and so his inner experience remains outside of the scope of this work. Contrary to the view that Yehoshua provides the Arab a central role in the story, it appears that his portrayal is rather limited and remains subservient to that of the guard and the issue of his relation to the forest.[38] Indeed, Yehoshua acknowledges that he introduced the figure of the Arab later because he thought that it is more credible than the depiction of a forest fire as a result of arson by a Jewish guard.[39]

In spite of the limited representation of the Arab's voice, *Facing the Forests* raises poignant issues that display the tensions underlying the relations of Israeli Jews and Palestinians who live in the same land but subscribe to competing memories and experiences. In fact, Yehoshua chose to highlight this message of the story when he used a quote from it as an epigraph for his polemic writing on the conflicting national claims to the land by the Palestinians and the Jews.[40] Thus, although he does not present the Palestinians' experience from their perspective, he nonetheless focuses on the suppression of their alternative memory and its impact on Israeli culture.[41] *Facing the Forests* therefore constructs the destruction of the Zionist monument as an act of liberation for the Arab ruins. "There, out of the smoke and haze, the mined village appears before his eyes, born anew in its basic outlines . . ." (233). The rebirth of the Arab village, however, remains constrained within the domain of symbolic representations. The village appears as "an abstract drawing, as all things past and buried." It is not the village that is brought back to life, but its memory, thus correcting the guard's ignorant comment earlier in the story about the lack of a local past.

Yehoshua thus examines the issues of memory and national redemption that are at the core of Zionist ideology, but deliberately shakes up the Zionist construction of historical progression from exile and destruction to national revival and construction. The association of the theme of national liberation with the Arab village provides an obvious example for this deliberate inversion of historical processes as constructed in Zionist memory. Moreover, this inversion is already suggested prior to the outbreak of the fire, when the guard discovers "small tins filled with kerosene" [*kupsao'ot pah ketanot*] (Heb. 111/224) from which the Arab ultimately produces "a great light" (231). These allusions to the Hanukkah miracle of oil also disclose the symbolic inversion that *Facing the Forests* creates: the oil used to light the ancient temple in celebration of Jewish national redemption is now used by an Arab to liberate the ruins of his village and destroy the forest, the "living temple" that represents Jewish national redemption. Furthermore, as a result of the fire, an Israeli tree is transformed into a traditional Jewish martyr "wrapped in prayer . . . going through its hour of judgment and surrendering its spirit" (231), and the Zionist forest is reduced to "smoking embers" [*udim ashenim*] (Heb. 119/232), a term often associated with Holocaust survivors. Thus, whereas the Zionist narrative depicts the period of exile and the Holocaust as leading to the foundation of the State, *Facing the Forests* associates contemporary Israeli symbols with exilic Jewish history, unsettling the historical sequence that Zionism constructed.[42] The same act that resulted in the display of the ruins that become a monument of a once thriving Arab village also leads to the creation of new ruins (the burned trees) that serve as a monument of the Zionist forest.[43] Yehoshua thus subverts the Zionist narrative that moves from destruction to construction by delineating a process that leads from one act of destruction to the next.[44] . . . The student's inner state of entrapment and aimless wandering becomes a mirror of the futility of a cycle of wars that continue to produce monuments of destroyed pasts. Within the broader scheme of meanings of *Facing the Forests*, the forest clearly continues to function as a national icon, yet its complex representation in this story reflects, and even predicts, the growing burden of the Israeli-Palestinian conflict that would further escalate during the post-1967 era.

Trees, Forests, and the
Israeli-Palestinian Conflict

The intertextual analysis of *The Founders* and *Facing the Forest* offers an interesting opportunity to explore the meaning of the forests as a national symbol mediating between nature and culture, past and future, memory and oblivion. Yet history does not allow us to contain this exploration within the domain of literary analysis. Themes that these literary words explore are part of a volatile political reality of the Israeli-Palestinian conflict, and the literary imagery draws upon and feeds into this reality. That a national conflict is played out in this arena highlights the role of trees and forests as bearers of national memories, symbols of collective identities, and markers of ownership over a contested land.

Uprooting trees and burning forests have assumed the meaning of aggressive acts of war within the Israeli-Palestinian conflict. Such acts took place during the Yishuv period, most notably during the Arab revolt of 1936–39.[45] The setting of forests on fire and the public response to it seemed to evoke Smolly's literary depiction in *The Founders*. This affinity is manifested in the rhetoric used in reference to the Balfour Forest. While the planting of this forest was celebrated by Yosef Weitz of the JNF as "the work of Creation" (drawing on the same biblical concept, *be-reishit*, that Smolly used in his title),[46] the communication regarding the loss of trees due to a fire in 1936 adopted mourning symbols usually preserved for human death, echoing Hermoni's view that "trees are like human beings" (Heb. 48): a picture of the burned trees of the Balfour Forest was followed by an announcement entitled *Yizkor*, the name of the traditional Jewish prayer for the dead; the announcement was printed within a black frame, as is the custom in the case of a person's death. The personification of the burned trees evokes traditional images of Jewish martyrs burned by fire for their faith, and the collective commemoration of the trees is similar in style to the commemoration of patriotic death in the contemporary Hebrew culture.[47]

During the 1980s and early 1990s, forests and orchards emerged again as a major domain of conflict between Israelis and Palestinians, stirring up deep emotions on both sides. Tree planting was used by Israel and by the Jewish settlers as a visible marker of ownership over land as well as by Palestinians who wished to prevent further confiscation of lands by Israeli authorities. Shaul Ephraim Cohen, who studied planting patterns in the Jerusalem periphery, made the following observation:

> Where the agriculture of the [Palestinian] village ended, it was met by young pines planted by the JNF. . . . A short distance from the last furrow of plowed dirt or row of olive trees, and often immediately adjacent to or even intermingled with them, were the first trees of a future forest. Further examination revealed an additional pattern. Where the JNF trees were somewhat recently planted, or other forms of Israeli presence had been initiated or expanded, there were signs of new or renewed use by the Palestinians—such as plowed but not yet planted fields, new saplings of olive and other fruits, or fencing and land reclamation.[48]

The strategy of tree planting triggered the counter-response of destruction of trees. The methods in this "tree-war" ranged from uprooting new saplings and cutting down older trees[49] to setting forests and fields on fire. In the summers of 1988 and 1989, the use of arson was particularly heavy, as it was embraced by the Intifada leadership and encouraged through the use of popular media.[50] The JNF referred to the proliferation of arson cases in its forests as "the Intifada against trees," and declared a new campaign entitled "A Tree for a Tree" [*Eitz taḥat eitz*], borrowing from the biblical phrase of "an eye for an eye." The campaign called for the replacement of a million burned trees by planting three million saplings, and the JNF encouraged the public to participate in the tree planting ritual of *Tu B'Shvat* 1989 to promote this afforestation project.[51]

The fires, as well as the JNF planting campaign, drew public attention to the national significance of forests. A newspaper article based on interviews with forest guards highlighted their devotion to their work and their awareness of its patriotic dimension, since "the forests are at the forefront of an historical struggle over land ownership."[52] Perhaps the largest and most damaging fire triggered by arson occurred in the Carmel forests in September 1989, drawing hundreds of volunteers to fight it and large crowds of visitors who came to see the destroyed forest.[53] Israelis responded to those arson cases that were classified as "nationalistically motivated" with tremendous anger and moral outrage, and there were reports about avenging fire by fire.[54]

The reactions to the fire that severely damaged the Carmel forests in 1989 raised themes that had appeared in Smolly's and Yehoshua's literary works, and seem to continue their dialogue about the symbolic meaning of burning forests. Consider, for example, two opposing views that were published side by side in the same Israeli newspaper:

> The horrible arson of the largest nature-reserve in Israel not only provides another proof for the PLO's double-talk and its lack of moderation, but also an example of a hatred toward the land [displayed] by the arsonists and their supporters. The irreversible destruction of the Carmel is not a protest against a foreign ruler and is not a violent objection to an occupier's luxurious civilization, but is rather a manifestation of a desire for destructiveness for its own sake. The readiness to demolish a unique landscape such as this bluntly shatters the myth that the Arabs belong to the place and we are like new Crusaders.[55]

While this writer interprets the Palestinians' fire as a display of their disregard for the country and its nature, and denies the possibility of political motivation, the other writer criticizes Israelis for "overreacting" to the burning forests when Palestinians suffer from injuries and deaths as a result of Israeli occupation:

> This week newspapers cried over the fires in the Carmel forests in terms preserved for the worst national disasters. . . . In spite of the sorrow and the rage over the loss of a piece of forest, it should be noted that these responses reflect a certain moral numbness. . . . One ought to remember that from September 1 to the 19th, nineteen persons were killed in the territories, including six children. One ought to remember that scores of people have been injured. One ought to remember that for the parents of wounded children, their families, and their people, crushed bodies outweigh all the forests in the world. And even if we believe that in spite of everything trees deserve immunity, we stand on shaky grounds. Since the beginning of the Intifada, the army uprooted tens of thousands of trees. These were not barren, but were fruit-bearing trees. Hundreds of dunams were poisoned by settlers as punitive actions [against the Palestinians]. And for the landscape, it makes no difference whether a tree is burned by fire or uprooted by a tractor's arm.[56]

The interplay of history, literature, and politics around the issue of the fires is manifest in other responses as well. Alexander Zeid's experience of witnessing his crops set on fire by Arabs in 1929— the climax of Smolly's novel—is quoted by a newspaper article as an example of the Arabs' recurrent use of fire as a political weapon.[57] Another article, borrowing Yehoshua's title "Facing the Forests," addressed the ways in which historical reality and literature intersect in the Israeli-Palestinian conflict. After describing the public response and her own grief over the loss of trees and animals in the Carmel fire, the writer adds:

> Therefore, I was shocked when a wrinkled old man from the [Palestinian] village of Batir showed to a television crew olive trees that had been cut down, and could not comprehend why anyone would conspire against his beautiful old trees that were cut down by the army to prevent their use as a cover by those who throw stones. . . . It appears that here, too, literature preceded reality. I felt as if I lived in a nightmare; that here, in front of my eyes, A. B. Yehoshua's story, *Facing the Forests*, is being recreated. No longer a nightmarish fictitious story but a reality. And I wondered, what did the writer, who lives on Mount Carmel, think and feel when the forests were burning.[58]

The interaction of literature and politics around the issue of arson was also brought to the limelight when an Israeli military censor charged an Israeli Palestinian writer for incitement against the State. The writer, Ednan Fa'our, published a story about cats who sacrifice their lives by spreading fires tied to their tails as a revenge against a wicked Sheik who took over their master's land. The charge of incitement to arson was later dropped by the State.[59] Reporting on this case, a known Israeli journalist pointed out the resemblance of Fa'our's story to the biblical narrative about Samson's vengeful act of setting the Philistines' fields on fire through the use of foxes (Judg. 15:4–5), and added that the censor's logic should have prohibited the inclusion of this text in an Arabic-language Bible.[60]

The "literary fires" depict a transformed landscape that changes— at least temporarily—the political reality that it symbolizes. Like the broader framework of the conflict of which they are a part, these fires replace death by death and create new monuments to represent both. *The Founders* articulates the Israeli belief in the power of renewal that was clearly most pronounced during the Yishuv period. But *Facing the Forests* reveals a greater awareness that the possibility of renewal does not obliterate the past and that the archeology of memory in the symbolic landscapes of the country represents multiple roots and multiple monuments. Thus, the memory of destruction will always be imprinted on the landscape underneath the signs of renewal, whether it points to the ruins of an Arab village, or to the scars that the forest fires have left.[61] Yet the liberation of memory in the acknowledgment of these ruins and scars may contribute to the possibility of a peaceful coexistence of Israeli Jews and Palestinians.[62]

A Tree for a Tree:
The Aggressive Nature of Planting

Shaul Cohen*

When you shall besiege a city a long time, in making war against it to take it, you shall not destroy the trees thereof by wielding an ax against them: you may eat of them, but you shall not cut them down, for is the tree of the field man that it should be besieged by you? Only trees of which you know that they are not for food may you destroy and cut them down, that you may build bulwarks against the city that makes war with you, until it falls.

(Deut. 20:19–20)

During his first and only visit to Palestine, Theodore Herzl planted a tree just outside of Jerusalem as a dual symbol. The tree represented the Jewish presence in Palestine, and also the agenda of the nascent Zionist movement, to reclaim and rebuild the land. Ironically, only a few years later Herzl's tree fell to a political ax; it was cut down, it is suspected, by a member of Jerusalem's ultra-orthodox Jewish community, which then, as now, opposed Zionism. The response of the Yishuv to that act of vandalism was also symbolic, and presaged a strategy for dealing with challenges to the symbols and constructs of the Zionist movement: where Herzl's tree fell, more than two hundred were planted in its place.

Eight decades later the trees planted by the Zionist movement, now in the form of the State of Israel, while retaining great symbolic power, convey a tangible presence in the landscape. As such, they are still the targets of vandalism, now on a nationalist background, as the territorial struggle with the Palestinians evolves. With the rash of forest arson which was a facet of the Palestinian Intifada, the Jewish National Fund (JNF) looked to local history, both ancient and more recent, and announced a program for responding to the latest challenge. Called "A Tree for a Tree," an obvious reference to An Eye for an Eye, the JNF vowed to plant ten trees for every tree that was burned. Thus, in the groves and forests of Eretz Yisrael, the more things changed, the more they remained the same.

This essay will detail the role of tree planting in shaping the political landscape of the area contested by Israelis and Palestinians, focusing on the aggressive aspects of a generally benign act. It will begin with a brief review of trees in pre-State Palestine, including their use as a political and economic tool by the Ottoman and British rulers of the area. This will be followed by a description of early planting activities in the Zionist program to gain and expand a foothold in Palestine. The national agenda of tree planting following 1948 is the next topic, followed by an examination of the current clash between Israelis and Palestinians in regard to planting activities.

The Background

As other essays in this volume have pointed out, the place of trees in Jewish and Israeli culture is rich and long. Biblical sources contribute to the powerful imagery of trees, and their multi-dimensional character. As indicated in the epigram above, trees were protected by law from wanton destruction, and their fate was metaphorically linked with that of man. The book of Isaiah states that "as the days of a tree shall be the days of my people" (65:22), and sees the co-existence of various tree species as a model for peace among human kind (41:19). Indeed the fortunes of the forests, like other natural elements in the contract between God and Israel, are linked to the fate of the nation; destruction follows transgression, regeneration comes with redemption.

Thus, while the Jewish people yearned for a land flowing with milk and honey, during the years of exile the landscape of Palestine reflected something less idyllic. Several decades before Herzl launched the Zionist reclamation project, Palestine was visited by traveling correspondent Mark Twain, whose commentary reflected the disappointment of Biblically based expectations.

> The further we went the hotter the sun got and the more rocky and bare, repulsive and dreary the landscape became. There was hardly a tree or a shrub anywhere. Even the olive and the cactus, those fast friends of a worthless soil, had almost deserted the country. No landscape exists that is more tiresome to the eye than that which bounds the approaches to Jerusalem.[1]

While the hyperbole is evident, it is true that the landscape of Palestine reflected the combination of neglect and abuse that characterized the area during the period of Ottoman rule (1516–1917). Twain's visit came shortly after a radical reformation in the Ottoman Empire, the Land Code of 1858, which was intended to stimulate rehabilitation of the landscape and an expansion of agriculture. The motivation for the 1858 Code was the desire to increase the productivity of the land, and thereby augment the coffers of the treasury through taxation. The fortunes of the Ottoman Empire, indebted as it was to European powers, was linked to the planters of trees, the harvesters of olives.

The Code delineated several classes of land tenure, distinguishing primarily various limitations and conditions for use of rural land. Inasmuch as most of the privately owned land in Palestine was in towns and cities (and relatively insignificant quantitatively), the small farmers, or *fellahin*, were growing on State lands. Such land, called *miri*, was largely indistinguishable from private property in that it could be bought and sold, left as inheritance, sub-divided, and so on. Yet, as State land (as it was later called), *miri* could be repossessed by the authorities if it was left fallow for three consecutive years. The clear intention of this provision was to keep the land productive, in terms of both agriculture and taxation. To maintain the link between the two, changes in use had to be permitted by the authorities, and the Code stated that

212

> without the permission of the official a person cannot make
> into a garden or vineyard the land he possesses by planting
> vines and different kinds of fruit trees. [If] he has done so with-
> out permission the government has the power during three
> years to make him pull them up. If three years have passed,
> and the trees have arrived at a stage to be a source of benefit to
> him, they should be left as they are . . . the freehold property of
> the owner. (I:I:XXV)

In effect, the government was allowing the acquisition of land
through the planting of trees, with the governmental veto rarely
exercised. The stage was thereby set for both legal and cultural
precedents for tree planting as a tool for establishing and legitimat-
ing a claim to the land.

Palestinian Tree Planting Gets a Push

With the inception of British rule under the League of Nations
Mandate for Palestine, tree planting in the countryside got a critical
boost. Administrators of the Mandate had a bureaucratic mentality
and were aware of the Ottoman goal of broadening the tax base
through the expansion of agriculture. They thus sponsored the cultivation of olive trees, on the one hand, and set up forest reserve
exclusion zones, on the other. This anticipated two themes that
would characterize the emerging conflict between Jews and Arabs,
namely, that tree planting could be a government supported activity which conferred land rights, while, at the same time, government tree policy was a tool to limit access to the land. The following
examples illustrate this point.

In order to encourage proper stewardship of the land, the Mandate conducted a variety of agricultural extension programs, teaching the Arab farmers of Palestine a variety of new or adapted
techniques for cultivating and harvesting their crops. As a component of this effort, olive trees were offered to villagers at a subsi-
dized price under the auspices of the "Olive Oil Committee" created
by the government. So successful was the subsidy that limits had to
be placed on the amount of trees available to individuals, and there
was constant difficulty in meeting demand. This led to rapid
expansion of the olive growing sector, and, in 1943, the Mandate

passed the Olive Control Ordinance and established the Olive Control Board to develop foreign markets for the crop and prevent a collapse of olive prices. The lesson learned by the farmers was that planting olives was a viable and preferred investment and, in keeping with the Ottoman Land Code, a practical way of strengthening or increasing land tenure.

The British observed the expansion of Palestinian tree planting with a mixture of satisfaction and alarm. The satisfaction stemmed from their desire to stimulate the economy, their alarm from the actual and potential land tenure consequences of the planting. Perceiving a need to protect open land from agricultural encroachment, the British turned to forest regulation as their primary tool. The declaration of forests reserves throughout Palestine was the tactic of choice, though such reserves were not required to contain even a single tree. The policy was explained in 1946 by the Mandate's chief forester as follows:

> The Forest Ordinance of 1926 provides for the demarcation and proclamation as a forest reserve of any waste forest land not being private property. In a forest reserve no cultivation is permitted and no grazing nor cutting except by a license issued by the Department. In practice, all local villagers are permitted to graze and cut, but not to cultivate, so that no new claims to ownership based on cultivation are allowed to arise. As a result . . . the rights of the state have been safeguarded, and the state still has the chance of afforesting and developing these uncultivated lands at some future date when circumstances permit.

It was a tactic already familiar to the Zionists, and in particular to their premier land agency, the Jewish National Fund.

Planting for a Foothold

Early in the twentieth century, tree planting became an element in the nation building program of the Zionist movement. The chief agronomist of the Zionist Federation explained the reasons for locating a grove near Kfar Dalib, on the route from Tel Aviv to Jerusalem: "I chose a place exposed to all passers-by in order that the neighbors [i.e. the local Arab population] as well as the passers-by will see that the Jews are reclaiming the land."[2] The two were obviously related, inasmuch as alerting the Arab population to the tenure of the land was an integral part of the reclamation. More broadly, tree planting served land reclamation through its use in draining swamps, stabilizing soil and dunes, providing windbreaks, and improving local hydrologic infiltration. Moreover, the skills gained through tree planting were seen as a useful precursor to more diverse agricultural occupations, and thus tree planting was considered a useful endeavor for new immigrants.

Many of the early leaders of the Yishuv brought with them from Europe an appreciation for forested lands, something which was notably lacking in Palestine. Thus the issue of beautification was also a factor in stimulating interest in afforestation, or reforestation. The two terms have slightly different connotations, which, in this case, relate to both perceptions and ideology regarding Palestine and Zionism. Afforestation is the extension, through human agency, of the forest to previously unforested lands. The concept which was promulgated by Ben-Gurion of "making the desert bloom" or the "greening of the wilderness" contained such an element. At the same time, the Zionist movement sought to "restore" the barren landscape of Eretz Yisrael to the cover that was described in the Bible, thus "reforestation."

Both approaches were part of the drive to redeem the land, and factored in later claims that, through stewardship of the land, the Jewish people earned the legitimacy of their political claims. Tree planting, from the outset, conveyed both practical and moral right to the Jews. That right was shared by the Diaspora community, which made its attachment to the land tangible through donations to the JNF. In another precursor of recent dynamics, donations to the JNF increased in the wake of forest arson, which was a component of the Arab Revolt of 1936–1939. The symbolism of the trees, and their utility in settling and controlling the land, was obvious, to Arabs as well as to Jews.

Consolidating Land in the New State

For the most part, Jewish tree planting prior to the War of Independence corresponded geographically with the areas of concentrated

Jewish settlement. Since there were too few Jews to create adjacent communities, forests were used to fill in the open spaces in the clusters which formed the Yishuv. The territorial imperative remained in the wake of the War and was, in fact, more pronounced in some ways, as the lands of displaced Arabs were put at the disposal of the State, thus necessitating a policy to direct their disposition. Some of that land was settled by Jewish immigrants who, as in the pre-independence period, were trained to plant trees in and around the communities which were created to absorb the human tide.

Much of this work took place in strategically important areas. Along the borders trees were planted to shield roadways from the view of hostile snipers, a tactic which was short-lived, due to various practical and esthetic complications. Another area which combined the strategic with the aesthetic was the Jerusalem Corridor. In light of the difficulty in maintaining the link between Jerusalem and the coastal plain during time of war, it was decided to clear the Arab population from their villages and settle the area with Jews. Here too, newly arrived immigrants were employed to plant trees on the land around the hilltops that would become home to the workers.

Planting was undertaken around Jerusalem as well, in an attempt to fulfill the Biblical description of the city that sits alone. Herein a time-tested British tactic was applied, i.e., the planting of trees to create a buffer. Earlier British plans had called for the planting of trees around one-half of Jerusalem and orchards around the other. This would maintain the visually distinct and open nature of the city's boundaries and highlight it in the landscape.[3] To the West, on lands which were part of the strategic corridor, six additional forest blocs were planted. These included Mevasseret Yerushalaim, Ora-Aminadav, Kaplan, Canada-Sataf, American Independence, and the Bar-Kochba Forest, ranging in size from 95 to 835 acres. An even larger forest was planted outside of Jerusalem, and with it another layer of symbolism was given to the trees. The Holocaust Martyrs' Forest, which ultimately exceeded 7,500 acres in size, was both memorial and statement about the future. The dedication of the forest states that:

> the Judean Hills and Jerusalem will again be rooted and afforested, again the branches of the Tree of Israel, those that were hewn in the great Holocaust and those that fell for the

216

freedom of the nation and the land, the souls of our holy ones and our heroes will live eternally with the green trees abundantly living—to reawaken the barren land and to fertilize the exiled of the nation.[4]

The announcement of the forest's creation spoke explicitly to the future and the purpose of forest planting:

> The memory of our six million holy ones will be eternalized in the trees which will be planted in the earth closest to the heart of each and every Jew [i.e., Jerusalem]. Their names will be sanctified for eternity by the tree which is renewed time after time with the passing of the year. 'Forest of the Holy Ones' will rise in the Judean Hills at the entrance of the capital of Israel and thus will serve as a practical contribution to the resuscitation of this important area.[5]

Along with all of the stated benefits that tree planting provided, the emerging state was also committed to providing recreation and open space to its growing urban population. Thus, alongside the political issues which contributed to the planting agenda, the creation of parks and groves, of scenic areas, and the planting of buffers and barriers to urban sprawl were also the purview of the JNF, which rapidly emerged as the primary tree planting agency. Indeed, Ben-Gurion's call to "green" the country was taken seriously, despite his somewhat unrealistic ambitions. As discussed elsewhere in this volume, tree planting became part of the national ethos, and Tu B'Shvat was elevated to the category of nationalist holiday.

The message of tree planting was intended for domestic consumption, but could be a signal as well. Forests were planted on the site of many Arab villages for which the displaced residents were given the legal status of "absentees." This was particularly true in the Galilee, but today one can find the remains of Arab villages in forests throughout Israel. One example of such a case, the most infamous, is Deir Yassin. A forest was planted on the slopes of the village, which became the Jewish neighborhood of Givat Shaul, though much of that forest was burned in the mid-1950s. On the other side of Jerusalem, Ben-Gurion directed the planting of orchards at the margin of Kibbutz Ramat Rachel as a message to the Jordanians regarding the Israeli agenda. Such planting was fairly typical in buffer zones and created a sharp image in the landscape, with forest on the Israeli side of the border, and barren land just across it. This led to a popular, though incorrect, explanation for the term "The Green Line." As an afforested boundary, it was, for the most part, a one-sided affair, as the Jordanians failed to answer in kind. As a result, "East Jerusalem" and, indeed, the West Bank remained largely devoid of forest trees during the period of Jordanian rule, 1948–1967.

Actualizing the Unification of Jerusalem

In the aftermath of the Six-Day War much was said about the unification of Jerusalem and the city's place as the eternal capital of the Jewish people. There was, however, a gap between the articulation of this belief and broad efforts to effect its realization. In fact, prior to 1967, a number of infrastructural linkages had remained between the two sides in an otherwise divided city. It was clear that such ties, relating primarily to subsurface systems such as the waterworks, needed to be augmented with a more tangible form of inter-connection. One such manifestation would be the construction of new Jewish neighborhoods in the newly accessible areas. Yet, despite the importance of the Jerusalem agenda, there was a lag in the provision of housing for Jews on lands added to the unified Jerusalem municipality. As in other areas of the State, tree planting was seen as a method of holding down unsettled land, thus providing a reserve for future development. As the reunification of the city emerged as a central issue in the Arab-Israeli conflict, the tree planting around Jerusalem gained political salience.

Under the stewardship of Teddy Kollek, then mayor of Jerusalem, tree planting took on an additional function. Kollek's vision for the city was of a mosaic, i.e., a whole composed of distinct and, critically, separate parts. For Jews and Arabs in Jerusalem, separation was something that had to be maintained.

There was little interaction, of course, during the years of division, but with the reunification of the city, the elimination of the no-man's land, the expansion of the municipal boundaries, and the growth of both populations, distance closed between the two sides. Kollek's mosaic stipulated not only separate neighborhoods, but buffers between the neighborhoods as well. This had long been a feature of colonial cities, particularly those of the British, wherein the design of the city distanced the indigenous population from the British population, and formalized class or ethnic distinctions in the city. Parks, boulevards, monuments, and groves were often used to this end, though the preference was to maintain open sight-lines in order to prevent surprise advances on the ruling quarter.

In Jerusalem trees were an obvious tool in preventing the fusion of Jewish and Arab neighborhoods that could result from creeping growth. In addition to providing a buffer (barrier) between neighborhoods, the forest would discourage cultivation and grazing on the periphery of Jewish neighborhoods, thus diminishing the likelihood of casual circulation near Jewish homes. From time to time, concerns were voiced that the forests were providing a haven for "criminal elements" (Jewish and non-Jewish), but this has been given little credence by the city and the Jewish National Fund.

Whatever the downsides, real or imagined, in siting forests on the edge of or between neighborhoods, the associated benefits have been seen as far more significant. Of them, the provision of green space and amenity has addressed a critical issue facing the city. Indeed, due to the lack of open space in the city, planning regulations call for a strip of green at the margin of any new residential development. Locating a neighborhood within an existing forested plot solves this requirement, as long as the whole of the grove is not consumed. Developments such as the Ramot neighborhood reflect such a course. Situated within the Jerusalem Corridor, close to the Palestinian villages of Beit Iksa and Nebi Samuel, Ramot has been built on land which, at least in part, was forested by the JNF beginning in 1970. Tree planting continues in that area today and is the source of a type of conflict which has, increasingly, come to typify the way that trees are incorporated in the struggle between Israel and the Palestinians for localized hegemony.

Reciprocal Planting

Israeli plans for settlement in the West Bank unfolded slowly, with the initial concepts taking on added vigor with a transition from the Labor Party to a Likud-led government in 1977. For Palestinians, what began as a slow and scattered process evolved into an apparently systematic effort to dominate as much of the land in the West Bank as possible. Faced with an increasingly aggressive settlement agenda, the Palestinians fell back on time-tested patterns of land tenure: if you wanted the land, put it into use. Though Palestinian villagers were usually vague in their understanding of Ottoman and British Mandatory land policies and laws, they did have an appreciation for the benefits that came from planting, and they retained the affinity for the olive that had been nurtured by the British.

Thus, as the frontiers of Israeli settlement began to encroach upon populated Palestinian areas, and as land was claimed for those settlements on the premise that it was unused State land, the villagers began to respond. Areas that the Israeli government argued was State land could, according to past patterns, be put into use by the villagers and, thereby, be protected from alienation. Inasmuch as the Ottoman Land Code was still the law of the land, at least nominally, trees that were planted and not challenged would confer legal rights to their owners. This facet of the law was not lost upon the PLO, which encouraged resistance to land alienation. To support the local population, the PLO offered subsidies to villagers for olive trees planted on land that was deemed in danger of Israeli encroachment. In such situations, olive saplings were provided through local Palestinian nurseries at a markedly reduced price, to be planted on the land in question.

The Israeli government attempted to forestall the acquisition of such rights by the Palestinians. To this end, they marshaled the existing law, added new security provisions, and linked these with technology, such as aerial reconnaissance photographs. The picture that emerged was one of competition in the landscape; both Israelis and Palestinians were planting trees to control land. Moreover, each side was planting with an awareness of the strategy, or at least a perceived strategy, of the other side.[6] Thus a jigsaw puzzle pattern sometimes emerged, with interlocking tree planting, generally

220

olive trees by the Palestinians and pine or cypress by the Israelis. Trees also bracketed residential areas, and even penetrated them, with Israeli houses reaching into a Palestinian orchard, or Palestinian houses into the margin of a JNF forest in the West Bank.

Reciprocal Destruction

The growing realization that trees were serving political purposes, both symbolic and practical, stripped them of their benign character, and made them objects worthy of "attack." Thus the Israeli government began a policy of uprooting trees that were located on particular plots of disputed land, such as in the case of the village of Katannah. The land of Katannah was divided by the Green Line in 1949, and many olive trees belonging to the villagers that were located on the Israeli side of the boundary were sold to a nearby kibbutz. With the effective dismantling of the Green Line after the Six-Day War, the villagers once again had access to their trees, and gradually they reestablished their use of the orchards. Realizing that Ottoman law would substantiate claims if the practice persisted, the government uprooted over three thousand trees and transplanted them to various sites around Israel. In addition to the uprooting of trees in a number of conflictual cases of this type, security concerns were also the basis of significant tree cutting (and bulldozing). This took place adjacent to Israeli settlements in the West Bank, along roadways, and the railway as well, out of concern, sometimes well grounded, that such groves had provided or could provide cover for terrorist attacks.

The obvious evidence of Jewish presence and intent conveyed by the forests planted by the JNF made them obvious targets for Palestinian fury, and also qualified them as eligible for the pranks of Palestinian children. Both took their toll on young trees and mature forests in the West Bank and in Israel. In fact, some areas planted by the JNF were targeted even as the planting was taking place and, with the departure of the work crews (often Palestinians!) at the end of the day, villagers would come and uproot that day's work. Goats and sheep were also brought to graze in newly planted areas, leading to the destruction of trees through both

221

trampling and mastication. Some of that planting was on land that was already in use for grazing by the Palestinians. Indeed, this was sometimes the reason that it had been planted.

More direct, however, was forest arson. For Palestinians, the torching of a forest planted by the Jews was a wonderfully symbolic act. It denied the Jews the practical benefits of the forest (some of which accrued to the Palestinian population as well, but no matter . . .), and it provided a catharsis, albeit a temporary one, in purging the Jewish symbol from their midst. Incidents of arson proliferated during the period of the Intifada, just as they had during the Arab Revolt against the Mandatory Government, from 1936 to 1939. And, as in that earlier period, the attacks on the forests created outrage in the Jewish community, both in Israel and abroad. The JNF capitalized on the publicity generated by the fires, and donations for tree planting increased dramatically during both these waves of arson.

The political aspect of the fires, and the planting which preceded them, was clear to all concerned. The poetry and rhetoric of the Intifada, often as disseminated in the leaflets of the uprising, praised the arson and called upon Palestinians to burn the land from underneath the Jews. The JNF responded, along with a call from President Chaim Herzog, for a planting response, namely, the Tree for a Tree Campaign mentioned at the beginning of this chapter. With this public articulation the planting, burning, and uprooting of trees in the West Bank proliferated, and sometimes devolved from organized activities with specific strategic objectives to arbitrary and punitive acts carried out by individuals acting on their own initiative. This came in addition to the official acts which were accelerating as a consequence of the Intifada.

A Green Belt for Jerusalem

Figures provided by Palestinian organizations claim huge numbers of trees (well over 100,000) uprooted by the IDF during the years of the Intifada. The army, while acknowledging a lack of firm statistics, strongly denies this number and says that it is wildly inflated. The JNF, for its part, concentrated planting activities in areas that were accessible to work crews, and easier to supervise following planting (i.e., less prone to attack). In practice this meant a concentration of West Bank planting in the area of Jerusalem, providing momentum for the "Jerusalem Green Belt." The concept of ringing Jerusalem in green stemmed from the Mandate period and British planners, but, until 1967, such work could only be done on the Western side of the city. Beginning in the early 1980s, plans were drawn and implemented for the extension of the Green Belt to include the expanded Jerusalem municipality. The boundary to the city after the Six-Day War incorporated many Palestinian villages and extended the length of the "border" with the West Bank. Thus, the tree planting in and around the city now included areas that were disputed between Jews and Arabs, at both the local and national level. (The Jerusalem planting was considered by the JNF to be exempt from the policy of not using the money from contributors for work conducted "outside" the Green Line, though often the sites were indeed in the West Bank.)

Tree planters and politicians shared an appreciation for the role that the forest could play in helping to determine hegemony over the land in and around the city, and the power that the trees had as symbols in the landscape. The trees were viewed as an effective wall or fence, demarcating where Palestinians could and could not go on the land.[7] There was, however, a surprising modus vivendi in the field. Palestinian villagers and JNF planters began to realize that the most effective strategy, for both sides was to avoid direct conflict with the other. Thus the jigsaw puzzle pattern emerging, with interlocking but rarely overlapping planting activities, pine and cypress for the Jews, olive and sometimes other fruit trees for the Palestinians. This pragmatic approach evolved without and at times in spite of the influence of the political echelon. Seemingly those working the land, Israeli and Palestinian, had reached a basic level of understanding, even within the context of the conflict.

Trees for the Future?

As Israel withdraws from many practical aspects of life in the West Bank, its planting agenda will contract accordingly. The Jerusalem

223

Green Belt remains a viable project, and it continues to grow into a tangible demarcation, visually separating the city from its West Bank hinterland in the Judean Hills. While the cessation of planting elsewhere in the West Bank will remove a source of friction between the two communities, the benefits that the forests provide might be lost to the Palestinians living there. Forests planted in the West Bank by the Jordanians between 1948 and 1967 were short-lived due both to improper care and deliberate consumption. The current peace process has demonstrated an awareness of environmental issues, however, and forests will be a component of that agenda.

Palestinians have already articulated a concern for the care of park areas established by Israel, and the lands planted by the JNF are a logical target of similar concern. In fact, the lands administered by Israel as State lands pose both opportunity and risk for the Palestinian Authority, as they constitute a vital resource and reserve for the Palestinians. Many Palestinians have acquired experience in tree planting while working for the JNF, just as Jewish immigrants did in an earlier era. Those workers can provide a base for the creation of a forest authority that will maintain and even expand the task of afforestation in the West Bank (and Gaza as well). The resources and experience of the JNF, however, could provide a critical assist to the nascent Palestinian effort. In that way the trees which, until now, have served as a barrier, could begin to provide a bridge, with benefit to all concerned. Perhaps then the words of the Prophet Isaiah would be realized and reflected in the works of the people of the land:

> I will plant in the wilderness the cedar, the acacia tree, the myrtle, and the olive tree; I will set in the desert the cypress, the plane tree and the larch together, that they may see, and know, and consider, and understand together. . . . (Is. 41:19–20)

Sun-Startled Pines

Zelda
translated from the Hebrew by Marcia Falk

Sun-startled pines
wafted a wild fragrance—
the same stunning strength
from the inmost flowering
made the world my home again
but did not reveal the core,
the divine intention
in budding and wilting plants.
And the point of my life
and the point of my death—
I will not know in this world.

Ancient Pines

Zelda
translated from the Hebrew by Marcia Falk

"And trees you're allowed to kill?"
blurted a small boy whose eyes looked pained.
When the snows melted,
grim men emerged from the ruins
to fell the ancient pines—
powerful trees—
that had responded to mountain winds.
Limber branches were crushed to dust
in the courtyards,
branches that had sketched in space
gentle motions of the inner flowering.
They tossed the pale-green shadow
in the trash,
and kicked at the fragrance, the sap.

Untitled

Zelda
translated from the Hebrew by Marcia Falk

I don't like all trees equally—
my soul befriends
a sickly pear tree.
Everything moves, changes place;
I and it are planted
in a courtyard stuck in space
above a dark pit.
(Each night, King David's violated daughter
yearns to die here,
because millennia cannot erase her shame.)
Yes, this is the very courtyard
but without the face I loved.
In this yard, I stand
before a tree whose end is near—
the crown of its freshness has fallen,
and its once sweet, once fragrant fruits,
which delighted and freed the soul,
are brown caves
swarming with tiny snakes.
But all this sorrow
belongs to quiet nights.
On the day of God's wrath,
I don't beg mercy for it,
I do not beg for it,
for my soul is removed from the plants.

And yet, how I suffered
when a small peach tree
that I raised in a bucket
was trampled
on the eve of Judgment Day.

Note: "King David's violated daughter" is Tamar, who was raped and then
scorned by her half-brother Amnon (2 Sam. 13:1–22).

226

I Know Nothing

Malka Heifetz Tussman
translated from the Yiddish by Marcia Falk*

Piously to embrace the tree,
to rest my cheek on brown bark,
to breathe, and to be quiet.
It's sad and good
in the rustle of branches.
In the swish of leaves, I say:
Here it's still.
In the spill of blossoms,
my thoughts are mild,
tranquil.

But
whether trees praise God
with the light of white petals—
this I don't know.
I don't know when they cry,
I don't know when they laugh,
I know nothing about such things.

part VI

Branches: Eco-Judaism

Early in the 1970s, there began to emerge a special literature that explored what Judaism had to say about the *adam-adamah*, human-earth, relationship. Some of it sprang directly from increasing public concern that new forms of human technology were damaging the earth. Some was a response to scientists who attacked Judaism and Christianity as the bearers of a destructive teaching that human beings alone of all creation bear the Image of God and that they should subdue the earth—a teaching that, the scientists argued, led philosophically to contempt for nature and practically to pollution and degradation of nature.

Two somewhat distinct Jewish approaches emerged, both interested in exploring Jewish responsibility for the whole of the planet, not only for the Land of Israel where Jews had again become historically responsible. Both approaches led to another burst of energy in the celebration of Tu B'Shvat.

Increasingly, the festival was seen to fuse the mystical with the eco-planetary, and so to include the trees of all countries as aspects of the Sacred Tree Above.

One of these new approaches we might call "Rabbinic Stewardship." Its proponents asserted that true Judaism was protective of the environment, bore no responsibility for the despoliation of nature that Western techno-industrialism was imposing, and should indeed be drawn on to protect the environment.

This approach emerged just about simultaneously with another kind of Jewish approach to the earth: It saw Rabbinic Judaism as an important source of Jewish concern for the earth, but one that was in itself insufficient to deal with the growing threats to the natural world posed by human technology. In response to this sense of insufficiency, several Jewish philosophies were put before the public that bespoke a love of the earth that went beyond most rabbinic teachings, drawing deeply on hasidic thought and on some kindred Western ideas. Martin Buber and Abraham Joshua Heschel, each in his own way, spoke out of these roots. Their work, along with some earth-focused elements of Zionism, fed into an emerging exploration of new approaches to Judaism as the *Havurot* and early Jewish-renewal energies, including feminist Judaism, grew in the United States in the early 1970s.

The proponents of Rabbinic Stewardship and the proponents of Jewish renewal were both attracted to recovering and renewing Tu B'Shvat, for somewhat different but overlapping reasons. Participants in the loose-knit Jewish-renewal movement were drawn to the drama, the depth, the beauty, and the intellectual power of the kabbalistic and Zionist ceremonial patterns embodied in Tu B'Shvat ritual and ceremony as well as to its hints of celebrating an earth in danger. The Jews attracted to Rabbinic Stewardship also responded to the possibility of drawing on Tu B'Shvat to focus on Jewish concerns for the earth.

In what direction will we see this rabbinic/nonrabbinic amalgam moving? What will be the future of this interest in Tu B'Shvat and in the emergence of a more ecologically concerned version of Judaism? Perhaps, Tu B'Shvat and its accompanying concern for the earth will simply join the more established Jewish festivals, with more vigor than it has had until now. Or possibly, these explorations are moving toward creation of an eco-feminist Judaism that may stand in part outside the Rabbinic Judaism on which it partly draws. They may be a signal that the crisis of the earth, along with other factors, is beckoning forth a new form of Judaism as the crisis of 2,000 years ago beckoned forth Rabbinic Judaism.

In the "branch" of the Tree presented in this section of the book, there is a range of these new approaches toward trees, toward Tu B'Shvat, and toward Torah. We want to call special attention to

230

the piece that ends the section, written by one of the editors, Ari Elon. It weaves together the threads of earthy Torah and wordy Talmud, mystical Kabbalah and physical Zionism. It looks deep into Tu B'Shvat/Yah B'Shvat for insight into the deepest dilemmas of the Jewish people and all earth today and of healing our deepest wounds.

If there is a moment in our generation when the branches high on the ancient Tree may reach deep toward the earth and hint toward the rerooting of the Tree and the regrowth of a new trunk— like the self-renewing banyan—we offer that essay as the nearest possibility.

I and Thou: A Tree

Martin Buber

I contemplate a tree.

I can accept it as a picture: a rigid pillar in a flood of light, or splashes of green traversed by the gentleness of the blue silver ground.

I can feel it as movement: the flowing veins around the sturdy, striving core, the sucking of the roots, the breathing of the leaves, the infinite commerce with earth and air—and the growing itself in its darkness.

I can assign it to a species and observe it as an instance, with an eye to its construction and its way of life.

I can overcome its uniqueness and form so rigorously that I recognize it only as an expression of the law—those laws according to which a constant opposition of forces is continually adjusted, or those laws according to which the elements mix and separate.

I can dissolve it into a number, into a pure relation between numbers, and eternalize it.

Throughout all of this the tree remains my object and has its place and its time span, its kind and condition.

But it can also happen, if will and grace are joined, that as I contemplate the tree I am drawn into a relation, and the tree ceases to be an It. The power of exclusiveness has seized me.

This does not require me to forego any of the modes of contemplation. There is nothing that I must not see in order to see, and there is no knowledge that I must forget. Rather is everything, picture and movement, species and instance, law and number included and inseparably fused.

Whatever belongs to the tree is included: its form and its mechanics, its colors and its chemistry, its conversation with the elements and its conversation with the stars—all this in its entirety.

The tree is no impression, no play of my imagination, no aspect of a mood; it confronts me bodily and has to deal with me as I must deal with it—only differently.

One should not try to dilute the meaning of the relation: relation is reciprocity.

Does the tree then have consciousness, similar to our own? I have no experience of that. But thinking that you have brought this off in your own case, must you again divide the indivisible? What I encounter is neither the soul of a tree nor a dryad, but the tree itself.

Trees for Life

Ismar Schorsch

As a U.S. army chaplain in Korea in the early sixties, I was stationed in Taegu, far south of Seoul. To get there after my arrival in Seoul, I took the train that ran straight down the center of the peninsula, cutting through a formidable mountain range. The landscape of South Korea is covered with mountains, and the railroad connecting the capital city of Seoul with the southern port of Pusan was one of the few positive legacies of Japan's long and oppressive occupation of the country before World War II. But what stirred my imagination far more than the network of tunnels was the unrelieved barrenness of the mountains. Without trees or vegetation of any sort, they were shrouded in shades of brown, the victim of human destructiveness.

Inevitably my mind jumped to Israel. Is this what its terrain looked like at the turn of the century before the Jewish National Fund set about to redeem and reforest the land, to elevate Tu Bishvat to the rank of a national holiday for planting trees, and to turn the Shakaidea, the almond tree, into a popular symbol?

The reforestation of Israel, one of Zionism's finest achievements, was born of ancient values no less than moderate ideology. Zionism repudiated the ghetto of eastern Europe with its confining and cerebral Orthodoxy but found in ancient Judaism's agrarian setting a religious language redolent with arboreal metaphors. For instance, the book of Proverbs chose to depict the Torah, the embodiment of divine wisdom, as a Tree of Life (3:18); adherence to the words of Torah held out the promise of restoring the Tree of Life lost in the primeval act of disobedience in the Garden of Eden. Jews reaffirm this belief in the synagogue by reciting that verse every time the Torah scroll is returned to the ark after a public reading. Another example of this metaphor is the seven-branched menorah; the ubiquitous emblem of Judaism in the Roman world, from the Arch of Titus, to the synagogues of Palestine, to the sarcophagi of the catacombs. Whatever meanings may have eventually been imputed to it, in origin and form the menorah suggests a life-bearing tree, a graphic symbol of the Torah as a divine medium of inexhaustible nourishment for this world and the world to come.

In this regard, a striking rabbinic phrase compares heresy to the destruction of trees. Of the four second-century rabbis who furtively indulged in mystical speculation (i.e. "entered the orchard"), only R. Akiva, we are told, emerged from the experience unscathed (*Hagigah* 14b). "Ben Azzai cast a glance and perished"; "Ben Zoma cast a glance and was impaired"; and Elisha ben Abbuya, who was to abandon Judaism, "cut down saplings" (*kitsets bi-neti'ot*). A later rabbinic text preferred to take this picturesque phrase as a metaphor and portrayed Elisha as a teacher who intentionally misled young students of Torah (*Song of Songs Rabbah* 7b).

My own inclination is to revel in the power and relevance of its concreteness: after all, saplings grow in orchards. To destroy trees wantonly is an act of disbelief, an affront to the Creator. The phrase assumes a link between faith in God and reverence for nature. Without a sense of the sacred, there are no limits to human behavior; everything is subject to human assault. Atheism paves the way for environmental degradation. Interestingly, modern Hebrew preserves the rabbinic metaphor in precisely its original sense: an act of religious rebellion.

Lest one think I overload this phrase with contemporary meaning, let me offer an example of rabbinic midrash that asserts the same link positively: namely, that to plant trees is a statement of faith. The midrash, a finely crafted homily full of surprises, extracts theological nuggets from an unproblematic verse. The verse reads: "When you enter the land and plant any tree for food, you shall regard its fruit as forbidden" (Lev. 19.23). The author of our midrash begins boldly by turning what appears to be no more than a sequence of events into a moral obligation, claiming that what God really said to Israel was the following: "Even though you find it [the promised land] filled with good things, you should not say, 'Let's sit back and not plant.' On the contrary, you must care about seedlings, (bi-neti'ot—the same word as above), for Scripture says: 'and you plant any tree for food.'"

In case we have missed his argument for stewardship, our preacher elaborates, "For just as when you [plural] entered the land and found seedlings planted by others, so you are obliged to plant for your children." The first half of verse 19, in other words, is not to be read declaratively, but imperatively. God expects us to turn over the land to the next generation, to our progeny, with all its resources intact. The land is not ours to dispose of, but only to make use of with reverence and responsibility.

Nor is this an obligation that lapses in old age. "No man should [presume to] say, " 'I am old. How many years do I have left? Why should I exert myself for others if tomorrow I may die?'" With this twist, the midrash has effected a psychological shift from the people as a whole to the individual. The general command to maintain the land in good order can be realized only if every Jew feels addressed directly. The welfare of the land is an obligation that devolves on everyone and from which no one is ever released, even in old age. Quoting Solomon, our midrash insists that God has wisely withheld from mortals the knowledge of when their time shall come and hence we ought always to affirm life by our actions. We are never free to desist from planting.

Like an accomplished preacher, our homilist then musters an unforgettable story to drive home his point. On one of his military campaigns to crush a rebellious province, the Roman emperor Hadrian met an old Jew planting fig shoots (again neti'ot te'ainim). Struck by the futility of his labors, the emperor stopped to inquire. "Why should you, an old man, exhaust yourself for others?" To which the man responded, "My Lord the King, indeed I am engaged in planting. If I should merit it, I will eat of the fruit of my shoots; if not, my children will eat them." After three years of warfare, Hadrian happened to return to the same spot, only to find the same elderly farmer. Recognizing the emperor from afar, the man filled a basket full of ripe figs from his first harvest (*bikkurim*) and offered them to the emperor along with a gentle reminder of their earlier conversation. In admiration Hadrian ordered his soldiers to fill the basket with gold coins and return it to the farmer.

The paradox is exquisite: a feeble, old Jew teaching the world's mightiest man of war a lesson about the limits of power. The land is not ours to lay waste. A concept of stewardship must define our relationship. The tale clearly implies that if instructed by God "to till and tend" His garden, human beings are duty-bound to preserve its capacity for sustenance, even when crippled by the infirmities of old age.

Still, the midrash does not leave it at that. Rather, our homilist closes with a wholly non-utilitarian argument both daring and novel: ultimately it is God's own behavior that should impel us never to cease from planting. "As if God said to Israel, learn from Me. For am I ever in need? And yet Scripture says: 'The Lord God planted a garden in Eden, the east'" (Gen. 2:8). To care for the earth ought to be an ultimate value inspired by the very lack of necessity for creation itself. The simple biblical narrative pulsates with theology. The garden of Eden looms as the paradigm for the ideal stance toward nature, a relationship based on altruism, not duty or self-interest.

In brief, this midrash, which packs an otherwise pedestrian verse with unanticipated meaning, suggests that our original phrase, "*kitsets b'neti'ot*—he cut down saplings"—is not a random metaphor. In the midrash our reverence for nature is validated by divine example; conversely, to ravage nature would make human beings the measure of all things. Caring for trees points to a living faith in God.

What may have triggered the articulation of this sermon was the devastation inflicted on the province of Judaea by the large-scale and futile rebellions against Rome in 66 and 32 under the Zealots and Bar Kochba. We know from the extensive account of this first revolt (Josephus) that the Roman general Titus denuded the environs of Jerusalem of trees for miles around in order to build the embankment for his siege of the capital.

The still larger scope and greater intensity of the Bar Kochba uprising unavoidably must have extended the damage to the environment. Hence, I choose to read our midrash with its pointed reference to Hadrian as expressing a muted protest over the destruction of the Judaean countryside, a deepened sensitivity to the sanctity of nature, and a plea for the reforestation of the land.

The passage of time has only added to the light of this incandescent midrash. As trees fall at the end of the twentieth century at an ever quickening pace, victims of the need and greed of humankind, they give incontrovertible evidence of the dismal fact that for us God is dead. Whatever we might profess in this post-rational age, our behavior exemplifies the absence of religious constraints to stay our hand. According to Lester R. Brown, the project director of *State of the World:*

> During the twenty years since the first Earth Day, in 1970, the world lost nearly 200 million hectares of tree cover, an area roughly the size of the United States east of the Mississippi River. Deserts expanded by some 120 million hectares, claiming more land than is currently planted to crops in China. Thousands of plant and animal species with which we shared the planet in 1970 no longer exist. Over two decades, some 1.6 billion people were added to the world's population—more than inhabited the planet in 1900. And the world's farmers lost an estimated 480 billion tons of topsoil—roughly equivalent to the amount of India's cropland.[1]

A century ago, already well into the scientific and industrial revolutions that set the modern era apart from all others, Nietzsche's madman rushed into the marketplace to declaim the death of God at human hands. But none of his listeners were able to catch the prophetic truth of his startling words, and he withdrew in despair.

"I come too early," he said then; "my time has not come yet. This tremendous event is still on its way . . . it has not yet reached the ears of man. Lightning and thunder require time, the light of the stars requires time, deeds require time even after they are done, before they can be seen and heard. This deed is still more distant from them than the most distant stars—and *yet they have done it themselves.*"[2]

In our day the thunder has finally caught up with the lightning. Our pervasive atheism is attested daily by our pillaging and polluting of the environment. In our minds the planet is ours to dispose of as we please. The arrogance of industrial society is untouched by any sentiment of reverence, interdependence, or eternity. The uniqueness of our blue habitat in the cosmos fails to move us to recognize the damage our technological civilization inflicts on its network of ecosystems.

And so indifferently we level an acre and a half of the earth's forests every second and some 17 million hectares of its tropical rain forests every year. Only half the original expanse of rain forest in the world is still standing, and much of that has already been degraded. In the Amazon, "the garden of the world" (William H. Edwards), the fate of the forest is sealed by the very building of a road. In the words of Andrew Revkin:

> With the coming of the road the owner no longer cared about a few tons of rubber or nuts. Now the value of the property would skyrocket, just as it had wherever a road had been cut into the forests of the Amazon offering profits of 400, 600, and not uncommonly 1000%. . . .The road determined the fate of that land as assuredly as a diagnosis of AIDS dictated the fate of a man.[3]

Around the globe nature is forced to give way before the relentless proliferation of human life. By the year 2000 the world's human population will have grown by another one billion to a total of 6.4 billion people, with one-half of that figure living in cities. And by the end of the next century under the best of circumstances, it is estimated that the number of human beings on earth will reach 11 billion.[4]

No one alive today can foretell whether the planet could ever support such numbers or whether any political system based on human rights could long function under the pressure of such massive human need. In the face of these ominous population trends, the relentless attack against abortion and family planning in the United States seems to me a reckless diversion from the real problem. Worse still, it has eviscerated the international leadership our government once provided in the vital cause of family planning.

A planet overrun by Homo sapiens will have less and less space for trees, other species, or even the presence of God. The Kabbalists of Safed long ago enriched the mystical thought of Judaism with the stunning concept of *tsimtsum*—an act of divine contraction prior to creation. If God were omnipresent, they reasoned, then how could the universe ever come into being? What kind of space would there be for it to fill? To address this conundrum, they came up with the idea of *tsimtsum:* the emptying of space for the existence of something other than God. The universe fills the void left by God's self-imposed exile. Creation begins with withdrawal.

No concept in Judaism's theological repertoire could be more relevant to our crisis of overpopulation. God again stands forth as the model for human behavior. The miracle of cohabitation with other living species, the beauty of collective I-Thou relationship with beings wholly different from ourselves, requires our self-limitation. If we were everywhere, our presence would herald the end of the teeming diversity of nature. Our fragile and unique habitat needs a reprieve from human assault. We, its most sentient creatures, must gain the self-mastery to rein in our personal wants, to reverse the growth of cities evermore uninhabitable, and to contain the explosion of our numbers. For us to heed the biblical injunction of planting trees, there must be soil in which to plant them.

The Redwood Torah

Arthur Waskow and Naomi Mara Hyman

In January 1997, more than 200 Jews gathered in far northern California to create and eat together the sacred meal of fruits and nuts and wines that celebrates Tu B'Shvat—the New Year of the Trees. They had gathered in a grove of ancient redwood trees. The redwoods stood above them, silent in their majesty—250 feet tall and more. They were, they are, the tallest living beings on dry land.

The celebrants intended to complete the seder by walking illegally onto the land of a corporation that was planning to log some of the last remaining stand of ancient redwoods that are in private hands. There they would plant redwood seedlings and risk arrest for trespass.

At this Redwoods seder, one of the editors of this volume, Naomi Mara Hyman, looked up at those great trees and said: "What would a Torah Scroll be like that had these *eitzim* ['trees'] for its *eitzim* [the wooden poles that hold the spiraling Torah scroll]? How grand, how tall would such a Torah be!" Then, looking at the crowd who had come to celebrate the seder, she said: "Each of us would be just the right size to be one letter in such a Torah Scroll!"

And that is what we are, of course: each one of us a letter in God's great Torah Scroll of all life on the planet. Yet being a letter is not enough. Nowhere in the Torah does a single letter stand alone to bear some meaning. In English, the word "I" is but a single letter, standing alone; but in Hebrew, even the word for "I" has several letters. No one, not even "I," can stand alone.

When one person, one corporation, like the corporation that claimed to own those redwoods, thinks it is a single letter that can stand alone, that single letter concentrates such energy that the letter turns to an engulfing flame, while all the words around it are reduced to paltry parchment—and to ashes. So the great Torah Scroll, the earth and the society in which we live, begins to burn. It is a community of lives—not an isolated life—that makes up words, verses, books of wisdom in the living Torah made of earth and air, wood and water.

The community of Jews that gathered in the ancient redwoods to live within that giant Torah Scroll came because they also live within the other ancient Torah, the weave of wisdom that Jewish tradition often calls the Tree of Life. If it were not for that Torah, there would be no Tu B'Shvat; no seder; no gathering of Jews to affirm that these trees were God's and should not be wantonly destroyed.

Which of these Trees of Life encompasses the other? Does the Jewish Torah live as one thread of human culture in the human strand of all the species that make up the weave of earth? Or do we see the forest as a "forest" because it lives with us within the weave of words and melodies, dances and desires, that human beings—in this case, Jewish human beings—use to recreate the world?

Each. Both. At moments of our history, our spiritual journey, we have focused on one Tree or the other. The mystics of Tzfat saw every earthly tree as simply fruit of the Tree Divine whose roots are in the heavens. The Zionist kindergarten teachers of Tel Aviv saw the notion of the Mystic Tree as a mystification to be healed by rerooting Jewish life in green earth.

241

We need to affirm them both. We need to call forth a Tu B'Shvat that affirms both Trees, affirms that the abundance that each grows from cannot keep flowing without the abundance of the other. The Tree of Life in scrolls of Torah, the living Torah inscribed in redwood majesty—the Jewish people, and the human race, will wither if we do not renew them both.

Tu Bishvat in the Redwoods: A Meditation Suite for the Earth

Composed for the Tu Bishvat Seder at Headwaters Forest, January 26, 1997

Marcia Falk

1
Here we are. We are here.
And why, when here, do we always want more?

2
Here you are, back
in the redwood forest—

how tall the fir trees,
how delicate the pines!

Standing on the winter-dark earth,
you suddenly know these trees

will be your gravestone.
Nothing stirs—but what

are those sounds?
You balance on the edge

while under your feet
the mushrooms smolder

and the unborn ferns
hum in their bed.

3

If you sit long enough in the woods,
nothing happens.

Just the earth's breath rising and falling
up and down treetrunks

which go copper-green in the air
as if oxidized.

Just your own breath warming a spot of earth
while your heart beats

and you begin, like all the creatures,
to repeat yourself—

the same thoughts entering your mind—
entering, leaving—

while yearnings rise and fall
like the tails of startled squirrels.

4

"'And trees—you're allowed to kill trees?'
a small boy blurted . . ."

5

*"You do not belong to you,
you belong to the universe,"*

*and you will be reclaimed
by its constant, ever-changing heart—*

*your wise body
and your spacious mind,*

*whether you are ready
or not*

*when you are joyful
or not,*

*even as you turn away—
to be buffeted*

*and set aloft,
a twig in the wind.*

6

*You take the long road on your walk today,
slowly threading back through the woods,*

*past the log cabin, locked, and posted
"Do Not Enter,"*

*and the posted tree
announcing its own end:*

*"Notice of intent to cut
growing wood and timber."*

*You vow that every day
you will post vigil*

as the hours slowly drop
from the slender length of tree,

one by one
by one.

7

In a naked slice of air,
a single blade proclaims dominion.

The silent flesh of the last living redwood
towering, alone.

Stones shift beneath the mold,
the earth's breath rises and falls.

Why has it gone so quiet?
What is left that we need to know?

Coda: A Dream of Recovery

The sky is soft as a grandmother's quilt.
The needles and fronds are soft, too.
They seem to heal you with their green fingers,
their heady perfumes rising.

The trees will open their arms,
the wind will catch you in its lap,
they will rock you, rock you like a baby
as you dreamed it in your deepest longing,

not as it happens when you wish for it
but as it's told in an old old story,
a story you were born knowing
and later forgot.

Nebuchadnezzar, Naḥman's "The Cripple," and Groundhog Day: A Meditation on Tu B'Shvat

Howard M. Solomon

Rabbi Naḥman of Bratslav's "The Cripple" begins with what seems to be the most fundamental of ecological imperatives. With his dying breath a wise man commands his sons: "You may earn your livelihood in other ways, but you must always try to water trees." But even more quickly than Adam and Eve were chased out of the Garden for failing to take care of the Tree that God had entrusted to them, the crippled son of Naḥman's tale finds himself in a terrifying forest, robbed and abandoned, beginning his quest to fulfill his father's command. "[W]hen he had nothing to eat, he started thinking what to do. And he threw himself from the wagon to eat grass. He spent the night in the field, lonely and frightened. His strength ebbed until he could not even stand, just crawl, and he ate the grass around him. As long as he could reach out and eat, he ate. After he had eaten all the grass around him and could no longer reach it, he moved himself further and ate there. And he ate grass for some time."

The two images in Naḥman's tale—tending trees and subsisting on grass—couldn't be more different. In the first, an upright man cultivates and waters trees. In the second, a crawling desperado barely survives on grass. In the first, we sense order, choice, taking responsibility for stewardship of the environment. In the second, we see a person reduced to instinct, starvation, mere survival.

These images in "The Cripple" are similar to those in the Book of Daniel's story of Nebuchadnezzar, from which Naḥman certainly drew his inspiration. Nebuchadnezzar, king of Babylon, dreams of "a tree in the midst of the earth . . . Its top reaching to heaven . . . visible to the ends of the earth. Its foliage was beautiful, and its fruit abundant; there was food for all in it." A heavenly voice commands the tree be cut down, and Nebuchadnezzar "be drenched with the dew of heaven, and share earth's verdure with the beasts." A year later, as he is contemplating his wealth and power, the dream is fulfilled: Nebuchadnezzar is "driven away from men, he [eats] grass like cattle, and his body [is] drenched with the dew of heaven until his hair [grows] like eagle's [feathers] and his nails like [the talons of] birds."

For the cripple and Nebuchadnezzar alike, the forest is a dream-world of shifting meanings, where cultivated fields and orchards suddenly give way to thickets of trees and wild grass, where boundaries between human and animal, God and nature, inexplicably dissolve. Rabbi Naḥman of Bratslav, one of the major figures of late eighteenth-century Hasidism and the second-century B.C.E. author of the Book of Daniel, both use the time-tested imagery of the forest journey to speak to us about spiritual loss and moral redemption.

But they speak to us in contemporary terms as well. The stories of Nebuchadnezzar and the cripple offer profound insights to Jews committed to ecological and environmental issues. More particularly, they suggest ways in which the festival of Tu B'Shvat can renew Judaism's relationship to the natural universe.

More than for other Hasidic masters, nature played a central role in Naḥman's personal and spiritual development. His discovery of nature as a young man was a dramatic turning point in his life: in Martin Buber's words, "the walls of [Naḥman's] spiritual ghetto tumbled down at once upon contact with the power of growing things" when he left the vibrant Ukrainian Jewish community of Medzhibozh to live in his father-in-law's village of Usyatin.

Naḥman taught his disciples that *hitbodedut*, the practice of daily solitary prayer, could be enhanced by the fullness of the great outdoors. "When man becomes worthy to hear the songs of the plants, how each plant speaks its song to God, how beautiful and sweet it is to hear their singing! And, therefore, it is good indeed to serve God in their midst in solitary wandering over the fields between the growing things and to pour out one's speech before God in truthfulness. All the speech of the fields enters then into your own and intensifies its strength." We should not be surprised, therefore, to find the characters of Naḥman's tales communicating with the Divine when they are in the solitary presence of animals, clouds, trees, etc. In "The Cripple," the hero's direct contact with God begins as he is crawling on the ground: he pulls up a stalk of grass and finds a magical diamond in its roots. By the end of the story, he is redeemed and is able to stand upright and walk. The long passage to redemption begins in the most abject depravity, "for a long time" eating grass like a beast of the field.

Crawling on all fours throws the cripple and Nebuchadnezzar into unmediated bodily relationship to the earth, a humbling (humus > "humiliate") which is the necessary first step in the spiritual quest. In the case of Naḥman's tale, the cripple's imperfect body tells us that he must undergo spiritual trial, beginning with humiliation, on the way to spiritual perfection. What, however, has Nebuchadnezzar done to deserve his humiliation?

Nebuchadnezzar perceives himself as the paragon of power and knowledge, indistinguishable from a tree which reaches "to heaven . . . visible to the ends of the earth . . . beautiful . . . abundant." He confuses himself with the Tree of Life—in essence, with God. God commands that the tree be cut down and Nebuchadnezzar live "in the grass of the field . . . with the mind of a beast . . . so that all creatures may know that the most High is sovereign over the realm of man, and He gives it to whom He wishes and He may set over it even the lowest of men."

Nebuchadnezzar's dream is a fantasy of male pride run amok ("greatness has grown to reach heaven, and dominion is to the end of the earth"), but not even Nebuchadnezzar can equal the Tree— the Tree of Good and Evil, the Tree of Creation. When the dream-tree is cut off at the stump, Nebuchadnezzar ceases to be part of human history. He is banished to a world of brutish survival: without past or future, isolated from other human beings, condemned to an unchanging, eternal present. In Carl Jung's words, Nebuchadnezzar "regressed even further back than the primitive and became completely inhuman . . . a complete regressive degeneration of a man who has overreached himself." His descent to the vegetative earth is as extreme as his imagined expansion into heaven—the first state begets the second.

Equating trees with manhood, and cut trees with severed masculinity, is an archetypal image in many cultures, and Nebuchadnezzar's dream draws on that imagery. The association is embedded in the Hebrew language as well: cutting off Nebuchadnezzar's manliness (*zachar*) severs him from history and memory (*zachor*). In biblical culture, as Howard Eilberg-Schwartz puts it, "one must have a member to be a member."

What poetic justice, that the despot who uprooted the Jewish people—itself metaphorized as a tree—should himself be cut down. But Nebuchadnezzar was guilty of destroying physical as well as metaphorical trees. When he uprooted cedar trees from their natural environment in Eretz Israel and transplanted them to the wet soil of Babylon, he violated the ecological principle that plants, crops, agricultural and social practices that are natural in one environment may be disastrous in another. No wonder, according to tradition, that the trees themselves rejoiced at Nebuchadnezzar's downfall!

Violating the natural order of things by exiling God's people from *ha-aretz*, the Land, Nebuchadnezzar becomes a symbol of violated categories, the incarnation of disorder itself. Chased from his palace, out of his mind, living like a "beast of the field" with hair "like [eagle's] feathers and . . . nails like [the talons of] birds," Nebuchadnezzar has become a monster, demonstrating ("monster" > "demonstrate") God's anger at those who violate Creation. If nature is indeed "a mirror of Israel, [and] Israel is also a mirror of nature," then Nebuchadnezzar is the most distorted representation of humanity imaginable.

Given the pastoral/agricultural context of Biblical culture, it is hard to imagine anything more degrading than being exiled from human company and condemned to graze on all fours. The curse resonates with image of the scapegoat, of base animal instinct obliterating all vestiges of human reason. But it is also important to recognize the ecological implications of the curse as well. Mishnah *Baba Kama* 7:7 speaks against "small cattle in *Eretz Yisrael*" because "small cattle," especially goats, consume vegetation all the way down to their roots. Elsewhere in the Talmud, the condemnation is even more categorical: raising small cattle in *Eretz Yisrael*—along with forging documents, giving false testimony, and cutting down good trees—is one of the four transgressions capable of weakening the Celestial Lights.

The law of *bal tashḥit*, which forbids wanton waste and destruction, derives from Deut. 20:19: even in war, destroying trees is prohibited. Cutting down a tree before its time is analogous to murder: "When a tree that bears fruit is cut down, its moan goes from one end of the world to the other, yet no sound is heard."[1] The equation of trees = grass = humanity is among the most powerful in Jewish tradition. If, as Isaiah said, "man is but grass," is God telling us to equate Nebuchadnezzar with those who eat human flesh? Eating grass seems to have taken Nebuchadnezzar to the very limits of shame and decency.

To the very limits of shame and decency, but not beyond. In spite of his deformed appearance and behavior, in spite of the inhumane regions he inhabits, Nebuchadnezzar always retains some vestige of human identity. His experience, as well as that of Naḥman's cripple, is less a punishment than an opportunity, less an endless curse than a means to an end. Both outcasts return from the wilderness. The cripple becomes able to stand, walk, and fight demons; he learns that working to bring about the age of redemption is what "watering trees" is all about. And Nebuchadnezzar too is redeemed: "When the time had passed, I, Nebuchadnezzar, lifted my eyes to heaven, and my reason was restored to me. I blessed the Most High, and praised and glorified the Ever-Lasting One" (Dan. 4:31). Redemption begins with humiliation and leads to humility: Nebuchadnezzar and the cripple begin their transformation when they connect with the earth in the most elemental way possible, on their hands and knees, like beasts of the field, eating grass.

The images of Nebuchadnezzar and the cripple remind us of the high cost of not taking care of trees: we cease being human when we neglect our responsibilities to the natural order. Just as significantly, these images remind us that if we are willing to connect with nature in a fundamental and sacred way, we can rediscover our lost selves.

And this is what Tu B'Shvat is all about.

Tu B'Shvat, the New Year of the Trees, is celebrated on the fifteenth of Shvat, in the wet and cold that follows the darkness of the Winter solstice. Historically, the full moon of Tu B'Shvat marked the beginning of the tax year in ancient Israel—according to the rabbis, the moment when the sap began to flow from the roots of the fruit trees into their branches. The festival of Tu B'Shvat was exactly six months from the full moon of Av, the midsummer festival of betrothals and weddings. And just as significantly, it was seven weeks from the beginning of Hanukkah.

For Diaspora Jews living in the European cold, Tu B'Shvat was a vivid reminder, even in the midst of darkness and exile, of the promise of putting down roots and flourishing in *Eretz Yisrael*.

With the kindling of the first light on the Menorah—the Menorah itself replicating the shape of a tree and the olive oil replicating its sap—nature's birth begins anew, discernible in the rising sap of the trees of Tu B'Shvat and the first premonition of spring. This seven-week dormancy from Hanukkah to Tu B'Shvat prefigures the more prominent seven-week dormancy between Pesaḥ and Shavuot—the forty-nine days from the despair of Egypt to the blazing radiance of the Torah at Sinai on the sixth of Sivan and the harvest of the first fruits of summer. The connection between Hanukkah/Tu B'Shvat and Pesaḥ/Shavuot becomes even more meaningful when we realize that *Eitz ha-Or,* the Tree of Light, is one of the favorite rabbinical synonyms for the Torah. The fruit trees of Tu B'Shvat precede the Tree of Light as surely as the first glimpse of Spring precedes Summer. The festival cycle replicates and reinforces the meteorological cycle: the covenant of the Jewish people with the God of Torah occurs only after we covenant with the God of Nature.

Like Jews, Christians also celebrate the first stirring of Spring within the darkness of Winter. Candlemas, the Feast of the Presentation of the Infant Jesus in the Temple, is celebrated on February 2, marking the end of Mary's forty-day *niddah* after Jesus' birth. Official church teaching associated the holiday with feminine fertility and the emergence of Spring. In late medieval Europe, however, popular observance focused less on the events of Mary's life and more on the pagan belief that hibernating bears (not groundhogs, as in Candlemas' American incarnation) would peek out of their caves and then go back to sleep until the emergence of spring six weeks later. Celebrations around the hibernating bear and the passage from darkness to light included singing, dancing, and feasting, but they also had a dark side. In many parts of western Europe, gangs of adolescent males masquerading as wild animals ridiculed unmarried women and attacked recently married husbands whose wives were not yet pregnant.

Candlemas revelers became transformed when they took on the identity of wild animals—like Nebuchadnezzar, crossing the thin membrane between human and animal, light and darkness, civilization and disorder. Nebuchadnezzar and other wild man images became increasingly popular in late medieval Christian culture—not only as emblems of madness, but also of sexuality and fertility—at the same time that formal Candlemas observance was becoming more and more profane. It is as if organized, "official" religion was unable to make the connections to nature that these popular images were able to make.

For Judaism and Christianity alike, Nebuchadnezzar has been historically a potent image. As a contemporary image for us and as a Tu B'Shvat meditation, Nebuchadnezzar's fate reminds us what we can expect if we do not take care of trees. It also reminds us, however, that we can reclaim our humanity if we turn from our pride and, in humility, eat like beasts of the field.

Animal metaphors are of great importance in the rituals and narratives of traditional Judaism. But Jews no more idolize animals than we idolize human beings—the Golden Calf account warns us what the fetishizing of animals can lead to. Anthropomorphizing animals may indeed connect us to the mysteries of nature and the seasons, but it can also degenerate into a superficiality which blurs those mysteries. Witness how the kitsch of Groundhog Day has obliterated the deep meaning of Candlemas for Christians: the mysterious potentiality of Mary's belly and Jesus' presentation in the Temple have given way to inane news reports from Punxsutawney, Pennsylvania every February 2, that the groundhog has seen his shadow and we can expect six more weeks of Winter.

Tu B'Shvat gives us a choice. If the festival continues to be a simple-minded Jewish Arbor Day, it will become to Judaism what Groundhog Day has become to Christianity, a day of kitsch and superficiality, cutting us off from our deepest spiritual roots. If, on the other hand, we approach Tu B'Shvat as a holiday of sacred ecology, it can enable us to reaffirm our relationship to God.

The stories of Nebuchadnezzar and the cripple warn us that the refusal to care for the environment leads to separation from God. But they also tell us that the way out of that separation is connecting with God through nature through planting, watering, tending trees. Tu B'Shvat is an opportunity, once a year, to renew that sacred partnership.

The New Year of the Trees

Marge Piercy

It is the New Year of the Trees, but here
the ground is frozen under the crust of snow.
The trees snooze, their buds tight as nuts.
Rhododendron leaves roll up their stiff scrolls.

In the white and green north of the diaspora
I am stirred by a season that will not arrive
for six weeks, as wines on far continents prickle
to bubbles when their native vines bloom.

What blossoms here are birds jostling
at feeders, pecking sunflower seeds
and millet through the snow: tulip red
cardinal, daffodil finch, larkspur jay,

the pansybed of sparrows and juncos, all hungry.
They too are planters of trees, spreading seeds
of favorites along fences. On the earth closed
to us all as a book in a language we cannot
yet read, the seeds, the bulbs, the eggs

of the fervid green year await release.
Over them on February's cold table I spread
a feast. Wings rustle like summer leaves.

Wisdom and the Two Trees

Alix Pirani

It is customary at Tu B'Shvat to celebrate the Tree of Life in all its mystical and symbolic meanings, and to eat and enjoy fruits. But

253

nothing is said, seemingly, of the other Tree that appeared in the Garden of Eden at the same time as the Tree of Life, nor of the fruit eaten and enjoyed by Eve and Adam. We need to be mindful of that Tree also, since its fallen fruits seeded ideas fundamental to Judaism, and attitudes which have alienated many Jews. And the Tree of Life itself has a rarely mentioned connection: in Proverbs it is identified with Wisdom—*Hokhmah*—a feminine figure whose divine and "human" features are celebrated with startling vividness in the first nine chapters.

> *Her ways are pleasant ways*
> *And all her paths peaceful*
> *She is a tree of life to those who grasp her*
> *And whoever holds on to her is happy (Pro. 3:17–18)*

In this familiar passage, *she* is the Tree of Life, not "it," as rendered in the Siddur, where "it" is Torah. *Hokhmah* was "translated" by the rabbis into Torah. But her complexity and significant creative power needs renewed attention, and we have to lament the obscurity she has been cast into. Her representation in *Mishlei* [Proverbs] reveals her as a divine being in her own right, co-creator of the world with the God of *Bereshit*, who is *Elohim*.

Indeed it is almost suggested—in chapter 8—that she was there first. The nearer one gets to the exact relationship between Hokhmah and Elohim, the more elusive the statements become, the more open to creative interpretation or biased translation. There are places too where it is unclear which of them is speaking to "the sons of men," charging them to attend to "my words"—"her wisdom"—"his commandments"—"my discipline." It sounds like a loving couple talking together to their child.

Mishlei is given scant place in the liturgy, so *Hokhmah*, apart from this concealed reference, is scarcely known. However, in the Beginning, God, we are told, put the Tree of Life in the middle of the Garden and the Tree of Knowledge of Good and Evil. Again the connection is elusive—this time, between the two Trees—and some say they are in effect one and the same. When Eve refers to the Tree in the middle of the Garden, she means the Tree of Knowledge. The separation/confusion of these two Trees is a basic perplexity of Judaism, for the one represents our idealism and the other our realism. The Tree of Life also has a spiritual and historical significance that extends far beyond the confines of Eden and the Jewish religion. Wisdom is present in both Trees, and infinite in time and space.

Tu B'Shvat gives us the opportunity to go back to the roots of Jewish tradition and reassess their meaning for us now. At the cold, cheerless time it occurs, we encourage trees to come to life again— real and spiritual plants, for there is no telling whether they have died at the roots or will survive the winter. The same may be true of our faith and of a Wisdom that has been buried out of sight.

We will have celebrated light in the dark days of Hanukkah, but in January/February there is no warmth: it is the most chilling, depressing time of year (the French call it *morte saison*) and we may wonder if spring will ever come. Often we ourselves are deeply dispirited, uncertain whether we will come to life again and not rot in the earth, as some bulbs do. This is for many the valley of the shadow of death, the valley of dry bones; we are starved of nourishment from the source, be it the sun or our own inner generative faith, the fire of the soul, as individuals, or as a community. At worst there is despair and suicide; at best, for those who cannot find or make artificial brightness and heat, paralysis and mindless hibernation.

This festival comes, after all, between two commemorations of persecution and survival. Hanukkah, for all its positive messages of inextinguishable light, is shadowed and overshadowed by the glamour and power of Christmas. Purim, a month after Tu B'Shvat, expresses an almost manic hilarity: a relief after the anxiety of being in a place of oblivion, as we emerge to the heady greeting of spring. Perhaps the absence of God's name from the book of Esther reflects the uncertainty and doubt we feel when, in the depth of our hopelessness, He seems not to be there and we are left to our own desperate devices, and to the ruthless politics of survival under the tyranny of a Haman, or Antiochus, or Hitler.

Even in our awareness of these two festivals we experience the difference: The spiritual idealism of the Tree of Life belongs with Hanukkah (and the menorah-*ḥanukkiyyah* has its connection with the Kabbalistic Tree); the secular realism of the Tree of Knowledge belongs with Purim. And the defiant, resilient ones in the Megillah are women.

What then do we find when we return to the Trees in the Garden of Eden and look at the soil in which the roots of our faith are nourished? Spiritual ecology demands that for religion to develop creatively what is decayed or rotten is allowed to die—made to die perhaps—and serve as compost, fertilizing new growth. The Kabbalistic Tree of Life is made up of Divine emanations called *sefirot.* At its base is *Malkhut,* which is sovereign territory, supportive ground, and the human expression of the divine in the corruptible world of the material. We shall see presently what that implies.

As symbolized, enshrined, in the Tree, Wisdom is the principle of balance and stability, and in the central pillar, of forward progress also, and of "networking," radiating out to the *sefirot.* And there is an unceasing flow, as all the energies return to her to reinforce the central work. As described in *Mishlei,* Wisdom represents Process itself, and the forward movement, the motivation, to keep learning. . . . "Let your eyes look forward/Your gaze be straight ahead. . . . Do not swerve to the right or the left." (Pro. 4:25–27) She is a celebrant of joy and beauty, so *Tiferet* (compassionate beauty) is at her heart in the Tree, facilitator of the cultivation of loving intelligence and virtue. Her paths are pleasant and bring peace, completion—as do the paths of the Tree. And there is the mystery of her connection with Him, and with the Tree itself: that is, in *Da'at* (intimate knowledge), where infinite and carnal knowledge exist together in a state of not-knowing—a place of intersexual encounter.

Da'at, in the year's onward journey toward the end of Adar, is where Tu B'Shvat is: a time for the death of previous consciousness, for loss of belief even in the Tree's process itself and its two-dimensional scripted function: comparable to the prescriptions and descriptions of our life in the past year.

The *sefirot* appear in each of the kabbalistic Four Worlds of reality: *Atzilut,* Spirit or Being; *Beriyah,* Intellect or Creativity; *Yetzirah,* Relationship or Formation; *Asiyah,* Actuality or Doing. The doubt inherent in *Da'at* inevitably precedes any genuine approach to enlightenment in *Atzilut.* In the area of *Beriyah* and creation, *Da'at* must be experienced when the image of God which once sustained us but has failed us needs to be revised, re-visioned. Shifting upward from one level to another, *Da'at* becomes the *Yesod,* foundation, of the next, inseminating new growth. By planting new trees, new images, at Tu B'Shvat, we lay the foundation for a new generation. The approach to *Atzilut* also needs the balancing of the two *sefirot Binah* (Discernment) and *Ḥokhmah*. Here *Ḥokhmah* is acknowledged as having a role within the system as well as "being" the system.

Returning to *Malkhut*, the area of practical concerns of rulership and territory, we see that the planting by God of the Tree of Life in the middle of the Garden was a political act: a guarantee of stability and progress, but a borrowed one: a transplant. This Tree had been a symbol of spirituality for centuries in many religions, notably connected with Goddess- and nature-oriented pantheism. Specifically, at the time God's domain was being established, were trees sacred to the Goddess Asherah. God was annexing and enclosing the symbol of the Goddess He intended to oust, but who was still an object of great devotion and homage. In time the defeated *Asherah*'s manifold aspects would be re-formed into the three main Hebrew feminine deities: *Ḥokhmah*, the Shekhinah, and Lilith. So the Tree of Knowledge of Good and Evil has to be, inevitably, the twin of the Tree of Life—knowledge of the previous regime of *Asherah* and *Ba'al* and of what was to become of it. And one mustn't forget that in regimes like theirs the gods were seen as having both good and bad characteristics.

The Tree of Life is a symbol of our desire for eternal values, life-enhancement, and confidence that what we do will contribute to divine purpose and make us "as if" immortal, like gods. It is a symbol of aspiration, and belief in the upward evolution of our species. Without that belief, that "uplift," we could be in despair. Human beings are unique in their capacity to symbolize, to imagine; as long as the Tree of Life is there we can use it for the development of human intelligence.

However, verticality—a particularly male concern—is not all, and the horizontal—divine immanence—needs acknowledgment. The other Tree is not about aspiration, but here-and-now reality, our connectedness with other life forms, death, the pain of living in the human brain and body, the consciousness that torments and plagues us instead of enlightening us. This Tree is often pictured with the serpent coiled around it, arising from its roots; but there had long been similar depictions of the serpent coiled around the Tree of Life. We shrink from the Tree of Knowledge even as we are drawn to it: its existence is one with its forbiddenness. No prohibition was put by God on the Tree of Life; only later did He show concern about protecting it from human inroads.

It seems that God put the Trees in the Garden to see what the couple would make of them, what meaning they would find for them, how far they might be edible, tangible, and how far symbolic. That is still our task. For each Tree can be identified with, and represent, God. The one is felt to be benign, life-enhancing: it inspires trust, creative endeavor, promises spiritual validity, and is a unified beautiful whole. The other is mysterious, not to be touched, a threat to life in spite of its attractive appearance; a repository of secret knowledge and unfathomable wisdom: not a unified whole because it contains death and disintegration within itself and is both tempting and forbidding.

Implicit in all this then, is not the question of whether Adam and Eve will die if they eat the prohibited fruit, but of whether the image of their God will die . . . just as the deities who held sway before Him had been condemned to die. It must still be our question today in a very secular world where the Tree of Knowledge dominates and access to the Tree of Life is barred.

The serpent exposes the fact that God's word can't be trusted, nor taken literally; it gets to the root of the paradox of symbolism, and its transformatory act reveals this God shockingly for what He becomes in the story: unloving, ill-tempered, jealous: a cursing, punishing parent-figure who virtually wipes out the two humans before they have developed personalities of their own. Adam and Eve are made to seem like unlovable, and unloving, sulky children, not adults.

There is no dialogue between God and these two humans, no acknowledgment that He is dependent for His survival on how they envision Him. Even with Cain, God could have dialogue; but not with Cain's parents. . . . And they are the original parents of us as Jews. The God of Eden, narcissistic father as He is portrayed, had created man in His own image; He was petulantly disappointed with these offspring, and with what this image of Himself reflected back to Him. He heaped imprecations on Adam and on the treacherous serpent and disloyal Eve, both of whom, in their connection with the Tree, must, as we shall see, remind Him of the missing mother.

Before considering the role of the serpent at the roots of the Tree of Knowledge, I have to stress how disastrous has been that image of a ruthless authoritarian God, which we seem now to take for granted, shrug off perhaps. It rooted itself in the Western psyche because it resonates with primary infantile experience and other psychological and social scenarios. It led to excessive guilt and self-hatred, spiritual paralysis, the subordination of women, and political abuse. These are still with us. The Christian doctrine of original sin was founded on it, as was an unholy attitude to our bodies and to incarnation itself. The breath, Neshama, soul, that was Adam's coming to life, inspiration, was virtually withdrawn as he was told he would return to the dust again.

Later, in the story of Job, we find this original image of a frightening God being confronted and engaged in a fundamental and mature way, but the primary model of a vengeful God who banished dissenters from His territory was followed ever after by totalitarian dictators, religious and political. And familial: a model for Jewish parents, whose disobedient children, having tasted of forbidden knowledge offered by wider society, marry non-Jews.

Planting trees has become one of the important ways for Israel to reclaim the desert, establish its living space. Eden was the first territory God filled with trees and designated to the humans: He then decided they had no moral right to it and expelled them. There followed an endless search for a Promised Land by a people who had an "expulsion complex" and believed they didn't deserve it. *Malkhut*, territory, is, in body terms, the seat, the bottom, the basic "tail end." It is a place of grounding and of defecation/expulsion and of the sordid practicalities in the world of *Asiyah* (Actuality or Doing). To hold on to territory and government involves deviousness and the dirty world of politics, no matter what idealistic banner is raised, based on worthy and genuine intentions. *Keter*, the crowning glory, is said to be in *Malkhut*. That is worth pondering on: it reflects how the Godhead was and is manifest on earth.

It was Mother Earth—*Adamah*—whose territory the God of *Bereshit* took over and called land, *Eretz*. Did He have a moral right

259

to it? It was from *Adamah* that Adam came: the Garden was given to him as a quasi-Paradise and his mother-culture was buried in its soil: the riches and the corruption of that culture: good and evil, the blessings and the ruthless injustice of nature and mother nature, out of which we have to learn moral and ethical ways of living. Just as we have to experience the negativity of *Da'at* on our way to *Atzilut* and *Keter*.

The two *sefirot*, *Binah* and *Ḥokhmah*, remind us that the wisdom and guidance we need on our way are there in the Tree if we look carefully. Not only is *Keter* in *Malkhut*, but so too, it is said, is the Shekhinah—she whose role it is to find form for the divine on earth. But I believe she is accompanied there by the dark aspect of the feminine, Lilith, who is reputed to have been made from the filth of the earth . . . and was eliminated from the system. Lilith is allied, equated even, with the serpent, but perhaps most tellingly she is in *Da'at*, a place of disbelief, loss of bearings: she who is closely connected with free sexuality and death in childbirth. Should the other tree be renamed the Tree of Death? It is here that the fear of death is first suggested. And challenged: for the threat of death may lead not to fear but to defiance—which a childbearing woman has to have—and it has been said that Eve's action proves that the existence of a death penalty is not a deterrent.

The serpent who comes to Eve is a spiritual symbol as old as the Tree of Life itself, powerfully connected with Goddess cultures: so God would be nervous about its influence in Eden. Serpents and snakes have always fascinated, because of their strong insinuating tactile slippery quality: a kind of reptilian instinctual knowing of bodylife, sensual-sexual, a bodylife which God cannot know, only "know about." As a symbol the serpent speaks of metamorphosis. It sloughs its skin; furthermore, though it has been "transcended" in evolutionary reckoning, it is still there, challenging us to assess what our human brains have achieved and to question how we may evolve further. The uroboric serpent also represents a cyclical awareness of time ("In my end is my beginning") which corresponds to the process of the Tree of Life, and other phenomena of timelessness interconnected with time—such as the snakelike umbilical cord in the seemingly timeless womb, which connects the fetus and its soul-memory of infinity with the body through which

260

it is coming into carnate time-bound existence. As *kundalini* energy in the spine, the serpent vitally connects the energies of the body, and this is visible in Wisdom's Tree, where the central pillar has the same spinal role.

The serpent is perhaps genderless, androgynous, without sexual identity. The banished Lilith, often depicted as the serpent in Eden, endures loss of identity in *Da'at*. *Da'at* is a place of body knowledge and any knowledge the Tree can't convey: the *sefirah* of the unconscious, and of the knowledge the Tree doesn't have. Lilith knew the secret name of God, and called it out, but it has remained a secret. What the patriarchs' Kabbalistic Tree didn't explicitly "know" yet unconsciously knew was the power of the feminine. Lilith and the serpent knew that in time the Goddess would return—as the women's movement is bearing out. That must cause a metamorphosis of the prevailing image of God. We are at present in *Da'at*: so is the whole world.

As a proud daughter of the great Creatrix, Lilith could not accept subordination by Adam; demonized, she became the legendary scapegoat for many of the ills and evils afflicting humanity which were omitted from the story of Creation. Once that story was told to human beings, cracks began to appear in it. The serpent—perhaps Lilith making mischief, perhaps the first Talmudic quibbler—questioned the storyteller's word, and Eve, who has been called the first scientist, tested it. God had, after all, not spoken to her but to Adam: the serpent did speak to her. In her "naked innocence" she could only use her own judgment, based on seeing that the Tree offered nourishment, beauty and discernment. She ignored the prohibition: the serpent has reminded her of her strength and her woman's familiarity with blood-loss, death and cyclical time, and has indeed led her into dis-grace and lost innocence: the knowledge of what a powerful patriarch can do to a woman who will not be a subordinate helpmeet. Eve had to learn her lesson. . . . "The beginning of wisdom? The acquisition of wisdom." In *Mishlei*, Wisdom insists on discipline as essential to learning.

Adam too is disempowered and these typecast guilt-ridden victims go forward to centuries of victimization by Christianity—Jews and women humiliated and slaughtered mercilessly in the Middle Ages and thereafter. But genocide has its precedents in the slaughters effected by their Biblical God, and in the ghastly plagues and epidemics that have ravaged, and still do ravage us. And still, as in Eden, we lay blame and suffer guilt feelings in a vengeance-oriented morality. It seems we cannot accept that pain is, simply, pain; nor accept the transpersonal forces of nature, of "the gods": we prefer feeling guilty and important to feeling helpless.

All these truths that lie in the Tree of Knowledge must be disagreeable to us as optimistic seekers after joy and enlightenment, wanting to celebrate and venerate the Tree of Life. In our suffering the benign, comforting, compassionate Shekhinah is available to us through the Tree, reassuring, motherly, mediating between a stern God and humans, a principle of light, *Hesed*, peace and shelter. But we must beware lest her fear of destructive forces—she fled when the Temple was destroyed—makes her blind to danger, over-protective, complacent even. Unlike Lilith, she is not acutely aware of the treacherous painful life of the body: she is "out-of-body."

My fear is that the male interpretations of Kabbalah, their reverence for the Shekhinah, and the Hasidic ecstasies associated with the Tu B'Shvat seder, evade the darker facts and may subtly reinforce the regime of a God who does not speak to Eve except in reproof. I see Lubavitcher men dancing worldwide with their Judaism, spreading the wise teachings of their Rebbe, but I rarely see or hear their women. Fundamentalism gets its license from the male God of Eden, claims exclusive rights to Tree of Life mysticism, and enables events such as the Hebron massacre.

The Shekhinah may bring us *shalom*—peace and a feeling of completion, of healing for our wounded and alienated souls and bodies. But wise *Hokhmah* knows that peace on an over-populated earth will never be permanent. Lilith is said by men to have spawned thousands of demons from men's sperm—and by women to have invented contraception. The implications are clear; and in her place at the base of the Tree she knows that some saplings, seeds, weeds, perforce die and rot because there is no room for them: they would impede healthy growth in select species.

Who is selected? Who is chosen to survive? Indeed there is a spiritual ecology that we can only submit to, trusting in its hardly imaginable purpose. Wisdom is that ecological balancing process. Since she was there to co-create the universe, then she must be restored to her place again next to the God who used her and then lost her. She can no longer remain hidden, because she is needed now for the task of re-creating our discredited religion.

I have come to realize that my respect for the Tree of Life as an awesome medium of spiritual intelligence and creative process, and my devoted, loving commitment to it, is the backbone of my religion. Here I can keep my dignity as an adult, body, mind and soul: a spiritual, political, imagining person. Wisdom bids me assess what the established God has come to stand for and what the relationship is between the two of them now. She bids me keep pushing at the thresholds of knowledge which has been withheld. She can only agree with Eve's eating of the Tree. In *Mishlei* she says nothing about exact truths, only about never ceasing to ask timeless questions and find timebound answers. So if we keep the image of the timeless Tree of Life always with us, and keep the image of the time-bound Tree of Knowledge alongside equally, we can go forward with the work of creation. And we need not lose regard for the God whose image can still be re-formed, an image to which we have given questionable homage. *Ehiyeh asher ehiyeh* (I will be who I will be) is, after all, His name.

At Tu B'Shvat let our blessing go to the select fortunate trees who survive the cheerless cold, to the people who survive loss of faith, and to the saplings and new ideas we plant. We wish them all *Ḥazak*, strength, for they will need it. . . . The full moon presides here, for she knows what it is to go into the shadow, to die and be born again. She bids us never lose hope, nor faith that our innate desire for wisdom will be answered.

 # The Human, the Tree, and the Image of God

David Seidenberg

Jewish mysticism imagines the cosmos to be a manifestation of the divine which unfolds through ten powers or qualities, which are called the *sefirot*. The world of the *sefirot* is typically pictured in terms of two forms: a cosmic tree and a primordial human body. The *sefirot* represent the way in which divinity becomes manifest in and cloaked by creation. They are seen as both emanated and eternal, created and pre-existent; as such, the *sefirot* become the pattern both for God and creation.

The Kabbalah maps the central *sefirot* onto the organs and limbs of a body that is in general, with some exceptions, seen as male: the three "brains" of "HaBaD," which are wisdom (*Hokhmah*), understanding (*Binah*) and knowing (*Da'at*); the right and left arms, which are *Hesed* and *Gevurah*, love and might; the heart-space, *Tiferet*, beauty; the legs, *Netsah* and *Hod*, eternity and majesty, and the phallus of Yesod, foundation. This structure is bounded above by *Keter* or crown, the primordial spark, and below by *Malkhut*, kingdom, which is conceived as a female persona and sometimes as the vulva in a female body. (The number of the *sefirot*, leaving out *Da'at*, is ten. *Da'at* was added in many kabbalistic systems as a kind of reflection of *Keter* above, which is sometimes seen as too refined to be counted among the lower *sefirot*. This is the source of the *Hokhmah-Binah-Da'at* triad with which many are familiar through Lubavitch Hasidism.)

The system of the *sefirot* is also imagined in terms of roots and branches, with the roots above drawing down the divine *shefa* or flow from the highest world, and the branches sustaining the most physical dimension of reality. The whole tree exists in order to produce the fruit of righteous souls and to sustain all of creation in this world.

These two pictures overlap most clearly in the central *sefirot*, which are described both as the trunk of a body and the trunk of a tree. It is this tree which we celebrate on Tu B'Shvat, the "New Year for the Tree," as Kabbalists understood the mishnaic phrase "*rosh ha-shanah la-ilan*." The way in which these forms overlap has three obvious implications: (1) the human is patterned in the image of both creation and God simultaneously, (2) creation in its totality is therefore also "in God's image," and (3) the tree itself is also created in the image of God.

A secondary implication of these images is that a human body and a tree share in one ultimate pattern. These conclusions are both radical and strange to someone unfamiliar with Jewish mysticism. Even after we become familiar with the texts of Kabbalah, we are still left pondering the question of what it all means.

Leaving aside until later in this essay the emphasis on the male body found in these texts, and a host of other problems (especially the strangely anthropomorphic picture of God which seems to contradict everything most of us have been taught about monotheism), this article will explore the most basic question: "How is a human like a tree?" or in the words of Deut. 20:19: *Ha-adam eitz ha-sadeh?*/"Is the tree of the field a human?" We will use this question to draw out insights about the centrality of the body in Judaism and the ecological interpretation of Jewish rituals.

The Central Column

Sefer Ha-Bahir, the Book of Brightness, which was redacted in the twelfth century but includes much older parts, is the earliest document to explore these themes, earlier even than the codification of the *sefirot*. In its beginning paragraphs, it describes a king playfully discovering a spring of flowing, living water as he begins to cut out the stone from which to build his palace. What does he do? He plants a garden, and a tree, to "delight the whole world."

The text, continuing in God's voice, tells us that the first thing God created, even before the angels, was this tree:

> "I am the one that planted this tree, for all the world to delight in him; and I hammered out all/*kol* with him, and I called his name "all/*kol*," for all/*hakol* depends on him, and all comes out from him. And all need him, and [to] him they look forward, and for him they wait. And from there grow the souls in joy. I was by myself when I made him. (Bahir, section 22)[1]

The tree of the Bahir eventually became synonymous with the *sefirot*. In the passage above, even though the tree has the otherworldly function of "growing the souls," it seems to be strictly a part of creation, brought into being for the sake of the world.

In the following passage we learn that this tree is also part of divinity. Here the Bahir is giving its interpretation of the word *ish*/ "man" in Exod. 15:3, which states that "YHWH is a man of war." The Bahir explicates that the third letter of *ish* refers to the tree:

> [A]nd Shin [in the word *ish*], what would it be? He said to him:
> The tree's root, for Shin [with its three extensions] would be
> like the design/*ayn* of the tree's root/*shoresh*.
>
> And what would the tree be that you spoke of? He said to him:
> The powers of the Holy One, this one on back of this one, and
> they resemble a tree, in that this tree, by means of the waters,
> brings out fruit. . . . They [the waters] are wisdom, and they
> [the fruit] are the souls of the righteous that grow from the
> spring. (Bahir, section 118–19)

"The powers of the Holy One," which are the channel for wisdom and creative power, are in the form of a tree. This tree appears
as a source of creation itself, and a direct emanation of God. However, this divine emanation, no matter how directly associated with
God, is still dependent on human action. Using the verse "*Tzaddik*
founds the world" (Pro. 10:25), the Bahir explains that "[there is] a
single column from the earth to the firmament, and *Tzaddik*, The
Righteous One, is its name, and when there are righteous peo-
ple/*tzaddikim* in the world, it becomes strong, and if not it becomes
weak." (Bahir, section 100)

The image the Bahir uses, "a single column from the earth to the
firmament," emphasizes that the tree, the column, the *tzaddik* and
man are all images in the Bahir of what connects the upper
and lower worlds, and of what is dependent upon both the
upper and lower worlds.

To the human eye, no creature embraces heaven and earth more
than a tree. A tree is poised in between worlds, its roots dividing
out smaller and deeper into the earth beneath until they seem to
dissolve in it, its branches soaring above us, full of leaves like hands
holding the sky.

This same sense of stretching characterizes human experience in
our most wakeful moments: the sense of being between, of stretching to embrace physical and spiritual. This sense is expressed in the
working of our minds and in our physical posture, stretched from
earth to heaven. The shape of the word for tree used here, *ilan*,
shows this same quality: the *lamed* stretching upward, the *nun*
probing downward. The tree and the human body both become
symbols for what unites the divine and the mundane, and for how
the worlds depend upon each other and flow toward one another.

Root and Branch

Kabbalah is not only interested in the cosmic tree as a symbol of divine connection. It also tries to understand this connection by reflecting on the anatomy of trees and of the human body. The Bahir continuously weaves together images of the tree and the human body, as we have already seen in the midrash on the word *ish*, above.

The "single column" we have read about is not just the trunk of a tree; it is also the spinal cord, one vertebra upon another, as was hinted at in the phrase "the powers of the Holy One, this one on back of this one, [which] resemble a tree." In this metaphor, the source of water or wisdom is the brain, and the spinal cord the channel, which carries the water to every part of the body.

The dynamics and dimensions shared by the tree, the human body, the world and God, are especially closely examined in the ritual of waving the *lulav*, which is so strongly connected to both the human body and to trees. According to *Sefer Ha-Bahir*, the myrtle, willow and *lulav* become like a human body when they are bound together:

> [I]t says, "Take . . . a branch of a tree thick-interlaced/*anaf eitz avot*" (Levi. 23:40). It must be that his branches are stretched around/over his main part. A *mashal*, to what does it compare? To a person, who has his arms and protects his head with them, and here his arms are two and his head makes three: *anaf* (willows) to the left, *avot* (myrtle) to the right, and *eitz* is found in the middle [the *lulav*]. And why is he [the *lulav*] called "a tree" [when he is only a single branch]? Because he is the root of the tree. (Bahir, section 176)

The three-word phrase from the Torah, *anaf eitz avot*, is traditionally understood to refer to myrtle branches, but the Bahir reads it as referring to all three species which are bound together. The binding of myrtle, willow, and *lulav* turns them into a single body. The *lulav* branch stands for the whole tree because it is its "root" (the place from which all new growth occurs), and so it is like a person's head, which stands for the whole person.

The cosmic axis is not only represented as a tree and a human body, but the symbols of the tree and the human are images which converge together in a single picture of the body. The Bahir identifies the fruit, heart, spinal cord, body, and root together in the following passage:

> Israel, holy ones, carry the body of the tree and his heart. As a heart is majesty/*hadar*, the fruit of the body, even so Israel bears the fruit of the tree of majesty (*peri eitz hadar* = *etrog*). As a date palm, its branches around [the crown] and its *lulav* in the middle, even so Israel carries the body of the tree: this is its heart. And corresponding to the body is the cord of the [spinal] column in a person, which is the root/*ikar* of the body. And just as *lulav* [can be] written, *lu leiv*/"to him a heart," even so the heart is tied to him [the spinal cord]. (Bahir, section 98)

This is reminiscent of the well-known midrash that also maps the ritual of the *lulav* to the human body (*lulav* branch to spine, *etrog* to heart, willow to lips, myrtle to eyes), but it is far more complex. Because the Jewish people carries the symbols of the heart, the *lulav* and *etrog*, in our Sukkot prayers, we collectively become the body of the divine *Tzaddik* who carries the heart. By the same token, we become the cosmic tree because we bear its fruit and branches.

A brief botany lesson from my friends on kibbutz: the *lulav* is the only place from which new branches grow in a date tree, though sometimes a baby *lulav* will grow from the base of the trunk to form a new tree. To take the central *lulavim* from a tree is to kill the tree (the *lulavim* we use on Sukkot are offshoots taken from the base). The main *lulav* is therefore like a heart: it contains all the vitality of the tree and all of its vulnerability.

The Bahir emphasizes that the heart is tied to the spine (we might understand this to mean: tied by the nerves to the spine), as the fruit is tied to the root by the tree trunk. This is important because according to Kabbalah, the sin of the Garden of Eden is not eating from the tree of knowledge, but separating the fruit from the tree; this separation is what brings death.

Israel repairs this sin when we unite the *etrog* with the *lulav*. We reconnect the fruit to the source of its vitality every time we do a mitzvah. The picture of inverted roots invoked by the word *eitz*, the word for tree used in the passages above, also teaches us to tap second roots, new roots, deep into the divine "above," like the long branching form of the final *tzaddi*.

268

The Opening of the Body

The metaphor of the heart is also a metaphor of the center branching out to touch every part of the whole. The human body is like a tree on the inside, each system branching into smaller and smaller vessels and spaces until every body cell is reached by the blood, every part touched by a nerve, every blood cell breathing as it passes by the tiny alveoli in our lungs. Every organ and gland has similarly branching networks which connect cells to ducts. Every part of the body is in connection with every other part, enabling it to fulfill its function for every cell. It is only because we are animals, "packaged" to move, as it were, that we don't see all our fractal branching, that our bodies appear to be smooth and rounded surfaces.[2]

Even the appearance of a clear boundary which our skin gives to our bodies is a kind of illusion. For every surface of the body, despite its apparent smoothness, is also a branching out, an extension of the senses, of breath and sweat and fluid, a casting out upon the world beyond the apparent boundary it represents. David Abram writes most eloquently:

> [T]he boundaries of the body are open and indeterminate; more like membranes than barriers, they define a surface of metamorphosis and exchange. The breathing, sensing body draws its sustenance and its very substance from the soils, plants, and elements that surround it; it continually contributes itself, in turn, to the air, to the composting earth, to the nourishment of insects and oak trees and squirrels, ceaselessly spreading out of itself as well as breathing the world into itself, so that it is very difficult to discern, at any moment precisely where this living body begins and ends.[3]

It is this openness, and our ability to reflect on this openness through the gift of insight and imagination, which makes the human body especially, along with other bodies, a metaphor for God's connection in the world, the infinity which unfolds within the finite.

When we shake the *lulav* we bring all these meanings together, the sensual and the metaphysical and the physical; the prayer for next year's rain and the living growth of last year's rain, which represents the body or cycle of the year; the plants of desert and mountains and river and plains, which represent the body of the land, together with our own bodies.

Every sense draws us out: the smell of citrus and the sweet smell of myrtle, the clattering sound of *lulav* fronds striking each other, the shapes of the different leaves, elongate, sword-like, rounded, red laced through the green of the willow, *hadas* in its three-foldedness, the feeling of an *etrog's* skin. The *lulav*, bound together with the other species, is like the opening of the body itself, opening through different senses, directions, and organs. As such it becomes an extension of our own bodies.

Other rituals and images can also be understood as analogues to the human body. Consider a tallit, which halakhically is literally like a body: it must be big enough to cover most of a person's body, shoulder-to-shoulder. As Arthur Waskow has explained, the *tzitzit* fringes are one of a series of mitzvot that teach us that there are no sharp corners, not to our faces, nor our bodies, nor our fields. The twilight-colored winding thread which some Jews still use draws us out (as the Talmud and the Bahir both explain) to the sea and sky and beyond, showing us how far our bodies connect beyond the boundaries of skin. The purpose of *tzitzit* is to teach us to remember, and they are a kind of model for memory itself: a knot which is fixed at the edge of the self, leading along multiple paths to the manifold of the world.

A Problem We Don't Like to Talk About[4]

Anytime we think about the meaning of the body we must also consider the meaning of gender. We noted above that the cosmic tree of Kabbalah is predominantly male. While the Bahir emphasizes that the date palm is a particularly appropriate image for the divine because "she contains male and female" (section 188), the central column or tree is primarily conceived of as a phallus from whose seed grows the souls of Israel and the righteous.[5]

In the Zohar and later Kabbalah this is emphasized to an even greater degree. For example, this is how the Zohar describes the genesis of the cosmic tree:

> The male is extended into Knowledge, so that the convocations and assemblies become filled from it. From the top of the skull the process begins, expanding throughout the body, going into the breast, the arms, everywhere. . . . Again does the male expand from both the right and the left. . . . When these two elements [of right and left] come together their union is called Splendor. This gives form to the entire body so that it becomes a great Tree, mighty, beautiful and fair. . . . The genital member of the male is the summation of the entire body.[6]

In the same passage we also read: "[W]hen the male couples with the female they actually become one body, and all the worlds are joyful because they receive blessing from the complete body." This is followed by the statement: "The beauty of the female is derived entirely from the beauty of the male." It would be easy for us, but false, to hold up the former sentence as egalitarian and to ignore the latter one.

The Bahir and the Zohar focus on the phallus as a symbol of divine emanation and blessing, perhaps because they emerged from circles of men who tried to understand the cosmos from the reality of their own bodies.

While zoharic and later kabbalistic literature also describes Malkhut, or Shekhinah, as female and even as a vulva, the female is never represented as a fully imagined body, with height, limbs, organs, etc., on par with the male. Elliot Wolfson, in his groundbreaking book *The Circle in the Square*, argues that this is because the female in Kabbalah is meant to be incorporated within the male, which is why we also find strange images of Malkhut as the corona of the phallus. He concludes that "[t]he phallocentrism of kabbalistic symbolism so overwhelms the perspective on gender that the female is reduced to an aspect of the male."[7]

How should we think of these images in terms of the politics of gender? Can we live with the unbalanced representation of male over female, and can we accept that our "gendered openings," the parts of our bodies through which we experience sex and gender, are so essential to the kabbalistic way of imagining God?

271

We are faced with difficult choices in the task of reinterpreting Kabbalah. Should we create a separate Kabbalah of the female body alongside the Kabbalah of the male body, one which develops the partial images we find in traditional Jewish mysticism? Should we psychologize the ideas of male and female, find ways for each person to identify with both the female and male within them, as has been done within Jewish Renewal? Should we dismiss Kabbalah because of its deep structure of sexual hierarchy and try to found a new mysticism?

The Kabbalah is rooted in ideas about gender and essence that egalitarian Judaism has mostly rejected. But an egalitarianism which ignores gender and sexual identity cuts itself off from a very deep source of meaning and power. Whether we make essential the diversity of male and female, or make light of this diversity, we end up by cutting ourselves off from the deep complexity of our bodies. In order to become fully cognizant of the openness of the body to the world, we must go beyond the Kabbalah's traditional focus on our gendered openings, but we may still learn much from the emphasis on what is open, relational, and unbounded about the body.

The constant flow and ebb which defines the lives of animal and human, plant and tree, the flow which fills the human experience with sacredness and anxiety and beauty and terror and hope, includes fertility and sexuality. One of the pitfalls of focusing on the problem of sexism in human society is that we may end up ignoring the broader context of the lives of animals and all other creatures. This problem has been widely explored in eco-feminist philosophy. The fact that the human body is analogized to a tree in Kabbalah also suggests ways in which we can explore this broader context.

By thinking more deeply about the meaning of sex and gender within Kabbalah we may find that the emphasis on the hierarchy of male over female becomes less prominent and more open to interpretation. Perhaps we can find new ways to explore the idea of gender, focusing not on the male or female per se, but on the uniqueness of each body, a uniqueness which includes sexual feeling and rapture, extension of self and enfolding of other.

It may be that we can understand the emphasis in Kabbalah on the male as a particular perspective on certain ways that the body communicates and nurtures through sexuality.

272

The way one's sense of self is "knit together" in moments of sexual union and pleasure, to use a phrase from the Zohar, is repeated on many levels of sensual experience and knowing. The challenge is to recognize this in and through our bodies, as physical, as male or female as they are, and in the bodies of other creatures, and not only through our ideas.

By doing so we may open ourselves up to the diversity of all creatures, each of which manifests an image of the divine. What Irigaray claims is true for women could then be true for both men and women, for all: "She finds pleasure almost anywhere . . . the geography of her pleasure is far more diversified, more multiple in its differences, more complex, more subtle, than is commonly imagined.[8]

Through careful meditation and reflection, we may find that the answer to the problem of gender in Kabbalah comes from within Kabbalah itself. This is not, however, an answer to a problem, only a prologue to a question we must continue to work on in our communities and our practices.

Ultimately, the struggle to understand the spiritual depth and meaning of the body must emerge from our own experiences and self-understanding.

Sensuous Minds

We open out to touch other creatures, other forms, and most importantly, the earth itself. Our rituals connect our bodies to the cycles of the earth; they are physical, not spiritual, ideas. Halakhah precisely defines the dimensions of each ritual: The inner leaves of a *lulav* must not be separated from each other, they must conjoin as one branch. The *etrog* must have its *pitom*, what remains of the ovary and the flower, intact.

Ideally, halakhic requirements define not just an idea or interpretation but an experience of meaning. These definitions teach us to bind the inside and the outside, the internal and the external, the physical and the spiritual, the sensible and the sensual. We are working to understand the phenomenology of ritual when we think about it this way. By doing so we also understand something about the nature of our consciousness and self. The human body, as we have understood it, is really a form for consciousness, a form which connects rather than contains. Irene Diamond talks about "the sensuous mind" in her work, a concept which is well suited to talk about the opening of the body as the form of consciousness.

The body and mind, the two which are one, are called by the one word *nefesh* in the Torah. The sensuous mind is the sensuous body. David Abram, drawing on the work of Merleau-Ponty,[9] helps us to understand this quality when he describes the body as an "open circuit":

> My senses connect up with each other in the things I perceive, or rather each perceived thing gathers my senses together in a coherent way, and it is this that enables me to experience the thing itself as a center of forces, as another nexus of experience, as an Other . . . [T]he intertwining of my body with the things it perceives is effected only through the interweaving of my senses, and vice versa.
>
> The relative divergence of my bodily senses (eyes in the front of the head, ears toward the back, etc.) and their curious bifurcation (not one but two eyes, one on each side, and similarly two ears, two nostrils, etc.) indicates that this body is destined to the world; it ensures that my body is a sort of open circuit that completes itself only in things, in others, in the encompassing earth.[10]

Ritual can teach us to open our thinking to this intertwining, to think "sensuously." It is no accident that the Jewish tradition even turns language itself into an offering of the body, in the prayer-meditation of the Amidah, which calls on us to move our lips, to say these words, to sway our torsos, to bow here. If our body is destined to the world, then somehow we can understand the world, even the world of prayer, through our bodies.

We might say that the body becomes one through perception, that the mind becomes one through reflection, and that this is what it means to "close the circuit." *Sefer ha-Bahir* sees a kind of circuit in ritual which is much greater than this circuit of human consciousness that unites perceiver and perception. In its language, ritual "unites the forms, powers, and holy ones." The Bahir, in its explanation of worship, claims that human ritual unites God's presence as well:

> And why is [a Temple sacrifice] called *korban*, "bringing near"? Only because it brings near the forms, the powers, the holy ones, as it's written (Ezek. 37:17), "And bring them near, one-toward-one to you, to [become] one tree, and they will be united by your hand." (Bahir, section 109)

The circuit of the cosmic tree runs between the divine self and the fullness of the world, a circuit which we complete through mitzvah. It is like tying a bundle of wheat stalks together so that it can stand. We end our prayers with a line that is resonant with this idea of uniting God in the world: "On that day YHWH will be one and his [sic] name one." According to some interpretations in Kabbalah, this means uniting the "powers," i.e., the levels of being between the spring and the souls and this world, so that by uniting them to become "one tree," we bring blessing to the world.

The Tu B'Shvat seder is one of the few Jewish rituals that focuses on uniting these levels consciously. As such, it gives us an opportunity to consider the tremendous connections between creatures and cosmos, between sustenance and sustaining forces, between human and tree and God's wisdom.

Yet the Tu B'Shvat seder is mainly a symbolic ritual, i.e., something that has meaning once a year when we think about its symbols. It is incumbent on us to connect to the deepest levels of action, of sustaining and witnessing and praying, in all moments, whether we find this by dwelling in the *sukkah*, or by taking care of people, or by meditating at sunset, in all the ways that our tradition commands us and in all the ways that the world itself teaches us.

This level can be found in moments of ritual, of righteousness, of sensing and being aware of our bodies. Such moments give us a glimpse into the unity of patterns and meanings bigger than our selves.

The unity of human and tree which is the basis of the kabbalistic Tu B'Shvat seder is not just a metaphor for how important trees are to us, but a meditation on the idea that both trees and human creatures are patterned after the life of the cosmos. By examining humans and trees together, we may understand something deeper about the meaning of the life we are given and its place in the life of the world.

From *The Wisdom of the Jewish Sages*

Rami Shapiro

Rabbi Jacob says:
If you are walking lost in wonder,
empty of self, and mindful of Reality,
and suddenly you interrupt this peace to exclaim:
"How beautiful is this tree! How magnificent this field!"
you forfeit life.
The intrusion of self and the imposing of judgment
separates you from Reality
and snares you in the net of words.
Be still and know.
Embrace all in silence.

Mishnah Avot 3:9

Re/Membering Nature

Rami Shapiro

A story is told about a rabbi and a gardener.

The rabbi was working with his gardener friend as the latter set out to plant several trees about his property. In the midst of their planting they heard a great tumult arising from the city, about a mile to the east.

Outside the city gates a massive cloud of dust arose as hundreds of people made their way out to the surrounding fields and farms. The rabbi and the gardener stopped their work to watch the approaching throng. Men, women and children were dancing joyously; their faces lifted skyward; their voices ringing with praise.

As the crowd drew near, its leaders called out to the rabbi and his friend: "Come quickly! The Messiah has arrived and we go out to greet him!"

The gardener tossed his hoe aside and made to join the crowd, but the rabbi laid a heavy hand upon the other's shoulder and bade him wait. In time the throng passed, and the two men were alone.

"How dare you keep me from the Messiah," the gardener cried out, his voice cracking with anger and despair.

The rabbi picked up the fallen hoe and handed it to his friend. "Messiahs come and go," he said softly, "but the task of planting never ceases."

Thus Rabbi Nathan reminds us: If you are planting a tree and they come to you saying: "Come and greet the Messiah," first plant the tree and then go meet him. Redemption is in the very act of planting.

Rabbi Nathan's pithy comment is the basis for this little tale. I imagine Rabbi Nathan half listening to a group of sages argue over when it is proper to greet the Messiah. One after the other, the masters of Torah offer objections to each other's positions. Their delight is in the quickness of their responses, the sharpness with which they deflate what on the surface seems a reasonable proposition.

Two things the sages take for granted: the first is that the Messiah will probably never show up; the second is that we must go out to greet him when he does.

This is the wonderful paradox at the heart of Jewish teaching. The world is not a case of *either/or:* either sin or redemption, either right or wrong, either good or evil. The world is not *either/or* but *and:* sin and redemption, right and wrong, good and evil. The God of the Jews is the imageless "And" that is infinite possibility.

When we forget the "And," however, we seek to impose the *either/or* idolatry of limited human reasoning. When the *either/or* takes hold, we take ourselves far too seriously, and inflict much unnecessary suffering on the world. When we insist that the world is *either/or,* we divide person and planet; we invent scarcity and the national boundaries needed to enforce it; we see the stranger as enemy and the other as stranger. When we fall into the trap of *either /or,* we replace virtue with law, symbol with sacrament, *aggadah* with *halacha.*

When our sages get caught up in the minutiae of their own *either/or* reasoning, their words become more important than the reality to which they once referred. It is then that the law becomes

God and God is reduced to law. It is then that the simple reality of everyday living is lost beneath the pseudo facts of legal fiction.

So I imagine Rabbi Nathan, a sage of "And," half listening to the *either/or* wranglings of his friends. Do we greet him first, or second? What if we are reciting the *Shema?* Or what if we are in the privy? Or what if we are planting a tree—

"Enough!" Nathan shouts, no longer able to ignore their foolishness. "First plant the tree," he yells at them. "Just plant the tree!" For a moment his friends stare at him, open mouthed, their attention pulled away from themselves and their cleverness.

""What are you saying, Nathan?"

"Listen: if you are planting a tree and the people come and tell you the Messiah has arrived, finish planting before you go to see him. That's all. Finish the planting."

"So, Mister Big Shot Sage, that's all? Just finish the planting? And where is this written?"

Rabbi Nathan smiles. He enjoys rattling his friends. He knows that they are just playing with this kind of *either/or* talk, though he fears that what is fun for them now will one day become deadly serious for their heirs. "People will remember our words," he would often caution his colleagues, "but who will pass on the laughter that accompanied them?"

"Messiah comes in response to one of two situations," Rabbi Nathan says to his friends. "If we fulfill our nature, Messiah will arrive. And if we totally degrade our nature Messiah will arrive. Now the question is: What is our nature, and what does it mean to fulfill or degrade it?

"What is our nature? Our nature is to plant. Is this not what *Torah* tells us? *Adam,* the human, from *adamah,* the earth. Adam the earthling raised up out of the dust to plant, till, and tend the Garden. When we cease to tend we cease to be *adam.* When we cease to be *adam;* we pervert our true nature.

"We fulfill our nature when we plant. We degrade it when we uproot. We plant when we live in a manner that reveals the connection between all things. We uproot when we live in a manner that separates and divides. We fulfill our nature when we make plain the interdependence of all things. We degrade our nature when we pretend to independence.

"We plant when we take our place in the world, recognizing that we are *adam* from *adamah*, earthlings at one with earth. We degrade ourselves when we insist upon being homeless, without place, aliens and strangers rather than gardeners and tenders. This is why we call God *haMakom*, the Place. Do we call God *That* Place, as if there was some place devoid of God? No! God is *the* Place, *this* Place, *every* place we happen to awaken to the interdependence of each and all."

Rabbi Nathan looked from one face to the other. His friends were listening, but were they hearing? For a moment he felt a terrible urge to make it all a joke, and let them get back to their discussion. He could tell himself that humor is the greater teacher. True enough, but Nathan was no humorist. He frowned instead of smiling, and plunged ahead.

"Messiah will come when we have totally lost our Place, for then we will have completely degraded nature, ours and everything else's. But even if Messiah did come then, we would be unable to go out to greet him. Why? We would no longer be able to recognize him. So long would we have devoted ourselves to rooting out the stranger that we would no longer recognize the face of the Friend. So busy would we be carving the earth into parcels upon which to build fences and house armies, that we would have no time to build a gate and welcome the other. The Messiah would arrive and none would care.

"But if we maintain the planting, if we attend to tending, we will attend to ourselves, to our true nature, and to the true nature of all things. When we attend to ourselves we see that we are *adam*, earthlings. When we see we are *adam* we suddenly see we are also *adamah*, earth. We will see that we are not alien to this world, but an expression of it. Just as the fig tree figs, so *adamah adams*, God peoples.

"When we see that *adam is adamah*, we cease to be separate from our Place. Ceasing to be separate, we cease to war within ourselves. Ceasing to war within ourselves we cease to war among ourselves. Taking our Place, or better discovering that *the* Place is *every* Place, we are no longer blinded by the false scarcity we invent to maintain the illusion of us and them, ours and theirs. No longer driven by the fear of having less, we can help all to have more.

"Coming to Place is coming to our senses. Coming to our senses is awakening to the wonder of being *adam/adamah*. Our whole being is alive as an expression of God. We suddenly know that God is all and all is God.

"And then we would have no need to stop our planting to greet the Messiah. For then we would greet the Messiah in each seedling we plant, in each sapling we water, in each tree we prune and harvest, in each face we meet. If you need to stop the planting to greet the Messiah, you are already lost, for you have already mistaken the Messiah for someone else. For the planting is Messiah. So too the planter and the planted. Finish the planting and then greet him, if indeed you still feel the need."

Rabbi Nathan turned back to the task at hand: bundling wood for kindling. His friends, stood quietly looking—first at Nathan, then at each other, then again at Nathan, and then again at each other. At last one of them spoke:

"But, what if you're planting and the High Priest comes to you and says, . . ."

Tu B'Shvat is not Jewish Earth Day. Tu B'Shvat is not a call to go back to Nature. Nature is not nostalgic. Nature doesn't long to go back to anything. To what would Nature return? Nature is acutely present. Nature tends to what is.

Tu B'Shvat is a call to return to our nature. Tu B'Shvat is an opportunity to recognize that we are *adamah;* to remember (literally to re-member, to put back together) the supposedly shattered self that pretends to be other than Nature. Tu B'Shvat is an opportunity to plant ourselves firmly in the Place that is every place, and to awaken to the fundamental unity of God, woman, man and Nature.

You and I are Nature! We are Nature's way of looking at herself, of thinking about herself, of recreating herself. We are Nature's way of tending; Nature's way of doing what must be done. If we are to fulfill our nature, we must reclaim the ability to attend. To attend means to be at the task of tending, to be at the work of doing what needs to be done.

How do we reclaim the ability to attend?

We must learn to take root. Socially, politically, and economically this means to take responsibility for the place in which we live: to hold fast the soil of community. Spiritually, it means to quiet the mind and be still.

We quiet the mind when we do what needs doing without self-conscious hesitation. When we act without hesitation we act without ego, without pride, without prejudice, without error. When we act without hesitation we act from the Whole for the Whole. When we act without hesitation we act as Messiah.

When we act this way we have no need to stop the planting to greet the Messiah. We know that Messiah neither leaves nor arrives. With Rabbi Nathan we know that redemption—awakening to the unity of each and All—is in the very act of planting.

Tu B'Shvat as a Visual, Mystical Rosh HaShanah

David Wolfe-Blank

Concept of a "Rosh" HaShanah

Mystically speaking, the fact that a new year is called a *rosh*, a head, rather than some other term, suggests that the New Year day is more than a *Reishit*, a beginning, but is rather a *rosh*, a brain having a holographic influence on the energies of the rest of the year. Hasidic and Kabbalistic thought teaches that the calendar affecting Rosh HaShanah (the first of Tishrei) embeds within itself a map of the rest of the year, each hour of Rosh HaShanah enfolding a week of the upcoming year, as the brain affects every nerve and system of the body, no matter how far in the distance. That is why Hasidim are so careful on Rosh HaShanah to avoid any idle chatter on these forty-eight hours—that some week in the middle of the year doesn't slip by in unconsciousness, in idle waste, parallel to the hour spent thoughtlessly on Rosh HaShanah.

281

"Rosh" Ḥodesh

"Rosh" Ḥodesh, the head of the month, contains a map of the rest of the month, a twelfth of the energy divided out of the package of energy given on Rosh HaShanah. This is further divided into week periods which correspond to the individual Shabbatot, each of them split into seven pieces (the seven days of the week) according to the Torah reading of the coming Shabbat. Shabbat both gathers from the past week all the holy energies gathered during the work week *(nitzutzot*—sparks), and also Shabbat starts off the flow of energy *(ki hi m'kor ha-berakhah*—for she is a source of blessing from the "Lekha Dodi" prayer) to the following week, as the new *Parsha* is begun to be read at Minḥa of Shabbat.

A Visual Curiosity

Given that every Rosh HaShanah has a "Rosh" effect on the rest of the year, that is, influences the rest of parts of the year like a head influences the body, I wondered what a visual plotting of Tu B'Shvat's effect on the holy days of the rest of the year might yield. I discovered a curiosity.

The graph resulting from the plotting of lines from Tu B'Shvat to the holy days and Shabbatot of the year resembles. . . . a tree! (See next page.)

This has to do with the placement of the holydays on the monthly moon map. Since more Jewish holy days fall on the fifteenth of the month (five) than on any other day of the month, plotting a line on the fifteenth of the month yields a strong trunk.

The farthest flung of the holy days from the full moon is Hanukkah, which hugs the end and the beginning of two months. This shows up as representing a maximum foliage spread. Since Hanukkah is the farthest holy day from Tu B'Shvat in time (about eleven months), if we place Tu B'Shvat at the bottom, the *Yesod*, the connector of the Tree to the bottom of the earth, then Hanukkah, farthest away, becomes the farthest flung, and widest spread top foliage.

Immediately preceding Hanukkah we have a similarly wide spread of holy days across a month. The holy days previous to

THE TREE OF TU B'SHVAT'S INFLUENCE
ON THE HOLY DAYS

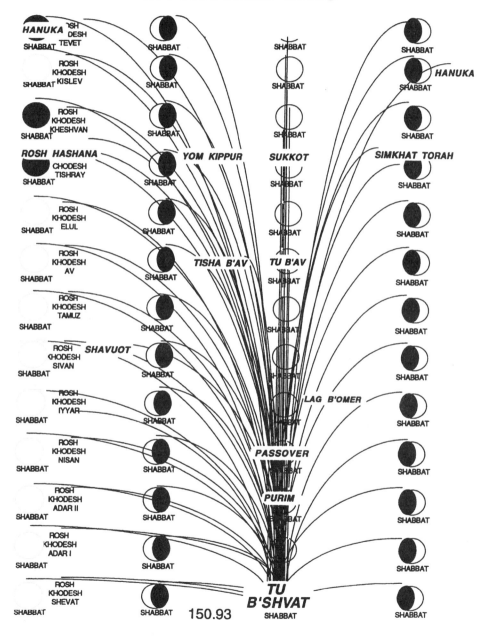

HANUKA SH
DESH
SHABBAT TEVET

ROSH
KHODESH
SHABBAT KISLEV

ROSH
KHODESH
KHESHVAN
SHABBAT

ROSH HASHANA
CHODESH
TISHRAY
SHABBAT

ROSH
KHODESH
ELUL
SHABBAT

ROSH
KHODESH
AV
SHABBAT

ROSH
KHODESH
TAMUZ
SHABBAT

ROSH *SHAVUOT*
KHODESH
SIVAN
SHABBAT

ROSH
KHODESH
IYYAR
SHABBAT

ROSH
KHODESH
NISAN
SHABBAT

ROSH
KHODESH
ADAR II
SHABBAT

ROSH
KHODESH
ADAR I
SHABBAT

ROSH
KHODESH
SHEVAT
SHABBAT

SHABBAT
SHABBAT
SHABBAT
YOM KIPPUR
SHABBAT
SHABBAT
TISHA B'AV
SHABBAT
SHABBAT
SHABBAT
SHABBAT
SHABBAT
SHABBAT
SHABBAT

SHABBAT
SHABBAT
SHABBAT
SUKKOT
SHABBAT
SHABBAT
TU B'AV
SHABBAT
SHABBAT
SHABBAT
LAG B'OMER
PASSOVER
PURIM

TU
B'SHVAT
SHABBAT

150.93

SHABBAT
SHABBAT
SHABBAT
HANUKA
SHABBAT
SIMKHAT TORAH
SHABBAT
SHABBAT
SHABBAT
SHABBAT
SHABBAT
SHABBAT
SHABBAT
SHABBAT
SHABBAT

283

Hanukkah are the holy days of the month of Tishrei, spreading out from the 1st of Tishrei to the 23rd (Simḥat Torah), which also become represented on this illustration as a wide spread of foliage.

Thus Tu B'Shvat's lines of influence to all other holy days looks more like a tree than any other holy day. If we were to do the same mapping process based on Rosh HaShanah we would find a different picture. Since Hanukkah is so close, the tree would spread out too quickly and then thin back to the right for Tu B'Shvat; Purim and Passover lean less to the left for Shavuot and Tisha B'Av. It would look like a funny bush. But then, Rosh HaShanah does not purport to be a New Year for Trees.

The Rings of Growth

Zalman Schachter-Shalomi

I thought that I was glad to see
a beautiful Midrash in a tree . . .

The sentence we use in singing the Torah back to the holy Ark—*Eitz ḥayyim hi?—lamaḥaziqim bah*—is generally thought to deal with the Torah. Reading it however in the context of the Book of Proverbs, it refers to *ḥokhmah*, Wisdom, Sophia. For those who see Torah and *ḥokhmah* as synonymous, this is no problem. However the Sages ob"m saw *ḥokhmah* as universal, something that gentiles share with Jews, whereas Torah is seen as more restricted to Jews alone.

Ḥokhmah is the innate wisdom in things that tells even the DNA and RNA what shape to give to growth. People speak of it also as the entelechy. Tu B'Shvat is the Yom Tov of that all pervasive *ḥokhmah*, the template of templates of all species, the morphogenetic field about which Rupert Sheldrake teaches us.

This *ḥokhmah* field is also the source of Torah and souls and issues from the unprecedented void. *Ha-ḥokhmah me'ayin timmatze.* The "daughter" *ḥokhmah* was founded by the "Father" the Infinite *Ein*

Sof. We are always newly and afresh issuing together from that which is yet to become. And we as part of her field of fields have our share in shaping it. And she is a Tree of Life.

There are times when we can see the souls as her leaves, her branches as the species, her roots, at times, rooted above and she, the Tree growing downward into differentiation. At other times we can see her as the co-evolution of life growing upward in consciousness. In either case there is the record of all growth in her rings and there is the mystery of the growing edge.

In Muir Woods in California there is a slice of a trunk of a redwood tree more than two thousand years old that had been sawed through and through. There is a legend beside it pointing to rings showing when great historic events occurred. The rings are not even. Those who know these things can tell about the climate in the years each one of these rings was first shaped. As I stood there and looked, I felt something shift in me.

I had often in my kitchen sliced an onion and seen how in the onion and other vegetables the rings evolve from the center of the onion: the newest ring is the nearest to the center. Not so in a tree. The tree grows from the growing edge, nearest the outside bark. The inner rings are from the youth of the tree and the outer ones are from the recent past. So every year a new ring begins at that growing edge. It is between the wood of last year's ring and the outer bark.

I stood and mused over that for a long time. In the back of my mind another phrase stirred that I had heard from the most recent Lubavitcher Rebbe, Reb Menachem Mendl the second, when I met him first in Marseilles, France, about ten years before he became rebbe. The phrase was (Deut. 20:19) *Ki ha-adam eitz ha-sadeh,* "For a person is like a tree of the field."

An aside: The original meaning of the sentence was as an ironic question, meaning to the contrary, i.e., a person is *not* like a tree, so when you fight a battle, laying siege at a city, do not cut down the trees—For is the tree the person of your enemy?—so let it stand; for you need to eat of its fruit. The *halakhot* that deal with the law of *bal tashḥit,* not to destroy anything useful, are all derived from the interdict to cut down only fruit trees. Other trees could by the simple original intent be cut and be used for firewood or to build

285

siege instruments and catapults. However, in our day we desperately need trees to absorb carbon dioxide and to give us the essential fruit of oxygen. Hence, each ecological contributor needs to be included in this law.

But in Hasidic tradition the sentence was read straight, as if it said that the tree *is* like a human being, and conversely a person is like a tree. This way of reading opened for me a huge territory of Midrash.

So here I was looking at that Sequoia and looking at the awesome mystery of the rings, of the way in which that tree had been a witness to so much history.

So, too, did I once feel the awe and impact of history when looking at the old, old Oak of Mamre—somewhere outside of Hebron. The Russian Orthodox have built a monastery nearby and the Arab kids sold little bags of acorns from that tree. I brought some acorns back and shared them with friends. I would hope that we could get some more acorns and plant one of the trees in every synagogue yard with a meditation bench below it and do *britot* and the reception of converts under them. (In places where the climate permits, or in greenhouses where it does not; it would also make sense to plant the Four Kinds—*etrog*/citron, date palm, myrtle and willow—so that we can be mindful of them, caring for them and seeing them grow the year round before using them at Sukkot.)

Sitting then under that ancient tree I affirmed my covenant with God—for under that tree Abraham our sire got circumcised and made his covenant and God and angels met him three days later at that place with the promise of new life. I could well appreciate a Buddhist's desire to visit the Bo tree in the Deer Garden under which Gautama experienced his awakening.

I suppose that traditionally we did not much celebrate Tu B'Shvat in the way of having rituals under trees. The climate in Eastern Europe did not encourage that and our shudder of *Asherah* worship prevented us in warmer climates. Now with eco-feminism as part of our consciousness and commitment we might reconsider our position in regard to this.

Mt. Tamalpais rises from Muir Woods, and as I climbed up to a clearing that day, I gave myself to a meditation on the rings of that tree as eagles soared in their circles.

Those days in the early '70s we had the notion of that radical immanence in which we believed everything comes from the deep center; hence the model was the onion. How come that the new ring does not begin at the center with a new shoot? This puzzled me. The more I began to delve in it the more the notions of interactivity presented themselves. The tree acted on the environment and the environment on the tree. They both evolved together and influenced each other.

I had learned that where the redwoods are concerned an occasional fire was an important way to stimulate new growth. The vital membrane of the meeting of the environment and the tree was in the growing edge. What is most alive in the tree is not its center. In some way the tree could not accommodate new growth like an onion. The center of the tree is the hardest, least flexible, the driest, the least juicy part. It could not allow each year for the inner core to issue new life. The inner core of the tree was too set, too static.

Yet this very quality is also the strength of the tree. The growing edge alone could not hold it up to stand rooted, enduring storms and weather. But the growing edge carries the life from the roots to the leaves and back. And yet the knotholes from which the branches issue forth go toward the center, the place where the growing edge was when the branch first sprouted. When a tree dies it is the growing edge that has died first. No more juice is raised from the roots, no more leaves the next year. It is sad to see a sturdy tree lose its life. I remember reading a novel in which a fundamentalist who suspected his brother of idolatrous tree worship cut out a circular band of the growing edge and murdered a tree.

I thought of how we as persons grow. Here, too, our encounters with the outer world stimulate the new ring of experience on the tree of our lives. What tells me most about myself and the way in which I grow in the world is neither my past nor my present outer possessions. It is the vital growing edge, the place where I am vulnerable and alive, where what happens on the outside impinges on me and where I digest and assimilate what happens on the outside. There, too, flows the nourishment from roots and leaves and the effect of the sunshine that comes to the roots.

I suppose that we have a greater choice than trees in the way in which we handle the toxic and the nourishing influences in our lives. So the present consciousness and attitude is the current growing edge of the psyche and the memories and impressions are the rings. Blessed are those who manage to keep the growing edge healthy. So the Book of Psalms opens:

> Blessed is the Person
> who did not walk the way of the malicious
> nor stand in the way of those who miss the mark
> nor sat to sneer and ridicule. . . .
> They shall be like a tree planted at the confluence of rivers
> fruiting in season whose leaves don't wilt.

They have a healthy growing edge.

A people, a religion has one too. The tree of tradition gets its strength from the core and the past. It endures the storms and stands rooted. And it needs the growing edge lest it die.

The co-evolutional truth is dawning on us from many quarters. Duane Elgin's book *The Awakening Earth* is a wonderful way to look at our evolution as a species.

Not only is the "tree" connected with the sun in her growth but also with the moon. This is the Jewish contribution to tree thought. Whereas most people in the world reckon the renewal of trees by the sun only, we place it in Hillel's way at the time of the full moon.

Tu B'Shvat can now become our Gaian *yom tov*. Look how well it is situated in our calendar; much of the celebrations of our calendar occurs on the full moon, the 15th day of the month. After the mid-winter solstice—Hanukkah—we come to Tu B'Shvat. The next month there is an increase; the holiday Purim in mid Adar is bigger, stronger, has more ritual and a book. Pesaḥ and Pesaḥ *sheini* come again on the full moon and these celebrations are highlights of the year. We have an early Sivan celebration at the close of the first quarter, and have to deal with calamity after the full moon of Tammuz. Once we get to the full moon of Av we tune in to ancient celebration connected again with trees and wood for the altar in Jerusalem. While mid Elul is quiet, after the full moon we have the Baal Shem Tov's birthday. The full moon of Tishrei brings us Sukkot. After that the full moon is quiet until the next Tu B'Shvat.

288

Here, then is a *remez*, a hint, a seed of much more in the growth of that new ring on that first full moon of Shvat.

Through Tu B'Shvat to Yah B'Shvat

Ari Elon

Part I: *Dubi-Shvat* / Teddy-Bear Shvat, the Festival of Bears

Dubi-Shvat[1] is Teddy-Bear Shvat, a sad little bear that can't go to bear kinder-Garden because he's always running away from the bad people that cut down the trees in his forest. If the bad people keep cutting down trees, Teddy-Bear Shvat won't have any forest left to play in, and there won't be any more bear kinder-Garden, and the bad people will take him and all the other little bears away from their mommies and daddies, and will put them in cages and send them to a zoo, and boys and girls from kinder-Garden will come and look at them all the time, and they'll never be able to get out of their cages and go back to their mommies and daddies. . . .

> Eliyah Elon, age 4, Kenesset Israel kindergarten,
> Elkins Park, Pennsylvania

In the past year, I have collected many stories, poems, songs, and midrashim about trees, forests, gardens, and Tu B'Shvat. I think Eliyah's midrash is one of the nicest. Not just because it is a fascinating collage of the kindergarten teacher's version with Eliyah's imagination (every midrash is a collage of the rabbi/teacher's version and the imagination of the student), but because it gives a fresh and dramatic meaning to such an obscure and mysterious expression as "Tu B'Shvat."

Eliyah, like every child, is by his very nature a *darshan*, an interpreter, a midrash-maker. The *darshan* interprets a particular phrase

289

when that phrase (or a part of it) is not clear to him. Sometimes the *darshan* merely plays the part of one who doesn't understand the obscure expression, and sometimes he really doesn't.

Eliyah, like all the kindergarten children, was unable to understand the *"peshat,"* the "plain meaning,"[2] of the concept "Tu B'Shvat." In order to understand such a concept, he would first of all have to understand what a date is. I don't know at what age a child becomes able to understand the *"peshat"* of, for example, January 12, but it is clear to me that kindergarten is early for that. The task of a child who needs to understand the *"peshat"* of a Hebrew date will be more complicated because he or she will have to translate the numbers into Hebrew letters. And when we're talking about Tu B'Shvat, the matter becomes really complicated because now, in addition to mathematics and *gematria,*[3] the child must also know an important principle in Jewish theology:

One neither says nor writes "Yah." Even in *gematria.* Therefore, in spite of the fact that the number thirteen is *yud-gimel (yud = 10 + gimel = 3),* and the number fourteen is *yud-dalet* (10 + 4), it is not permissible that the number fifteen should be Yah—*yud-heh* (10 + 5), but rather Tu: *tet-vav* (9+6).

Why? Because the combination *yud-heh* forms a name of God, the shortened form of the explicit name, *yud-heh-vav-heh* and this combination, every Jewish boy and girl must know, is the most depended upon, the most yearned for combination. For that exact reason, it is totally forbidden.

The midrashic technique that Eliyah chose to use is a well-known technique called *midrash al tikri*—"read not thus" midrash. The fixed formula of these midrashim is "read not *x*, but rather *y.*" In rabbinical literature, there are hundreds of *al tikri* type midrashim, the most dangerous of which I love very much: "And this is the Torah which Moses placed before the children of Israel— *vezot ha-torah asher sam Mosheh lifnei benei Yisrael:* read not 'sam— placed, but 'sam—drug. For one with merit, it becomes a life-giving drug, for one without merit, it becomes a fatal drug, . . ."

Eliyah's midrash, by contrast, is: "Read not 'Tu B'Shvat,' but rather 'Teddy-Bear Shvat.' He did not actually say, "Teddy Bear"; he said "Dubi," his own hearing of the Hebrew *"Tu B."* Why do I translate this as "Teddy-bear"? Because *Dubi,* in Hebrew, is a children's name for a little bear, either living or stuffed, as a teddy bear.

Eliyah is a great expert on bears—teddy or otherwise. He is surrounded by them. They star in at least ten of his books and four of his tapes. They are printed on his sheets, his plates, his cups, and his clothes. There is no reason, therefore, that the bears should be prevented from also entering into his repertoire of holidays, and certainly not a holiday whose name has such a Teddy-Bear Shvat ring to it.

By the way, according to the same stringent logic that lies behind the concept of "Tu B'Shvat," Eliyah himself should be called "Elitu," or even "Kelitu." Eliyah, whose name contains two explicit divine names (El and Yah) within it, does not yet know that behind his festival of bears and forests, Yah is hiding. Like the rest of the kindergarten children, he still doesn't know that one must hide oneself from the presence of that alluring and dangerous holiness that is concealed not only in the explicit name "Yah B'Shvat," but also among the great trees of this holiday.

Indeed, this holiday, more than any other, conceals within itself the fear of our longing for that which is forbidden, for that which is lost. And there is a connection between that longing and the expulsion from the kinder-Garden, which threatens Teddy-Bear Shvat. Tu B'Shvat, more than any other festival, is a festival of Yah—a festival of protest against the expulsion from the Garden, and a festival of the never-ending longing for the Garden, and of the inexhaustible strivings to return to it.

Tu B'Shvat and Yah B'Shvat (The Two Creation Stories and the Three Movements of the Creation Symphony)

THE FIRST MOVEMENT ("GOD"):
(Its beginning:) When *God* began to create heaven and earth. . . ."

(Gen. 1:1)

(Its end:) The heaven and the earth were finished, and all their array. On the seventh day *God* finished the work that He had been doing, and He ceased on the seventh day from all the work that He

291

had done. And *God* blessed the seventh day and declared it holy, because on it *God* ceased from all the work of creation that he had done.

(Gen. 2: 13)

THE SECOND MOVEMENT ("LORD GODS = YHWH GOD"):
(Its beginning:) Such is the story of heaven and earth when they were created. When the *LORD God* made earth and heaven. . . .

(Gen. 2:4)

(Its end:) And the *LORD God* said, Now that the man has become like one of us, knowing good and bad, what if he should stretch out his hand and take also from the tree of life and eat, and live forever!" So the *LORD God* banished him from the garden of Eden, to till the soil from which he was taken. He drove the man out, and stationed east of the garden of Eden the cherubim and the fiery ever-turning sword, to guard the way to the tree of life.

(Gen. 3:22–24)

THE THIRD MOVEMENT ("LORDS = YHWH"):
(Its beginning:) Now the man knew his wife Eve, and she conceived and bore Cain, saying, we have gained a male child with the help of the *LORD*."

(Gen. 4:1)

(Its end:) And to Seth, in turn, a son was born, and he named him Enosh. It was then that men began to invoke the *LORD* by name.[4]

(Gen. 4:26)

In the end, it will become clear to us that there are two Tree Festivals: "Tu B'Shvat" and "Yah B'Shvat." These two festivals fall on the same day of the year (the fifteenth of Shvat), and there is a complete and powerful opposition between them. The written Torah does not actually deal with either of these two festivals, but they are very ancient, with their origins in Genesis. Indeed, as we shall see, there is a direct link between these two festivals and the two different stories of Creation that appear one after the other in the beginning of the book of Genesis—Tu B'Shvat is the festival of the trees that were created, according to the first story, on the third day; Yah B'Shvat is the festival of the tree of life and the tree of knowledge of good and bad and the rest of the trees of the Garden of Eden that were created, according to the second story, on an unknown day.

In the end, we shall arrive at the beginning, and it will become clear to us that everything to be said here about trees, ecology, nature, and *tikkun olam* flows from the fascinating dialectic between the two stories of creation, or, more precisely, from the fascinating manner in which the editor of the book of Genesis bridged the two differing creation stories which she had before her. That editor, it will become clear, used the two creation stories to fashion a dramatic symphony in three movements, which is spread across the first four chapters of the book of Genesis. The first movement of the Creation Symphony is the story of God; the second movement is the story of YHWH God, while the third movement is the story of YHWH.

In the first movement of the symphony, everyone is afraid—including the narrator—to call YHWH by name. The world described in the first movement is the world of a generic, anonymous, and perfect God who created a generic, anonymous, and perfect man in His image. There is no conflict in this movement and certainly no drama.

At the beginning of the second movement, the drama breaks out before the idyllic scene that was portrayed in the first movement. The narrator of this movement dares call YHWH by name, but is careful for the entire length of the movement to add the noun God to the proper name YHWH. The conflict between the generic noun God and the proper name YHWH is a reflection of the similar conflict that takes place within the souls of this movement's heroes. In the course of this movement, the man, the woman, the snake, and the trees move from sterile generality to painful and yearning concreteness.

The third movement begins with Eve's great boldness, in that she is the first individual to call YHWH by name. This movement ends with the statement, "It was then that they began to invoke YHWH by name," which is applied to the generation of Enosh.[5]

The sentence, "It was then that they began to invoke YHWH by name" is the climax and the conclusion of the Creation Symphony. This sentence forms a repeating refrain in every generation, based on the repeated daring of many individuals to look straight into the face of existence and call It by name.[6]

Yah B'Shvat is the festival for all these individuals in each generation. Tu B'Shvat is the festival for everyone else. . . .

The Four Tikkunim

Yah B'Shvat, therefore, is the hidden name of this holiday; Tu B'Shvat is its revealed name. The very existence of the name Tu B'Shvat is the best indication that something is being covered up here. The concept Tu B'Shvat is a product of the twentieth century (or, with effort, one might find hints of it in the nineteenth century; I haven't yet found any). Before they began calling this day Tu B'Shvat, they called it the "Fifteenth of Shvat," or just "Fifteen."

One can speak in general of four revealed, historical manifestations of this day:

1. The Fifteenth of Shvat of the Sages (which we first read about in the Mishnah, which may be ascribed to the second century)
2. The Fifteenth of Shvat of the kabbalists (the students of the AR"I—end of the sixteenth century)
3. The Tu B'Shvat of the Zionists (end of the nineteenth century)
4. The Tu B'Shvat of the environmentalists (end of the twentieth century)

The first three of these were born in the Land of Israel. The last incarnation was born in the United States (and it, clearly, sets the tone for this anthology).

Each of the four incarnations contains a fundamental innovation relative to the previous traditions. Each of these innovations emphasizes a different *tikkun*, a different repair/remedy/healing.

The emphasis of the Fifteenth of Shvat in the Mishnah (or the First of Shvat, according to the House of Shammai) is on social *tikkun olam*. There exists a fundamental injustice, which indeed has no complete solution (*"the poor shall never cease out of the land"*—Deut. 15:11) but allows for the possibility of much *tikkun*. The sages of the Mishnah suggest effecting this *tikkun* through the imposition of taxes in the form of tithes, *terumot*,[7] corner gleanings, and the like. The Fifteenth of Shvat is one of the most important days for reminding society to take a frank reckoning of itself. On this day, all who have gardens are supposed to go down to their garden to count up all the fruits and profits that were gathered in the course of the year, and to reserve the required portion for the benefit of those who have neither garden nor fruit to eat from it.

The sudden appearance of the idea of a "New Year for the tithing of trees" on the mishnaic landscape is sufficient in itself to teach us about the social revolution that the Sages of the Mishnah effected through their relationship to the priestly monarchic conception of tithes and *terumot*. In the Bible there is no mention of such a day, and the fact of its establishment testifies to a need to give more force to social and religious taxes that will improve the situation of those in need.

In contrast to the mishnaic Sages' social *tikkun*, the emphasis of the kabbalist Fifteenth of Shvat is on theo-cosmic *tikkun*. The world was devastated as a result of the taste from the Tree of Knowledge, and by the resultant expulsion from the Garden of Eden. The kabbalists (the students of the AR"I) took it upon themselves to repair this devastation by means of numerous rituals spread about their calendar *(tikkunei hatzot*—midnight vigils; *tikkun le-eil Shavuot*—midnight study session for Shavuot, and the like). The Fifteenth of Shvat is a day on which many kabbalists try to get as close as possible to the Garden of Eden, to taste of its fruit, and to heal its damaged trees. They do this with a long, drawn-out Tu B'Shvat seder, at whose center they taste the fruits of this world and say blessings over them using techniques of special mystical meditations directed towards the fruits of the heavenly worlds.

The custom of eating fruit on the Fifteenth of Shvat is absolutely novel relative to the Mishnah and to the rest of the known rabbinic literature (halakhah and aggadah). The Tu B'Shvat seder, with its extended ritual of mystical meditations, is an absolute innovation relative not only to rabbinic Judaism, but also relative to earlier Kabbalah. (Neither the Zohar nor any of the Kabbalah prior to the AR"I relates at all to the Fifteenth of Shvat.) Add to this the fact that the original Tu B'Shvat seder (from the book *Ḥemdat Yamim)* is ascribed to Nathan of Gaza[8] (even if the ascription cannot be proven), and we get a hint of the messianic-Sabbatian potential hidden within it, which is certainly a form of rebellion against the halakhic Judaism of the Mishnah and the *Mishneh Torah.*

295

The Zionist Fifteenth of Shvat is a day of national-historical *tikkun*—of healing from the devastations of the exile, whether these resulted from external causes, such as oppression and anti-Semitism, or from internal causes, such as the religious, halakhic leadership. More than any other day, this day symbolized the longing of the Zionists to be healed of their Diaspora characteristics, to be joined anew to a patch of earth, of land. On this day, the Zionists taught themselves and their children to color the Land of Israel green with the planting of thousands of trees. They would thus—so they believed—again take possession of their homeland by making the desert bloom. Likewise—so they hoped—they would teach themselves and their children to stop their exilic floating and finally land on solid ground.

The rebellious nature of the Zionist Tu B'Shvat relative to the prior biblical, halakhic, and kabbalistic perspectives is patently obvious. The planting ceremony (ritual?) is a definite innovation in the landscape of Jewish ritual. As we will see below, it was imported at the end of the last century from rites celebrating spring and May Day and "slipped" into the traditional Fifteenth of Shvat.

The environmentalist Fifteenth of Shvat is a day of ecological *tikkun olam*, of repairing the planet, which has been appallingly devastated over the course of the last century by the human race. Beginning in the seventies, environmentalists started to cry out and warn us against cutting off the branches that we were sitting on. Some of the Jews among those who sounded that alarm felt a need to express themselves in the terminology of their own culture. That is how Tu B'Shvat became more and more the central day of environmental awareness in the Jewish year. More and more Tu B'Shvat seders began to take on an environmental character, and recently, Tu B'Shvat has even been declared "officially" to be the Jewish Earth Day.[9]

The environmentalist Tu B'Shvat, in my opinion, gives us a picture of a rooted Jewish paradigm in conflict with both Zionist Judaism (post-Zionism?) and halakhic Judaism (neo-halakhism?). The conflict with Zionism is expressed, to take one example, in the change of Tu B'Shvat into a universal Earth Day, rather than a day only for the earth of the Land of Israel. Similarly, the environmentalist Tu B'Shvat is in direct confrontation with halakhic Judaism

296

because the environmentalist Tu B'Shvat understands the halakhic essence of the holiday to be *mitzvot* that apply to the world as a whole and not only to the Land of Israel—the message of the environmentalist Tu B'Shvat is that one must interpret the word "land" not just as the Land of Israel, but as Earth, as the world. This, of course, is in direct conflict with the traditional, halakhic viewpoint. For the groups behind the environmentalist Tu B'Shvat, this conflict is part of the attempt to fashion an entire system of alternative halakhah, which is expressed, for example, by the ethical claims for an eco-kashrut that goes beyond food to other "fruit of the earth" that we consume, like coal and oil and paper.

We have before us, then, four different types of *tikkun*: social, theological, national-historical, and ecological. These four types of *tikkun* signify not only four different "Tu B'Shvats," but also four different world views. Every one of these four viewpoints constitutes a revolutionary change relative to the views that preceded it. Within each of these revolutionary changes is a veiled or open rebellion. The change and the rebellion become expressed in a characteristic ritual, which is innovative in comparison with the previous incarnations of this day.

It is possible, therefore, to see in each of the four different Tu B'Shvats a weaving of rebellion and continuity. I personally have a problem with that pair, "rebellion and continuity." It's too black-and-white and has the stale taste of Modernism. However, I am interested not in doing away with it, but rather in adding to it the pair "dismantling *(peruk)*-repairing *(tikkun)*," which is my attempt to capture in a Hebraic idiom two extremely significant post-Modern concepts: Deconstructionism and Reconstructionism.

Based on the above clarifications, I would like to make the following claim: (1) Each of the four Tu B'Shvats described above is a *tikkun* (reconstruction) of one (or more) of the prior Tu B'Shvats. (2) A necessary condition for each of those *tikkunim* is the dismantling (deconstruction) of the conceptual universe out of which one (or more) of the previous Tu B'Shvats was built. In other words: We're not speaking of only remodeling the past, but of also dismantling the entire structure. Often the dismantling is liable (likely?) to end up destroying the ceremony or occasion; just as often it is likely to end up transforming and renewing it. In the case

297

of Tu B'Shvat, we are witness to a series of transformations that spreads out over nearly 2,000 years (or more).

Incidentally, it is critical to point out that as opposed to (or even because of?) these various incarnations of Tu B'Shvat, it remains without any significance until this very day from the standpoint of post-talmudic halakhah. One can't rule out the possibility that it was exactly because the post-talmudic, rabbinic halakhah found no use for this day that it proved to be so fascinatingly fruitful and still, I believe, is bound for a no less fascinating future.

If God Created the Sky and the Land, Who Created the Outland?[10] (Mitzvot That Hang on the Land and Mitzvot That Hang on the Sky)

Any commandment that hangs on the land is only performed in the Land and if it does not hang on the land, it is performed both in the Land and outside the Land.

Mishnah Kiddushin 1:9

Shalom, children, says Tu B'Shvat to Hagi and Hagit. My name is *Hag Ha'ilanot,*" "Tree Festival," but I'm better known by the widespread name, Tu B'Shvat. I'm different from the rest of the Jewish holidays, because I am a holiday of the Land of Israel. While all the rest of the holidays are celebrated also outland, I am principally celebrated in the Land of Israel.

Rabbi Menahem Hakohen, *Sefer Hehagim* (*Liladim*), p. 31

For, in truth, a man is called a tree of the field, as it is written (Deut. 20:19): "Trees of the field are human." It's just that he is an upside-down tree, for the tree has its roots stuck below in the land, whereas man has his roots above, for the soul, which is his root, is from heaven. And the hands are the branches of the tree, the feet are the branches off the branches, his trunk is the center of the tree. And why is he an upside-down tree? Because the tree's roots are below for the tree's life is from the earth, while the life of a person's soul is from heaven.

Maharal of Prague, *Netsah Yisra'el*, p. 47, section 7

The sages of the Mishnah decided to make the Fifteenth of Shvat a determinative day for tithes of fruit trees. They did this alongside thousands of additional determinations, which formed, in the first centuries of the common era, the significant book of halakhah called the Mishnah. The core of these sages' activity took place in the Landofisrael[11] following the destruction of the second Temple. In the course of the end of the first century and the entire second century (and a bit of the third) they laid out the six *Sedarim* (Orders, Volumes) of the Mishnah, which include many thousands of *halakhot*[12] dealing with every area of life. The halakhah that speaks about the Fifteenth of Shvat as a determinative day for tithes of fruit trees appears at the beginning of Tractate *Rosh HaShanah,* which is one of the twelve tractates that make up *Seder Mo'ed*—Festivals, which traditionally is the second of the six *Sedarim* of the Mishnah. In spite of the fact that the only mention of the fifteenth of Shvat in the Mishnah is in the Order of Festivals, nowhere does the mishnaic, talmudic, or midrashic literature relate to Tu B'Shvat as a holiday. The most important *Seder* to delve into if we want to understand the many-branched associations of the mishnaic (and talmudic) Tu B'Shvat is *Seder Zera'im*—Seeds, the first of the six *Sedarim. Seder Zera'im* is mainly about "commandments whose obligations concern the plants of the land, such as: *kil'ayim* (cross-breeding), *shmita* (sabbatical years), *orlah* (the first fruits of a tree), *terumot* (free-will offerings), *ma'asrot* (tithes), and the rest of the laws of gifts (gifts to the poor).[13]

Therefore, in order to deepen our knowledge of the halakhic reality of the Fifteenth of Shvat as the New Year for Tree Tithing, *Seder Zera'im* will be the most important requirement. A close reading of the chapters of *Seder Zera'im* also becomes a journey into the gardens, fields, orchards, and plantations of the Land of Israel in the period of the Mishnah. "Does not the scent of the fields rise up from the flower-beds of the Mishnah in *Seder Zera'im?*" asked Chaim Nachman Bialik in his introduction to the edition of *Seder Zera'im* with vocalization of the Hebrew and explanatory commentary. (It may be worth pointing out that already in 1932, Bialik published the first vocalized edition in history of *Seder Zera'im.*)

Lo and behold, the Mishnah itself already established the many mitzvot related to *Seder Zera'im* as "mitzvot that hang on the land." Which means that the mitzvot in *Seder Zera'im* apply as a halakhic system *only* to the Land of Israel, and the rule of tithing, for example, is not in force, from the halakhic standpoint, in the "outland."

Which means that, from a halakhic standpoint, Tu B'Shvat has (almost) no significance outland. The midrashic joke "If God created the sky and the land, who created the outland?" has, in my opinion, vast political and ideological implications, and its very existence points to the Zionist fixation in which Israelis grow up, which bases the concept "land" on the concept "Landofisrael." But the very possibility of such a joke flows from the fact that the word "land" in the terminology of halakhah, as well as in contemporary Hebrew terminology, has almost the sole meaning, "Land of Israel."

So it is possible to interpret the phrase, "mitzvot that hang on the land" according to its halakhic-historical *"peshat,"* namely as mitzvot whose existence is based on the settlement of the Land of Israel, but it is also possible to interpret it otherwise. It is possible to interpret it according to its linguistic *"peshat,"*—mitzvot that hang on the earth, that is, on the lands of all who dwell on earth. In other words, mitzvot that don't hang on the sky.

I propose to speak of two types of commandments—two types of mitzvot—facing the human species for us to be conscious of the ecological disaster that is happening to us:

A. Mitzvot that hang on the sky. B. Mitzvot that hang on the land.

I don't intend by this to propose this pair as a replacement for the well-known pair "mitzvot between one person and another" versus "mitzvot between a person and God," but to suggest an additional perspective, and to make the following claim: Just as the concept "between one person and another" has a cosmopolitan ethical significance, which is not based on the cultic practices of this or that religion, so should the concept "mitzvot that hang on the land."

It seems to me that part of the reason that we are now living in the shadow of ecological disaster is that over the course of many generations, the system of human-land relationships got crushed between the two great systems of person-God and person-person. The law code—the *shulḥan arukh*—of the whole civilization (at least western, so-called Judeo-Christian civilization) is littered with the smallest details of rules of obligations between people and God or between people and people. As opposed to that, "traditional" environmentalists who wish to hang ecological obligations on ancient halakhic trees face over and over again the fact that they have almost nothing to hold on to. In the Jewish system of halachah, for example, *bal tashḥit*—do not destroy—is almost the only anchor (and it, too, is very problematic, if we begin to take a close look at it[14]).

"The heavens belong to the LORD, but the earth He gave over to man" (Ps. 115:16). The commandments between a person and his/her heavens vary so much between different faiths and religions, and we must learn to value and honor that variation and to foster religious pluralism. But it is necessary to arrive at a consensus as soon as possible about the obligating halakhah regarding the meaning of the phrase, "but the earth He gave over to man."

The heavens are infinite; on the other hand, there is only one earth. And that is exactly the reason that when we are dealing with the land, the earth, we must come up with a unified halakhah that is binding on everyone who lives on this land, this earth. That is exactly the reason that the human species must urgently lay out for itself a new, binding, *shulḥan arukh*—a new, binding code of conduct—and to fashion a full system of enforcing that *shulḥan arukh*.

That, in my humble opinion, is the realistic halakhic midrash that we must derive from the expression "mitzvot that hang on the land." Opposite it, one may stand the surrealistic, aggadic midrash from the Maharal of Prague:

> For, in truth, a man is called a tree of the field, as it is written (Deut. 20:19): "trees of the field human." It's just that he is an upside-down tree, for the tree has its roots stuck below in the land, whereas man has his roots above, for the soul, which is his root, is from heaven. And the hands are the branches of the tree, the feet are the branches off the branches, his trunk is the center of the tree. And why is he an upside-down tree? Because the tree's roots are below for the tree's life is from the earth, while the live of a person's soul is from heaven.

A man has—so the Maharal of Prague teaches us—roots in heaven and he is planted in heaven but is also connected to the earth. He is hanging with his head caught in the thicket of the earth just like Absalom was caught in the branches of the terebinth and like the ram from the binding of Isaac was caught in the thicket. Across the face of the earth is a giant thicket, on which all of the mitzvot from *Seder Zera'im* hang and in which they are all caught. The Gemara in the Tractate *Pesaḥim* tells us of Rav Yosef, the son of Rabbi Yehoshua b. Levi, who managed to recover from a fatal illness. After he recovered, the following dialogue took place between the father and the son:

Father: "What did you see?"

Son: "An inverted world is what I saw. Upper ones below and lower ones above."

Father: "My son, a righted world is what you saw."

We will never know who is right: the father or the son? And we can never determine with certainty whether our present world is right side up or upside down. One thing we can determine: Ours is a world of mirrors—the roots of its land are reflected in the roots of its heavens, and the commandments that hang on the land have the sole purpose of reminding us that the land hangs on—depends on—the commandments. The land on which we are trying to live hangs on the mitzvot that we fulfill—whether the mitzvot between a person and her heavens or the mitzvot between a person and his fellows.

The land hangs on the mitzvot that hang on the land. . . .

The Children of the Green Ḥeder

I want to examine closely the phenomenon of the Zionist Tu B'Shvat in general and the phenomenon of tree plantings in particular. Until the end of the nineteenth century there was no connection between the fifteenth of Shvat and planting. More than that: I don't know of any Jewish ritual connected with plantings— neither in the context of Tu B'Shvat nor in any other context in the course of the year. In contrast, in the course of the twentieth century, tree planting became one of the most important Jewish rituals, and the central ceremony of Tu B'Shvat. Beginning in the twentieth century, plantings became the most basic, defining characteristic of Tu B'Shvat in Israeli culture. For example, this is how Tu B'Shvat is defined in the Even Shoshan Dictionary: "Tu B'Shvat—the New Year of Trees. Celebrated in Israel in various settlements with the planting of trees, especially by school children."

Among the many volumes of the well-known and authoritative *Sefer Ha-mo'adim*[15], edited by Levinski, is the most significant Israeli

Tu B'Shvat anthology yet written. It is a rich anthology, published in 1954 and edited by Levinski during the first years of the State of Israel. To the best of my knowledge, that anthology has not been updated, nor has any other significant anthology been written, which fact has enormous significance, of course, with regard to the present state of Tu B'Shvat in Israeli society. A large portion of the anthology is dedicated to trees and fruits in general, and particularly to the trees and fruits of the land of Israel. Another section is dedicated to the three first historical incarnations of Tu B'Shvat that we recounted above. The fourth, environmentalist, incarnation was not yet born in 1954, and the almost complete absence of environmental topics shows the almost complete lack of awareness of the topic in the early fifties.

And as to the first three incarnations, a quick glance at the table of contents is enough to convince us that we have before us a clear preference for the Zionist Tu B'Shvat over its predecessors. Levinski dedicates five pages to the mishnaic (rabbinic) incarnation of Tu B'Shvat, ten to the kabbalist incarnation, but thirty-three pages to the Zionist incarnation with its plantings. Alongside this is a no less significant attempt to form some continuity between the different Tu B'Shvats with the goal of blurring the significant conflicts between them. And so, in accordance with this Zionist myth, each and every Jewish child participates in the birth of an actual tree. He/she plants it and is thus supposed to become a complete partner in the work of Creation.

The titles that Levinski awards these three incarnations are no less interesting: To the mishnaic Tu B'Shvat, he awards the title "Aforetimes in Israel: Tu B'Shvat—The Tree's New Year"; he calls the kabbalist incarnation "In the Kabbalists' Camp: The New Year of Fruit and Tree"; The Zionist Tu B'Shvat, in contrast, merited the title, "At the Return of Zion's Captives: The New Year for Planting."

The revolution that stands behind the other title on the page—*At the Return of Zion's Captives*—is no less significant, for, as we all know, the original verse that Levinski is interpreting here is a verse from the Songs of Ascents, "at YHWH's return of Zion's captives." This midrash combines within itself the powerful brazenness of the Zionist leaders and thinkers with their obsessive and repressed fear of heaven. YHWH didn't return Zion's captives and neither did any other god. Not even the "rock of Israel." Zion returned herself. That is all of Zionism on one foot. The ideologists behind the Zionist Tu B'Shvat revolution erased the word YHWH or Yah. They didn't want to deal with it at all. The phrase "at the return of Zion's captives" is trying to hide the same thing that the phrase "Tu B'Shvat" is trying to hide—the explicit name—and the fear of not only pronouncing it, but even relating to it at all. The "secular" fear of heaven is greater and more frightening than the "religious" fear of heaven—the latter are afraid to mention the explicit name of their God, the former are afraid to mention God at all. These and those are afraid of the phrase "Yah B'Shvat" as of fire!

Returning to the innovation of the plantings, Rabbi Ze'ev Yavetz, director of the Zichron Ya'akov school, along with his students held what is now accepted to be the first planting ceremony in 1890. In the words that he wrote for the Newspaper *Ha'aretz* one year later, Yavetz clarifies the motivation behind his initiative:

> For the love of the saplings, . . . the school must make a festival of the day that was set aside from ancient times in Israel as the New Year of Trees. To gracefully and beautifully arrange the trees, saplings, lilies and flowers, just as they do in Europe on the first of May.[16]

In this small selection, we notice several things. First of all, the need to plant and to "repair" the barren land. Likewise, we can see the educator's recognition of the power of ceremony, and his understanding that new paradigms are best introduced by way of children and by way of ceremonies. In addition, we see in a fascinating way how one moves a mythic ceremony from the European First of May to Tu B'Shvat in the Land of Israel.

In 1907 (or 1908) a glorious planting ceremony took place in Mikveh Yisrael, in 1910 the first planting ceremony in Tel Aviv was recorded, and in 1913 the Hebrew Teachers of Jerusalem brought their students into the Zionist consensus of planting on Tu B'Shvat.

Tu B'Shvat is apparently the only Jewish festival that was declared a *festival* by the teachers' union. More than that: Tu B'Shvat is the only Jewish holiday that is openly designated as a children's holiday. Even the Even Shoshan Dictionary, the most accepted dictionary of the renewed Hebrew language, describes Tu B'Shvat as a holiday of schoolchildren. In 1910, two years after the Organization of Teachers in the Land of Israel declared Tu B'Shvat to be a planting festival for children, the first planting festival was magnificently celebrated in Tel Aviv, the "first Hebrew city." In honor of this festival, the poet S. Ben Tzion composed this song to the famous melody of *"Oyfn Pripitshek*—the Ḥeder Song."

> *Open fields and green trees, children carry spades, there the teacher to the students teaches* alef-bet.
> *This is the Torah, gentle children, study, do not spurn, plant and sow this land, the spring dove returns.*
> *This tree*—alef, *this tree* bet—*even* gimel—*a tree, tree letters in a green book as far as eye can see!*
> *This is the Torah . . .*
> *On this land our fathers spilt sweat and milk and blood—let spring come, let it blossom, as the nation blooms.*
> *This is the Torah . . .*

Exactly because of its simplicity, this song highlights the Zionist revolution's force of protest and rebellion. "This is the Torah" which S. Ben Tzion placed (do not read "drug," but rather "placed") before the new children of Israel who carry spades on their shoulders in the infinite, green, spaces of learning that replaces the damp and dark *ḥeder*. And this is the new alphabet that the new rabbi teaches the new students: *Bet*—tree, *gimel*—tree, all the letters—tree. The new rabbi and the new students will plant all these new letters in the earth and will write from them a completely new Torah. The new Torah scroll won't be a yellowing antique—it will be a "green book as far as the eye can see," and this green book will bring spring.

Tu B'Shvat is the swallow that announces the coming of spring. Tu B'Shvat is the first point in the dark tunnel of winter at which we begin to see the light of spring. The winter, à la Ben Tzion, is of course the Exile, which is expressed in pale children of the *ḥeder* who are forced to recite their *alef-bet* from yellowing and ancient Torah scrolls.

The new children of Tel Aviv will bring spring. They won't go to *ḥeder* but will plant so many trees that the land will awake from its long winter sleep, green and blossoming. And will awake into the blossoming spring.

S. Ben Tzion is part of a generation that went through "*ḥeder*-trauma." This Bialik-like model of a three-year-old boy who is brought to the *ḥeder* and taught *alef-bet* is intimately tied up with tearing the boy away from trees and nature. They take all the children out of the world of trees and put them in the world of letters in order to put them through the Spartan survival ordeals of the People of the Book. The best of them will be sorcerers of letters, will be *talmidei hakhamim,* will be kabbalist mystics, will be Rabbi Akivas with the Holy Blessed One as a study partner. How will the Holy Blessed One be their study partner? By tying crowns that they will untie. Those who pass all the tests will be rewarded by becoming eternal, pale, bent children who play Scrabble with God. These chosen Yah-children will remain solitary in their caves (or on their roofs) and bury themselves in a complete obsession with letters.

The *talmidei hakhamim* and kabbalists are the letter-elite of the people of the Book. It is a lonely elite who lives the life of eternity in the kabbalists' cave and gives itself the challenge of changing all the world's objects into letters, which will become part of the express name of God. They do not allow themselves to go outside the cave to see nature and trees as they are in themselves. All those trees and hills are, according to them, nothing more than a foggy and dull copy of the transparent Torah, which is a magical combination of flowering letters. If the kabbalists said: Forget about the trees and rocks and go to the letters, for everything is letters and everything is combinations, S. Ben Tzion comes along and says, forget about letters and go to trees. In his simple song, S. Ben Tzion tries to travel the whole way back from the letters to the trees.

In the Tu B'Shvat seder, the kabbalists try to turn trees and fruit into letters, out of which to make holy combinations. When we try to imagine a Tu B'Shvat seder, we must picture kabbalists tasting fruit with palpable devotion, where every chew is filled with intense concentration and intention to change the fruit being chewed into letters that will blossom in the air, rise up to heaven, pour their abundance into the upper worlds, and reach the most hidden corners of the God who is nothing other than a Book, nothing other than a Combination of Letters.

We need to stop this obsession with letters, says S. Ben Tzion in his way, as Berditchevsky, Tchernichovsky, Bialik, Gordon, Brenner, and many others said each in their own way. We need to take the letter-genie out of the bottle and free this people from its letter *dybbuk*. That *dybbuk* is dangerous; it leaves us in exile; it leaves our potential leaders in their caves cut off from the real world and absolved of historical responsibility or political involvement. We need to take all the little children on Tu B'Shvat and bring them out to open places, to the infinite, green *ḥeder*. Every child will take a shovel and will plant a letter.

We do not write letters, says Ben Tzion to the children of Tel Aviv in 1910, we turn them into tender saplings and plant them.

Tu B'Shvat, the Festival of Children

In 1908, the Organization of Teachers in the Land of Israel first declared regarding the Fifteenth of Shvat "that from now on, [the Organization] will make it a 'festival of plantings' for children."

From seder Tel Aviv, A. Druyanov, editor

Tu B'Shvat—the New Year of Trees. Celebrated in Israel in various settlements with the planting of trees, especially by school children.

Even Shoshan Dictionary

Kakh Holkhim HaShotlim—**Here Come Planters**

Kakh holkhim hashotlim
ron balev ve'et bayad
Min ha'ir umin hakfar
Min ha'emek umin hahar
be-tu tu tu tu, be-Tu B'Shvat

Here come planters spade in hand,
see them swinging bravely by,
little trees they bear on high,
on *ḥamishah asar* B'Shvat
on tu tu tu tu, on Tu B'Shvat.
What has brought you planters here?
We strike the rocky mountain side,
Drain the marshes far and wide,

on ḥamishah asar B'Shvat
on tu tu tu tu, on Tu B'Shvat.

Hashkediyah Poraḥat—Tu B'Shvat Is Here

Hashkediyah poraḥat
veshemesh paz zoraḥat
tsiporim merosh kol gag
mevasrot et bo heḥag.
Tu BiShvat higia, hag ha-ilanot!

The almond tree is growing,
a golden sun is glowing;
The birds sing out in joyous glee
from every roof and every tree.
Tu B'Shvat is here,
hail the trees' New Year.

Let's make the land a garden,
with water from the Jordan;
And our land will flow once more
with milk and honey, as of yore.
Tu B'Shvat is here,
hail the trees' New Year.

The truth is that it is not just Tu B'Shvat that is a children's holiday, but all Jewish (and non-Jewish) holidays are, in the end (and the beginning), children's holidays. When I was a boy, I was convinced that the word *yeladim*—"children" was synonymous with *yehudim*—"Jews." This was the result of an irreconcilable difference of opinion between two of my nursery school teachers regarding the correct words to a particular song: One insisted that it should be sung "*ḥag Purim ḥag Purim ḥag gadol la-yeladim,*" while the other refused to give in and continued to sing "*ḥag Purim ḥag purim ḥag gadol la-yehudim.*"

(Incidentally, in the context of that confusion, I was convinced as a child that the correct words to the Havdalah ceremony for the end of the Shabbat were "*la-yeladim haytah orah ve-simḥah ve-sason vikar, ken tihyeh lanu*—the children had light and happiness and joy, so may we"[17] and for many years, I wondered in amazement where all those happy children who had it so well could be.)

But it is not just Purim that is a children's holiday, even Tisha B'Av is. If we do a close reading, for example, of the midrash in Lamentations *Rabbah*, which describes how God leans over the Holy Temple that He had just destroyed with His own hands and weeps bitterly, we can't help but be reminded of the heart-wrenching cries of a little boy who has destroyed with his own hands his most beloved toy . . .

In short, it is certainly reasonable to claim that in the end (and in the beginning), all of the holidays were created as nourishment and compensation for the frustrated child within each of us. In this essay, we won't journey to the chaotic depths of our souls to understand that each of our earnest attempts to struggle with some holiday or ceremony is another attempt to return to the Eden of our lost childhood. Occasionally, it will suffice to illustrate that claim by way of our holiday, Tu B'Shvat, as I hinted at, for example, in the above section on the expulsion of Teddy-Bear Shvat from the (kinder)Garden.

And so, just like every Jewish child in Israel (and in the world), I too knew to declare that Tu B'Shvat is the festival of trees. And just like every other child, I didn't know that only at the beginning of the twentieth century did Tu B'Shvat become a festival at all, in particular a festival of trees. And apparently, there's nothing wrong with that—after all, not even the eldest among us were children before the beginning of the twentieth century . . .

Even so, I felt a need to write a few words in a previous section about Yavetz, Ben-Tzion, Levinski, and the rest of the inventors of the festival of trees and the festival of plantings, in spite of the fact that, or maybe because, they spent their childhoods in the nineteenth century. Before the children of the twenty-first century arrive, so I thought, a few words should be dedicated to the children of the nineteenth century that renewed the Hebrew language, renewed the Hebrew land, renewed the Hebrew festivals, and invented, as we said, the festival of trees.

Two other children of the nineteenth century who designed Tu B'Shvat, the festival of children and the festival of trees, for us, were Yitzhak Shinhar and Yisra'el Dushman. The former composed *"Kakh Holkhim Hashotlim*—Here Come Planters" and *"Hashkediah Poraḥat*—Tu B'Shvat Is Here."* In the Israeli hit parade of Tu B'Shvat songs, there is a perpetual rivalry between these two songs for first

309

place. When they are placed side by side, they look exactly like eternal twins. Each has three stanzas of five lines each, and the last line is sung twice as a repeated refrain after each verse.

These two repeated refrains provided the key phrases of Tu B'Shvat for the nostalgia of the children of the twentieth century who grew up in Israel: *"Tu B'Shvat higia, ḥag ha-ilanot*—Tu B'Shvat is here, Hail the trees' New Year," and *"Be-Tu Tu Tu Tu be-Tu B'Shvat*—On Tu Tu Tu Tu, on Tu B'Shvat." As to the importance of "Tu B'Shvat is here, Hail the trees' New Year," one may rely on Yom Tov Levinski's description of the Fifteenth of Shvat, 1949, which was "celebrated in Jerusalem with extraordinary ceremony such as the city has not known for many generations." That day was chosen as the official opening day of the first Knesset of the State of Israel, and the fact of that choice indicates the centrality of Tu B'Shvat in the consciousness of the new state's spiritual and political leaders, who themselves were the pioneering children of the nineteenth century. This is how Levinski describes the events of that day:

> Still in the early hours of the morning, Jerusalem's children were seen passing by in large groups, each by their standard, dressed splendidly in Scout's uniforms, saplings in hand. The kindergarten children, crowned with garlands and holding flowerpots, crossed the streets singing and shouting for joy: "Tu B'Shvat is here, Hail the trees' New Year." At nine o'clock, the orderly processions of schoolchildren and youth organizations began—young planters with shovels and hoes in one hand, and saplings in the other. At ten o'clock, the procession of planters from the young generation was received by Prime Minister David Ben Gurion. On that day thousands of trees were planted throughout the country in honor of the Knesset.[18]

So the first Tu B'Shvat in the history of the State of Israel is often described as an unforgettable day on which kindergarten and elementary schoolchildren crowded the walkways while singing "Tu B'Shvat is here, Hail the trees' New Year," and watching the thrilling parade that passed before them. And in the parade were bigger children, shovels in one hand and saplings in the other, striding at attention to a marching rhythm and singing *"Kakh holkhim hashotlim*—Here come planters."

I added that last part from my memory; Levinski didn't write it explicitly. I added it because I remember exactly how the bigger children passed before me on King George Street on the way to Ben Gurion and sang themselves swinging bravely by, little trees they bear on high, on Tu Tu Tu Tu, on Tu B'Shvat . . .

For the sake of precision and academic integrity, I must specify that the planters' parade that I remember didn't take place on Tu B'Shvat 1949, since I was born a little more than a year later (Iyyar, 1950). But I remember as if it happened today, how I, as a young student in Jerusalem, joined the crowd on the sidewalk of King George Street on Tu B'Shvat 1956 or 1957, and I was singing "Tu B'Shvat is here, Hail the trees' New Year," and watching in admiration the bigger children marching like soldiers on the way to Ben Gurion. I remember as if it happened today, their leader roaring "left-right-left" like an important commander, and the children walking in a straight line and singing "Here Come Planters," holding the shovels on their shoulders as if they were swords. And I remember as if it happened today how I dreamed of the day on which I too would march "left-right-left" through the streets of Jerusalem, a song in the heart and a shovel in hand. On Tu Tu Tu Tu. Like a soldier.

But it never happened. As a big boy, I never once got to participate in a Tu B'Shvat planting ceremony, and it goes without saying that I have never marched in a planters' parade. One of the reasons is tied to the fact that I studied in the public religious schools and that the administration of my school had a very ambivalent relationship to the planting ceremonies. On the one hand, my school was Zionist, and, of course, supported the settling of the Land and making the desert bloom. On the other hand, the planting ceremonies had connotations that were too secular and foreign. The same applied, by the way, to the first-fruits ceremonies on Shavuot, which also were characteristic of the kibbutz movement and the secular Land of Israel. Those two ceremonies seemed to me to be classical representatives of a magical and ritualistic secular world. Although I wasn't exactly a *"ḥeder bocher,"* the Jewish ceremonies of my youth were nevertheless associated with books, with the confines of the classroom, with the complete separation of men and women. (I studied in an all-boys' school.) The planting ceremonies and first-fruit ceremonies of the secular children, and especially the kibbutz children, ignited my imagination; to an urban Orthodox child, they modeled the possibility of unconstrained Jewish ritual.

311

In reality, it turns out that my idealization of the planting ceremony (and the first-fruit ceremony) was exaggerated. Later, I came to know that the whole enterprise of the plantings began to lose steam by the late fifties. In the introduction to the Tu B'Shvat anthology published in 1960 by the Inter-kibbutz Festival Commission, the editors, Aryeh Ben-Gurion and Tsevi Shua, warn that "it's become routine, and since, with the passage of time, planting has ceased to be a compelling cause, a careless attitude is noticeable."

Nine years later, in the third edition of the same anthology, the warning has become an overwhelming concern: "We weren't able to ignore the clear signs of 'aging' in the 'Festival of Trees' which had been so particularly beloved by our children and our community in years past."

The quotation marks around the words "aging" and "Festival of Trees" are the authors' own and it is worth paying attention to them. It seems that not only had the "children of the green ḥeder" from 1910 aged by 1969, but the first children's holiday in history had also aged with them. Slowly, it becomes clear that this holiday is not as well loved by the children (nor the educators) of the fifties and sixties as it was by the generations of children that preceded them. This fact causes the editors to make the following heartfelt appeal: "We appeal to the holiday activists[19] and the educators to struggle anew with this wonderful holiday, and not to bury it just because there are no more plots of land near the kibbutz that are suitable for planting trees. We have the opportunity to develop the celebration of this holiday in multiple and colorful ways while remaining true to its traditional values."

The planting ceremonies, so it seems, had already ceased to be a compelling cause by 1960. It is very possible that Tu B'Shvat, 1949, the day on which the Israeli Knesset was founded, was the high point of this day as a "festival of trees," "festival of plantings," and "festival of children." The euphoria of planting began at the start of the twentieth century, grew through its first half, reached a climax with the founding of the State, and toward the end of the fifties began to die out.

Suddenly, people sober up from the intoxication of the plantings. There are even criticisms from experts pointing to the destructive nature of the mass plantings:

> When I hear "Tu B'Shvat," I see before me thousands and thousands of trees that were planted throughout the land on past Tu B'Shvats, that didn't even last a year. Is that what you call teaching the love of trees and a connection to trees, when you plant entire forests and abandon them on the same day? Ever since I woke up and saw the fate of those trees and the feeling of disrespect that they plant in the children, I have been against Tu B'Shvat plantings.[20]

These critical words are presented by the famous naturalist Azaryah Alon in his piece, "Who needs Tu B'Shvat?" In this piece, Azaryah Alon tries to claim that there is a need for Tu B'Shvat, and he tries to convince his professional and kibbutz colleagues that Tu B'Shvat shouldn't be allowed to die. The piece is laid out in the manner of talmudic-fictional argument and presents a disagreement between those who oppose Tu B'Shvat and its supporters. There are four speakers—two against and two for. The significant point, for our purposes, is that even those who speak in favor of the continued existence of Tu B'Shvat agree completely with the criticism. Their main point is that the way the holiday is celebrated should be changed, but it shouldn't be eliminated. It is striking that all the participants in the argument criticize the phenomenon of mass plantings on Tu B'Shvat, whether because of the principle of *bal tashḥit* or out of the following reasoning:

> The whole enterprise of planting on Tu B'Shvat is unjustifiable from the beginning: It is not at all a suitable day for planting. Conifers and deciduous broad-leaves need to be planted long beforehand; the former so they can take full advantage of the winter rains and the latter because, by that time, they already need to be setting roots and budding. And trees that are transplanted in clods or pots, like citrus trees—the time hasn't come yet to plant them.[21]

Suddenly, after fifty years of mass plantings on Tu B'Shvat, the experts come in and claim that Tu B'Shvat is not at all a suitable time for planting. After fifty years, it turns out that behind the righteous and vital passion for planting and making the desert bloom, a great ignorance was hiding. Not only ignorance of the talmudic sources, but also of the ecological realities of the Land of Israel.

313

That ignorance is astonishingly beautiful and moving. It contains within itself the whole story of the *ḥalutzim*, the Zionist pioneers. These children of the nineteenth century successfully sought to create, at any cost, a planting ritual for Tu B'Shvat. And they didn't know, or didn't want to know, about the basic contradiction between the fifteenth of Shvat and the planting of trees.

Indeed, nowhere in the talmudic literature, or in the post-talmudic literature, does it refer to the Fifteenth of Shvat (or the First of Shvat) as a day for planting trees. The original Fifteenth of Shvat was spoken of as the New Year for *planted* trees and not for the planting. This day has to do with the relationship of the planted tree to the rainwater that flows in its vessels and veins; this day has to do with the relationship of the planted tree with the formation of its new fruit; this day has to do with the renewal of the tree and the renewal of its fruit. On this day, as it were, the tree plants itself, renewing its own fruitfulness. On this day, the tree goes through a thrilling process with itself—humans need not get involved. There is nothing to be done except to watch, to pay attention, and to learn. On this day, one must protect the tree from any interference. Protect it and watch.

Not coincidentally, Azaryah Alon is the person who was most identified in Israel with the protection of nature. He was a founder and leader of the Society for the Protection of Nature *(Ḥevrah Le-ha-ganat Ha-teva)*. As such, he also protects Tu B'Shvat from its opponents. But he joins with them and takes the lead in their opposition to the mass plantings on Tu B'Shvat. He suggests rooting out the plantings. Rooting them out and healing them.[22] Here are his words in their entirety:

> I certainly understand the anger that has been directed against the paradigm of mass plantings, but that is a disease that can be healed. And people are healing it. We can do without having every child plant a tree, and make do with a symbolic planting, appropriately done with prior planning as to who will take care of the trees in the future. Let's choose an appropriate plot of land, which didn't come into existence for Tu B'Shvat, but for the relevant purpose, and we'll plant trees for which the season is appropriate. If necessary, we'll stand ten children by each tree, and each one will participate in the planting with a handful of dirt, but besides them, there will be an appointed adult who will plant the

tree. But beyond that: who said that planting is required at all? Let's go out to the field or the hill, and see the plants where they awaken and grow. Instead of breaking off almond branches to put them in jars and sing *"Hashkediyah Poraḥat*—The Almond Tree Is Growing," let's go to the tree, look at it, and enjoy it without breaking it. Anything can be done poorly or done right—including Tu B'Shvat. Let's do it right and have a joyous holiday.[23]

It is worth noticing the last line: "Let's do it right and have a joyous holiday." It sounds like "Let's have a kosher and joyous holiday."[24] Or more precisely, "a kosher and joyous Tu B'Shvat" (or even more precisely "a kosher and joyous Yah B'Shvat"). It is said by a leader of the Society for the Protection of Nature in an attempt to build a bridge over the absurd chasm of natural destruction that is connected to the celebration of Tu B'Shvat. Out of great love for the idea of nature, we harm it, says the environmentalist, and the harm does not really result from bad intentions, but from ignorance.

The suffocating love of nature is a legacy from the children of the nineteenth century and from all those whose urban (and Orthodox) experience caused them to love nature out of hatred for urban claustrophobia. They escaped to nature, escaped the experience of confinement, but they harmed nature out of love for it. For, really, they loved the idea of nature—nature in the abstract. A child who loves a flower might pick it, exactly like a kitten might kill a bird while trying to play with it. But love that is grown-up and responsible is not suffocating. There was something childish and suffocating about the love of nature of the children of the nineteenth century. The exodus to open spaces was like a great escape from the ghetto, from the *ḥeder,* from oppression. But they didn't know exactly what to do with nature. They never ceased being passionate about it. You can pick flowers out of love for them; you can in the same way display a stuffed antelope in your parlor—this too can be defined as love of nature. The criteria change from generation to generation. What was once permitted, lovely, and romantic (picking flowers) became one generation later a serious crime (from a legal standpoint) and something that is not done from the standpoint of moral society. The same is the case, for example, with smoking in public, or throwing away paper or glass or plastic—whatever can be recycled.

New facts are always coming to light that bring about new attitudes and that result in new ethical criteria. There will always be direct, moral confrontation between the sacred ritual of the past (whether distant or recent) and the ethical claims of the present and the future. The greatest problem is what exactly do we do with this confrontation, and what do we sacrifice? Contemporary ethics? Inherited ritual? Both? Neither? How? How much? What's the limit? Is there a limit?

"Anything can be done poorly or done right—including Tu B'Shvat. Let's do it right and have a joyous holiday"—so our rabbi and teacher Azaryah Alon instructs us. Here there is an explicit call for what, twenty years later, Arthur Waskow and Zalman Schachter will call "eco-kashrut." The actual practice of Tu B'Shvat had been completely outside Azaryah Alon's ethical and spiritual universe— it harmed nature! But the Tu B'Shvat that Azaryah Alon and his generation grew up on had become a symbol of the new Israeli and the return to nature! There is a fundamental contradiction between the nature ritual and nature itself. What do the zealots who are interested only in contemporary ethics suggest? They say: Our ritual has come to an end, for the ritual is not ethical. It accomplishes a perverse goal. Children relate to delicate saplings as if they were disposable toys. What was good for our parents (the children of the nineteenth century and the "children of the green *ḥeder*") is not good for our children and that's all there is to it! Who needs Tu B'Shvat? Tu B'Shvat isn't necessary. . . . Azaryah Alon disagrees with them. He understands that rituals are necessary to teach children to love nature. Rituals do not sprout up *ex nihilo;* they are part of a symbolic structure with ancient roots. He can totally identify with the choice to make Tu B'Shvat a day of trees and nature. (He knows well that the original Tu B'Shvat was not a nature holiday, nor a tree holiday, nor the New Year of Nature.[25] He is aware of the fact that ritual is inherently risky—especially if one declares education to be one of its goals. With ritual, as with any art, there is a danger that the symbol will come to overpower that which is symbolized. That the abstract concept will overpower the concrete object. Just as there is always the danger that in the name of the love of humanity, "humanists" with beautiful souls will (spiritually, physically, or economically) harm actual human beings, so there is

316

a danger that in the name of the love of nature, actual nature will be harmed. Such is the nature of ritual—it distances itself from the actual in order to draw near to it. Azaryah Alon well understands that for the benefit of nature, we must dedicate at least one day a year that is as ancient and traditional as possible. Hc knows that the Jewish tradition provides Tu B'Shvat for this purpose. He knows that the Jewish tradition, by its very nature, is compelled and able to take any holiday or ritual out of its historical context and to work it into a new ethical and aesthetic shape.

So, as forcefully as one must protest against the ethical defects that a holiday like Tu B'Shvat brings with it (and all the more so holidays like Purim, Hanukkah and Pesaḥ), one must defend its right to continued existence. Its right is our obligation—our obligation toward ourselves, toward our children, and especially toward the child within each of us. We must cultivate the choice of Tu B'Shvat as the day of trees and nature. We must deepen our connection with this holiday, with its help to strengthen the connection of every girl and boy with trees and with nature. At the same time, we must be eternally vigilant. It is forbidden that a holiday be allowed to overpower us—that is a clear formula for chauvinism. It is equally forbidden that this holiday (any holiday!) be thrown into the trash heap of history—that is a proven formula for collective suicide, for cutting off the branch we are sitting on (if I may use a Tu B'Shvat metaphor).

On Tu B'Shvat, Kill the Arabs, Rat-a-Tat-Tat
(Be-Tu Tu Tu, Ha-Aravim Yamutu)

When I quoted above "Here Come Planters," I avoided the wretched and venomous variation, "on Tu B'Shvat, kill the Arabs, rat-a-tat-tat,"[26] which was appended to it at some point and became an integral part of the repressed and unwritten reality of Israeli culture. I don't know when or by whom this addition was made, nor how, if at all, it would be possible to check such a thing. In any case, I remember singing those words myself, both with neighborhood children and with other schoolchildren (in unofficial contexts, of course). In an improvised study of adults who grew up in Israel, I found, first of all, that all of them, without excep-

317

tion, remembered "Here Come Planters" as an integral part of their childhood experiences. Likewise, I found that all of them, without exception, remembered the version, "on Tu B'Shvat, kill the Arabs, rat-a-tat-tat." Some of them were rattled by the admission, some were amazed at how successfully they had repressed that evil version, some admitted that it was the most significant line from the song engraved in their memories, and some admitted that it was one of their most significant memories of Tu B'Shvat from childhood.

I am one of the latter. I admit that that accursed line refuses to leave me alone, and it seems to me that it is one of the main reasons that I have tried for many years to repress Tu B'Shvat as much as possible. In the last section we spoke of the ecological devastation that resulted from the Zionist Tu B'Shvat's "planting *tikkun*." In this section I want to deal with a devastation that is much deeper and more bewildering.

Tu B'Shvat is identified with *tikkun olam*, with love of Creation. Tu B'Shvat is a song of praise for nature and for the entire universe. Yah B'Shvat, which is supposed to be one great Halleluyah, becomes a poisonous, hate-drenched song that all the children of Israel sing with idiotic and miserable humor, a song hoping for the death of all the Arabs. No *tikkun* in the world can succeed if it continues to be accompanied by a line such as this that so thoroughly fashioned us. We must confess that this line exists deep, deep within us. We must admit that deep, deep within us there is hatred and fear of Arabs in general and strangers in particular. It is not sufficient to make politically correct statements about peace and friendship. We must deal with the hatred and fear. We need to engage in a deep and complex process of national, collective, therapeutic work in order to uproot them from within us.

As part of our therapeutic work, we will have to take a journey to our collective memory. "On Tu B'Shvat, kill the Arabs, rat-a-tat-tat" is definitely part of the memory of those of us who grew up in Israel. All of us, without exception, have to lie on the analyst's couch and sing that line over and over in order to descend to the roots of our hatred and fear.

But our collective memory reaches back much, much further than children's songs of the early to mid-twentieth century. Some of the principal layers of our collective memory are the Tanakh, Talmud, and midrash. It would be impossible to bypass these sources and to complete a successful process of national healing. We need to turn them over and over in order to locate everything ugly that is hidden deep in our souls as well, of course, as everything lovely and noble.

For this we must know (and what follows is intended not only for the Israelis among us, but also for, perhaps especially for, all those American liberal, post-halakhic, neo-halakhic, new age [choose one of the above] Jews who have already been working many years with these sources): Jewish communities who want to use these sources in a process of healing cannot make do with only collecting the many wonderful, humanistic passages while avoiding the existence of those passages that are antihumanist, antifeminist, antiliberal, antipluralist, and so on and on. Such a process is liable to be at least as dangerous as one that avoids the sources altogether. It's impossible to sweep everything negative or ugly under the rug. It's forbidden! If it doesn't blow up in our faces, it will blow up in the faces of our children.

I want to illustrate my point with a comparison of two midrashic sources that are connected to the Torah portion *Beshallah,* which is centered on the Song at the Sea following the splitting of the Sea of Reeds and the drowning of the Egyptians. The Shabbat on which this portion is read is traditionally called *"Shabbat Shirah*—the Song Shabbat," and more than a few commentators have pointed out the fundamental connection between the Song Shabbat, which is always adjacent to Tu B'Shvat (either before or after), between the song of praise that the children of Israel sang at the sea, and the song of Yah B'Shvat, in which "all of Creation, trees and plants and all living things, begin to sing the song of spring."[27]

In the context of the splitting of the Sea and the Song that follows, we meet two midrashim with exactly opposite messages. In the first, humanist, midrash, we read: "At that time [when the children of Israel sang the Song at the Sea], the ministering angels sought to sing a song before the Holy Blessed One. The Holy Blessed One said to them, 'The work of my hands is drowning in the sea, and you would sing before me?!' On the basis of this midrash, Rabbi Yonatan explains the halakhic fact that one doesn't recite a full Hallel on Pesaḥ "because the Holy Blessed One does not rejoice at the downfall of the wicked."

On the other hand, in the *Mekhilta*[28] on this Torah portion, the following midrash appears:

> *And He Took Six Hundred Chosen Chariots.* Whose livestock drew the chariots? Should you say they belonged to the Egyptians—has it not already been said: "And all the cattle of Egypt died" (Exod. 9:6)? Should you say they belonged to Pharaoh—has it not already been said: "Behold, the hand of the Lord is upon thy livestock" (Exod. 9:3)? Should you say they belonged to the Israelites—has it not already been said: "Our livestock also shall go with us; not a hoof shall be left behind" (Exod. 10:26)? To whom then did they belong? To those "that feared of the Lord among the servants of Pharaoh"[29] We thus learn that even those that feared the Lord among the servants of Pharaoh became a snare for Israel. In this connection R. Simon the son of Yoḥai said: "Kill the best of the goyim! The best of serpents—smash its brains."

This strange and convoluted midrash, although its last line makes one shudder, is relatively well known, and it too is part of each of our repressed collective memories (at least for the Israelis among us). "Kill the best of the goyim" has the same ring as, how can I say this, . . . "A good Arab is a dead Arab," which I have heard thousands of times in my life (in the army, in the street, on the bus, in a taxi, etc.).

In short, my central claim is that in order to deal with the fixation on hating Arabs that is planted within us, it is not sufficient to reach back to the recent past of our collective memory and deal with "a good Arab is a dead Arab" and with "on Tu B'Shvat, kill the Arabs, rat-a-tat-tat." In this context, we must take several steps back to reach at least as far as Shimon bar Yoḥai's "kill the best of the goyim," which warned us as early as the second century against entanglement with any goy—even (or maybe especially) the "good goyim." It's not clear who the dangerous "good goyim" were from whom bar Yoḥai deflected his generation of second-century Israel. In contrast, it is clear who the "good goyim" were who cooperated with the Jews at the time of the Exodus. In addition, it is perfectly clear who the dangerous "good Arabs" are whom so many Jews try to warn us about on the bus, in the street, in the taxi, in the reserves, from the podium of the Knesset, and from the preaching pulpit of the weekly Torah portion. Let's be honest: How many times has each of us heard the thesis that it is impossible to trust the Arabs, that even the "good Arabs" will take the first opportunity to stick a knife in our backs, and that these "good Arabs" are taking advantage of our naiveté and our gentle spirits in order to get us to return the territories to them and in order to make it easier to liquidate the State of Israel, the Jewish People, and so on and so on.

So, first of all, we must take every opportunity to show the other side of the weekly-Torah-portion coin. First of all, on the Song Shabbat, we must quote as much as possible statements like: "The work of my hands is drowning and you would sing?" or "Do not rejoice in the downfall of your enemy" or "You shall love the stranger (not the proselyte but the alien who lives among you), for you were strangers in the land of Egypt.[30] First of all, we have to find a way to speak a humanist weekly Torah portion in the taxi and on the bus, in the street and at the demonstration.

I have no doubt that if we do not find our way back to the weekly Torah portion, everything will be lost. But, as I said, that is not enough. We must—even the most "leftist" among us—recognize the existence of the "Arab hater" in us and nurse ourselves with these sources. We need not do this, apparently, on the street corner and not, apparently, with small children. In hidden closets, perhaps, in workshops for parents and educators, and maybe—who knows?— on Shabbat, in numerous minyanim and *havurot* of a self-renewing Judaism, between the weekly Torah portion and the haftorah. . . .

Part II: The Midrash of Tikkun

Therefore Rabbi Shimon b. Yoḥai would say: "Kill the best of the goyim."

Mekhilta derabbi yishma'el, Parashat Beshallaḥ

He [Bar Yoḥai] said to him [his son]: "Women are light-headed."

Talmud *Berakhot* 33b

Rabbi Shimon b. Yoḥai says: "When Israel does the will of the Omnipresent One, their work is done by others. . . . and when Israel doesn't do the will of the Omnipresent One, they do their work themselves."

Talmud *Shabbat* 35b

Rabbi Shimon b. Yoḥai said: "Learn my ethical principles, for my principles are loftier than Rabbi Akiva's highest principles."

Talmud *Gitin* 67a

Rabbi Shimon b. Yoḥai said: "I saw the elite and they are few. If they are a thousand, my son and I are among them; if a hundred, my son and I are among them; and if only two, they are me and my son."

Talmud *Sukkah* 45b

Rabbi Shimon b. Yoḥai says: "One who is walking along studying and interrupts his study to say, 'how lovely that tree is' or 'how lovely that field is,'—Scripture considers such a one to have forfeited his life.

Mishnah *Avot* 3:7

They [b. Yoḥai and his son] lived twelve years in the cave. They came out. They saw people plowing and sowing, and they said, "They ignore the life of eternity and busy themselves with the life of this world!" Wherever they cast their eyes immediately burnt up. A heavenly voice came out and said to them, "Have you come out to destroy my world? Go back to your cave." They returned and stayed (in the cave) twelve more months. It is said that the decree for the evil in Gehenna is twelve months. . . .

Talmud *Berakhot* 34a

Rabbi Shimon b. Yoḥai is in urgent need of a lot of *tikkun*. The above collection of sayings cannot be coincidental. It's hard to think of a more chauvinist statement than "kill the best of the goyim," or more misogynist than "women are light-headed." It's hard to think of a more parasitic expression than "When Israel does the will of the Omnipresent One, their work is done by others," or of more sarcastic arrogance than "Learn my ethical principles, for my principles are loftier than Rabbi Akiva's highest principles."

Almost all the above statements have become classics of rabbinic literature and, certainly, an integral part of our collective (repressed?) memory. It is understandable and natural that such problematic statements have been subject to many conflicting interpretations—open admiration here, recoiling rejection there, and many stripes of apologetics in between. Part of the admiration as well as part of the criticism flow, in my opinion, from hatred and fear, and in each of the apologetic approaches, there is, of course, a drop of truth. After all, that's the task of apologetics—to stress the hidden positive behind the revealed negative; to show that the context in which the words were said was totally different from our context, and the like.

These three channels of reaction—admiration, rejection, and apologetics—are the three channels that we occasionally witness in reaction to some "religious" provocation that is tossed into the Israeli cultural space. The script is more or less fixed: Every few days some "religious" provocation falls on us with a provocative quote from the traditional sources ("the one who violates the Sabbath shall surely be put to death! . . ."), and the representatives of the three eternal Israeli camps—the admirers, the recoilers, and the apologists—immediately rush to react. The admirers turn yolky eyes upward and lift their heels, saying "Holy Holy Holy"; the recoilers turn yolky eyes downward and rush to be appalled; and the apologists—"religious" and "secular" from the "hidden center"— rush to set things in perspective and warn the two sides not to reach hasty conclusions. After a few days, the episode will be forgotten and will make way for the next provocation.

This dynamic can be explained in more "professional" language. The provocateur takes a quotation that originated either as midrash or as a halakhic statement and puts it forward as *peshat* that is applicable here and now. The representatives of the appalled recoilers immediately pick up the phone to their journalist—even if they had time to check the quote in the original, they don't know how, and in any case, they also accept it as *peshat*. Most of the blind admirers, too, are uninterested in opening a page of Talmud, and they too, of course, accept things as *peshat*. The admirers, therefore, seek to apply the provocative quote here and now in a monstrous halakhic state. The recoilers, in contrast, seek to cut off all contact with this whole primitive business. Both of them relate to the quote *solely* as part of a normative-authoritative system (halakhah) that must be accepted or rejected. Both of them totally ignore all of the psychological layers of their selves that are folded into this collective memory (what is the internal significance of "violation," of "Sabbath violation," of "holy," of "shall surely be put to death," of "Sabbath," etc.). The apologists, too, ignore the psychological implications of the provocative quotation and try to bring calm to the situation by pointing out the difference between the political-historical reality of "then" and the political reality of our day, and they try to convince the two sides that one doesn't rush to apply such things here and now. Therefore, they too relate to the quote solely as a halakhic statement, as *peshat* from the past that is not relevant (yet?) to the present.

Not one of these public reactions has the intention of going to the depths of the collective memory of "kill the best of the goyim" or "women are light-headed" or "the one who violates the Sabbath shall surely be put to death" for psycho-midrashic therapy.

The response of the satirists—all those who each weekend, in every medium, put out convoluted midrashim that work the recently quoted text into various, conflicting absurdities—is a completely different response. Satire, in essence, turns the perplexing quotations spoken in the course of the week by public figures into silly absurdities. It does this, partly, as a healthy way of dealing with the dark side of our collective soul, which gains expression in the pitiful pronouncements of our leaders.

The phenomenon of Israeli satire based on quotations from Torah or midrash is to me one of the most interesting phenomena in the entire dynamic of so-called "secular" Israeli culture and one of the most fascinating embodiments of the midrashic phenomenon. The myriads of "secular" Israelis who read satire do not know that they are reading midrash. But satire, by its very nature, is midrash. It takes a sacred *peshat* and elaborates one aspect of it *ad absurdum*, or it leaves it exactly as it was written but changes "just" one letter. For example, the midrash that defines Torah as a drug because it says "*Ve-zot ha-torah asher sam*—This is the Torah that is a drug" is nothing other than a delightful and tragic satire. The same is true of b. Yoḥai's midrash that resulted in the conclusion "kill the best of the goyim." That *pilpul*[31] in the *Mekhilta* about "where did the Egyptians get six hundred chariots" is a crazy satire that bears comparison with the best of Monty Python. Anyone who knows about the phenomenon of the *Purim-shpiel* in the world of the yeshivot can better understand the latent potential for satire in the study of Torah. A *Purim-shpiel* is essentially standup comedy performed by *talmidei ḥakhamim* using the same techniques of *pilpul* of which they are the masters and which they use day and night—when they lie down, when they rise up, and when they walk by the way.

It is possible, in my opinion, to read hundreds of passages of Talmud and midrash as satire.

In short, the Torah and the rest of the sacred sources are no more than a gold mine for satirists whose art is to reduce the sacred to the absurd. The technique of satirical midrash can be described as a sort of deconstructionism. The best satirists are professional dismantlers of linguistic patterns. Like any good *talmid ḥakham*, they also have the ability to spot the weak point in a sacred or binding text and to press it *ad absurdum*. That, on one foot, is the structure of many talmudic passages—on the basis of the canonical, binding text of the Mishnah, for example, a whole lot of scholars engage in *pilpul*, looking for its many weak spots, and begin to pose to one another all the imaginable difficulties and questions that there could be.

In short, a good scholar is necessarily a potential satirist, and it isn't totally coincidental that a number of the best satirists in Israel studied (or were forced to study) Talmud as children. As for other good satirists, it is completely clear to me that their souls are the lost incarnations of the spirits of the hundreds of Babylonian talmudic scholars who were punished for turning their Torah into a delightful word game and ignoring their responsibilities as public leaders. In general, when I read the Israeli Friday papers during these crazy days, I have the feeling that a convoluted talmudic negotiation is taking place above the burning head of the Jewish people between right-wing provocateur *talmidei ḥakhamim* and left-wing satirist *talmidei ḥakhamim*—a sort of heavenly deconstructionist yeshiva. My suspicion grows stronger and stronger that there's a conspiracy here, a secret network of provocateur and satirist scholars who, from above, are pulling the strings of the State of Israel, its leaders, and its citizens.

Satire is the air that every democratic society breathes, and satiric midrash is necessary, in my humble opinion, for the transformation of Israel's Torah from a dangerous and ossified source of authority into a source of delightful inspiration. For the many of us who enjoy satire, it is a true Sabbath delight. I can testify that for me and a number of my best friends, there are several satirical columns that we meticulously read every Shabbat, studying them closely as if they were the weekly Torah portion. In spite of all this,

325

as against all this, I will permit myself to say the following, although I know it will sound preachy:

We cannot suffice with midrash that dismantles (deconstructionist midrash). We must start on a deeply communicative journey of midrashim that repair (midrashim of *tikkun*). We urgently require many *batei midrash*[32] for *tikkun,* and we need to teach ourselves to be, pardon the expression, constructive. We need to teach ourselves to be post-cynical, not just post-Zionist. Blind admiration, recoiling rejection, apologetics, and satirical midrash are the four current Israeli paths to Israel's Torah. We need to pave the fifth path—the way of constructive midrash. Constructive midrash does not relate to b. Yoḥai as a historical figure who needs to be placed before an investigation committee (He said it/he didn't say it . . . What he said was very good/very bad . . . He meant something else . . . His words were taken out of context, etc., etc.). It also doesn't relate to him as to a political figure who must pay the price (resign, for example) for his wretched words. B. Yoḥai is not exactly Ezer Weizman . . .

Actually, b. Yoḥai and Ezer Weizman do share something in common, and it hinges on the fact that both of them are national, cultural symbols—icons. Words that are ascribed to them have an excellent chance of reflecting the nation and culture that stand behind them and of becoming part of its collective memory.

The charm and charisma of Ezer Weizman and the fact that he is the anointed president of the people of Israel give his words as much force as if they had been uttered by us, particularly by the male sabras (Ashkenazim?) among us. That's why this is such a bewildering business—it's not nice to hear yourself suddenly emitting some misogynist exhaust—after all, you are a known feminist. . . . Weizman's off-the-cuff remarks are a living reminder to each of us that there is an enormous, unavoidable gap between the political-ideological "me" and the psychological "me." It reminds me, for example, that in spite of all my endless statements and declarations, within me there is a chauvinist, a homophobe, a misogynist, a racist, a patriarchalist, an elitist, and so on.

But only Weizman has the necessary charisma, standing, and ability to actually fly the plane. B. Yoḥai too. This man who said, "kill the best of the goyim" and "women are light-headed" had much more than plain charisma—there was holiness and a rare spiritual power within him. He rode the heavens. He was divine. Open up any edition of the holy Zohar, and you'll find on the first page that that holy book was written by the divine and holy *tanna*, Rabbi Shimon b. Yoḥai.

The Zohar, which is ascribed to b. Yoḥai, is the most quoted book of *tikkunim* in the kabbalist Tu B'Shvat seder. The author of the Tu B'Shvat seder connected each fruit that is eaten in the course of the ceremony to a quotation from the Zohar, which is to be read carefully and with concentration in the process of eating the fruits, in order to accomplish *tikkun olam*.[33]

The Tu B'Shvat seder is described by the kabbalists as an additional great *tikkun* in a cycle of important *tikkunim* that were established by the AR"I and his followers as part of the general system of *tikkun olam*. The great grandfather of kabbalist *tikkun*-doers is, of course, b. Yoḥai himself. There is something bewildering in the fact that such a great, divine maker of *tikkunim* is associated with such an unreconstructed set of statements. Actually, though, behind that great bewilderment hides a great hope. In the end, it is exactly b. Yoḥai's bewildering statements that reveal the great "human" recesses of a man considered by many to be the most holy and divine of all the sages and mystics. It is exactly the enormous defects within the enormous holiness that, in a truly mythological way, allows each of us to see the reflection of our repressed collective memory, where the noble and the ugly are all mixed together. In the end, all the children of Adam were created in the divine image of b. Yoḥai: women and men, Jews and Arabs, those who vote for Meretz and those who vote for Moledet.[34] Even Ḥabad Hasidim. The bottom line is that our collective memory is not comprised only of racism, chauvinism, and homophobia—it also includes holiness. Also purity. Also a deep spiritual thirst, and also, if you'll pardon the expression, God. Halleluyah! (I mean praise Yah, not praise Tu.)

And in order to praise Yah, we do not need to be born again, we don't need to change our area code, and we don't even need to change our outward appearance (to cut our hair, grow a beard, add a layer of clothing, or the like). All that is necessary is to actualize the spiritual potential that is within us. To accomplish a great and fundamental *tikkun* on the b. Yoḥai that is in each one of us. To pull up the baobabs and water the rose.

Master of the Universe,
What Are You Destroying the World For?!

How, then, shall each of us heal the damaged b. Yoḥai within us, in order to actualize all the holiness embodied in it? There are, of course, many possible ways to do it, and I have no intention, heaven forbid, of presenting recipes. Nonetheless, I am interested in illustrating, with b. Yoḥai's help, one possible path to *tikkun*, for b. Yoḥai did, indeed, go through a most dramatic process of personal *tikkun*. That process is described in the famous story that appears in Tractate *Shabbat* of the Babylonian Talmud.

It is a very long story relative to the hundreds of Talmudic stories—more than a whole page long! (The average length of a story in the Talmud is seven or eight sentences.) I dedicated the longest chapter in my book *Alma Dee* (published in English as *From Jerusalem to the Edge of Heaven)* to the analysis of this story, and I must admit here that I paid little attention there to b. Yoḥai's process of *tikkun*. Mostly I paid attention to the impressiveness of the "unreconstructed" b. Yoḥai's creative-spiritual power, which allowed him to use Torah study as a refuge from public responsibility.

In order to clarify what I just said, I should confess that any connection that I developed to *tikkun olam* in *Alma Dee* was extremely cynical and slick. It is true that I occasionally mentioned the need to be active in the sociopolitical *tikkun* of this world, but that was just in order to satisfy an obligation and in order to pay lip service to the frustrated, political "me."

The approach that I developed in *Alma Dee* was pessimistic, "Tel-Avivi," and vain. This world is lost and there is no room for *tikkun*. Its God is dead and should be properly buried, and we should recite for Him, *"Yitgadal ve-yitkadash shemei rabah be-alma dee."* This Mourners' Kaddish, which may be translated, "Magnified and sanctified be His great name in the D world," is an opening into the revelation of *alma dee*—a fantastic and remote world, cut off entirely from the lost world, which is called "World B." Instead of wasting energy on the *tikkun* of the lost world, it's best to invest all of one's assets in *alma dee*—the D world, where everything is enchanting and marvelous. There, and only there, God is living forever and ever, and there, and only there, His great name is magnified and sanctified. How does one make such an investment? By joining Rabbi Akiva, Abaye, Rava, b. Yoḥai, and the rest of the Sages in the Olympus of the heavenly *beit midrash.*

Alma Dee, in short, is my very personal variation on the Garden of Eden or the mystical Orchard called "Paradise" or Olympus or the Cave. It is a song of praise and legitimation for all the individuals who redeem themselves by avoiding their responsibility to redeem the Other and to repair the world. The great heroes of *Alma Dee* are those individualist *talmidei ḥakhamim* who are described in the stories of the Babylonian Talmud, and at their head: b. Yoḥai.

I admit that for all the years during which I wrote *Alma Dee*, I admired bar Yohai and sought to draw near to him and his circle. I remember the terrific jealousy I bore toward him for having the courage to say out loud what I never dared to—that I wished my work would be done by others, so that I could give myself over to my private creativity and redeem myself. And the world can go to hell!

I remember my fantasy, the Arkia[35] fantasy, in which I cut off contact with the Land and with the outland, with the fruit of the Land and with the common people of the Land, and with the commandments that are connected to the Land, and in which I wander and float in my Arkia olympus and study in *ḥevruta*[36] with the Vilna Gaon, Rabbi Akiva, Moses, and b. Yoḥai. A thrilling internet connects me and them—I tie crowns for them, and they untie all the knots that hover excitedly with me, via e-mail.

To illustrate, this is what I wrote about the classic cave scene of the story (scene 3):

> If it had been up to me, I would have chosen this fantastic scene as the outer cover of the Talmud, for it encapsulates the essential desires of the devoted *talmid hakham.* . . . What is missing from this picture? We have a father and a son naked in a cave studying Torah and covered up to their necks with sand. . . . The sand covers them like an amniotic sac. An amniotic sac connected to the carob tree and the spring that give them everything that they need. By means of this incredible envelope, they are cut off from the world of reality and take off inward—to all possible worlds.[37]

In the scene that precedes the cave scene, bar Yohai and his son are hiding in the *beit midrash,* and every day the woman in their lives (wife and mother) arrives and brings them a loaf of bread and a jug of water. At a certain point, they decide not to take any risks

329

and they go hide in the cave. Their reason: "Women are light-headed; they may give her grief and she will then reveal where we are."

I approached the phrase "women are light-headed" with apologetic silence. In contrast, this is what I wrote about the transition from the *beit midrash* scene to the cave scene:

> There is a fascinating change of functions: *The cave assumes the role of the* beit midrash; the divine female (Torah) takes over the role of the human woman; the *carob tree takes over for the bread and the spring for the jug of water.* This is an absolute return to first principles. Spring water is more natural than jug water, the carob more natural than the bread, the cave than the *beit midrash,* and the primeval goddess than the real woman . . .

The cave is explicitly described as an ideal existence. A veritable paradise. A father and son naked, a carob tree, and a spring. A divine female. This is paradise after the fruit of knowledge has been eaten. A paradise of knowledge and study. They have nothing in the world but four cubits of the tree of knowledge. And beyond the tree of knowledge is the revolving and flaming sword of the Romans.

Here, in my opinion, is encapsulated the spiritual impulse for the formation of the Talmud and the kabbalistic literature that follows it—the attempt to return to the Garden of Eden without relinquishing the ability to eat continually from the tree of knowledge. The attempt to make the square round. To have your cake and eat it too.[38]

And that, of course, is the secret behind the magic of the Orchard, that mysterious Paradise into which b. Yoḥai's four teachers entered by one path and from which they exited by four separate paths.

And here, in my opinion, lies the secret of the spiritual impulse behind the creation of the kabbalist *tikkun Tu B'Shvat*—the Tu B'Shvat seder.

The whole enterprise of the *tikkun* on the night of Yah B'Shvat is an attempt to return to the Garden of Eden in order to taste all the fruits of the Tree of Knowledge that are contained in the Zohar, in the Talmud, in midrash, and in the Tanakh. Esoteric kabbalists enter the Garden of Eden's orchard on this night, taste all the permitted fruit, and recite blessings over them with great concentration. In order to taste the fruit, they read the story of b. Yoḥai and his son in the cave and read many portions of the Zohar that were revealed to b. Yoḥai in the cave, and very slowly, the fruit they are eating is transformed into divine fruit, and they, together with b. Yoḥai, his son, and the rest of the community, continue to perpetuate the recipe for tasting the fruits of the Tree of Knowledge tarrying in the Garden of Eden. It is a viable recipe. It has proved itself through generations of *talmidei ḥakhamim* and kabbalists. It is possible to enter the Garden of Eden and eat from the Tree of Knowledge. Period. There are just two serious problems that result:

A. There's the problem of getting out.
B. There's the problem of those who are left behind (the other 99.9 percent).

And, it should be understood, there is a tragic connection between these two problems. In every generation, many individuals succeed in tricking the revolving and flaming sword and accomplishing dramatic individual break-ins to the Garden of Eden. A few of them succeed in finding the way back. But then they become convinced that they have left their sons and daughters and spouses on the other side of the revolving and flaming sword. An entire people—so they are convinced—is left behind the revolving and flaming sword. An entire world. Most of those who return won't be able to bear the load. At best, they'll cease to function. In general, they become menaces to the public welfare.

> After twelve years of splendid isolation, [b. Yoḥai and his son] come out of the cave and see people plowing and sowing. They are not able to make peace with the wretched sight of people sunk to their necks in the vanities of this world. They begin to burn up the plowers and the sowers. As they burn them up, they murmur in amazement mixed with anger, *"You ignore the life of eternity and are busy only with the life of the world!"* The life of the world is agriculture, commerce, prayer, or any other occupation that isn't the study of Torah. Only those who are never diverted and remain continually in the study of Torah can be counted among the gods, the denizens of the *beit midrash* who live the life of eternity. Certainly those who spend twelve years in a cave absolutely absorbed in the process of studying Torah.

Rabbi Shimon b. Yoḥai said, "I have seen the elite and they are few. If there are a thousand—I and my son are among them. If there are a hundred—I and my son are among them. If there are two—they are my son and I."

331

He and his son. . . .

He and his son hover for twelve years in a limitless number of possible worlds. They cease to consider what life is like for people who are buried in the miserable world of actuality. As a result, when they emerge from the cave after twelve years, they look upon any occupation other than Torah study as worse than a waste of time. As corruption and sin. They have an inner sense that nobody who passes up the life of eternity has any right to exist. They have no tolerance for the world as it is, so they burn everything. They find themselves intensively engaged in the destruction of the world.

> Like creatures from outer space, they descend into misery, and their eyes beam deadly rays. Every place they glance burns up. It is true that *"talmidei hakhamim* bring peace to the world," but sometimes they lose control over themselves and sow destruction. Sometimes they have to descend into the cold world because of the astonishing heat of Torah study, and they may react with violent anger against those who dare to sever them from the umbilical cord that connects them to that marvelous carob and the spring. Just so, babies—were they not born blind and miserable—would burn us up with their eyes because of the violent separation that we impose on them.[39]

At this point, God has no choice but to put an end to b. Yohai and his son's destructive rampage.

> *"A voice came out and said, 'Have you come out to destroy my world? Go back to your cave.'"* Go back to your cave. Go back to your infinite number of possible worlds. You cannot function in the real world. You cannot even accept its right to exist. You are dangerous to the existence of my world. You might destroy it . . .[40]

And this is one of astonishing junctures in the story, whose essence, as I said, is *tikkun olam.* In fact the verb *tikkun* appears ten (!) times in it, although the combination *tikkun olam* never appears. On the other hand, the combination "destruction of the world—*hakravat olam*" cries out from the heart of the story and is, as we will see further on, the personal turning point of b. Yohai from a *talmid hakham* engaged in destruction of the world to a *talmid hakham* engaged in *tikkun.*

B. Yohai is not the only *talmid hakham* with sufficient power to destroy the world. One of the other such *talmidei hakhamim* is Eliezer b. Hyrcanus, as is related in the famous story of "Akhnai's

Oven." After the other Sages excommunicated Rabbi Eliezer, Rabbi Akiva expressed the concern "lest someone improper go to tell him [about the excommunication] and he ends up destroying the world." Indeed, the fact that a proper person (Rabbi Akiva) went to tell Rabbi Eliezer about the excommunication prevented the destruction of the entire world, but didn't manage to prevent the terrible devastations that took place that day—a third of the crops were destroyed, all of the dough fell, many other devastations took place, and the worst of all: "Wherever Rabbi Eliezer turned his eyes, was burned up." Exactly as in our story—b. Yoḥai and his son leave their cave of Paradise and see people who dare to plow, to sow, to plant, and to engage in the other vanities of this world— they can't bear such a sight and "wherever they turned their eyes, burned up immediately." God, too, is described more than once as a "creator and destroyer of worlds" and as one who not infrequently threatens to destroy the world or to return it to the emptiness and void. Without a doubt, this trait, too, makes b. Yoḥai and Rabbi Eliezer divine beings.

Another story describes how God becomes furious while Rabbah b. Naḥmani is dying and hurls a great storm upon the world, which causes a certain Arab and his camel to fly from one bank of the river to the other. After the Arab lands, he turns to God and says:

"Master of the Universe, the whole world belongs to you, and Rabbah b. Naḥmani belongs to you; you are Rabbah's and Rabbah is yours—what are you destroying the world for?!"

The fact that the story continues indicates that this wonderful Arab's appeal calmed the storm and annulled the destruction of the world at the hands of God.

In the context of the above sources, it is worth looking at the following midrash:

> When the Holy Blessed One created the original Adam, God took him around to all the trees in the Garden of Eden and said to it, "Observe how lovely and excellent my creations are, and everything that I created, I created for your sake; take heed not to damage or destroy my world, for if you do, there will be no one to repair it for you."

This wonderful midrash is one of the most outstanding quotations from any source in all the Tu B'Shvat seders that I have seen over the past year (numbering more than forty). It is rightly adopted by environmentalists as one of the most relevant midrashim, and scholars love to point to it as an example of the personal responsibility that "Judaism" places on every individual. Only it's worth noting that this midrash is speaking about the trees and the Garden of Eden, and the first human, as we know, has already managed to damage them, so apparently, according to this midrash, there's no one to fix things up. In *Bereshit Rabbah*, for example, we get the news that "ever since the first human sinned, the lights have been damaged, and they won't return to their repaired state until the son of Peretz (the Messiah?) comes."

In short: If we put aside for a moment our mission to find midrash of *tikkun*, and we wear the *wissenschaft* dunce cap and examine with a magnifying glass the context in which this midrash was written, there is a high probability that the damage being referred to is not ecological, but theological. According to this scholarly *peshat*, we're dealing here not with a suggestion for political-educational *tikkun* aimed at strengthening environmental awareness, but with a written invitation to all future mystics to concentrate on meditative intentions and to put together combinations of letters for the purpose of repairing the world and the Divinity.

The following description will suffice to illustrate these last ideas:

> [Rabbi Meir said:] When I arrived at Rabbi Yishmael's, he said to me: "My son, what is your work?" I told him: "I am a copyist." He said to me: "My son, be careful at your work, for your work is the work of Heaven, lest you leave out a single letter or add a single letter—and you end up destroying the whole, entire world."
>
> Talmud *Eruvin* 13b

The "whole entire world" is a very narrow bridge suspended over nothingness. The whole entire world is nothing but a combination of letters. It is obvious and known before our Throne of Glory that if but one of the letters were to be ruptured or obstructed, it would be impossible to survive and stand in our world for even a single hour.

So what kind of *tikkun* are we talking about in the end, and what kind of power was there in the eyes of b. Yoḥai, the great grandfather of all letter-combiners, when he left the cave and saw people repairing plow handles and plows and horseshoes? Who would not have been horrified as they adjusted each horseshoe by the terror-spreading appearance of the furious b. Yohai, and where would we all be now had the voice not stopped him at the last minute? . . .

The divine voice was there, thank God, for the purpose of rebuking and punishing him, and in order give him and his son the sentence of the wicked and send them down to Gehenna. The voice transformed the cave from an Eden of letters into a burning hell and imposed twelve months of being burned on b. Yohai/Arkia and his son, for having with their own eyes burned the plowers, the sowers, and the planters. The path that returns from the Garden of Eden to this world must pass through hell. All the holy destroyers must know that if they ever expect to engage in the *non* (social, ecological, national, political . . .) of *this* world, *too,* they need to be roasted in the smelting furnace of hell. If they can't take it, they can continue playing Scrabble in the heavenly Arkia, and blossom like gladiola with the rest of the letters that sprout in the air.

B. Yohai agreed to learn from the experience in hell. His son refused. After the twelve months of hell, the voice returned and proclaimed: "Leave your cave!" They again went out to the plowers, the sowers, the carob planters, the gladiola growers, and the rest of the common people who dare to look this world in the eyes and to live their temporary lives here on the ground.

Once more, [the son] begins to sow destruction wherever he glances. His father is forced to follow behind him to undo his destructions. *"Every place that Elazar would strike, b. Yohai would repair, saying, 'O my son, you and I are sufficient for the world.' . . . "* The son still refuses to accept the right of any world to exist that isn't a world of Torah study. With great patience, the father walks behind the son and rebuilds what he destroys and tries to convince him: *"You and I are sufficient for the world;* it is enough that the world has two *talmidei hakhamim* like us. The two elite. We shouldn't get angry at the limited inhabitants of this world. They are extremely simple and fragile. They do not have the capacity to love the process of studying Torah and to rejoice with the Torah of Study. They cannot be cut off from their daily life. . . . We have to accept them as they are. We have to behave with caution and restraint. Any careless move of ours could bring catastrophic destruction on them."

In the end, the son is somehow convinced, and he disappears from the story. Bar Yohai is left alone to go through the next stage, the stage of *tikkun.*

A Verbal Minefield

There appears, then, a section of text that I completely ignored in *Alma Dee;* I didn't even include it in my quotation of the story itself. Here is how the story in its entirety appears in the Talmud:

> [B. Yoḥai said:] Since a miracle happened to me, let me go and repair something, as it is written (Gen. 33:18), "And Jacob came in peace/whole" and Rav said: whole in his body, whole in his property, whole in his Torah. [And it is further written in that verse about Jacob] *Va-yiḥan et pe-nei ha-ir* [normally translated along the lines of "he camped facing the city," but our text offers other interpretations:] Rav said: He minted a coin for them, and Shmuel said: He established marketplaces for them. And Rabbi Yoḥanan said: He fixed up bathhouses for them.[41] He said: Is there something that needs fixing? They said to him: There is a place (in Tiberias) that is in doubt as to its impurity, and the priests have the extra burden of going around it . . .

I left this strange midrash, which connects b. Yoḥai's deeds of *tikkun* with Jacob's deeds of *tikkun*, out of *Alma Dee*. The "official" reason for the omission stemmed from the mistaken view of literature that I had then, according to which this midrash wasn't an integral part of the story. Now, I want to "repair" that which requires *tikkun* and to show that the midrash on Jacob is the key to the whole story.

By the way, the version of the cave story that appears in *Bereshit Rabbah* comes at the point of the verse (Gen. 33:18), "he camped facing the city," and it is nearly certain that the connection between b. Yoḥai and Jacob is older than the very different version in the Babylonian Talmud, with which we are dealing.

So b. Yoḥai learns the necessity of *tikkun* from Jacob, and this strange parallelism between b. Yoḥai and Jacob says, *"Drash me, tell my story."* First of all, it must be pointed out that according to the literary understanding of the Rabbis, our forefather Jacob was a *talmid ḥakham* who studied Torah, or, more precisely, Gemara, all day and all night. It is also true, by the way, of other biblical characters, such as David and Joshua, that they were none other than brilliant *yeshiva bochers* who made hair-splitting arguments about such tractates as *Bava Metzia, Makkot, Niddah, Ḥullin,* and so on.

Jacob was, therefore, a *talmid ḥakham*, "a dweller of tents," who sequestered himself in the tent of Torah and studied day and night. He fled from Esau (who is the archetypal Roman in rabbinic literature) and spent fourteen years detached from the world at the *beit midrash* of Shem and Ever. After that, he returned home and, after wrestling again with Esau and with God, he became Israel. As Israel, he recognized his obligation to become a person of deeds (more like Esau[42]), to take on responsibility, to stop being a *talmid ḥakham* astronaut. Recognized and acted. As soon as he arrived in his home city, Jacob began to make practical improvements, to accomplish tangible *tikkunim,* in order to make the day-to-day life of its citizens easier. Jacob the tent-dweller, the pure, the impractical, flees from Esau, from action; he tries to dig himself deeper in the tents of Shem and Ever, to remove himself from this world into the Torah and its letters. But the demands of this world (wives, concubines, children, crooked father-in-law, sheep, etc.) are stronger than his desire to escape, and in the course of the years of his flight, he learns to deal with action and practicality. He learns to make peace and accept his inner Esau. In the end, he no longer feels a need to flee this world—his ability to wrestle with God and be Israel is also his ability to love his own practical side.

What does he do after he returns to the city? He mints coins, establishes markets, fixes up bathhouses. He becomes a political activist and does everything he possibly can to improve the quality of life and to repair the world.

And b. Yoḥai passed through the same sequence as Jacob. He also fled from practicality and criticized the Romans (the Esau-ists) for their *tikkunim,* as opposed to Rabbi Judah, who praised these *tikkunim.* B. Yoḥai was able to find fault with all of them. (They established bridges to collect tolls, bathhouses for their own pleasure, markets as a place to settle their prostitutes. . . .) As a result, the (practical) Romans threatened his life. B. Yoḥai escaped from before the threatening practicality in the cave of words and letters. After thirteen years, he left the cave with the resolve to accomplish practical *tikkunim.* Exactly like Jacob and the Romans, he, too, took it upon himself to establish markets. He put himself at risk and acted vigorously (politically!) for the sake of a real *tikkun* in the Tiberias market, which would make the daily lives of its citizens much easier. The situation in this market was apparently intolerable. The stringent rabbinic authorities had declared the area impure for fear that there might have been corpses buried there. In cases of possible, but unconfirmed, impurity, a majority of authorities tend not to take any chances and to rule stringently. This ruling created difficulties for movement from place to place, for the possibility of development and construction, and for the daily life of the city. With the strength of his *pilpul,* b. Yoḥai found a way to remove the uncertainty and declare the lower market of Tiberias pure.

There is great danger in the seclusion of a *talmid ḥakham* in his cave. The more he secludes himself, the more he is liable to shrug off responsibility, and to devote himself to barren, verbal *tikkun.* B. Yoḥai overcame the danger and came out sweeter than before. He completely exhausted his ability to do verbal *tikkun* in order to do a practical *tikkun* that made a great contribution to the citizens of Tiberias. B. Yoḥai taught himself to repair markets.

The metamorphosis of b. Yoḥai from a verbal repairman (one who does *tikkun* for letters) to a practical repairman (one who does *tikkun* for markets) is expressed by the key sentence of this story: "Since a miracle happened to me, let me go and repair something."

The Aramaic word, which is here translated as "something"—*milta*—has the simultaneous meanings "word" and "thing." The same is true of the Hebrew word "*davar.*" This fundamental connection is not merely linguistic, it is an integral part of our most deeply rooted Hebrew culture and certainly comprises one of the most collective of each of our memories. Our culture was capable of drawing thousands of midrashim out of this fact—beginning with midrashim indicating that the world was created through speech, and ending with midrashim indicating that the whole entire world is nothing but speech, and nothing but a combination of letters.

When we read about b. Yoḥai leaving the cave of letters after thirteen years and deciding to repair *milta,* it's not clear to us whether a verbal or physical *milta* is meant. But when we read that, exactly like the Romans and like Jacob, he too repaired markets, it becomes clear that we are talking about a practical *tikkun* "on the ground." What made b. Yoḥai go from being an entrenched verbal repairman to an integrated practical-verbal repairman? The miracle. (Since a miracle happened to me, let me go and repair *milta.*)

The last thing[43] that remains for us to clarify in order to understand the meaning of *tikkun* in this story is: What is the miracle that happened to b. Yoḥai?

I believe the answer hinges on the narrator's words that precede the sentence, "Since a miracle happened to me. . . ."

Previously, when Rabbi Shimon b. Yoḥai would pose a difficulty, Rabbi Pineḥas b. Yair would answer him with *twelve deconstructions*. And afterward, when Rabbi Pineḥas b. Yair would pose a difficulty, Rabbi Shimon b. Yoḥai would answer him with *twenty-four deconstructions*.

In preparing the Hebrew (and then English) translation of this story for *Alma Dee,* I turned the Aramaic word *peruk*—"dismantling/deconstruction" into the "Hebrew"[44] "*teruts*—response." Now, I want to do a *tikkun* in the translation and leave the word *peruk*—"deconstruction." The pair "difficulty-deconstruction" is most significant, and I would like to deal with them in the following manner:

There is a fundamental difference between the pair difficulty-deconstruction and the pair question-response. The latter pair is two-dimensional and parochial relative to the first. "What time is it?" is not a difficulty, just as "It's seven forty" is not a deconstruction. Difficulty and deconstruction are far beyond the domain of informative trivia, and they may be found in either one of the two following problematic domains: the problematic existential domain, and the problematic domain of Torah study. In these two domains, a "difficulty" points to a fundamental flaw in the system, and the only way to deal with that flaw is through the deconstruction of the entire system.

It's not easy to be a poser of difficulties. Not everyone is able to do it. The silent majority is unable to pose difficulties and prefers to accept things as they are. In the best case, it is like the Haggadah's simple son: able to ask a question or two. Only *talmidei ḥakhamim* and revolutionaries permit themselves to pose difficulties. Only they permit themselves to turn the system over and over and to put their finger on the weak link that is hidden in its depths.

Those who deconstruct systems are rare experts. A minority in a minority. Before he entered the cave, b. Yoḥai didn't know how to deconstruct. Only to pose difficulties. He was, for sure, an excellent poser of difficulties—for every single *milta*, he would find twelve fundamental difficulties—but he wasn't able (or didn't want?) to engage in deconstruction. B. Yoḥai's great miracle hinges not only on the fact that he learned the secret of deconstruction, but that he learned to be a virtuoso deconstructionist—for every single difficulty that Pineḥas b. Yair would pose for him, he was able to find twenty-four deconstructions, deconstructions of deconstructions, and so forth.

I would like to consider another use of the Hebrew word *peruk: peruk mokshim*—sweeping for and eliminating mines. There's much more than just an associative connection between the *peruk kushiyot*—"deconstruction of difficulties" of talmudic Aramaic-Hebrew and the *peruk mokshim*—"sweeping for and eliminating mines" of Israeli military Hebrew. The verbal field of the deconstruction of difficulties is the exact reflection of the physical field of minesweeping. Both of these fields are extremely existential and both are dangerous and murderous. Crushed limbs fly over both of them, and awful cries of pain, anger, and terror are ripped from them, and suspicion and abysmal fear. Life and death are in the hands of language to at least the same extent as they are in the hands of the minesweeper. The responsibility assigned to the verbal minesweeper is no less great than that assigned to the deconstructor of explosive difficulties.

In short: Both with the physical *tikkun* (minesweeping) and with the verbal *tikkun* (deconstructing difficulties), we are definitely involved in the saving of lives, and only the combination of these two will allow for a full *tikkun olam*.

In recent years, a pointed debate has been carried out between post-modernist philosophers over whether there can be a responsible and constructive deconstructionism. I personally feel with all 248 of my limbs that there exists a kind of devoted deconstructionism that is a great mitzvah and a preserver of life. True minesweeping. The b. Yoḥai that left the cave was that sort of a devoted deconstructionist. He made use of all his consummate skill to deconstruct verbal constructs in order to declare the market in Tiberias pure and to improve the lives of its citizens. He made use of all the powers of deconstruction that he had learned in the cave to take a stand at the political front as a lone purifier against a multitude of defilers.

This literary figure of b. Yoḥai who knows how to mix practical *tikkun olam* with verbal *tikkun olam* must be a model that guides us when we speak of *tikkun olam* on Yah B'Shvat. The great challenge that lies before us is to fashion a *tikkun* for Yah B'Shvat that contains a vital and relevant mixture of political-practical *tikkun olam* and verbal-spiritual *tikkun olam*.

Our current poverty is illuminated by the various historic reincarnations of Tu B'Shvat. Each of the incarnations we've spoken about moved the center of gravity toward one of the two types of *tikkun* to the neglect of the other.

The kabbalists inherited a Tu B'Shvat of tangible trees and fruits from the *tannaim*. They turned all these trees and fruits into words and letters and raised them up to heaven. So that in the beginning of this century, S. Ben-Tzion and his comrades came and brought all the heavenly letters down to earth and taught (in the green *ḥeder*) the new children of Tel Aviv to plant all those letters in the soil of Tel Aviv.

If we add a little surrealist-dreamy turquoise to this pendulum, we get a kind of Tu B'Shvat that moves between kabbalist believers who plant trees in the sky and Zionist believers who plant letters in the ground. In the end, that's what I want to believe; that we're dealing with believers. We're not dealing with rogues who manipulate little children and common people. We're not dealing with a fox and a cat that entice Pinocchio to plant his gold coins deep in the earth. But that is more or less what actually happened. The trees that the kabbalists planted in the sky left the Diaspora Jew alienated from nature, while the letters that the children of Tel Aviv planted in the ground left them and the following generations alienated from their language and its sources. The Jews who planted trees in the sky floated among those trees as in Chagall's paintings. The Jews who planted letters in the ground tramped about on them and lost the ability to fly. If we don't succeed in uniting the *tikkunim* and giving them vital and relevant depth, we'll continue, at best, to swing on the surrealistic Tu B'Shvat pendulum of the previous generations.

And the precious, gritty sand will continue to run out of the sacred hourglass.

The running grit is the political and verbal *tikkunim* that we fail to accomplish.

The sacred hourglass is language and the world.

part VII

Fruit of the Lovely Tree:
Tu B'Shvat Itself

From the Root and Trunk, biblical and rabbinic, and from each of the branches of our Tree of Torah—kabbalistic, Zionist, Eco-Torah—have come some contributions to the practice of Tu B'Shvat in our generation—the fruit of all these generations.

This section presents some teachings toward the actual celebration of Tu B'Shvat today. We begin with—of course!—blessings, in new shapes drawn from earth by Marcia Falk. Then we turn to Ellen Bernstein, who was among this generation's pioneers in renewing the celebration of the Tu B'Shvat seder. She gives us a "recipe" for shaping our own Haggadah for the seder, drawing on the kabbalistic seder that emerged from Tzfat (Safed) and pointing it toward protection of the earth. Like most recipes, this one has a basic structure and suggestions for how to spice it up yourself.

Then come a series of essays, meditations, and teachings for use in the celebration, ranging from blessings over the fruits and nuts of the seder to poetry from within and beyond Jewish life that celebrates the earth and trees, to questions about *tzedakah* (the socially responsible use of money) on Tu B'Shvat, to the celebration of the seder at a place on earth that is in danger of eco-destruction, to suggestions for children's education. There are even recipes, in the more literal sense, for some traditional Tu B'Shvat meals. And there are songs for the seder—or for planting a tree.

343

Blessings for the Seder

Marcia Falk
From The Book of Blessings

BIRKAT P'RI HA'EYTZ

N'vareykh et eyn haḥayim
matzmiḥat p'ri ha'eytz.

BLESSING OVER THE FRUIT OF THE TREE

Let us bless the source of life
that nurtures the fruit of the tree.

BIRKAT YAYIN

N'vareykh et eyn haḥayim
matzmiḥat p'ri hagefen.

BLESSING OVER WINE

Let us bless the source of life
that ripens fruit on the vine.

Cooking Up a Tu B'Shvat Seder

Ellen Bernstein with Hannah Ashley

Why a Tu B'Shvat Seder?

Why not just plant a tree and eat some fruit? Because a *seder* is a ritual that makes an idea tangible. On *Pesach,* we use all of our senses to transform a trip to the dinner table into a journey of liberation. We eat horseradish in order to really taste the bitterness

345

of slavery; we see *haroset* and envision the labor of our ancestors, laying bricks with mortar; we drink wine to experience in our bodies the giddiness of freedom. We also tell the story of the exodus from Egypt so that we have words to understand these sensations intellectually. Slavery and freedom, as concepts (and realities), may be difficult to grasp when we are fortunate enough not to be experiencing them at that moment. The Passover seder engages our minds with a saga, while our bodies respond directly, almost bypassing the brain, to the sensations they are taking in.

The intention of a Tu B'Shvat seder, also, is to make an idea concrete. That idea is this: God is the source of all life, and therefore every tiny piece of creation is infinitely valuable. Taking this idea a step further, the seder speaks to human responsibility: Nature is a grand web in which everything is connected to everything else, and every small action that humans do reverberates all over the universe. . . .

How does a Tu B'Shvat seder teach this message? By engaging us intellectually, emotionally, spiritually, and physically with something as small as a raisin or a walnut. At this seder we

- learn about the connections among all creation through text study from a variety of sources—traditional Jewish writings, American authors, environmentalists.
- open our hearts with music, art, meditations and a beautiful environment.
- expand our spirits when we say blessings over many different kinds of fruits and nuts, sometimes as many as thirty or forty, and over four cups of wine. Aryeh Kaplan writes:

> The most important discipline of Judaism . . . involves the blessing. When a blessing is recited before eating, then the act itself becomes a spiritual undertaking. Through the blessing, the act of eating becomes a contemplative exercise.[1]

- nourish our bodies from many sources in the web of life when we carefully eat the food and wine we have blessed. Kaplan explains:

> Just as one can contemplate a flower or a melody, one can contemplate the act of eating. One opens one's mind completely

to the experience of chewing the food and fills the awareness with the taste and texture of the food. One then eats very slowly, aware of every nuance of taste.[2]

This is not just *noshing!* We see the abundance of figs and oranges on the table, we hear the cracking of walnuts, we smell the unique fragrance of fresh strawberries, and taste all the varieties of fruits before us. This meditation on food is the central ritual of the Tu B'Shvat seder. Each berry and nut is the proverbial "grain of sand" in which to know the world.

How to Deliver This Message?

The entire seder can be a "contemplative exercise" if a holistic sacred space is created. All the senses are fully engaged in a well-orchestrated seder. Powerful rituals are most often part theater, and planning does not detract from the spirituality of a ritual; it demonstrates respect and seriousness. Remember that "seder" means "order." A poorly planned event, or one that is supposed to happen "spontaneously," may end up being disappointing.

Some people may be more interested in emphasizing the environmental education aspects of the seder. However, the strength of using a seder, as opposed to a book or a play, to teach about ecology, is that a seder speaks to spiritual values. It is important, therefore, that the Jewish soul of the seder not be lost.

The soul of the seder concerns "The Four Worlds." The Kabbalists who originated the tradition of a Tu B'Shvat seder defined four levels of meaning in all experience, which they called "worlds." In this seder, each world is also connected to a particular element, and the environmental aspect of that element is explored.

Assiyah, the world of	Action	Earth	Winter
Yetzirah, the world of	Emotion	Water	Spring
Briyah, the world of	Thought	Air	Summer
Atzilut, the world of	Spirit	Fire	Fall

These spheres form the structure of the *seder*, making it a four-part ritual. In each section, the particular essence of that world is illuminated through readings, activities, blessings, and foods.

A Tu B'Shvat seder can be held at any time or place, indoors or out-of-doors, with any number of people of all ages.

Food

Food and drink engage participants on a *physical* level. All fruits are divided into categories representing the first three worlds. The fourth world, *Atzilut,* has no fruits because it is pure spirit and cannot be represented physically. The three "lower" worlds are ordered according to how close they are to the world of pure spirit. The further away they are, the more protection the holiness within that world needs. The edible part of each fruit—the flesh or the meat—represents holiness while the inedible portion—the shell, skin, or pit—represents protection.

Assiyah, being the furthest away from perfection/God-energy, is represented by fruits or nuts with an inedible outer shell and an edible inner core: pineapple, coconut, orange, banana, walnut, pecan, grapefruit, star fruit, pine nut, Brazil nut, pistachio.

Yetzirah has enough God-energy to surround its protective parts with holiness, but still needs some protection. It is represented by fruits with edible outer flesh and pithy, inedible cores: olive, date, cherry, loquat, peach, apricot, jujube, persimmon, plum, hackberry.

Briyah, being the closest to pure spirit of the three lower worlds, is represented by any fruits which are edible throughout: strawberry, grape, fig, raspberry, blueberry, carob, quince.

Some people use the fragrance of flowers, incense, or spices, or just a burning candle, to represent the final world. This seder leaves *Atzilut* completely without symbolism.

Preparing the fruits can be a big job if you're having a large crowd. Cut the fruits into bite-sized portions, especially if you have an abundant variety. Organize the fruits according to "worlds." Five to ten types for each "world" is customary. However, fewer is certainly acceptable, especially if you're buying local or organic produce. Be sure to let participants know about the food choices you've made; this is a good opportunity for education.

We also drink four cups of wine (or grape juice) to symbolize the four seasons: white wine for the winter slumber; red wine for the vital life force. First we drink one cup of white wine as a reminder of winter, then a cup of white wine with a dash of red for spring; red with a dash of white for summer, and pure red for autumn.

Setting, Music, and Art

The setting and artistic parts of the seder engage participants on an *emotional* level. Any space with a beautiful and peaceful atmosphere—one evocative of nature—will do. Candles, flowers, table-cloths, artwork, and branches will enhance the aesthetic experience.

The seder is a perfect opportunity for people to express their love for nature in whatever way they know best. Local musicians, artists, or dancers may want to compose pieces specifically for the event. The *kavannah*, or intention, of the artwork, songs, or movements as well as the setting and the food is to help participants experience the four "ways of being" into which the *seder* is divided.

Study and Blessings

Like the original Kabbalistic seder, much of this *seder* is devoted to writings from traditional Jewish sources, plus modern thinkers, poets, and environmentalists. The juxtaposition of Biblical/Jewish readings and readings on ecology and nature is a dramatic way to teach about the environmental aspects of Judaism. Study engages participants on an *intellectual* level.

Blessings, and then contemplative eating, either in silence or with music or focused conversation, culminate each section of the seder. These allow for experiencing the seder, and its implications, at perhaps the deepest, the *spiritual*, level.

349

Tu B'Shvat Seder

Ellen Bernstein

The seder has three parts: an explanation—the why and how of the seder—an opening blessing, and the main body of the seder. The body of the seder is again broken down in four parts, according to the four worlds.

I. Introduction

Said Rabbi Simeon: "Mark this well. Fire, air, earth and water are the sources and roots of all things above and below, and all things above, below, are grounded in them. And in each of the four winds these elements are found—fire in the North, water in the South, earth in the West; and the four elements are united with the four winds—and all are one. Fire, water, air and earth: gold, silver, copper and iron: North, South, East and West—altogether these make twelve, yet they are all one." (Zohar, Exod. 23b)

Read "Why a Tu B'Shvat Seder?" section here, or your own explanation of why the holiday is celebrated in this way. Explain or read about the concept of the Four Worlds.

II. Opening Blessing

R. Nachman of Bratslav used to say: Know that every shepherd has a unique niggun for each of the grasses and for each place where they herd. For each and every grass has its own song and from these songs of the grasses, the shepherds compose their songs.

. . . Would that I merited hearing the sound of the songs and praises of the grasses, how every blade of grass sings to the Holy One of Blessing, wholeheartedly with no reservations and without anticipation of reward. How wonderful it is when one hears their song and how very good to be amongst them serving our Creator in awe.[3]

350

Read Blessing section of *"Peri Eitz Hadar,"* (see p. 135) or say your own blessing to open the *seder.*

III. The Four Worlds

If there is a leader, s/he may lead the group in the *meditations* at the beginning of each world, and the *kavannot* before the blessings. The group as a whole *sings;* please embellish on the ideas for music! Distribute the *readings* in each world—embellish here, too. . . . from your own sources—before the beginning of the *seder* so that as many people have parts as possible. Other activities, such as dancing, storytelling, etc., should be inserted into the appropriate world. The *blessings* may be found at the end of the *seder.*

Assiyah: The World of Earth

Meditation

Earth is the rhythm of our feet on the Mountain. In this world, we bless the physical: our bodies, our land, our homes. It is our connection to the Earth that inspires Action.

Songs

Tzadik KaTamar; "You Shall Indeed Go Out with Joy"; "Inch by Inch" (The Garden Song); a dance with a strong beat.

Readings

There never seems to have been any doubt that Rocks came before living things—that they were in a sense, the first beings. In the oldest myths Rocks are tricky objects. Sometimes alive, or at least inhabited by spirits, they could move around and turn into other things. Monotheism quieted them down. They became Rocks of Ages, symbols of heavenly permanence and power, eminences for saint and prophet to stand on, foundations for temples and churches.

Evolution seems to have reversed this trend towards quiescence and Rocks are on the move again. Although we no longer see them as animate, we know that some of them once were alive, that many will be alive again as their elements break down into soil and are taken up by plants, and that they are constantly on the move. Rocks have regained respect in the past century or two. They are not just inert stuff to be blasted through or piled up into buildings. They have a slow life of their own. They *form, mature and age,* and their movements affect the lives of plants and animals enormously.[4]

And the Lord GOD took the humans and put them into the Garden of Eden to dress it and to keep it. (Gen. 2:15)

In nature, what dies and decays provides the fertility for that which is to continue.

At one time farmers respected these processes and used them to advantage. Farming is no longer a way of life, no longer husbandry or even agriculture. It is big business. . . . agribusiness. Agribusiness does not love the land. It treats soil as a raw material to use up. The result of the exploitation of the soil is:

1. soil erosion
2. soil compaction
3. soil and water pollution
4. pests and disease due to monoculture
5. depopulation of the country
6. decivilization of the city.[5]

And the Land shall not be sold in perpetuity for the Land is mine: for you are strangers and settlers with me. (Lev. 25:23)

Blessings

For Assiyah, we eat nuts and fruits with a tough skin to remind us of the protection the earth gives. Through this act, we acknowledge that we need protection in life, both physical and emotional. We bless our defense systems. They are holdovers from an earlier time when they helped us to survive.

Say one of the *brachot* over fruit.

Eat the fruits with hard shells on the outside and soft fruit on the inside.

Our first cup of wine is white. In winter, when nature is asleep, the earth is barren, sometimes covered with snow.

Say one of the *brachot* over wine.

Drink the first cup.

Yetzirah: The World of Water

Meditation

Yetzirah is the world of formation and birth. Water, the fluid element, gives shape to all matter. Our hearts are folded rivers: our bones are spiraling vortices: knots in trees are recycling eddies.

From water, the heart pours forth blessing and emotion. At this time we honor the watery ones: the phytoplankton who produce most of our oxygen, the sea creatures: dolphins, whales and seals subject to our unconscious wastefulness, the salmon whose lives are interrupted by dams.

Songs

Ushavtem Mayim, Atsei Zeitim Omdim

Readings

The letter *mem* derives its name from *mayim*, the Hebrew word for water. The letter also represents the *Mikvah* (the ritual bath) and the womb. Water is the place of birthing and rebirthing.

"Mayim" shares the same root as the word for What, *"Mah."* When a person immerses in water, he is nullifying his ego and asking "What am I?" Ego is the essence of permanence while water is the essence of impermanence. When a person is ready to replace his ego with a question, then he is also ready to be reborn with its answer.[6]

> *Nothing is weaker than water;*
> *Yet, for attacking what is hard and tough,*

353

Nothing surpasses it, nothing equals it.
The principle that what is weak overcomes what is strong,
And what is yielding conquers what is resistant,
Is known to everyone.
Yet few men utilize it profitably in practice.
But the intelligent man knows that:
He who willingly takes the blame for disgrace to his community
    is considered a responsible person,
And he who submissively accepts responsibility for the evils in
    his community naturally will be given enough authority for
    dealing with them.
These principles, no matter how paradoxical, are sound.[7]

From the forested headwaters to the agricultural midstream valleys to the commercial and industrial centers at the river's mouth, good and bad news travels by way of water. Did my toilet flushing give downstream swimmers a gastrointestinal disease? Did the headwaters clear-cut kill the salmon industry at the river's mouth? Did my city's need for water drain off a river and close upriver farmland that fed me fresh vegetables? Did a toxic waste dump leak into the groundwater table and poison people in the next county? Watershed consciousness is, in part, a promotional campaign to advertise the mutual concerns and needs that bind upstream and downstream, instream and offstream peoples together.

This journey is right out your window—among the hills and valleys that surround you. It is the first excursion of thought into the place you live. It focuses on where your water comes from when you turn on the faucet; where it goes when you flush; what soils produce your food; who shares your water supply, including the fish and other non-human creatures. The watershed way is a middle way, singing a local song, somewhere close by, between Mind and Planet.[8]

. . . All the rivers run into the sea, yet the sea is not full. Unto the place where the rivers come, thither they return again. . . . The thing that has been; it is what shall be; and that which is done is that which shall be done. (Eccle. 1:5–9)

Blessing—*Bracha*—comes from *Breicha*—a pool. Each person has her own pool inside, which is her pool of Blessing.[9]

A person who enjoys the pleasures of this world without blessing is called a thief because the blessing is what causes the continuation of the divine flow of the world.[10]

Blessings

For *Yetzirah,* we eat fruits with a tough inner core and a soft outer. Through this act we acknowledge the need to fortify our hearts. With a strong heart and a pure vision we can pull down the protective outer shell. Our lives grow richer and deeper as we become available to the miracle of nature which surrounds us.

Say one of the *brachot* over fruit.

Eat the fruits which are soft on the outside and have hard pits on the inside.

As spring approaches, the sun's rays begin to thaw the frozen earth. Gradually, the land changes its colors from white to red, as the first flowers appear on the hillsides. So, our second cup will be a bit darker. We pour a little red wine into the white.

Say one of the *brachot* over wine.

Drink the second cup.

Briyah: The World of Air

Meditation

Air is the stuff hopes and dreams are made of. Air is the work manifesting as the world. Close your eyes and take a breath. As you inhale, know you are being breathed by the earth. Let the breath out and visualize your next step to beautify the Garden.

Song

Lo Yisah Goy, instrumentals, *niggunim*

Readings

Then the Lord God formed the human of the dust of the ground, and breathed into the nostrils the breath of life; and the human became a living soul. (Gen. 2:7)

In Arabic, the wind is *"ruh,"* but the same word also means "breath" and "spirit," while in Hebrew, *"ruach"* enlarges the sphere of influence to include concepts of creation and divinity. And the Greek *"pneuma,"* or the Latin *"animus"* are redolent, not just of air, but of the very stuff of the soul.

Without wind, most of Earth would be uninhabitable. The tropics would grow so unbearably hot that nothing could live there, and the rest of the planet would freeze. Moisture, if any existed, would be confined to the oceans, and all but the fringe of the great continents along a narrow temperate belt would be desert. There would be no erosion, no soil, and for any community that managed to evolve despite these rigors, no relief from suffocation by their own waste products.

But with the wind, Earth comes truly alive. Winds provide the circulatory and nervous systems of the planet, sharing out energy information, distributing both warmth and awareness, making something out of nothing.[11]

> *Thirty spokes share the wheel's hub*
> *It is the center hole that makes it useful.*
> *Shape clay into a vessel;*
> *It is the space within that makes it useful.*
> *Cut doors and windows for a room;*
> *It is the holes which make it useful.*
> *Therefore profit comes from what is there;*
> *Usefulness from what is not there.*[12]

> *I live life in growing orbits*
> *which move out over the things of the world.*
> *Perhaps I will never achieve the last,*
> *but that will be my attempt.*
> *I am circling around God, around the ancient tower,*

and I have been circling for a thousand years.
And I still don't know if I am a falcon
or a storm, or a great song.[13]

Every part of the vegetable world
is singing a song
and bringing forth a secret
of the divine mystery
of the creation.[14]

Blessings

For *Briyah* we taste fruits that are completely edible. In this world, where God's protection is close at hand, we can let go of all barriers and try on freedom. We are co-creators with God and each of our thoughts becomes Action.

Say one of the *brachot* over fruit.
Eat the fruits which are soft throughout.
In summer, when vegetable and fruits are abundant, we are re-minded of the richness of life. We drink red wine with a dash of white.
Say one of the *brachot* over wine.
Drink the third cup.

Atzilut: The World of Fire

Meditation

There's a fire alive within every living cell of every being. The car-bons we eat burn in the presence of the oxygen we breathe, giving us the energy to be. This spark of light is our connection to the Divine.

Song

"In Your Light Do We See Light," "This Little Light of Mine"

Readings

And the angel of the Lord appeared unto him in a flame of fire out of the midst of a bush; and he looked, and, behold, the bush burned with fire, and the bush was not consumed. (Exod. 3:2)

Had I not seen the sun
I could have borne the shade
But Light a newer wilderness
My wilderness has made.[15]

I have never understood why so many mystics of all creeds experience the presence of God on mountain tops.

Aren't they afraid of being blown away?

It often feels best to lie low, inconspicuous, instead of waving your spirit around from high places like a lightning rod.

For if God is in one sense the igniter, a fireball that spins over the ground of continents, God is also in another sense the destroyer, lightning, blind power, impartial as the atmosphere.[16]

And it shall come to pass, if you shall hearken diligently unto my commandments which I command you this day, to love the Lord your God and to serve him with all your heart and soul, then I will give the rain of your land in its season, the former rain and the latter rain, that you may gather in your corn, and your wine and your oil. And I will give grass in your fields for your cattle, and you shall eat and be satisfied. Take heed to yourselves, lest your heart be deceived, and you turn aside, and serve other gods, and worship them. (Deut. 11:13–16)

Today, like every other day, we wake up empty and frightened. Don't open the door to the study and begin reading. Take down the dulcimer.

Let the beauty we love be what we do. There are hundreds of ways to kneel and kiss the ground.[17]

Master of the Universe
Grant me the ability to be alone;

May it be my custom to go outdoors each day among the trees and grasses, among all
    growing things and there may I be alone, and enter into prayer to talk with the one
    that I belong to.[18]

Blessings

As summer turns to fall, plants are preparing seed for the next cycle of nature. We too must nourish the world for the coming generation. Just as the natural world goes through changes to achieve its full potential, we also need to change: we need to get rid of anger, envy and greed so that we can be free to grow. When we do this, we will become very strong, healthy trees, with solid roots in the ground and our arms open to the love that is all around us.

At this level we go straight to the fourth cup, which we drink full strength red.
    Say one of the *brachot* over wine.
    Drink the fourth cup.

At the end of the *seder,* a fuller meal using the foods that are mentioned in the quote, ". . . a land of wheat, and barley, and vines, and fig trees, and pomegranates; a land of olive oil, and honey; a land in which thou shalt eat bread without scarceness," can be eaten. Some suggestions are: challah, mushroom-barley soup, cheeses and honeycake.

Traditional *brachah* over the fruit:
    Ba-ruch ata A-do-nai El-o-hay-nu mel-ech ha-olam bo-ray pree ha-etz.
    Praised are you, Eternal, Our God, Ruler of the Universe who creates the fruit of the tree.

Alternative brachah over the fruit:
    Brucha at Yah, El-o-tay-nu ruach ha-olam bo-rate pree ha-etz.
    Holy One of Blessing, Your presence fills Creation, You create the fruit of the tree.

Traditional *brachah* over the wine:
Ba-ruch ata A-do-nai El-o-thay-nu mel-ech ha-olam bo-ray pree ha-gafen.
Blessed art thou, O Lord our God, Ruler of the Universe who creates the fruit of the vine.[19]

A Circle of Friends: Tu B'Shvat for Small Children

Elisheva Kaufman

Invite children outside to find a class tree which you will adopt for the year. You may want to designate this area as your outdoor class meeting place. Throughout the year you may share nature stories here, do artwork, have special gatherings, record seasonal observations, etc.

Walk to your class tree. Ask students to join hands around it forming a circle. You may ask them (one task at a time) to: observe, smell, feel (light, shadows, wind, warmth, silence, group energy) and listen. When silent observations are complete, you may ask, "What have you learned about our tree by: looking, smelling, feeling, listening?" These subtle sensations about the class tree may allow for special feelings to arise regarding the children's relationship to nature. Allow for some time to express this in picture form, poetry, or song.

The children may create a circular story after their silent observation experience. Perhaps the circular story is about the life of the tree from seed to now. The first student contributes a sentence to get the story started in the seed stage. Each student adds a sentence, weaving together a story in the round, which tells about this tree. Children may record these circular stories as well as their observations of circles in nature in their nature journals.

While visiting this tree throughout the year, take the opportunity to look for examples of circles in nature, i.e., cycles of seasons, leaves decompose into soil and soil is nourishment for the tree, acorns feed the squirrel and the squirrel is a planter of acorns when

360

they are hidden for a food reserve, trees cleanse air and send it forth for humans, humans breathe cleansed air and send back carbon dioxide for the tree to convert, nutrients recycle when the dying tree returns to the earth its own trunk, etc. Discuss what it means when things work in a circular pattern or rhythm.

Plants and Trees in Winter: Tu B'Shvat for Older Children

Elisheva Kaufman

And Elohim said,
Let the earth sprout forth vegetation,
Plants that have seeds, and
Trees that have fruits with seeds of its own kind, . . .
and Elohim saw that this was good.
And it was even and it was morning, the third day.

Gen. 1:11

Thus the Torah understands plants as the basis for all life, since they were created on the third day, just after the waters were divided above and below the firmament. Plants are grouped into three main kinds:

* vegetation,
* plants with seeds, and
* trees bearing fruit.

These three groups give us understanding of basic plant forms and processes:

Vegetation includes bacteria, fungi, mushrooms, algae, seaweeds, mosses, lichens, and ferns.

Plants with seeds includes all flowering plants and shrubs with green stems.

Trees includes plants with sturdy wooden trunk-stems supporting leafy growth and bearing cones or fruits with seeds.

Our planet supports a richly diverse plant kingdom on which we are dependent for our very existence. Plants are found throughout all regions of the land and sea. Although we can look at plants from the simpler to the more complex, each plant's relationship to the whole is as part of an interconnected web. The activity of the simplest forms of non-green plants, such as bacteria and fungi, are as important to the whole ecosystem as the majestic trees.

As we look more closely at the winter life of basic plant types, we remember that every part of the earth is part of this great living earth body. The winter life of plants, is of course, much quieter than the great activity in the rest of year. Now the earth seems more still, as if it has breathed in its energy below the roots of the trees. But don't be fooled! There is a great deal to see and discover on the old rotting logs, the pinecones, moss and ferns poking out beneath the melting snow, the dried old plants and the striking silhouettes of winter trees.

Caring for a Tree of Life

Elisheva Kaufman

The lights (i.e., sun, moon and stars) of the world suffer when a beneficial tree is harmed.

Talmud *Sukkah* 29a

When a fruit-bearing tree is chopped down, a crying voice is heard from one end of the world to the other, but it is not audible to the human ear.

Pirke de'rebbi eli'ezer 34

This article supplies elementary-school teachers with projects, including some directions to give the students and some explanations for the teachers.

How can we give back to the trees? How can we care for them? How can we tell if a tree is healthy? The most important indication of tree health is abundant, full leaves and a sturdy, intact trunk. Since the forest is a home of so much life, the names of the different layers of the forest remind us of the parts of our home:

1. Canopy—the upper leaves that receive full sunlight
2. Forest floor—the shady ground that receives little direct sunlight

Stand back and look at the tree's height relative to its neighbors. How much sunlight does it receive? Walk all around your tree. Look at its top from many different angles. How much of the tree is full with leaves? If only the lower branches look dead, don't worry. It is normal for these branches to die from lack of sunlight. Is there much leaf damage from insects? Is the bark wounded? Is there any shelf fungus? Is the soil around the roots loosened to absorb rain?

Invite a local agricultural extension person to visit you to talk about caring for local trees and plants. How can wounds be covered? Can you gently loosen the earth around the roots? The tree may brighten up with a birdhouse or feeder to care for its birds.

Find the same kind of tree in a range of environments—a forest, meadow's edge, protected area, or exposed field. Notice how the tree in the crowded, mature forest grows tall with foliage at the very top. Compare this to the same type of tree in an open meadow. Notice how the exposed tree is rounded, with a full growth of leaves. Can you find a tree on a windy hillside? How does this tree respond to the constant sun and wind on one side? Be a plant detective, and search out a plant in various environments. Notice how the sun-filled environment creates thinner leaves, and shade draws out fuller, rounded leaf growth. Why?

Tree Discovery Activities

For we are as the trees of the field, this indicates that our life depends on the trees.

Sifre Judges 23

Growing Trees

Gather tree seeds. Wherever you live, you will find trees with seeds to gather. Pot young tree seedlings that are growing too close to their mother. Dig a deep, generous circle around the sprout or sapling to take it up from the soil. Care for the seedlings indoors for the winter. Set them outdoors in a special place next Spring. Or gift them to family and elderly people who are not able to get out into nature.

Research Trees

Determine which part of the tree products come from. The crown of the tree give fruits; nuts; seeds; drinks like cola, coffee, chocolate; milk from coconuts; shelter; leaves for compost; bark mulch; etc. Trunk and sap of the tree give maple syrup and sugar, rubber, chewing gum, paper, and wood for building many things. Roots of a tree give the gifts of medicines and dyes, not to mention root beer!

Tree Books

Make your own unique Tree of Life books using leaf rubbings, bark rubbings, illustrations of tree shapes, pressed dried leaves, illustrations, and stories and legends about the tree's qualities. Each type of tree can have its own book with the qualities of the tree celebrated within it. Or make chapters for each tree within a large tree book. Look at the leaf, twig, and branch arrangements. Make Tree of Life books on how insects, earthworms, birds, animals, and human families need and help each other.

Making a family tree book during the same period of study is a rich complement to tree studies.

Preserving Leaves in the Book

If you want to preserve a leaf in your book and still feel it, you may use a decoupage fixative to preserve the leaf that has been pressed in a thick book or a flower press, and attach it to the page. If pressed leaves are placed within contact paper, the preserved leaves will last forever, though you can no longer touch the leaf. Pressed leaves may be ironed between wax paper, and attached to sturdy, decorated cardboard frames. Laminated leaves eventually will fade to brown over time. Rubbings made from leaves can be used in your book as well. When your leaf samples are ready, try to determine the special characteristics of each leaf.

Being with a Tree of Life

> All of the trees, plants, and spirits that dwell in nature conversed with one another. The spirit that lives in the trees and nature conversed with Humankind, for all of the Beings in nature were created for mutual companionship with Man.
>
> *Gen. Rabbah* 13:2

You can relate to a tree on many levels. Find a tree whose gesture and mood feel special to you. Touch and smell it. Feel its silent, growing being. Stand near it. First become more aware of yourself, moving your awareness from your feet up throughout your body. Become aware of your breath. Feel the Earth with your feet and extend tiny rootlets out, growing down, down into the soft soil. Draw your sustenance from the earth. Draw the earth energy up, up until it courses within you. From your head, visualize long filaments emerging, branching up to the sky, connecting you with the cosmos. Let your breath quiet with the tree's giving breath. Allow the warming sunlight to lighten you. Let the tree's movement move with you, reaching between heaven and earth. Be with the tree. Then become aware of your own self, your own heartbeat. Listen to the sounds around you. Slowly open your eyes.

Stand back from your tree. Experience it as a life form with awareness and spirit, that silently senses and responds to you with fellowship.

Try to draw it from a place where you can see its wholeness. Your thoughts and responses may become poetree! As you move more closely to the tree, notice the pattern of the leaves growing on the branches. You might keep the sketch of the tree and mount some of its leaves, bud or blossoms to the sketch.

> And it is said of Hillel, that he did not omit to study any of the words of the Sages, even all the languages, even the speech of mountains, hills and valleys, the speech of trees and herbs, the speech of wild beasts and cattle, the speech of melody and of parable.
>
> Why did he study all these? Because it is stated,
>
> The Lord was pleased, for His righteousness sake, to make the teaching great and glorious (Isa. 42:21).
>
> *Soferim* 41b

Giving Back

So many people take from nature without awareness of the consequences. How can we bring our children outdoors and gather the fruits of the earth for art, healing, and learning—while cultivating sensitivity and an ethic of giving back? The following talmudic parable provides us with guidance:

> A man was journeying in a desert. He was hungry, weary, and thirsty. He found a tree whose fruits were sweet, its shade pleasant, with a stream of water flowing beneath it. He ate of its fruits, drank from the water, and rested under its shade. When he was ready to continue his journey, he said, "Tree, O Tree with what shall I bless you? Shall I say to you, 'May your fruits be sweet'? They are already sweet. That your shade be pleasant? It is already pleasant. That a stream of water may flow beneath you? Lo, a stream of cool water flows already beneath you. Therefore, I say, May it be God's will that all the shoots taken from you will be like you."
>
> B. *Ta'anit* 8a–b

Discovery Activities

1. Divide into pairs. One will be a tree, the other will gather from the tree. First gather roughly from the tree, without sensitivity to the tree. How does it feel? Then practice gathering gently and firmly, with respect and gratitude to the spirit of the tree. How does it feel? Switch roles. Talk about this experience.

I found that it felt good to have someone gently gather my bark and leaves, sort of like a haircut and grooming, or a back scratching. I sense that trees enjoy being appreciated and used well by us.

2. Practice blessing a plant when you receive something from it or eat it. The blessing provides a vital stream for elemental beings around the plant, the guardian angel of the plant to restore itself by drawing down the *shefa*, the divine flow. It is much easier for me to bless silently. I feel shy saying these things aloud, although I know that our sages teach the importance of speaking blessings out loud. Talk about this with your rabbi.

Surely it has been taught, if one buys a tree for felling, he must leave at least one handbreadth of the trunk from the ground, so that the trunk will send forth new shoots to renew itself. Of the trunk of the sycamore two handbreadths of the trunk of virgin sycamore tree—three handbreadths, of reeds and vines—from the knot above it, from the place where the plant begins to branch out. However, in the case of date palms and cedars, he may dig into the ground and uproot them, because their stock does not renew themselves from the root.

B. Ta'anit 25b

Gathering Tips: Only take a little bit from a place, making sure that there are enough plants left to continue growth in that place. Whenever possible, gather the leaves, not the entire plant. Return its seeds to the earth if you take a plant.

Thank and bless the plant for giving itself to you. Thank the Creator for creating the plant, and for being there to continue the species.

Be a Tree Theater

Become a Tree of Life. Fashion a crown of birch bark gathered from the ground near a birch tree, festooned with pressed, waxed leaves, and dried winter plants. Wear branches with leaves attached on arms and hands. Wrap the body with brown fabric as a trunk. Help the children to explain the basic function of different tree parts to their classmates. Older children may want to use branches, wire, fabric, and papier-mâché to make life-sized tree puppets or sculpture.

- Crown—branches and twigs which hold leaves
- Trunk—supports crown, carries minerals and water up, food down
- Roots—supports tree, absorbs minerals and water, stores food
- Outer bark—provides protection from fire, disease, insects
- Inner bark—sends food down to roots from leaves
- Cambium—the tree rings which produce inner bark and sapwood
- Sapwood—brings minerals and water up to leaves
- Heartwood—hard core which provides inner support

After telling the children a tree tale, encourage them to create their own tree myths and legends. Create a "Voices of the Earth" theater, using the "Be a Tree" costumes.

Indoor Forest Corner

Make an indoor forest in your room. Can you find cut tree stumps to bring indoors? Bring in fallen branches, bark (forage fallen bark from trees or wood piles), nuts and pinecones, stones or fallen bark covered with lichen or mosses (mist regularly), seeds, and special treasures from the forest floor to decorate the forest corner. Make a recording of environmental sounds of the forest in your classroom forest for special effects.

Keep a mystery bag in the classroom forest. Each day place a different object from the forest in the bag for students to feel and identify. The same idea can be expanded to include smells of the forest. Jars with holes in lids placed inside the mystery bag may contain a variety of changing materials, e.g., decomposing leaves, pine needles, wintergreen leaf, herbs, etc.

Tree of Life Art

Make branch weavings with fallen winter branches and natural materials woven into the colored yarn wrapped around the branch. Make tree bark rubbing stationery, leaf and branch pattern puzzles.

Nature Trail

Create a nature trail on school grounds, around the block or in the nearest woods. Take hikes to decide the areas that have special interest for the children. Encourage the children to explore and to see nature anew. Mark the places with child-made explanatory wooden signs. Students may make their own numbered tree and plant identification signs. Let them make a map marking the numbered signs.

Make a Tree of Life Trail guide booklet for school and community use. Draw and record details of special characteristics of these trees, e.g., insect and animal homes, branch patterns, bark textures, mosses. Choose several of these notable characteristics to share when leading a Tree Trail Tour. Prepare to lead Tree of Life Trail tours for other students, family, and friends of the neighborhood! Remember to do a trial run of activities on the Tree Trail before the official opening day.

- Prepare tree foods to serve at the festival. Try maple products, nuts, fruit salads, guacamole dips, coconut milk and meat, almond butter.
- Plan activities for those on the Tree Trail Tours, like doing bark rubbings along the way. You can really see tree bark textures. A large sheet of easel paper may be fastened around the tree for group rubbings. Have crayons handy and replace the easel paper as it gets used. Save for piecing together later as a giant tree rubbing banner, complete with tree-safe graffiti!

Measuring the Height of a Tree

Measure the length of a tree's shadow. Measure the length of your shadow. The tree's shadow is how many times the length of your shadow? The tree's height is this number times the length of your height.

Rotting Log Terrarium

Recycle a large gallon jar with a lid, or a two-liter plastic soda bottle. Place a one-inch drainage layer of gravel or coarse sand in the bottom. Cover with a layer of dead leaves. Next comes a thin layer of charcoal chips, for odor absorption. Add potting soil. Find an interesting piece of old decomposing tree limb. Place the rotting log inside the jar. Mist to keep moist. You may like to add small stones, tiny pinecones, or student-made clay creations for the rotting log village. Screw on the lid and keep the jar away from direct sun or your log might cook. Students enjoy observing the terrarium daily with a hand lens, recording and illustrating observations in a journal.

Once a week, you may remove the rotting log carefully. Now everyone can get a close-up look and record the goings on and any changes in appearance, odor, texture, color, emerging plants or critters who may live there.

A "dead tree" makes great contributions to the forest long after its own growing days have ended. It gives back and provides food and place for many diverse and amazing animals and plants!

Bringing a Tree of Life Home

Take the children out to a woods to find a young sapling to thin, or a sturdy branch to bring back. Explain how thinning helps to reduce the competition for light and nutrients in the forest. It lets the remaining trees have more available light and nutrients. When uprooting, carefully dig a wide circle to encompass the entire root system. Place the uprooted tree on a large cloth, gather up the corners, and return to school.

Transplant the tree in a sturdy soil-filled container in the classroom. The children may decorate it with seasonal or holiday themes. Children may add changing leaves, snowflakes, buds, nesting birds, etc., which reflect their observations of changing seasons. You might create a moss garden (mist daily) beneath it with foraged acorns, stones and crystals, fallen leaves, fungus, critters made from natural objects (pinecone animals, milkweed pod mice), etc. Older children may use the indoor tree habitat to learn about trees as mini-habitats for many kinds of life.

Growing an Indoor Garden

Take a winter hike to gather tree and wildflowers seeds from the dried winter plants outdoors to plant in an indoor garden. If you gathered seeds in the Fall, did you remember to let them winter-over in the freezer or outside? Examine the seed shapes and methods of dispersal when you come back in. Are the seeds jumpers,

370

hitchhikers, spinners, floaters or what? Plant the tree seeds to raise saplings for an outdoor garden project.

Vegetables for an indoor garden harvest salad may be planted at Tu B'Shvat time to be tended and harvested during the *Omer*. Ask the children what vegetables they like to eat. Try fragrant herbs of the children's choice for a *havdalah* bouquet. Parsley, chicory and romaine lettuce may be planted for *karpas* at the seder. Can you find a horseradish root to plant in the garden?

Sow seeds in six-inch pots filled with moist germinating mix. There are many container varieties available today in seed catalogues. You may also enjoy trying varieties available from seed catalogs in their "Baby Vegetable Collection" of miniature carrots, beets, scallop squash, onions, lettuce and bush beans. Pole beans or grape vines may be grown in pots down below the indoor garden and left to trellis their way upward to the indoor garden lights. You may begin herbs, sunflowers, vegetables and flowers to transplant for your outdoor garden after Passover.

Resources:

> *Gro-Lab Teacher's Manual: A Complete Guide to Gardening in the Classroom*, National Gardening Association, 180 Flynn Ave. Burlington, VT 05401. They also provide a newsletter and support workshops.
>
> Regional Natural Organic Farmers Association (NOFA) chapters offer a wellspring of friendly organic gardeners. NOFA is keenly interested in supporting agriculture in the classroom, and you are likely to find good local support and guidance.
>
> Your local agricultural extension agent.

Nature Journals

Students who learn directly from experience and hands-on explorations outdoors will need a way to keep records of their activities and projects. A nature journal can support teachers in expanding beyond grades toward portfolio and project-based assessment.

A big, blank artist's sketchbook can help the children organize their nature observations, experiments, research, drawings, maps, poetry, stories, rubbings, pressed plants, leaves and projects. Nature journals may be brought out regularly when the children go outdoors.

Covers

Encourage each person to make his or her book as special as possible. Before anything goes inside, spend time covering the journals with fabric or recycled gift wrap. Students may enjoy gathering fallen bark from under birch trees for title plates. Soak the bark in water for up to an hour. Press between thick books. When dry, the flat bark may be cut into any shape. After you glue the plate onto the books, press again overnight. Handle it carefully; the bark may be brittle. Please do not peel the bark directly off the trees, as this takes away the tree's protection from insects and disease.

Page Borders

Use rulers to mark off margins around the pages. Decorate the borders with rhythmic designs and thematic patterns. If crayons are used, a watercolor wash over it looks especially bright.

Nature Paper

To make paper for the journal, save the fibrous paper from the recycling bin (paper towels, construction paper, napkins, etc.) Add water and mash. Blend up well. Experiment adding bits of ferns or delicate pressed flowers. Put a nylon screen tacked onto a wooden frame into a flat pan. Pour a thin layer of the paper mash over it. Lift the screen and press out the water. Let dry in the sunshine or a warm place. Carefully peel off.

Finishing the Books

At the end of the year, unwrap the metal spiral binding of the sketchbook and have the children sew the books back together with embroidery thread. This gives a special finishing touch to the nature journals.

The Cycle of Life

"Rabbi Yitzḥak Eisik said,
The motto of life is "Give and Take."
Everyone must be both a giver and a receiver,
in living circle.
He who is not both is a barren tree.[1]

Although the tree reflects a quality of rooted peace, it is an active, dynamic organism with constant inner movement. Trees are our planet's main mechanism for maintaining and regulating the delicate balance of the elements. On a global level, it is estimated that 75 acres of forest are being destroyed each minute, or about 5,000 square miles every month. The crisis of global warming, loss of soil due to erosion, poor air quality and acid rain are directly proportional to our critical and increasing destruction of trees.

The primary cycles that take place within the tree have a theme of the elements:

The water cycle: Plant roots drink up water in the soil and transpire it back to the atmosphere.

The earth cycle: Old plants decay and regenerate into a renewal of life in nutrient-rich soil.

The air cycle: Trees breathe in carbon dioxide, break it down, and return oxygen for animals and people to breathe. They then breathe out carbon dioxide.

The heat cycle: Primary radiant energy from the sun turns into food and plant life.

Cycle of Life Discovery Activities

1. Research a tree cycle, and the impact of modern life on that cycle. Create a display, sculpture, art project, play or song to dramatize the cycle, the problems, and a creative solution.

2. Contact the American Forestry Association, P.O. Box 2000, Washington, D.C. 20013, or call 900-420-4545 (there is a charge for this call, which supports the reforestation program) to find out about its Global Releaf Program.
3. Contact the Jewish National Fund to learn how to support reforestation.
4. Read *The Man Who Planted Trees*, by Jean Giono (Chelsea, VT: Chelsea Green, 1987), and plant as many trees as you possibly can!

Tree Talk

Each kind of tree expresses a unique mood in its gestures and character. Ancient biblical people were sensitive to the qualities and spirit of plants and drew on this common experience throughout biblical teachings. Some examples:

Olive Tree—light, peace, good deeds

> The dove which brought an olive branch in its beak to Noah, brought light to the world.
>
> *Tanḥuma, Tetzaveh,* 5:1

> . . . There were two olive trees beside the menorah, one on each side. I asked the angel, "What do these mean my lord?" . . . "This is the word of the Lord, Not by might, nor by power, but by my spirit" says the Lord.
>
> Zech. 4:2-6

In addition to supplying oil for the purest light, the leaves of the olive tree dance and shine in the wind, evoking a feeling of movement and lightness.

Oak—inner strength, courage, deep-rooted endurance

> Joshua wrote these words in the book of the law of God. He took a great stone and set it up under the great oak tree that was by the sanctuary of the Lord.
>
> Josh. 24:26

In Genesis 13:18 and 18:1, Abraham prayed at sacred oak groves.

Date Palms—purposeful, victory

> Like the date palm of which nothing is wasted. Every part is useful; its dates are for eating, its *lulavim* are for blessing, its branched fronds are for thatching, its fibers are for rope, its webbing is for sieves, its thick round trunk is for building. And so it is with people; every person is significant to the whole. There is a purpose for each part of creation.
>
> *Bereshit Rabbah* 41

Almond —steadfast, reliable hope

> Moses came to the Tent of Meeting. Behold, the rod of Aaron was budding and bloomed blossoms and bore ripe almonds.
>
> Num. 17:23

> God said, "Jeremiah, what do you see?" "I see a branch of the almond tree." "Yes, and I too am watching to see that my words come true."
>
> Jer. 1:11-12

Willow—gentle healing of sorrow, moon-like renewal

> As a tree planted by the waters that spreads out its roots, and does not see the coming heat. Its foliage does not wither.
>
> Jer. 17:8

> And we hung our harps upon the willows and wept for Zion.
>
> Ps. 137:1–2

Tu B'Shvat Seder for Children

(Around a table set with a white cloth, decorated with flowers and boughs of green)

BLESSING:

May it be Your will, Blessed Source of Life,
that by eating and blessing of the fruits of the Tree,
that we may be filled with strength
for goodness, for blessings,

for good life and for peace.
May we be deep-rooted trees planted
in the soil of our friendship together.

In the dark of the winter season, in the hush before the quickening of spring, we come together in the quiet moments before life renews itself in warmth and light.

There are three kinds of fruits from the Tree and fruits of our good deeds:

Fruit which are completely edible (grapes, figs, etc.)
Fruit with an inedible pit (dates, olives, etc.)
Fruit with an inedible peel/shell (oranges, bananas, etc.)

May the stony pits and hard shells help bear good fruits for everyone.

Let us celebrate the circle of the seasons:

1. Drink the first cup of white juice.
   Sing a Winter song.
   Enjoy the fruit.
2. Drink a second cup of white juice with drops of red juice mixed in.
   Sing a Spring song.
   Enjoy the fruit.
3. Drink the third cup of half red and half white juice.
   Sing a Summer song.
   Enjoy the fruit.
4. Drink the fourth cup of red juice with drops of white juice mixed in.
   Sing a Fall song.
   Enjoy the fruit.

We will close with a circle dance of the seasons.

Getting to the Root
of the Tree of Life—Outdoors

Michal Fox Smart

"Why is the Torah described as a Tree of Life?"

"Because it is so deeply rooted." "Because it draws sustenance both from the earth below and from the Heavens above." "Because every leaf of every tree is different, just as the Jewish community is diverse and yet part of a unified being." "Because it provides shelter and nourishment to human beings, and other creatures." "Because when one explores it carefully, all kinds of treasures are found." "Because in order to survive, it must be both securely anchored and able to be flexible." "Because for as long as it lives, it grows, adding layer upon layer. . . ."

These insights into the nature of Torah have been shared by students I have instructed on Jewish wilderness trips over the years. They illustrate just one of the many educational benefits of conducting Jewish education in the outdoors—the opportunity to become acquainted with fellow creatures and natural processes, and consequently also to deepen one's understanding of Jewish tradition, which is replete with references to them.

Both biblical and talmudic writers appear to have been astute observers of the natural environments in and near which they lived, and Jewish sacred texts are addressed to an audience intimately familiar with the landscape of *Eretz Yisrael*. There are, for instance, some 120 names of animals (excluding synonyms) in the Bible—mammals, birds, and reptiles being well represented.[1]

Moreover, these texts do not merely depict natural phenomena; they rather embrace external ecological reality as an opportunity to express eternal truths and spiritual reality. Animal behavior and the characteristics of specific plants are incorporated into moral exhortations within the Bible ("Go to the ant, you sluggard, and consider her ways, and be wise" [Pro. 6:6]), and are used as metaphors for both human beings ("The righteous man flourishes like the palm tree. He grows like a cedar in Lebanon." [Ps. 92:13]) and the divine ("As an eagle stirs up her nest, broods over her young, spreads abroad her wings, takes them, and bears them on her pinions, so the Lord alone did lead him."[Deut. 32:11–12])

These passages use the presumably familiar images of the natural landscape to express more abstract religious concepts, in a manner characteristic of Jewish writing. The educator Steve Copeland writes, "What perhaps most characterizes mythopoetic or religious man is his metaphoric imagination. Behind forms he sees meanings. Behind natural appearances he encounters spiritual values. Every external phenomenon bears him (Greek, *pherein*) to an inner reality behind or beyond it *(meta).*[2]

This poses a dilemma to today's Jews. For not only are many of us unfamiliar with the particular landscape of Israel, we have become alienated from any natural landscape whatsoever. When we read, for instance, that the Torah is "a tree of life to them that hold fast to it," the reference holds little meaning for us. Ironically, some of us understand the abstraction "Torah" better than the living tree that was meant to represent it. Others are distanced from both ends of the sentence, so that neither "tree" nor "Torah" is evocative or richly understood. In either case, the power of traditional metaphor is lost.

The rabbis in fact described Torah as a *pardes,* an orchard. Today, as ever, fully entering the orchard of Torah requires venturing beyond the classroom and synagogue walls. One of the gifts of Jewish outdoor education is an opportunity to rediscover the power of our tradition's metaphorical language. An instructor must strive first to reintroduce his or her students to the natural landscape, enabling them to gain the personal familiarity with other creatures and natural processes that is requisite to deeper insight. This entails basic environmental education—for instance, learning the parts of a tree and how they function, observing the unique traits and behaviors which identify individual plants and animals, and understanding the dynamic processes which have shaped the landscape into its present form.

The dominant contemporary mindset, however, does not predispose students to view the natural landscape also as a window into the transcendent. In addition, therefore, one needs actively to nourish students' metaphoric imaginations and sense of wonder. Thoughtful facilitation of the outdoor experience can help students to see themselves reflected in the world around them; to perceive the multiplicity of meanings suggested by the various faces of the landscape around them and to appreciate the miracle of the everyday.

At this stage, the educational goal is not to impart information but rather appreciation; and an instructor without much ecological knowledge can teach a great deal by sharing his or her spiritual sensitivity and imagination. In preparing students to spend time quietly and/or alone, one can share Heschel's sense of radical amazement, or Buber's conception of an I-Thou encounter. Groups can recite traditional liturgy, which blesses God for the daily re-creation of the world, the arrangement of stars in the evening sky, and the countless miracles that are with us each moment of every day.

With minimal training, teachers can facilitate one of several activities designed by myself and others which incorporate the recitation of traditional blessings with sensory awareness exercises and exploration of the landscape. After reading passages from *Perek Shirah*, a section of traditional Ashkenazi prayerbooks which recounts the unique song of praise that each creature sings, one can invite students to write the song of praise they imagine emanating from a particular rock, flower, or animal that has captured their attention. In these ways, the natural world in all its diversity and wonder comes alive to students. Ideally, they will come to appreciate their own aliveness, and their own participation in the miracle, as well.

While this learning is extremely valuable in itself, the lessons come full circle when students take that new body of knowledge and metaphoric imagination and return to traditional texts. After engaging in such experiential learning, I love to present traditional metaphors in Scripture or liturgy to my students and invite their interpretations. Their understanding of Torah, as well as my own, is continually enriched by each person's insightful responses.

At times, making these connections can be personally transformative. On a recent course in North Carolina, our group spent an arduous Friday hiking through a forest ravaged by winter storms, climbing over, under, and through massive trees which had fallen. The next morning, during Shabbat services, we discovered a small tear in the scroll of our *Sefer Torah*. While processing this difficult situation, one student—who had voiced frustration and resentment of Jewish tradition to that point—offered an additional insight into the metaphor we'd been discussing. For, she recognized in that moment, just as these trees which were so old, massive, and seemingly impenetrable were downed in a winter storm, so, too, the Torah is fragile. Like the natural world itself, in each generation, it is ours to protect.

Food from the Sacred Tree

Gil Marks

HALVA DI GRIS (MIDDLE EASTERN SEMOLINA PUDDING)

Although Westerners are most familiar with halvah as a sweetened sesame confection, the name actually refers to a variety of sweetened cooked grain confections popular throughout central Asia and the Middle East. Ironically, although halvah originated in the Middle East and Ashkenazim only recently became familiar with the sesame variation, the word entered the English language by way of Yiddish, as the confection was common in Jewish delis.

The semolina in this firm pudding, also called *halva aurde sujee,* is toasted in fat, then steamed to plump the grains. It is popular in Iran and central Asia, where it is served at most celebrations, particularly Purim and Hanukkah. Raisins (about ¾ cup) are simmered in the sugar syrup for Tu B'Shvat. Greek Jews make a version using milk for Shavuot, Hanukkah, and other dairy meals.

3 cups water (or 1½ cups water and 1½ cups milk)
1½ cups sugar
1 cup (2 sticks) butter or margarine
1½ cups coarse or fine semolina (not semolina flour)
½ teaspoon ground turmeric
½ to 1 cup coarsely chopped almonds, pistachios, walnuts, or any combination (optional)
1 teaspoon rose water or vanilla extract
1 teaspoon ground cinnamon or ½ teaspoon ground cardamom

1. Bring the water and sugar to a boil. Reduce the heat to very low, cover, and let stand while preparing the semolina.
2. Melt the butter or margarine in a medium saucepan over medium-high heat. Stir in the semolina and turmeric. Reduce the heat to low and cook, stirring constantly, until golden brown, about 20 minutes. If using the nuts, add them halfway through the toasting.
3. Return the syrup to a boil, then slowly stir into the semolina. (Be careful, since the mixture will splatter.)
4. Cook over low heat, stirring constantly, until the liquid evaporates and the mixture comes away easily from the sides of the pan, about 5 minutes. Stir in the rose water or vanilla and cinnamon or cardamom.
5. Remove from the heat, cover with a damp cloth, replace the lid, and let stand for at least 30 minutes. Serve warm or at room temperature. Spoon the halvah into serving dishes; or press into a large mold or several small molds, let cool and invert onto serving plates. Makes 6 to 8 servings.

Variations:

Indian Raisin-Coconut Semolina Halvah: Cook 3 tablespoons raisins, 3 tablespoons grated coconut, and 1 teaspoon grated orange zest with the sugar syrup.

Halva aude Birinj (Persian Rice Confection): Substitute 1½ cups rice flour or cream of rice for the semolina and increase the amount of rose water to 1 tablespoon.

KOFYAS (MIDDLE EASTERN SWEETENED WHEAT BERRIES)

Wheat berries are unprocessed whole wheat with only the outer husk removed. Their nutty flavor and chewy texture are delicious alone or mixed with other grains. They are available in health food and Middle Eastern stores. It is advisable to purchase grains from a source with a high turnover in order to ensure freshness. Store in the refrigerator or freezer. Add wheat berries to salads, soups, stews, casseroles, and puddings.

Since wheat berries resemble teeth, Sephardim customarily serve them at a party to honor a baby's first tooth. Sweetened and mixed

&

with fruits and nuts, they become a holiday dish—called *kofyas* in Turkey, *assurei* (from an Arabic word for "ten") or *koliva* in Greece, and *korkoti* in Georgia—for Tu B'Shvat and Rosh HaShanah. A similar Turkish pudding made from cracked wheat or bulgur is called *prehito* or *moostrahana*.

1 pound (about 2 cups) whole wheat berries
8 cups water
About 1½ cups sugar or honey
1 to 2 teaspoons ground cinnamon
2 cups raisins or dried currants
     (or 1 cup raisins and 1 cup chopped dates)
2 cups chopped mixed nuts
     (any combination of walnuts, almonds, pistachios, and pine nuts)
Pomegranate seeds for garnish (optional)

1. Soak the wheat berries in water to cover overnight. Drain. (Without presoaking, the cooking time can take up to 5 hours.)
2. Bring the wheat berries and 8 cups water to a boil, reduce the heat to medium-low, and simmer, uncovered, until tender but still slightly chewy, about 2 hours. (For a firmer texture, add salt to the cooking liquid.) Drain.
3. Add the sugar or honey and cinnamon, and stir over medium-low heat until the sugar or honey melts, about 2 minutes. (The wheat berries harden a bit when the sugar is added.)
4. Remove from the heat and stir in the fruit and nuts. Serve warm, at room temperature, or chilled. Mound the *kofyas* on a serving plate, and, if desired, garnish with the pomegranate seeds. (*Kofyas* is commonly garnished with similarly shaped pomegranate seeds.) Makes about 9 cups; 6 to 8 servings.

Variations:

Sleehah (Syrian Anise-Flavored Wheat Berries): Add ¼ cup anise seeds (*shimra* in Arabic) before cooking the wheat berries, or add ½ cup anise liqueur and, if desired, 1 teaspoon rose water with the fruit and nuts.

Delights of the Tu B'Shvat Table

Gilda Angel

International Potpourri

- Kibbe ib Gheraz (Syrian Meatballs and Cherries)
- M'rouzya Tajine (Moroccan Beef Stew with Prunes and Quinces)
- Bulghur Pilaf (Syrian Cooked Cracked Wheat)
- Havij Edjah (Persian Sweet Carrot Omelet)
- Desser Miveh (Persian Fruit Salad)
- T'mar Baba (Iraqi Date-Filled Pastries)
- Moostrahana/Prehito (Turkish Wheat Pudding)
- Syko Glyko (Greek Fig Preserves)

> . . . . a land of wheat and barley, and vines and fig trees and pomegranates; a land of olive trees and honey.
>
> Deut. 8:8

The *seder* is generally conducted in the presence of family and friends. It is meant to provide a joyous, communal spirit. Stories are told and songs are sung. The biblical and talmudic teachings regarding fruits and vegetables reinforce the meaning of the holiday. And of course, the special dishes developed in some Sephardic communities add to the festive atmosphere. Turkish Sephardim, for example, eat *moostrahana,* also known as *prehito,* a pudding made from cracked wheat. As might be expected, entrees prepared with fruit are particularly popular on Tu B'Shvat.

Among Iranian Jews, it has been customary for mourners to provide fruit for others either in the home or at the synagogue. After passages from the Zohar have been recited in memory of the deceased, the mourner says a blessing over the fruit which is then served with wine. Besides the seven food species grown in Israel, others native to Iran are also in evidence.

383

Sephardim in Turkey and many other places make special efforts to involve their children in the Tu B'Shvat celebration. Long tables of fruits and sweets are arranged in each home. Children eat their fill and are given bags of fruits and sweets to take with them when they leave.

The recipes in this chapter are drawn from a number of Sephardic communities. They are all prepared with fruits, nuts or wheat. While each recipe would make a fine addition to your Tu B'Shvat holiday table, it is *not* recommended that you serve all of these dishes at one meal.

KIBBE IB GHERAZ (SYRIAN MEATBALLS AND CHERRIES)

Cherries, wine, and cinnamon are combined to make an unusual sauce for well-spiced meatballs.

2 pounds lean ground beef chuck
2 tablespoons temerhendy* or 1 tablespoon prune butter and
    1 tablespoon apricot butter
3 tablespoons water
3 tablespoons wheat germ
½ teaspoon ground allspice
¼ teaspoon pepper
½ teaspoon ground cumin
1¼ teaspoons salt
2 tablespoons pine nuts (pignolias) (optional)
3 large onions, chopped
¼ cup vegetable oil
2 cans (16 ounces each) dark sweet Bing cherries
¾ cup sweet wine
3 tablespoons sugar
3 tablespoons lemon juice
1 teaspoon ground cinnamon

1. Combine meat with *temerhendy,* water, wheat germ, allspice, pepper, cumin, salt, and pine nuts. Form into 1-inch balls.
2. In large skillet, sauté chopped onions in oil over medium heat. Push onions aside and sauté meatballs until browned on all sides.
3. Drain cherries, reserving liquid. Pit cherries and set aside. Add liquid to meatballs in skillet. Add wine, sugar, lemon juice, and cinnamon. Cover and cook 1 hour over low heat. Add cherries

and cook, uncovered, additional 10 minutes. Serve over rice. Makes 8 servings.

*Available in Greek and Middle Eastern grocery stores.

M'ROUZYA TAJINE
(MOROCCAN BEEF STEW WITH PRUNES AND QUINCES)

In this recipe, pears may be substituted for the quinces, since quinces are in season for such a brief period. Serve with rice or steamed couscous.

1 pound prunes, pitted
3 pounds beef chuck, cut into 1-inch cubes
1/4 cup vegetable oil
1 teaspoon salt
1/2 teaspoon pepper
1 teaspoon paprika
1/2 teaspoon ground ginger
2 large onions, finely chopped, divided
1/4 cup chopped fresh parsley
1 stick cinnamon
1/4 teaspoon ground saffron (optional)
2 1/2 cups water
1 pound quinces or Seckel pears
3 1/4 teaspoons ground cinnamon, divided
1/2 cup sugar
1/4 cup honey
1 tablespoon sesame seeds

1. Soak prunes in cold water. Cover and set aside.
2. In large saucepan, brown beef in oil over medium heat. Add salt, pepper, paprika, ginger, half the chopped onion, parsley, cinnamon stick, and saffron. Add water and bring to boil. Cover and simmer 1 hour.
3. Add remaining chopped onion and additional water, if necessary to prevent sticking.
4. Continue cooking 1 additional hour, or until meat is tender and sauce has thickened.
5. Meanwhile, prepare quinces. Peel, quarter, core, and place in small saucepan with 3 teaspoons cinnamon, sugar, and water to cover. Poach until tender, about 20–25 minutes.

6. Drain water from prunes and add prunes to meat along with remaining 1/4 teaspoon cinnamon and honey. Simmer, uncovered, an additional 20 minutes, until sauce has been slightly reduced.
7. Toast sesame seeds in clean, dry skillet. Cook over low heat a few minutes, shaking pan gently, until seeds are lightly toasted.
8. Place meat and prunes in serving dish. Arrange quinces or pears among chunks of meat. Pour sauce over and sprinkle with sesame seeds. Makes 8 servings.

Note: If using pears, the poaching time will be slightly shorter.

BULGHUR PILAF (SYRIAN COOKED CRACKED WHEAT)

Bulghur, cracked wheat, is used in many ways—in salads, breads, and with meat. In this recipe, bulghur serves as a side dish in place of rice. A delicious fruited variation follows the basic recipe.

1 medium onion, finely chopped
1 cup chopped celery
4 tablespoons vegetable oil
2 cups coarsely ground bulghur*
3 cups vegetable or chicken broth
1½ teaspoons salt
¼ teaspoon pepper
1 teaspoon thyme
½ teaspoon ground cumin

1. In heavy saucepan, sauté onion and celery in oil over medium heat until translucent. Add bulghur. Stir well and fry 3–5 minutes, or until bulghur begins to crackle and turn brown.
2. Add broth. Mix well and bring to boil.
3. Stir in seasonings, cover tightly, and simmer over low heat 20–25 minutes, or until all liquid has been absorbed. Remove from heat and allow to cool, covered, 10 minutes. Serve immediately. Makes 8 servings.

Variation: Substitute 1 teaspoon cinnamon and ½ teaspoon allspice for thyme and cumin. Add 1 cup raisins and 1 cup chopped apricots to bulghur after it has cooked 10 minutes. Continue cooking 15 minutes longer. Cool, covered, 10 minutes. Meanwhile, sauté ⅓ cup sunflower or sesame seeds and ⅔ cup walnuts or pine nuts in ¼ cup margarine for 5 minutes, or until golden. Stir into fruited bulghur and serve.

*Available in Greek groceries and health food stores.

HAVIJ EDJAH (PERSIAN SWEET CARROT OMELET)

This omelet may be prepared in advance and reheated in the oven. It is an excellent side dish for a meat meal, or it may be served as dessert.

1 pound carrots
3 tablespoons margarine
2 large onions, chopped
1 cup pitted dates, chopped
½ cup currants
Juice of 1 lemon (about 2 tablespoons)
5 eggs
¼ teaspoon salt
¼ cup slivered almonds

1. Peel and grate carrots coarsely. Sauté 2 minutes in margarine over medium heat. Add onions and cook, stirring constantly, until onions are golden. Add dates, currants, and lemon juice, and simmer over low heat until tender.
2. Beat eggs with salt and pour over carrot mixture. Continue to cook over low heat until eggs are set. Invert on serving plate and sprinkle with almonds. Makes 8 servings.

DESSER MIVEH (PERSIAN FRUIT SALAD)

A melange of fruits is dressed with orange juice and almonds. Vary the fruits according to seasonal availability—melons, plums and peaches in summer, strawberries or kiwi fruit in spring.

2 seedless oranges, peeled and sectioned
2 apples, peeled, cored and thinly sliced
2 bananas, sliced
2 cups chopped pitted dates
1 cup chopped dried figs or apricots
1 cup orange juice
1 cup chopped almonds or grated coconut

1. Place fruit in serving bowl. Pour orange juice over fruit and mix gently.

2. Garnish with almonds or coconut. Cover and chill several hours before serving. Makes 8 servings.

T'MAR BABA (IRAQI DATE-FILLED PASTRIES)

These yeast pastries have a date-walnut filling.

Pastry:

1 package active dry yeast
1 teaspoon honey
1 cup warm water (105°–115°F.)
½ cup vegetable oil or melted margarine
1 teaspoon salt
4 cups all-purpose flour

Filling:

½ pound pitted dates
3 tablespoons vegetable oil
3 tablespoons water
1 teaspoon ground cinnamon
¾ cup chopped walnuts

1. Dissolve yeast and honey in water. Stir in oil and salt. Add flour, 1 cup at a time, mixing well after each addition.

2. Knead 5 minutes on floured surface, adding more flour if necessary. Dough should be soft and easily workable.

3. Place dough in large, oiled bowl. Turn to grease all surfaces. Cover with clean dish towel and allow to rise in warm, draft-free place 1 hour, or until doubled in bulk.

4. Meanwhile, prepare filling. In saucepan, combine dates, oil and water. Place over low heat and mash with wooden spoon until a soft, workable pulp is formed. Stir in cinnamon and nuts. Remove from heat and cool slightly. While still warm, form into 24 1-inch balls. Set aside.

5. After dough has risen, punch down and divide into 24 pieces. Flatten each piece into a circle and place a ball of filling in the center. Close dough over filling and roll between palms of hands until filling is completely enclosed and surface of dough is smooth. With fork, pierce each *baba* several times. Preheat oven to 350°F.

6. Bake on lightly greased baking sheets in preheated oven 30 minutes. Remove to racks and cool completely. Makes 24.

MOOSTRAHANA/PREHITO (TURKISH WHEAT PUDDING)

The base for this unusual pudding is cooked cracked wheat, sweetened with sugar and honey. Walnuts and cinnamon enhance the flavor.

1 cup finely ground bulghur*
4 cups water
½ cup sugar
½ teaspoon salt
2 tablespoons honey
1 teaspoon ground cinnamon
1 cup walnuts, finely chopped, divided

1. Cook bulghur in water over moderate heat 30 minutes, stirring frequently.
2. Add sugar and salt. Cook additional 10 minutes.
3. Remove from heat and add honey, cinnamon, and 1/2 cup walnuts.
4. Dust 9 x 9-inch pan with additional cinnamon. Pour in wheat mixture. Top with remaining 1/2 cup walnuts and a sprinkling of cinnamon. Cover and chill several hours. Cut into squares to serve. Makes 8 servings.

*Available in Greek groceries and health food stores.

SYKO GLYKO (GREEK FIG PRESERVES)

The superb flavor of this fig preserve is achieved by the addition of walnuts and aniseed.

2 pounds dried figs
2 cups water
3 cups sugar
Juice of 1 lemon (about 2 tablespoons)
½ teaspoon ground aniseed
1 cup coarsely chopped walnuts

1. Sterilize seven 6-ounce glass jelly jars in boiling water for 3 minutes. Set aside.

2. Remove and discard stems from figs. Cut figs into small pieces.

3. In heavy saucepan, combine water, sugar, and lemon juice. Boil 5 minutes. Add figs and cook over low heat 30 minutes, stirring occasionally. Add aniseed and walnuts. Simmer an additional 5 minutes. Remove from heat, stir, and spoon into sterilized jars. Seal with lids according to manufacturer's directions. Makes seven 6-ounce jars.

Ever Since Eden: Trees, Tradition, and Tu B'Shvat

Everett Gendler

Ever since Eden, trees have played significant roles in the human drama as portrayed biblically and developed by later Jewish tradition. The enigmatic episode revolving around the Tree of the Knowledge of Good and Evil, and the Tree of Life—with their simultaneous attraction and danger for humans, establishes early the intriguingly ambiguous character of trees for Jewish thought.

On the one hand, the tree as image often conveys a sense of approbation. Those who "delight in the law of the Lord" are

like trees planted by streams of water,
which yield their fruit in its season,
and their leaves do not wither. (Ps. 1:3)

The righteous flourish like the palm tree,
and grow like a cedar in Lebanon. (Ps. 92:13)

These well-known honorific tree images from Psalms are also found in the Prophets.

[Those] "whose trust is the Lord . . . shall be like a tree planted
*   by water,*
sending out its roots by the stream.
It shall not fear when heat comes,

and its leaves shall stay green;
in the year of drought it is not anxious,
and it does not cease to bear fruit. (Jer. 17:7–8)

Here the trees are similes for the faithful in God.

On the other hand, the tree as image can equally convey strong disapproval.

For the Lord of hosts has a day
against all that is proud and lofty, . . .
against all the oaks of Bashan. . . . (Isa. 2:12–13)

Yet I destroyed the Amorite before them,
whose height was like the height of cedars,
and who was as strong as oaks. (Amos 2:9)

Along with these images of arrogance come associations with idolatry.

For a spirit of whoredom has led them astray,
and they have played the whore, forsaking their God.
They sacrifice on the tops of the mountains,
and make offerings upon the hills,
under oak, poplar, and terebinth, because their shade is good.
    (Hosea 4:12–13)

. . . on every high hill, on all the mountain tops, under
every green tree, and under every leafy oak, wherever
they offered pleasing odor to all their idols. (Eze. 6:13)

Or the self-same Jeremiah:

On every high hill and under every green tree
you sprawled and played the whore. (Jer. 2:20)

In light of this profound Biblical ambivalence towards the tree as a symbol, how could faithful Jews expand a Rabbinic agriculture-tithing calculatory device into a full, celebrative New Year of the Tree? Without necessarily subscribing to the exact terms put forward by J. Pedersen in describing the perceived power within trees—"the soul of the tree . . . the tree as a whole, but . . . also . . . the dominant will, or rather the upholder of, the psychic whole constituted by the life of the [tree . . .]"[1]—it is hard to deny the ability of the tree to represent "the living cosmos, endlessly renewing itself."[2] Mysteriously drawing moisture and nutrients from depths defying our observation, self-supporting in reaching heights at times almost beyond our measure, long-lived yet bountifully generous in their gifts to us, trees do, indeed, seem numinous in essence. This quality may help account for both the initial attraction of the tree and its later abjuration within Jewish tradition as one school of Yahweh purists came to construe this numinous quality as competition with rather than a reflection of the power of the Creator.

The initial attraction is well attested. "Abraham built three altars, one in Shechem . . . one in Ai . . . and one in Hebron," says a Midrash.[3] What the Midrash does not state, but the Biblical text substantiates, is that at each of these three places, stately terebinth or oak trees stood as the designating feature of the sites.

An oak or a terebinth tree stood at Shechem, the site of God's first promise of land to Abram, just after he had left Ur of the Chaldees.

> Abram passed through the land to Shechem, to the Terebinth of Moreh, the Oracle's Oak. At that time the Canaanites were in the land. And the Lord appeared to Abram and said, "To your offspring/seed I will give this land." So he built there an altar to the Lord, who had appeared to him.
>
> Gen. 12:6–7

An oak or terebinth tree stood at Bethel-Ai, the site of God's further specification of the promise.

> From there [Shechem/Oracle's Oak] he moved on to the hill country on the east of Bethel, and pitched his tent, with Bethel on the west and Ai on the east; and there he built an altar to the Lord and invoked the name of the Lord.
>
> Gen. 12:8

The further details of the promise are found in Gen. 13:14–15, 17. That a prominent oak did, indeed, stand at Bethel-Ai is attested in Gen. 35:8: "Deborah, Rebekah's nurse, died, and she was buried under the oak below Bethel, so it was named Allon-bacuth, the Oak of Weeping."

And a grove of oak or terebinth trees stood at Mamre, where Abram settled after the promise at Bethel-Ai, and where he carried out the covenental circumcision of himself, his son Ishmael, and all the males in his household (Gen. 17:23–18:1; cf. Rashi on 18:1, establishing that the circumcision did take place at the Oaks of Mamre). It was here, also, that Abraham first acquired land, publicly witnessed: the burial site of Sarah, "in the cave of the field of Machpelah facing Mamre (that is, Hebron)." (Gen. 23:19) With the exception of Rachel, the other matriarchs and patriarchs were also buried in the cave of the field of Machpelah, before Mamre with its grove.

> There they buried Abraham and Sarah his wife; there they buried Isaac and Rebekah his wife; and there I [Jacob] buried Leah.
>
> His [Jacob's] sons . . . buried him in the cave of the field of Machpelah . . . in front of Mamre.
>
> Gen. 49:31; 50:13

It is hardly an exaggeration to assert that at each of these defining occasions at the birth of the Jewish people, trees stood as stately, silent witnesses.

Throughout early Israelite life, the vibrant forces within notable trees drew into their locale important functions in the life of the people.

Joshua chose Shechem for the sacred compact with the people of Israel to "put away the foreign gods that are among you," and the rite included the following:

> So Joshua made a covenant with the people that day, and made statutes and ordinances for them at Shechem. Joshua wrote these words in the book of the law of God; and he took a large stone, and set it up there under the oak in the sanctuary of the Lord.
>
> Joshua 24:25–26

The angel of the Lord who appeared to Gideon "came and sat under the oaks at Ophrah" (Judg. 6:11). It is "by the oak of the pillar at Shechem" that Abimelech is made king of Shechem (Judg. 9:6). A Diviners' Oak (*Elon-me'onenim*) is a recognized landmark used to describe strategic movements in a battle (Judg. 9:37). In her judging of Israel, "Deborah, a prophetess . . . used to sit under the palm of Deborah between Ramah and Bethel in the hill country of Ephraim; and the Israelites came up to her for judgment" (Judg. 4:4–5).

Saul, in his search for his father's lost donkeys following his anointing by Samuel, is told by the latter that he will encounter "three men going to God at Bethel" at the Oak of Tabor (I Sam. 10:3) preceding his meeting with "a band of prophets" (I Sam. 10:5). At their death, Saul and his sons were buried "under the oak in Jabesh" (I Chron. 10:12). "The man of God" who prophecies against Jeroboam was found "sitting under an oak tree." (I Kings 13:14). These and other examples make understandable why one philologist speculates that the derivation of the Hebrew word for terebinth, *elah*, comes from *El*, divine.[4] Some numinous connection with trees does seem evident in all these instances.

This sensed association with the Divine receives interesting support in later Jewish tradition also. In a vastly learned, meticulously researched and carefully argued essay, the late Morton Smith makes a compelling case that the menorah, a stylized tree, is a symbol of God for Jews during the Greco-Roman period, a symbol biblically based and rabbinically sanctioned.[5]

Encounter

It seems fair to say that one source of Tu B'Shvat flows from this sense of encounter with the numinous through the agency of the tree. Supportive of such an understanding is this citation from the Zohar included in *Peri eitz hadar*:

> By the word "tree," he also referred to the Holy One, who is the tree of life for all."[6]

Note also the remark of R. Shimon:

> There is a mighty and wondrous tree in the celestial sphere which supplies nourishment to the beings above and below."
>
> Zohar II, 58b

Even more striking is the bold reminder in *Peri eitz hadar* that "the *gematria* (numerical equivalent) of *ilan* (tree) is YAHDWNHY" (the

Hebrew spellings of the four letter words for LORD and GOD in alternation, a favored devotional device in mystical prayer). The numbers, 91 in each case, are indeed equivalent.[7] This is surely as bold an identification of the tree with the Divine as can be imagined.

Inspiration

It should not be surprising, then, given this assertion of the Divine nature of the tree, that it is seen as serving a divinatory function as well.

> Wherever Abraham took up his residence he used to plant a certain tree, but in no place did it flourish properly save in the land of Canaan. By means of this tree he was able to distinguish between the man who adhered to the Almighty and the man who worshipped idols. For the man who worshipped the true God, the tree spread out its branches and formed an agreeable shade over his head; whereas in the presence of one who clung to the side of idolatry the tree shrank within itself and its branches stood upright. Abraham thus recognized the erring man, admonished him, and did not desist until he had succeeded in making him embrace the true faith.
>
> Zohar, 102b

The literal acceptance of this description may give us pause, but perhaps we should be equally hesitant to dismiss out of consideration the core assertion of the Zohar: by association with the tree we are sometimes gifted with insights that might otherwise be beyond our ken. In Norse mythology, Odin wins the secret of the runic alphabet by virtue of Ygdrassil, the World Ash; in Buddhist tradition, Gautama gains enlightenment beneath the bo tree; in Biblical tradition, as we have seen, patriarchs and prophetess, teachers and diviners, judges and angels regularly sit beneath oaks, palms, and terebinths. Is this legendary evidence to be entirely disregarded?

Contemporary testimony offers further support for the deep-rooted sense that something of insight/intuition/revelation is granted us through trees. This is the reflection of the photographer Cedric Wright:

395

Consider the life of trees.
Aside from the ax, what trees acquire from man is
*   inconsiderable.*
What man may acquire from trees is immeasurable.
From their mute forms there flows a poise, in silence, a lovely
*   sound and motion in response to wind.*
What peace comes to those aware of the voice and bearing of
*   trees!*
Trees do not scream for attention.
A tree, a rock, has no pretense, only a real growth out of itself, in
*   close communion with the universal spirit.*
A tree retains a deep serenity.
It establishes in the earth not only its root system but also those
*   roots of its beauty and its unknown consciousness.*
Sometimes one may sense a glisten of that consciousness, and
*   with such perspective, feel that man is not necessarily the*
*   highest form of life.*
Tree qualities, after long communion, come to reside in man.
As stillness enhances sound, so through little things the joy of
*   living expands.*
One is aware, lying under trees, of the roots and directions of
*   one's whole being.*
Perceptions drift in from earth and sky.
A vast healing begins.[8]

This is the reverie of the Yiddish poet Yehoash:

MYSTERY

I don't know how it was:
Upon the ground
I lay—warm summer-night
Wrapping me round.
I hear the boughs above,
The grass below,
Whisper and call
In speech I did not know.
Then someone out of me

Spoke answeringly.
Long, long I heard both voices blending, blending,
Uncomprehending.⁹

It would seem that thoughtful moderns might well join traditional mystics in this meditative reflection:

> *Maker, Shaper, Creator and Emanator of Worlds above and*
>   *below . . . All in wisdom formed. . . .*
> *diverse, yet destined to be One:*
> *You have caused trees and vegetation to spring forth from the*
>   *earth, in stature and splendor,*
> *to provide humans with wisdom and understanding.¹⁰*

Appreciation

> *God gave Solomon great wisdom,*
> *discernment, and breadth of understanding*
> *as vast as the sand on the seashore . . .*
> *He would speak of trees,*
> *from the cedar that is in Lebanon*
> *to the hyssop that grows in the wall;*
> *he would speak of animals, and birds, and reptiles, and fish.*
>
> I Kings 5: 9,13

Prominent among the characteristics of Solomon's wisdom was his vast, detailed knowledge of the world of nature. Flora and fauna were so familiar to him that he could speak of them with authority. That such sensitivity to the qualities of each particular wood was not unknown is clear from other pages of the Bible. The differentiated use of acacia, cypress, cedar, and olive wood in the construction of the Tabernacle and Solomon's Temple is one example (cf. Exod. 25:10, 23, etc.; 1 Kings 6:9, 15, 23, etc.).

Impressive as was Solomon's knowledge of the great trees such as cedars, equally so was his acquaintance with lowly shrubs such as hyssop, whose purifying use is well attested biblically. (cf. Exod. 12:22, Lev. 14:4, 6, 49, 51–52; Num. 19:6, 18; Ps. 51:9). It was a knowledgeable naturalist who occupied the seat of power at that time.

This tradition of respect for particularity and appreciation of each natural element in its individuality is reflected in the Tu B'Shvat seder ritual. One notices the categorization of the fruits of trees according to the arrangement of their edible and inedible portions: an inedible shell outside but edible flesh within, the world of *Asiyah*; an edible outside but with an inedible pit inside, the world of *Yetzirah*; and edible both as outside flesh and inner pit, the world of *Beriyah*. Ten examples of each category are recommended for eating: grapes, figs, apples, etc., for the last; dates, olives, apricots, etc., for the middle; nuts, coconuts, pomegranates, etc., for the first. Also figuring in the ceremony are four cups of wine or grape juice, first white, the second white with some red added, the third with more red added, and the fourth mostly red with just a bit of white remaining. Thus is the ripening cycle mimed, from the wintry white of frost, snow, or ashen branches, through the blossoming of spring, to the fruiting of summer, and the full, red ripening of autumn. The eating and drinking, preceded and followed by blessings and readings, focuses awareness on both the wonder of the growth cycle and the tastes or textures of the various fruits and nuts.

Appreciation is enhanced by the deliberate and aware mode of eating. As we chew we are asked to remember that "the 32 teeth correspond to the 32 times the name of God is mentioned in the story of Creation."[11] Appreciation is also enjoined by the citation from the Jerusalem Talmud:

> *Said Rabbi Ibun: A person is destined*
> *to give account for innocent delights*
> *which his/her eyes beheld but his/her*
> *mouth did not taste."*[12]

This aspect of Tu B'Shvat seems to me epitomized in Rilke's Sonnet XIII of the First Part of "Sonnets to Orpheus."

> *Banana, rounded apple, russet pear,*
> *gooseberry . . . Does not all this convey*
> *life and death into your mouth? . . . It's there! . . .*
> *Read it in a child's face any day,*
> *when it tastes them. What infinity!*
> *Can't you feel inside your mouth a growing*

mysteriousness, and, where words were, a flowing
of suddenly released discovery?
Dare to say what "apple" has implied:
Sweetness, concentrated, self-repressing,
slowly yielding to the tongue's caressing,
growing awake, transparent, clarified,
double-meaning'd, sunshine-full, terrestrial:
O experience, feeling, joy,—celestial.[13]

Preservation

Encounter, Inspiration, Appreciation: all are occasions of receiving, the demand, if any, being that we accept the gifts, the bounty, the blessings. But there is reciprocity as well: a measure of response is asked, the acceptance of active responsibility for the preservation of the wonder.

> *One who enjoys the delights of this world without reciting a*
> *blessing is called a thief, for only by means of the blessing is*
> *the sustaining heavenly flow maintained, and the power of*
> *the guardian spirit of that fruit is renewed; so the fruit is*
> *nourished by this flow, and its power to grow renewed."*[14]

The blessing here referred to is simply the blessing traditionally recited before eating fruits of trees: *borei peri ha-eitz*. However, one may assess the Kabbalistic doctrine of the various trees having guardian spirits whose powers are released and recycled by humans reciting the prescribed blessing before eating, one fact is incontestable: depending on our awareness of the vegetation cycle and our intervention in it, the fruitfulness of the earth will be affected for good or for ill. Healthy topsoil is alive, of course, teeming with microorganisms and earthworms that maintain its productivity. When nourished by organic matter and covered by plant life that protects it from erosion by wind and water, the soil is constantly renewed and remains fruitful over decades, centuries, even millennia. When subject to thoughtless exploitation by humans—deforestation, overgrazing, overcropping, monoculture, herbicide, and pesticide overuse, etc.—then the land becomes inert, lifeless, and the flow of sustenance from and to the soil suffers fatal interruption.

Is not such injurious intervention, interrupting the fructifying life flow, indeed, a case of global theft? Possibilities blighted and promises withered, our planet rotates less richly garbed, less fetchingly bedecked by virtue of energy squandered, vitality stolen. Centuries before the development of environmental language, the mystics intuitively grasped this cosmic truth and gave it ritual expression.

And today? At the confluence of the streams of mystical tradition, environmental awareness, and Israeli focus, the current is strong and the water fresh. Millions of trees are planted in Israel on Tu B'Shvat become Arbor Day, while in Jewish communities throughout the world financial support is offered for the reforestation. The ritual eating of dried fruit in religious schools is often accompanied by rainforest charts and preservation projects, and may include one further innovation. The brittle *bokser* of earlier years is, of course, still there as a threat to the teeth, but often now it is accompanied by carob-covered peanuts and raisins, or carob chips, straight from the local health food store—sure signs of dietary change. Tu B'Shvat seders are more widely offered, with several haggadot now available and more likely to appear, and a significant component of many is likely to be a focus on a current environmental issue. At the same time, some celebrants may emphasize the meditative possibilities provided by the categories of fruit, drawing analogies with personal defenses that may be summoned in various circumstances as contrasted with others. At another seder the focus may be on the mystery of the seed, survivor of the death of one life cycle and bearer of life to the new. The spiritual diversity of this celebrative efflorescence bids fair to rival the vegetational diversity traditionally celebrated by Tu B'Shvat.

The mystery of the seed and the image of the "mighty and wondrous tree in the celestial sphere which supplies nourishment to beings above and below": how beautifully they are evoked, enacted, and joined on this New Year of the Tree. It is as if the third day of Creation were with us afresh, and we were proclaiming anew the wonders of vegetation and plants, earth and trees, seeds and fruit. (cf. Gen. 1:11–12, where these six terms occur nineteen times in two short verses).

The pull of earth is strong, the rhythms of the year compelling. In the words of Edith Sitwell:

> *Gestation, generation, and duration—*
> *The cycles of all lives upon the earth—*
> *Plants, beasts, and men, must follow those of heaven;*
> *The rhythms of our lives*
> *Are those of the ripening, dying of the seasons,*
> *Our sowing and reaping in the holy fields,*
> *Our love and giving birth—then growing old*
> *And sinking into sleep in the maternal*
> *Earth, mother of corn, the wrinkled darkness.*
> *So we, ruled by those laws, see their fulfillment.*
>
> *. . . Love is not changed by Death,*
> *And nothing is lost and all in the end is harvest.*[15]

Tu B'Shvat Meditation

Susan Singer

This meditation brings together the symbols of planting and new growth with this Kabbalistic teaching: When we attune ourselves to the powerful energies that are available on the Fifteenth of Shvat, the New Year of the Trees, we can receive additional support for what is important to our well-being.

The mystics believe that this is the one day when the earth is not permitted to receive nutrition for itself, but must send the new growth upward. The trees receive an infusion of celestial forces, and spectacular potential for new growth becomes revealed. When we are willing to align with our own potential for new growth at this specific time, the Kabbalists remind us that we too can prosper.

Meditation

Close your eyes and relax as we concentrate on our breathing. Let's now focus on our breathing as we prepare for a garden journey. Now follow your breath as it travels down into your body as you inhale and up as you exhale. Like the way nutrients flow down through the deep roots in the trunk of a tree . . . and out to the branches . . . down to the roots . . . out to the branches . . . down to the roots . . .

Imagine a lush orchard, rich with every flower, tree and fruit, those nourishing to the eye and those nourishing to the taste.

All seasons are represented in the garden. See and anticipate spring in the foreground, sproutings of tender new shoots. And in near to spring are the lush colors of summer with shiny leaves of every shade of green and tree branches hanging low, graced with fruits of every variety. In the distance see and know the deep colors of the fall.

As we roam in the garden, I am delighted to see that winter work has begun in a quiet corner. I notice the dead leaves and branches, last year's growth, have been cleared and cut in little pieces to fertilize the soil and prepare it to receive the new seeds or saplings for this year. The garden has been winterized, the soil fertilized, making it richer with nutrients and oxygen. Feel and smell the soft ground underfoot.

Everything a gardener needs is here. The tools are nearby, gleaming and ready, in a beautiful container. I notice the size and texture, and each tool so finely crafted.

I think of a corner of my life, where there are two projects that I want to take root. One inner and spiritual, and one a project that has been on my "to do" list just waiting for me to lovingly recognize it. Think of your own list now! I have room in my garden to nurture both. *Barukh ha-Shem*. This is the time to plant my yearnings, and appreciate creation all around me.

Seeds of new projects, aspects of my life that I really want to take root. Shekhinah, light of my soul, divine mother of the earth. I praise you, bless my endeavors.

Protect them like the ground in winter with its hard protective covering which nurtures the life within—like a child in the womb.

With a blessing, place it in the soil. With loving hands I plant a new sapling, a new seed. Thank you, Shekhinah, for the tools to work my garden. Thank you, God, for the beauty and bounty of life and for the tree of life, the Torah from which blessings flow.

Open your eyes when you are ready and tell someone near you the seeds of one project that you want to take root.

Judaism, Vegetarianism, and Tu B'Shvat

Jonathan Wolf and Richard H. Schwartz

All of the holidays in the Jewish year are (or can be) vegetarian occasions. For instance, every one of the obligatory foods and beverages at the Pesah seder is vegetarian (in fact, vegan). Many Jewish communities around the world follow the custom of eating dairy foods for Shavuot. Dishes containing oil, as well as cheese or milk (such as latkes with sour cream), are traditional for Hanukkah. The "Good luck" foods eaten (with special "wishes" for the year) by many on the first night of Rosh HaShanah, including apples dipped in honey, are vegetarian (except for those who eat the head of a fish or goat). Even the prescribed menu of the *Seudah Mafseket* meal immediately before the fast of Tisha B'Av, a hard-boiled egg (which some dip in ashes), is vegetarian fare, if hardly a feast.

Indeed (as one of the authors of this piece, Jonathan Wolf, has demonstrated in twenty years of vegetarian Shabbat and holiday gatherings and banquets at his apartment in New York City, the very first of which was a Tu B'Shvat seder in 1976), every event on the Jewish calendar can be joyously and sumptuously celebrated with vegetarian foods.

On the other hand, there is no food made from meat which is currently required on any occasion, nor even one which is widely associated with a particular day. And in the absence of a Holy

403

Temple in Jerusalem and of animal sacrifices (which, by the way, Rav Kook, the great chief rabbi of pre-state Israel and advocate of vegetarianism, wrote would *not* be reinstituted in the rebuilt Third Temple—because the moral development of humanity and of the Jewish people over the centuries will have rendered the killing of a fellow creature repugnant), there is no obligation that anyone who finds it objectionable should eat meat of any kind on any holy occasion—Sabbath or festival.

The Most Vegetarian Holiday

Of all these potentially or intrinsically vegetarian moments, the Jewish holiday which is arguably the most thoroughly vegetarian in its menu and meaning is Tu B'Shvat. We eat a cornucopia of fruits from trees; we celebrate Creation and the natural world; we recognize the Source of all bounty and pronounce blessings of thanks over fruits and nuts and fruitful beverages; we connect with the Land of Israel and with the promise and responsibility it embodies; we consider fellow humans who are less blessed than we and their needs and hungers.

In the Tu B'Shvat seder, the medieval ceremony which has been revived in recent years to become the major form of celebration of the day, we eat in a particular order the nuts and fruits of the Bible and Talmud; we study verses and midrashim about Creation, the Land, its produce, and its laws; and we make a special effort to recite as many *berakhot* as possible over fruits and wines (or grape juice). These are all thoroughly vegetarian activities, and they express the fundamental values within Jewish tradition which encourage Jews to become vegetarian.

Blessings

A prominent and recurrent element in the Tu B'Shvat seder is the *berakhot* which are spoken prior to the tasting (in designated order) of each of the different fruits, nuts, and cups of wine.

The idea of saying blessings before and after eating any food (as well as in connection with certain acts of seeing, of smelling, of hearing, and of bodily functioning) is a profound act of theology-in-action which Judaism introduced to the world. The Talmud says (in a statement alluded to in the text of *Peri Eitz Hadar*, the original published Tu B'Shvat seder text) that any person who enjoys the pleasures of this world without reciting blessings of thanks over them is a thief. Another Talmudic discussion reconciles two seemingly contradictory Bible verses: "The earth and its fullness are Adonai's" (Ps. 24:1) and "The heavens are Adonai's heavens, but the earth is given to human beings" (Ps. 115:16) by stating that we become entitled to use and "own" the earth by reciting blessings over its produce.

A Vegetarian Hierarchy

The system of blessings established by the Rabbis indicates the relative importance of different kinds of foods in Judaism. That hierarchy shares (and perhaps expresses) vegetarian values and priorities. When confronted with the choice of which food takes priority over others and is recognized with a longer, more specialized blessing, we are provided by Jewish tradition with the following order of primacy:

1. Bread: for which we say the *berakhah, ha-motzi lehem min ha-aretz* (which is recited over bread made from the five primary species of grain: wheat, barley, rye, oats, or spelt);
2. Wine: *Borei peri ha-gafen* (recited over wine [or juice] made primarily from grapes);
3. Cake: *Borei minei mezonot* (over pastries, crackers, and other baked goods [other than bread] made from the five grains);
4. Fruit: *Borei peri ha'eitz* (over fruits and nuts which grow on trees);
5. Vegetables: *Borei peri ha'adamah* (over salads, beans, non-baked grains, certain seeds and melons, and other vegetables which grow from the ground);

405

6. Everything else: *She-hakol niheyeh be-dvaro* (over all other foods, including water, meat, fish, broth, and cheese).

A similar order of priority is ordained in Jewish law for blessings recited *after* the eating of food (in fulfillment of the Torah's command, "And you shall eat, and you shall be satisfied, and you shall bless Adonai your God for the good Land which was given to you". (Deut. 8:10) Following meals which include bread, we read the entire lengthy *birkat hamazon* grace after meals; following wine or pastry or the seven species of fruit identified with Israel, we say the paragraph-long *Berakhah Aḥronah*. But after eating or drinking tomato juice or milk or eggs or lamb chops or tuna fish, we recite only the one-sentence *Borei nefashot* blessing.

The complex arrangement of *berakhot* makes an implicit statement about which foods are most prized, most weighty, most meaningful in Judaism. The foods accorded greater status are uniformly vegetarian (indeed, vegan) ones, while meat and fish are lumped together with every miscellaneous concoction at the bottom of the blessings-of-food chain. (This is not to say that any blessing which we receive or which we recite is really unimportant: Rabbi Abraham Joshua Heschel once observed that, since we pronounce the *She-hakol* blessing [praising God, " . . . by Whose word everything exists"] over the simplest beverage, the Jew sees the entire world in a glass of water.)

All of the blessings set down to be repeatedly spoken at the Tu B'Shvat seder (over fruits, nuts, wines) are recited over "important"—vegetarian—foods and drinks (as are all the *berakhot* at the Passover seder, after which the Tu B'Shvat ceremony was modeled).

Which Fruits First?

The word "seder," of course, means order; how did the kabbalists of Tzfat (who created the Tu B'Shvat seder in the sixteenth century and centered it around studying, eating, saying blessings over, and praying for the welfare of fruits and trees) decide on the order in which the fruits should be read about, praised, and eaten? Which fruits should come first? And a related question: if you have before yourself a table full of all kinds of fruits (as we try to arrange on Tu B'Shvat), which should you select first and pronounce the *berakhah* over, according to Jewish law?

There is a specific answer to this question. (Supposedly, it was sometimes used as a test by wealthy *balabatim* in the Middle Ages to evaluate the level of Torah learning of potential sons-in-law: they would set before them platters of fruit and see if the young men knew which to choose and say the blessing over first).

The most honored fruits in Judaism are those mentioned in Deuteronomy 8:7–8 as exemplifying and representing the Land of Israel: "For Adonai your God is bringing you to a good land, a land of rivers of water, of fountains and deep pools that spring out of valleys and hills. A land of wheat and barley, of grapevines and figs and pomegranates, a land of oil-olives and dates." The seven kinds of produce referred to in this verse are known as the *sheva minim*, the seven species associated with *Eretz Yisrael*.

Two of them, of course, are grains, and those two—wheat and barley (along with rye, oats, and spelt)—are the grains over which we say *Ha-motzi* and *bentsch*, the grains which can become *ḥametz* on Pesach (and which therefore can be used to make proper matza), and those from which we must remove *ḥalla*. The remaining five tree-fruits are the royalty of the Jewish fruit world, after the eating of which we must recite the lengthy *berakhah ahronah*; and, if given the choice of various fruits, we choose these five—grapes (or raisins), figs, pomegranates, olives, and dates—over any others. But among these five . . .? Which is truly the king/queen of fruits?

Jewish law instructs us (as those medieval suitors hopefully were aware) that the priority among these fruits depends upon their proximity to the word "land" (*eretz*) in Deut. 8:8. So central and powerful is the idea of the holiness of Israel that the importance of these fruits varies according to how soon after the word "land" they appear in the Biblical verse.

The word "land" appears twice, and the olive is mentioned immediately after its second appearance, while all the other four fruits are at least one word separated from the "land." Thus the order of primacy among the five fruits which are among the "seven species" is: olives, then dates (which are mentioned next), then grapes and figs and pomegranates (which are listed, in that order, following the wheat and barley, at the beginning of the verse).

And indeed the Tu B'Shvat seder of the Kabbalists begins with wheat and barley, followed by olives, dates, grapes, figs, and pomegranates in that (mandated) order. The seder continues with fruits which are spoken of elsewhere in the Bible (primarily in the Song of Songs): etrog, apple, walnut, and almond; followed by fruits mentioned in the Mishna (carob—long identified with Tu B'Shvat—and pear); and eight other fruits of historical and mystical significance, most of which do not even have real Hebrew names: azarole, quince, cherries, crabapple, nuts (pistachios?), hackberry, and lupine.

What a vegetarian festival of fruitly ideas, significations, and tastes!

Designated Blessers

Ordinarily, when one has a banquet table full of many varieties of fruit set before one (admittedly not a common occurrence, though perhaps somewhat more frequent among vegetarians), Jewish law directs that one recite only a single blessing over all of the fruit, or over the most important one (determined according to the standards just described). In fact, it would be a *berakhah le-vatalah* (an unnecessary blessing, therefore speaking God's name to no purpose) to recite the blessing over fruits several different times at one sitting.

But the medieval authors of the Tu B'Shvat seder, because they wanted the occasion to produce the maximum focus and intent and outpouring of blessings and benefits for the fruit and the trees on their New Year's, prescribed differently at this seder. They directed that one participant who has not eaten any of the previous fruits, and has not answered "amen"(with the intent of joining in) to the previous blessings, be held aside to recite the blessing over each successive fruit so that the number of properly said blessings be increased.

Similarly, for each of the four cups of wine (their number echoing the Pesach seder, but in this case their color mystically changing from all white, to white-with-a-drop-of-red, to half-and-half, to red-with-a-drop-of-white): someone who has not yet drunk any wine nor included him/herself in the previous wine blessings recites the *brakha* each of the last three times (though the wine-blessers *are* permitted to eat each of the fruits as its turn comes up).

Ecology, the Land of Israel, and Vegetarianism

All the Biblical holidays are connected to the natural cycles of the Land of Israel, and even those Jewish holidays which arose later tie in with the seasons and landscapes of Israel. But the occasion on the calendar which most closely relates to the ecology of the Holy Land is Tu B'Shvat, and it has been adopted by modern-day Zionists and Jewish environmentalists because of this theme. The same motifs also connect Tu B'Shvat to vegetarianism. Israel is identified in the Torah (in the verse which became the centerpiece of the Tu B'Shvat seder) as the source of the Seven Species, and also as the land "flowing with milk and honey (which refers not to bees but to date paste)" (in Exodus 3:8 and a dozen other places), but never by the beef or lamb or mutton of its animal inhabitants. The Spring imagery of the Song of Songs bespeaks the lush natural beauty and flora of the Land; the sensuous foods described are all fruits. Many of those lyrical verses appear in the text of the original Tu B'Shvat seder, and all describe vegetarian delights.

Glossary

Bentsch (Yiddish): recite the Grace After Meals (or other blessings).
Balabatim (Yiddish): householders, businessmen of substance.

Ḥalla (Hebrew): portion of dough commanded to be separated (originally for the Holy Temple).

Ḥesed (Hebrew): kindness, active caring.

Vegan (English): a diet which is totally vegetarian, excluding all milk products and eggs.

Sources of Further Information on Vegetarianism and Tu B'Shvat

Books on Judaism and vegetarianism from Micah Publications include: *Judaism and Vegetarianism* by Richard H. Schwartz (1993); *Judaism and Animal Rights* by Roberta Kalechofsky (1992); and *Rabbis and Vegetarianism* by Roberta Kalechofsky (1995). Micah Publications can be reached at 255 Humphrey St., Marblehead, MA 01945, (617) 631-7601.

The Jewish Vegetarians of North America publish a quarterly newsletter. They can be reached at 6938 Reliance Rd., Federalsburg, MD 21632, (410) 754-5550; E-mail: imossman@skipjack.bluecrab.org

The International Jewish Vegetarian Society publishes a quarterly magazine at 853/5 Finchley Rd., London NW 11 8LX, England.

Some of the most outstanding books, pamphlets, and guides about ecology in Judaism and Tu B'Shvat are published by Neot Kedumim, the Biblical Landscape Reserve in Israel. American Friends of Neot Kedumim can be reached at Steinfeld Rd., Halcott Center, NY 12430, (914) 254-5031; Fax: (914) 254-4458.

Recent books on vegetarian issues include:

Lappe, Frances Moore. *Diet for a Small Planet* [20th Anniversary Edition]. Ballantine Books, 1991.

Rhodes, Richard. *Deadly Feasts*. Simon and Schuster, 1997.

Rifkin, Jeremy. *Beyond Beef*. Dutton, 1992.

Robbins, John. *May All Be Fed*. William Morrow & Co., 1992.

Singer, Peter. *Animal Liberation* [revised edition]. Avon Books, 1990.

New Traditions for Tu B'Shvat

Rami Shapiro

Humans are celebratory beings. We need to affirm the possibilities of holiness amidst the hope and horror of history. Holy days are a way of exploring the deeper realities of everyday life in a manner that sanctifies the ordinary as an extension of the extraordinary. To do this successfully, however, holy days must address the ordinary facts of everyday life. When the address is disrupted, the holy day loses its power. To revive a holy day we must revive the address from which it originally grew. Tu B'Shvat is a case in point.

Tu B'Shvat is a holy day marking the rising of sap in the trees of ancient Israel. It is entirely tied to the seasons of a particular bioregion and continues to speak powerfully to the Jewish citizens of that bioregion. The problem with Tu B'Shvat arises when we try to transplant the holy day from one bioregion to another.

When I think back to Tu B'Shvat as celebrated in my suburban Conservative shul in western Massachusetts all I remember is an essentially meaningless exercise of vicariously observing the rebirth of Israel's forests in the dead of North American winter. What makes perfect sense in Israel becomes a caricature of piety in my home town. When I was very young it was fun. But fun only goes so far. When I was old enough to understand the meaning of the holy day I was old enough to see the ludicrous nature of our celebration.

I outgrew the holy day, and I am not alone. Ask Jewish adults about Judaism and most will offer a pre-teen picture of religion that lays claim to little but an ever diminishing nostalgia. The tragedy of contemporary Judaism is that we have reduced it to child's play. As we grow up we grow out of Judaism.

When the best we can do at Tu B'Shvat is plant seedlings in paper cups because the ground outside is ice hard, we are engaged in imitation Judaism. Imitation Judaism replaces the power of Tu B'Shvat (and every other holy day) with sentimentality and nostalgia. The holy day is trivialized. The congregation is infantilized. And the healing power of Tu B'Shvat is lost.

Tu B'Shvat is a celebration of the first stirrings of spring. It honors the rising of tree sap, the resurrection of life, the return of wakefulness. It heralds a general rebirth of life, and holds out the promise of new becomings. As such its timing is linked to its bioregion. In Israel Tu B'Shvat is real. It makes sense. Planting trees in Israel on the Fifteenth day of the month of Shvat means planting trees in a soil eager to embrace them. Tu B'Shvat returns us to the soil, it reminds us that we are rooted in soil. It reaffirms that we are *adam*, earthlings, whose obligation it is to plant, cultivate and guard *adamah*, the earth, until we have created a new Eden.

None of this happens in paper cups. So let's change it. Let's tap the primal power of the day, the affirmation of new beginnings, and recreate Tu B'Shvat for ourselves in our place and our time.

When thinking about re-creation we are faced with two choices. On the one hand, we can abandon the Israel connection and celebrate Tu B'Shvat at different times in different places, allowing nature, not nostalgia, to set the date for heralding spring. On the other, we can keep the connection via the date and imagine new ways by which to honor that date.

If we abandon the Israel connection we lose Tu B'Shvat. Tu B'Shvat is not a name but a date (the Fifteenth of Shvat, the Eleventh month of the Hebrew calendar). If we change the date common sense would require us to rename the day. Changing the date so that the holy day made environmental sense in every community would also introduce calendrical variations that would divide Jewish communities and deprive us of a common liturgical cycle. While this might make good sense from an environmental point of view, it makes no sense if we hope to maintain a cohesive world Jewish community.

If we would retain community we have to maintain the calendar connection and broaden the context of the holy day. I suggest that regardless of where on the planet we Jews live, all of us can set aside the Fifteenth of Shvat to honor the regenerative potential of nature by turning our attention to those forces that seek to destroy that potential.

If we recast Tu B'Shvat as a day for environmental awareness, will we lose the connection to trees and Israel? Not at all. These become viable examples of how Jews in a given bioregion celebrate and honor the holy day. Ritual diversity replaces halakhic conformity; what unites us is the date, the history, and the common sources (natural and liturgical) from which we draw our inspiration and material. We share, if you will, a common trunk and allow the branches to develop in whatever way is right for them.

I am a rabbi of a small Reconstructionist shul in Miami, Florida. Tu B'Shvat for us comes at a good time in the Gaian cycle. We could focus on trees and leave it at that. Yet for the past dozen years or so we have seen Tu B'Shvat as an opportunity not only to celebrate the regenerative powers of nature, but to confront the forces at work to defeat those powers. In addition to traditional Tu B'Shvat seders, and tree planting (we urge members to plant three trees each year: one in Israel, one at home, and one in the community), we also take our congregation "on the road" and hold our Shabbat morning service closest to Tu B'Shvat at a site connected with endangered species or environmental crisis.

Our first Tu B'Shvat Shabbat found us on a boat floating down the Miami river. Our liturgy linked the traditional Hebrew prayers with the issues surrounding the not so slow death of this once vibrant waterway. We saw the dying, said our *mi shebeirakh* for life in the midst of this unnatural decay. Our service addressed the world around us, spoke truth to power, and held out hope for redemption. Following the service we heard from experts on the river's restoration and learned what we could do to help save its life.

Over the years we have made Shabbat with butterflies, manatees, alligators, and the Florida panther. We have wrestled with the moral dilemmas of zoos and confronted the ethics of dining high on the food chain. We have davened outside fast food hamburger restaurants and studied the devastation to both person and planet that excessive meat eating causes. We have explored the dying coastal reefs in glass bottom boats; wandered the Everglades with more than a minyan of gators, mosquitoes and snakes; tasted the richness of diversity at the Rare Fruit and Spice Tree Park; and measured the renewal of vast gardens in the aftermath of Hurricane Andrew. We have heard from advocates for dolphins, vegetarianism, and organic farming. We have committed our community and ourselves to eco-kashrut (ethical consuming), *bal tashhit* (ending waste) and *tza'ar ba'alei hayyim* (protecting animals). We have made Tu B'Shvat a time for facing harsh realities, affirming nature's regenerative capabilities, and accepting our personal and communal responsibilities for the health and diversity of our neighborhoods and our world.

413

For us Tu B'Shvat is once again relevant, powerful, challenging, and healing. And all because we choose to honor intent over content. We see Tu B'Shvat and all of our Jewish holy days as Jewish expressions of a universal longing for holiness. When deciding how to honor that longing we place holiness uppermost and measure tradition against how well it speaks to holiness in our place and time.

We learn from the past; we study tradition; but in the end we see these as informing us of intent and not limiting us to content. We believe that our link to other versions of Tu B'Shvat is our shared desire to tap this particular day and its history as our vehicle for exploring the interdependence of *adam* and *adamah*. We believe that this link allows our expression of Tu B'Shvat to be considered authentic for it carries forward in our particular community the universal thrust of Judaism in all communities: *tikkun ha-olam*.

The key to the success of our Tu B'Shvat programming is three-fold. First there is the powerful awakening that happens when we hold Shabbat services at a site of nature's endangerment. By affirming the Power that makes for Creation, and reminding ourselves of our responsibilities for that Creation in the midst of environmental breakdown and tragedy, we cannot help but be moved to act to effect *tikkun* (healing) in that spot.

Second, there is the spiritual connection. As educated South Floridians, we are not unaware of the harsh truths of our local environmental problems, but our awareness is secular not spiritual. It leads to working on nature rather than with nature. It perpetuates the illusion of separation, and does nothing to reclaim the greater unity of *adam* and *adamah*. Linking the political with the spiritual makes the healing of the earth a matter of personal holiness. Standing on top of Trash Mountain (our local megadump) and affirming the Messianic promise of the kingdom of heaven, we cannot help but take responsibility for recycling and reducing consumption. The health of the planet becomes vital to the spiritual well-being of the person.

Third, there is the Jewish connection. Rediscovering the interdependence of all beings is at the heart of spiritual awakening; doing so as Jews is at the heart of personal and communal Jewish renewal. Too many of us have compartmentalized our lives and boxed Judaism away from the everyday. To find that Judaism speaks powerfully to the issues of the day is to find our Jewish identity pushed to the forefront of our consciousness.

While in no way adhering to the rigors of halakhah, members of my congregation embrace eco-kashrut as a principled way of life. They do their best (each in her own way) to eat lower on the food chain, to buy only what is needed, to see that what they buy is produced, prepared, shipped and used in a manner that respects both the planet that births it and the people that shape it. And they do so because their Judaism compels them to do so. By tapping into local problems, reframing them as part of global renewal, linking them to spiritual practice, and discovering that all of these are present in Judaism, we make the most cogent argument for remaining, becoming, and becoming more actively Jewish.

For us Tu B'Shvat is an opportunity for celebration. We stand in solidarity with nature and take up the challenge of personal and planetary renewal. This has nothing to do with imitation. This has everything to do with reclaiming the essential meaning and vitality of a holy day and applying it to issues of immediate concern. The suffering of the earth, the imperfections of earthlings are not cause for despair, but calls for action. We celebrate the transformative power of God. We celebrate the regenerative power of nature. We celebrate the *tikkun* power of humankind. We do not bemoan what is but see what can be. To set aside a day of this kind of power is to foster a Judaism one can never outgrow.

Sharing God's Fruitfulness

Arthur Waskow

Who could imagine a band of mystics choosing April 15—Income Tax Day—to make a festival for celebrating the rebirth of God?

Yet that is what the kabbalists of Tzfat did in the sixteenth century when they recreated Tu B'Shvat. Tu B'Shvat, the full moon of
midwinter, had been important only in Holy Temple days, in the
calendar of tithing. It was the end of the "fiscal year" for trees. Fruit
that appeared before that date was taxed for the previous year; fruit
that appeared later, for the following year.

The Talmud called this legal date the "New Year for Trees."

But the kabbalists saw it as the New Year for the Tree of Life itself—for God's Own Self, for the Tree Whose roots are in Heaven
and Whose fruit is the world itself and all God's creatures. To honor
the reawakening of trees and of that Tree in deep midwinter, they
created a mystical seder that honors the Four Worlds of Acting, Relating, Knowing, and Being. These Four Worlds were enacted with
four cups of wine and four courses of nuts and fruit (moving from
less permeable to more permeable, and after three courses of tangible fruit, ending with fruit so permeable that it was intangible—
for the Fourth World of Being, Spirit).

The symbolic system of this seder held still deeper riches: echoes
of generation and regeneration in the worlds of plants and animals.

- Nuts and fruit, the rebirthing aspects of a plant's life cycle, are
  the only foods that require no death, not even the death of a
  plant. Our living trees send forth their fruit and seeds in such
  profusion that they overflow beyond the needs of the next
  generation.
- The four cups of wine were red, rose, pink, white. Thus they
  echoed generation and regeneration among animals, including
  the human race. For red and white were in ancient tradition
  seen as the colors of generativity. To mix them was to mix the
  blood and semen that to the ancients connoted procreation.

Why then did the kabbalists of Tzfat connect these primal urg-
ings toward abundance with the date of tithing fruit? Because they
saw that God's *shefa*, abundance, would keep flowing only if a portion of it were returned to God, the Owner of all land and all
abundance.

And who were God's rent collectors? The poor and the landless, including those priestly celebrants and teachers who owned no piece of earth and whose earthly task was to teach and celebrate.

These mystics saw a deep significance in giving. They said that to eat without blessing the Tree was robbery; to eat without feeding others was robbery. Worse!—because without blessing and sharing, the flow of abundance would choke and stop.

Tu B'Shvat approaches once again. The trees of the world are in danger; the poor of the world are in need; the teachers and celebrants of the world are at risk.

Give! Or the flow of abundance will choke on the friction of its own outpouring, and God's Own Self will choke on our refusal of compassion.

Etz Ḥiyyim Rabbah: 1.1

Joel Lurie Grishaver

BACK IN THE SIXTEENTH CHAPTER OF FIRST CHRONICLES KING DAVID WAS JAMMING. HE WAS ON HARP. HE DID THE WORDS. ASAPH FOUND THE GROOVE WITH HIS CYMBAL. ASAPH DID THE CYMBAL — DAVID DID THE SYMBOLS. JEIEL, SHEMIR-A-MOUTH, MATTIT-YAHU, AND ELIAB KICKED IN ON HARP. BENIAN, OBED-EDOM AND JEHIEL SYNCOPATED THEIR LYRES. LITTLE BENAIAH AND JEHAZIEL (AKA THE PRIESTLY BROTHERS) WERE THE HORN SECTION. DAVID SANG: **PRAISE ADONAI. CALL ON GOD'S NAME.** THE WHOLE BAND LEANED INTO THEIR MICROPHONES AND ECHOED HIM. DAVID SANG: **THE WHOLE EARTH SHOULD SING TO ADONAI.** EVERYONE JOINED IN. MIRIAM AND THE TIMBRELLETTES PICKED UP THE BEAT AND ADDED THE HIGH HARMONY. DAVID SANG: **LET THE HEAVENS REJOICE. LET THE EARTH EXALT. LET THE SEA AND EVERYTHING IN IT THUNDER. LET THE FIELDS SING THEIR PART.** SHEMIR-A-MOUTH WAS REALLY WAILING — BLASTING OUT HIS FILLS. SWEAT WAS POURING DOWN. THE BAND WAS IN THE GROOVE. **WHEN GOD COMES CLOSE — ALL THE TREES OF THE FOREST WILL SHOUT FOR JOY.**

IN THE VIDEO, THE BAND WAS SUDDENLY BEING BACKED BY A WHOLE ORCHESTRA OF TREES. IN THE VIDEO, AN OLIVE GROVE BECAME A GOSPEL CHOIR. IT WAS DOO-WOP ALL THE WAY.

WHEN GOD COMES CLOSE—ALL THE **TREES** OF THE FOREST WILL SHOUT FOR JOY.

IT WAS FALL WHEN ADAM AND EVE WERE KICKED OUT OF THE GARDEN. FALL
IS NO TIME TO PLANT. IT WASN'T THE HAPPIEST OF HIGH HOLY DAYS. BUT,
STILL, ADAM HAD TO SMILE, JUST A LITTLE—HOPING THAT GOD WOULDN'T
NOTICE. THIS WAS THE SECRET. OVER HIS NEW FOUND NAKEDNESS WENT THE
FIG LEAVES. OVER THE FIG LEAVES WENT THE SKINS GOD HAD GIVEN.
HOWEVER, AMONG THE LEAVES WAS A SMALL FIG. AMONG THE LEAVES WAS
ADAM'S CHANCE TO GROW HIS OWN TREE OF LIFE, HIS OWN TREE OF
KNOWLEDGE. GOD SMILED, ENJOYING THE FACT THAT ADAM THOUGHT HE
WAS PULLING A FAST ONE. BUT GOD LOVED IT WHEN A PLAN CAME
TOGETHER.

GOD HAD SAID, "BY YOUR LABOR SHALL YOU EAT...BY THE SWEAT OF YOUR BROW SHALL YOU GET FOOD." THAT NEXT DAY, ADAM PLANTED THE SEEDS IN THE GROUND. HIS FINGERS BLED FROM THE DIGGING. HIS HEAD WAS DRIPPING WITH SWEAT. AND, LIKE IN A FAIRY TALE OR A DISNEY MOVIE—A SINGLE SWEET SWEAT DROP FELL ON THE SEED, AND LIKE MAGIC, OR PERHAPS LIKE TORAH, THE SEED BEGAN TO GROW. EVERY DAY HIS LABOR AND HIS SWEAT WATERED THE SEED, WHICH GREW OVER THE WINTER INTO A TREE.

BY YOUR **LABOR** SHALL YOU **EAT**...BY THE **SWEAT** OF YOUR BROW SHALL YOU GET **FOOD.**

IT WAS ON THE EDGE OF SPRING. IT WAS ON THE 15TH OF SHEVAT, THAT THE FIRST BUD OF FRUIT EMERGED ON THE FIRST TREE EVER CULTIVATED BY HUMAN HANDS. ADAM AND EVE AND CAIN AND ABEL (AND ABEL'S DOG CANINE) ALL SANG AND DANCED AND CELEBRATED AND PRAISED GOD. **WHEN GOD COMES CLOSE—ALL THE TREES OF THE FOREST WILL SHOUT FOR JOY.** IT WAS A HOPE. IT WAS A MEMORY OF WALKING IN THE GARDEN. IT WAS A DREAM. IT WAS A PRAYER. IT WAS A PROPHECY.

WHEN GOD COMES CLOSE—ALL THE TREES OF THE FOREST WILL SHOUT FOR JOY.

ONE TREE BECOMES MANY TREES. THAT IS THE WAY OF WISDOM. SOME FRUIT OF THIS FIRST TREE CARRIED NOAH AND FAMILY AND CREW THROUGH THE DELUGE.

ABRAM PRACTICED HOSPITALITY UNDER THE SHADE AND INSTRUCTION OF ANOTHER GROWN FROM THE SAME ROOTS.

ANOTHER FRUIT BECAME THE STAFF BY WHICH MOSES BROUGHT GOD'S POWER DOWN TO EARTH. AS THE TREES OF KNOWLEDGE SPREAD,

DEBORAH LEARNED FROM ONE. AMOS LEARNED HOW TO BE A PROPHET FROM OTHERS.

SIR ISAAC NEWTON LEARNED THE TORAH OF GRAVITY FROM ONE.

MARTIN BUBER TALKED TO GOD BECAUSE THE TREE ACROSS THE STREET WAS THE INTERMEDIARY.

JOHNNY TREE-MANE UNDERSTOOD THE TORAH OF DEMOCRACY FROM ANOTHER.

ROBERT FROST CAME TO GRIPS WITH HIS MORTALITY AND HIS SOUL AS SNOW FELL ON SOME, UNDERSTOOD THE BITTER SWEET TRUTHS OF THE PAIN AND JOY OF GROWING FROM OTHERS WHICH HAD BORNE UP UNDER THE WEIGHT OF MANY WINTERS.

MANY TREES— MUCH TORAH.

EACH TREE, EACH PIECE OF LIFE, WAS GROWN WITH THE TOIL AND PAIN OF EVE'S CHILDREN, WITH THE SWEAT AND EFFORT OF ADAM'S OFFSPRING. EACH 15TH OF SHEVAT, NEW FRUIT OPENS.

DAVID AND HIS BAND SANG WAY BACK IN THE SIXTEENTH CHAPTER OF FIRST CHRONICLES **WHEN GOD COMES CLOSE—ALL THE TREES OF THE FOREST WILL SHOUT FOR JOY**—WE ARE STILL LEARNING TO SING, DANCE, AND GROW OUR PART OF THE SONG FIRST SUNG ON THE FIRST TU B'SHVAT. LISTEN TO SHEMIR-A-MOUTH WAIL.

WHEN GOD COMES CLOSE—ALL THE TREES OF THE FOREST WILL SHOUT FOR JOY.

FORESTS REJOICE
from Psalm 96

© 1997 Geela-Rayzel Raphael

Chorus:

Az Y'ranenu kol atzey ya'ar! (2 times)

Crickets chant in rhythmic sound
Leaves are rustling on the ground;
Moss sits silent in meditation
All a part of Divine creation!

Butterfly flits in ecstacy
Squirrel and deer chime in harmony;
Spider spins with deep devotion
Wolves howling in wild commotion.

Fireflies praise with flickering lights
Bear dances with delight;
Insects buzzing as the percussion
The forest sings in exultation.

427

SHIR LASHKEDIYA
(Song of the Almond Tree)

© Fran Avni, music
words adapted by Tova Shimon

GO FORTH IN JOY
from Isaiah 55:12

Music by Yitzhak Husbands-Hankin

© 1993 Yitzhak Husbands-Hankin

(continued)

429

THE FIFTEENTH OF SHEVAT

Words and music by Ellen Allard

© 1997 8OZ Music

(continued)

Trees, Earth, and Torah

Tu B' Shevat come join us if you please. Our
se - der starts at night - fall when the stars they do ap -pear, our friends & fam - ily join us at this
fes - tive time of year. Our voi - ces rise to - ge - ther for the bles - sings loud and clear,
Tu B' Shevat we share our hol - i - day a - vec plai - sir. Love - ly glow - ing can - dle light and
flowers in full bloom, love ly bowls of fruit, so ma ny nuts we will consume. Love ly shades of wine to drink with
oth - ers in the room, when the seder's fin - ished ou - r lives will re - sume. Tu B' Shevat the

birth-day of the trees. Tu B' Shevat come join us if you please. A -no-ther

sim-ple way to cel-e-brate go out and plant a tree, it's a sim-ple way to cele-brate in

your lo-cal - i- ty or sim-ply plant a tree in Yis - ra - e - l don't you a-gree,

it's im-por-tant, it's a mitz-vah of the 1st de-gree, please re - mem-ber that the trees are so im-

por-tant to us all, re- mem-ber too the plants and an - i - mals all large and small. Re-

mem-ber to take care of eve-ry thing, keep on the ball, from Tel A - Viv, to Pa - ris, from De-

(continued)

troit to Mon-tre-al. Tu B' Shevat the birth-day of the trees.

Tu B' Shevat come join us if you please.

We'll Tu B' Shevat.

This song can be found on the recording *Sing Shalom: Songs for the Jewish Holidays* by Peter and Ellen Allard. To order the tape or CD, call Sounds Write Productions, Inc. at 800-976-8639.

THE BEAR IN ME

by Shefa Gold

© Shefa Gold, words and music

Walking through a Philadelphia snowstorm on the morning of Tu B'Shvat, I was feeling angry and cynical. How could I celebrate the birthday of the trees when I could barely see them through the snow? And besides, they looked almost completely dead to me.

As I surrendered to the wind and came close to a large oak, I sensed something stirring. I closed my eyes and leaned in to the tree. The stirring was both in me and in the heart of the oak. In me the feeling was like a bear waking up after a long hibernation. I heard the growl of new life emerge from my own depths.

In the tree a similar waking up was happening as the sap was secretly rising inside, giving invisible life to the tree in anticipation of Spring. In that moment the secret of Tu B'Shvat was revealed to me—and I could truly celebrate the reality of new life within, even before it could be seen from the outside.

(continued)

Refrain:

Though the winter wind still blows
My heart is thawing with the Spring that it knows
Though the winter wind still howls
The bear in me wakes up and growls

A CHANT FOR TU B'SHVAT
from Psalm 104
Yeesb'oo Ahtsay Adonai—
The Holy One's trees will be satiated.

Chanted at Tu B'Shvat in the Redwood, 5757.

© 1999 Naomi Steinberg, ASCAP

Try chanting call and response in two groups for fifteen minutes.

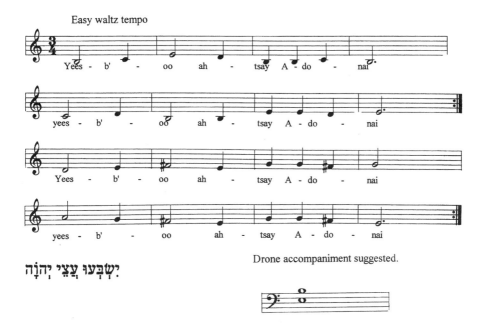

יִשְׂבְּעוּ עֲצֵי יְהוָֹה

ROOTS
Shorashim

Words and music by Fran Avni

© Fran Avni

Roots she cried —— O I am like a bran-ched tree ——

Leav- ing blo- soms in the air —— mid- way twixt earth and sky — and there hang

I no- thing holds me —— No- thing holds—— me ——

Sho- ra- shim —— Sho- ra- shim —— Etz Cha- yim ——

Etz cha- yim —— beyn a- da- ma beyn a- da- ma u- veyn sha- ma- yim —— u-veyn sha-

ma- yim ba- a- vir —— ba- a- vir —— t'lu- ya a- ni —— t'lu-

ya a- ni — mah yach- zik o- ti mah yach- zik o- ti mah yach- zik o- ti mah yach

ziko- ti —— Sho- ra-shim! ——

This song can be heard on a recording of the same name, released on the Tara Music label. For information call 800-Tara-400, or contact FAVNI @ aol.com.

TREE, TREES, TREES

© 1990 Fran Avni (SOCAN)

(continued)

439

This song can be heard on *Daisies and Ducklings* released by Lemonstone Records, P.O. Box 607, Côte St. Luc, Quebec H4V 2Z2 Canada.

ETZ HAYIM HI
from Proverbs 3:17, 18
Returning the Torah to the Ark

Music and English by Hanna Tifere
arranged by Harley Rothstein
© 1984 Hanna Tiferet Siegel

Proverbs describes the great value of wisdom and Torah in the feminine. As we hold the Torah close and honor the source of all that nourishes and sustains us, we feel blessed by the beauty and simplicity of Her truth.

(continued)

Trees, Earth, and Torah

She is a Tree— of Life more pre - cious than gold——

Hold her in your heart and you will un-der - stand—— Etz ha - yim hi——

Her roots are deep and wise, her bran - ches filled with light—— and

last time only (slowly)

all her path-ways are peace.—— Etz ha - yim hi——

OLAMAMA

Music and lyrics by Hanna Tiferet
arranged by Fran Avni

© 1993 Hanna Tiferet Siegel

(continued)

Refrain:

Olamama Olamama, I love you so
Olamama Olamama, just wanna let you know
Olamama Olamama, You bless my soul
You're the Mother of All
Spring Winter Summer and Fall
I love you so

I love to run through a field where
 the wildflowers grow,
To swim in a lake and to slide on
 the snow,
To drink the sweet water that flows
 in a stream,
Oh how you bless me.
I love the wind that blows through
 the trees in a storm,
Lying on a beach in the sand when
 it's warm,
The whales and dolphins that
 drive in the sea,
Oh how you bless me.

Refrain

I love the chirp of a cricket, the
 "ribbet" of frogs,
The purr of a cat and the barking
 of dogs,
The quiet of rabbits, the buzzing of
 bees,
Oh how you bless me.
I love snakes and lizards, coyotes
 and bears,
'Though I have to admit that at
 times I get scared
But I know we're all part of one
 great family,
Oh how you bless me.

Refrain

I love the sound of the rain as it
 falls on my roof
And the magic of rainbows that
 always brings proof
That behind every cloud You shine
 radiantly
Oh how you bless me.
I love to get up real early and see
 the sun rise,
Or stay up so late, the moon closes
 my eyes,
To wish on a star for the things
 that I dream,
Oh how you bless me.

Refrain

I love to feel my feelings, the good
 and the bad,
Sometimes I'm happy and
 sometimes I'm sad,
That's how I learn who I am,
 what I need,
Oh how you bless me.
I love the gift of this world. How
 you bless everyone
With the air we breathe and the
 light of the sun.
I'll take good care of the Earth,
 and good care of me too.
That's how I bless you!

Refrain (2 times)

444

V'AKHALTA

from Deuteronomy 8:10, A Birkat Hamazon

Music and English by Hanna Tiferet
arranged by Nomi Fenson

© 1992 Hanna Tiferet Siegel

V'-a - khal - ta v'-sa - va - ta, u - vey - rakh - ta___ v'-a -
khal - ta, v'-sa - va - ta, u - vey - rakh - - - ta. V'-a -

ta. We ate when we were hun - gry and now we're sa - tis - fied We
Hun - ger is a yearn - ing in bo - dy and soul
Gi - ving and Re - cei - ving we o - pen up our hands From
We share___ in a vi - sion of whole - ness and re - lease Where

thank the Source of Bles - sing for all that S/He___ pro - vides.
Earth, Air, Fi - re, Wa - ter and Spi - rit make___ us___ whole.
Seed - time through Har - vest we're part - ners with___ the___ Land.
ev - 'ry child is nou - rished and we all live___ in___ peace.

(continued)

445

Refrain:

> *V'akhalta, v'savata, uveyrakhta (4 times)*

We ate when we were hungry
And now we're satisfied
We thank the Source of Blessing
For all that S/He provides.

Refrain *(2 times)*

Hunger is a yearning
In body and soul
Earth, Air, Fire Water
And Spirit make us whole.

Refrain *(2 times)*

Giving and Receiving
We open up our hands
From Seedtime through Harvest
We're partners with the Land.

Refrain *(2 times)*

We share in a vision
Of wholeness and release
Where every child is nourished
And we all live in peace.

Refrain *(4 times)*

ETZ HAYYIM

Rabbi Margot Stein
Arr. by Ronald Fischman

part VIII

Seeds: Sources for Learning and Doing

RESOURCES

Environmental Organizations, Publications, and Videos

There are a number of organizations and books that will provide further information from year to year about Judaism and the earth, and about celebration of Tu B'Shvat, as follows:

- Broadest among these is an umbrella organization, the Coalition on the Environment and Jewish Life (COEJL), 443 Park Ave., South, New York, NY 10026; COEJL@aol.com; (212) 684-6950, ext. 201.

  COEJL is itself part of a broader coalition, the National Religious Partnership on the Environment. In the larger grouping, other components are the U.S. Catholic Conference, the National Council of Churches, and the Evangelical Environmental Network. COEJL works under the direction of representatives of the Jewish Theological Seminary, the Religious Action Center of Reform Judaism, and the Jewish Council on Public Affairs. Its sponsors include almost all the national Jewish organizations in the United States.

  COEJL works on legislative advocacy, liturgical materials keyed to the Jewish calendar, guides to eco-sensitive living, and conferences of Jewish communal leaders, rabbis, theologians, and eco-activists. It has a growing number of local and regional affiliates. Rather than try to list these, we urge people to check with COEJL for such contacts.

- The Shalom Center, 7318 Germantown Ave., Philadelphia, PA 19119; Shalomctr@aol.com; (215) 247-9700, ext. 25. The Shalom Center is especially interested in developing theology and eco-kosher life practice adequate to the present ecological crisis and in applying Jewish communal ethics to responsible corporate action.

- One of the earliest Jewish earth-oriented groups, Shomrei Adamah, is now mainly a support group for Teva Learning Center, 50 West 17th St., 7th floor, New York, NY 10011; tevacenter@aol.com; (212) 807-6376. Teva is especially concerned with teaching environmental ethics to young Jews and integrating direct outdoor experience with Torah.

- Yetziah/Jewish Wilderness Journeys is housed at Camp Isabella Friedman, 116 Johnson Rd., Falls Village, CT 06031; Yetziah@aol.com; (860) 824-5991. It specializes in river and other wilderness trips that integrate Torah study with nature experience.

In Israel, the most important environmental groups are as follows:

- Society for the Preservation of Nature in Israel (*Haganat Hateva*), 4 Hashfela St., Tel Aviv 66183, Israel; for hikes and trails, (03) 638-8677; for environmental action, (03) 375-063; with an American affiliate at 28 Arrandale Ave., Great Neck, NY 11024; aspni@aol.com; (212) 398-6750.
- Israel Union for Environmental Defense (*Adam Teva v'Din*), 317 HaYarkon St., Tel Aviv 63504, Israel; (03) 546-8099. IUED is an active legal support and challenge center for neighborhoods and towns whose eco-systems are being endangered.
- Jewish National Fund (*Keren Kayemet l'Yisrael*), with an American affiliate at 42 East 69th St., New York, NY; (212) 879-9300. JNF has made tree planting in Israel one of its major programs. There has been some controversy over JNF's behavior toward heavily Palestinian areas.
- Heschel Center for Nature Studies, Yavneh 1, Tel Aviv, Israel. (03) 620-1806; heschel@netvision.net.il. The Heschel Center does eco-theology, applying Torah to issues of the earth.
- Arava Institute for Environmental Studies, Kibbutz Ketura, DN, Hevel Eilot 88840, Israel; (972/2) 735-6666; arava@netvision.net.il. Regional center for conservation and environmental protection activities; accredited program in environmental studies (taught in English).
- EcoPeace: Middle East Environmental NGO Forum, P.O. Box 55302, East Jerusalem 97400, Israel; (972/2) 626-0841; ecopeace@netvision.net.il. Egyptians, Israelis, Jordanians, and Palestinians working together to promote ecologically sound development in the Middle East through research, education, and advocacy.

- Neot Kedumim, P.O. Box 1007, Lod 71100 Israel; (972/8) 233-3840. Nature reserve dedicated to restoring the flora and fauna of biblical Israel; publications.

Several books have appeared in recent years to address eco-Jewish concerns and they are as follows:

- Ellen Bernstein, ed., *Ecology and the Jewish Spirit: Where Nature and the Sacred Meet* (Woodstock, VT: Jewish Lights, 1997), includes essays on how a number of individual Jews have been awakened to and have responded to a sense of healing the earth as an aspect of Jewish life and thought.
- Marge Piercy, *He, She and It* (New York: Knopf, 1991), a novel set alternately in the Prague of the famous Golem and in the late twenty-first century (in the newly independent Jewish city-state of Tikva, located on the hills where Boston used to be before global warming), it addresses the dangers at political, psychological, and spiritual levels of out-of-control technology and the possibility of a *mentshlich* technology.
- Richard H. Schwartz, *Judaism and Global Survival* (Atara, 1987).
- Arthur Waskow, *Down-to-Earth Judaism* (New York: Morrow, 1995), looks at a number of Jewish life-path issues with special regard to the effects of the earth-human relationship.
- Arthur Waskow, *Godwrestling—Round 2* (Woodstock, VT: Jewish Lights, 1996), puts forward a Torah-rooted theology of eco-Judaism.
- Arthur Waskow, *Seasons of Our Joy* (Boston: Beacon Press, 1982, 1990), views the cycle of Jewish festivals in part as an attunement to the spiritual meaning of the sun-moon-earth cycles. It was the first English-language festival book ever to treat Tu B'Shvat as part of the regular cycle of Jewish festivals.
- David E. Stein, ed., *A Garden of Choice Fruit: 200 Classic Jewish Quotes on Human Beings and the Environment* (available from Shomrei Adamah; see list above).
- Louis I. Rabinowitz, *Torah and Flora* (Sanhedrin Press, 1979).
- Nogah Hareuveni, *Tree and Shrub in Our Biblical Heritage* (1984). Order from Neot Kedumim (see above).
- Roger Gottlieb, ed., *This Sacred Earth: Religion, Nature, Environment* (Routledge, 1995).

- *Judaism and Ecology*, a study guide produced by Hadassah and Shomrei Adamah; available from Department of Jewish Education, Hadassah, 50 West 58th St., New York, NY 10019.
- Ellen Bernstein and Dan Swartz, eds., *Let the Earth Teach You Torah* (available from Shomrei Adamah; see above).
- Arthur Waskow, *The Earth Is Filled with the Breath of Life;* overview of theology and practice of Eco-Judaism; pamphlet available from Shalom Center (see above).
- *Operation Noah*: two pamphlets on biodiversity and protection of endangered species from a Jewish standpoint—one on contemporary science, action, and program ideas; one on Jewish texts and sources; available from COEJL (see above).

There are two excellent handbooks for action in Jewish communities as follows:

- *To Till and to Tend*, published by COEJL (see above).
- Naomi Friedman and De Fischler, eds., *The Green Shalom Guide;* available from Washington Area Shomrei Adamah, 706 Erie Ave., Takoma Park, MD 20912; (301) 587-7535.

Special issues of two Jewish journals have addressed these questions:

- *Melton Journal* of the Melton Center at the Jewish Theological Seminary (Spring 1991 and Spring 1992).
- *Conservative Judaism* (Fall 1991).

And there are also several videos on this subject:

- "Visions of Eden: A Jewish Perspective on the Environment" (1997, VHS, 60 minutes). Documentary on Judaism and ecology produced by the Jewish Theological Seminary, COEJL, and ABC Television. The program follows a group of Jewish leaders, including rabbis and leading environmentalists, on an overnight backpacking journey along the Appalachian Trail. Available from JTS Communications Office; (212) 678-8020.
- "The Earth Is the Lord's" (1997, VHS, 60 minutes). Jewish Theological Seminary of America; for all ages; tells the Creation story and the importance of protecting all of God's creatures.
- "Keeping the Earth" (1996, VHS, 27 minutes). National Religious Partnership for the Environment (NRPE)/Union of

Concerned Scientists (UCS). Narrated by James Earl Jones, with prominent religious leaders and scientists. Middle school–adult. Order from UCS, 2 Brattle Square, Cambridge, MA 02238-9105, or call (617) 547-5552.

Tu B'Shvat Seder Haggadot

In the last generation in the United States there has been a fruitful flowering of haggadot for holding Tu B'Shvat seders. Perhaps the earliest, the third edition of which was published in November 1975 by the Jewish Community Center of Wilkes-Barre, PA, was by Seymour Hefter. It referred to varicolored wines and four (not three) settings of fruit (fresh, canned, dried, and nuts, rather than thick-skinned, etc.), but it did not mention the Four Worlds and it focused on the Land of Israel.

In 1979 the Diaspora Yeshiva in Jerusalem published in English *Tu B'Shvat: A Mystical Seder for the New Year of Trees*, edited by Yehoshua Bergman and Dennis Berman. This followed the kabbalistic pattern.

In the January-February 1984 issue of *Menorah* there appeared probably the first Tu B'Shvat haggadah showing an interest in global ecological questions, written by Devora Bartnoff and Mordechai Liebling.

The first breakthrough into broad public consciousness of a ecologically focused Tu B'Shvat haggadah came in 1988 with Ellen Bernstein's *The Trees' Birthday: A Celebration of Nature*. Its success led to Bernstein's creation of Shomrei Adamah.

The new interest in Tu B'Shvat stirred others to create new haggadot. In 1989 the Central Conference of American Rabbis published *Seder Tu BiShevat: The Festival of Trees*, by Adam Fisher. The Women's League for Conservative Judaism published *The Fruits of Our World* (undated), by Lois Silverman.

Since then there have emerged a profusion of family, congregational, and institutional haggadot. Among the most interesting are Avital Plan's haggadah for the Berkeley-Richmond Jewish Community Center in California: Louis Berman's *The Festival of Fruit* (Carob Tree Press, 2115 Washington Ave., Wilmette, IL 60091), which draws from a great deal on Sephardic family traditions; and an unusually beautifully illustrated haggadah by Mitchell Flaum.

Tree Planting

Since trees are the centerpiece of Tu B'Shvat, some sources of action and study might also focus on trees, whether Jewish or not. The following notes by Neal Shapiro may be useful to that end:

> Trees are not only beautiful, they carry out many environmentally beneficial functions. They absorb carbon dioxide, the major greenhouse gas (up to 50 pounds per tree each year) from the atmosphere, and release oxygen. They retain moisture in soils, hold topsoil in place, and provide shade, cooling, and food. Trees are also a renewable resource.

> Planted in strategic locations around the home or office building, trees can help save energy. The best locations are on the west and south sides of buildings. This reduces the amount of solar energy that heats structures in the summer, thereby reducing the amount of fossil fuel needed to generate electricity for air-conditioning.

> According to one estimate, three mature trees planted near a house can save, in annual air-conditioning expenses, about as much as it costs to run a refrigerator for a year. The extra shade will increase home comfort for those who do not have air-conditioning.

Sources of information on planting trees include:

- Local nurseries or gardening supply stores for suggestions on appropriate species for particular environments.
- Earth Access, 87 Cherry St., Cambridge, MA 02139. Send $1 for "The Wood Report," a list of alternative rain-forest products. This group suggests avoiding tropical hardwoods such as ebony, lanan, mahogany, padauk, purpleheart, rosewood, teak, and wenge because these woods most likely come from unregulated or mismanaged logging of tropical rain forests.
- Global ReLeaf Program, American Forestry Association, P.O. Box 2000, Washington, D.C. 20013; (800) 368-5748.
- Greenbelt Movement, P.O. Box 67545, Nairobi, Kenya.

- The New Forests Project, International Center for Development Policy, 731 Eighth St. SE, Washington, D.C. 20003; (202) 547-3800.
- Worldwatch Institute, 1776 Massachusetts Ave. NW, Washington, D.C. 20036; (202)452-1999. Worldwatch Paper #83, *Reforesting the Earth,* by Sandra Postel and Lori Heise.

Organizations that plant trees:

- Earth Access, see above.
- Friends of Trees, P.O. Box 40851, Portland, OR 97240; (503) 233-8172.
- Global ReLeaf Program, see above. A $5 contribution will plant one tree: (900) 420-4545.
- Greenbelt Movement, see above.
- The New Forests Project, see above.
- Philadelphia Green, The Pennsylvania Horticultural Society, 325 Walnut St., Philadelphia, PA 19106; (215) 625-8280, Ms. Susan Phillips.
- TreePeople, 12601 Mulholland Drive, Beverly Hills, CA 90210; (213) 273-TREE or (818) 753-4600.
- Trees Atlanta, 96 Poplar St. NW, Atlanta, GA 30303; (404) 522-4097.
- Trees for Houston, P.O. Box 13096, Houston, TX 77219-3096; (713) 523-8733.
- Worldwatch Institute, 1776 Massachusetts Ave. NW, Washington, D.C. 20036; (202) 452-1999. World-watch Paper #83, *Reforesting the Earth,* by Sandra Postel and Lori Heise.

Action groups focused on trees include the Rainforest Action Network, 221 Pine St., #500, San Francisco, CA 94104, www. ran.org, and (specially concerned with the redwood forest) Headwaters Action Alliance, www.HeadwatersForest.org.

CREDITS

Biblical passages excerpted from TANAKH: The Holy Scriptures. Copyright © 1985 by The Jewish Publication Society. Used by permission of The Jewish Publication Society.

"Birkat P'ri Ha-eytz/Blessing Over the Fruit of the Tree" and "Birkat Yayin/Blessing Over Wine" by Marcia Falk, from *The Book of Blessings*. Copyright © 1988 by Marcia Lee Falk. Reprinted by permission of the author.

"Delights of the Tu B'Shvat Table" by Gilda Angel, from *Sephardic Holiday Cooking: Recipes and Traditions*. Copyright © 1986 by Gilda Angel. Reprinted by permission of Decalogue Books. For additional information or to obtain a copy of *Sephardic Holiday Cooking: Recipes and Traditions*, contact Decalogue Books, 7 North MacQuesten Parkway, Mount Vernon, NY 10550.

"Food from the Sacred Tree" by Gil Marks, from *The World of Jewish Cooking*, published by Simon and Schuster. Reprinted by permission of Simon & Schuster, Inc. from *The World of Jewish Cooking* by Gil Marks. Copyright © 1996 by Gil Marks.

"From the Wisdom of the Jewish Sages" by Rami Shapiro. Copyright © 1995 by Rabbi Rami Shapiro. Reprinted by permission of Bell Tower, published by Harmony Books, a division of Crown Publishers, Inc.

"The House of the World" by Aryeh Wineman, from *Mystic Tales from the Zohar*, published by The Jewish Publication Society. Copyright © 1997 by Aryeh Wineman. Reprinted by permission of The Jewish Publication Society.

"I and Thou: A Tree" by Martin Buber. Reprinted with the permission of Scribner's, a Division of Simon & Schuster, from *I and Thou* by Martin Buber, translated by Walter Kaufmann. Translation copyright © 1970 by Charles Scribner's Sons.

"Sun-startled Pines,""Ancient Pines," and "Untitled" by Zola. "I Know Nothing" by Malka Heifetz Tussman, translated by Marcia Falk from *Selected Poems of Malka Heifetz Tussman*, published by Wayne State University Press. Reprinted by permission.

"Is the Tree Human?" by Eilon Schwartz, previously published as "Bal Tashhit: Thickly Describing a Jewish Environmental Precept" in *Environmental Ethics*. Reprinted by permission of the author and publisher.

"Israel: Orchard and Vineyard of God" by Howard Eilberg-Schwartz, from *The Savage in Judaism*, published by Indiana University Press. Reprinted by permission of the author and publisher.

"Midrash on Trees" from *The Book of Legends Sefer Ha-Aggadah: Legends from the Talmud and Midrash* by Hayim Nahman Bialik and Yehoshua Hana Ravnitzky. English translation copyright © 1992 by Schocken Books, Inc. Reprinted by permission of Schocken Books, distributed by Pantheon Books, a division of Random House, Inc.

458

"The New Year of the Trees" by Marge Piercy, from *Available Light*. Copyright © 1988 by Middlemarsh Inc. Reprinted by permission of Alfred A. Knopf, Inc.

"Shir LaShkeydiya" by Tova Shimon. Used by permission of the author.

"The Souls of Trees" by Howard Schwartz, from *Gabriel's Palace: Jewish Mystical Tales* by Howard Schwartz. Copyright © 1994 by Howard Schwartz. Used by permission of Oxford University Press, Inc.

"Thou Shalt Not Destroy" by Norman Lamm from *Faith and Doubt*, published by Ktav. Copyright © 1971. Reprinted by permission of the author and publisher.

"The Trees of Eden in the Kabbalah" from *The Messianic Idea in Judaism* by Gershom Scholem. Copyright © 1971 by Schocken Books. Reprinted by permission of Schocken Books, a division of Random House, Inc.

"Trees for Life" by Ismar Schorsch, published by *The Melton Journal*. Reprinted by permission of the author.

Every effort has been made to contact the copyright holders for the works which appear herein. If any omissions are brought to our attention we will correct them in our next printing.

NOTES

Part II

Howard Eilberg-Schwartz, "Israel: The Orchard and Vineyard of God"

* Excerpted from *The Savage in Judaism* (Indiana University Press).

[1] Asaph Goor and Max Nurock directed my attention to this source. Goor and Nurock, *The Fruits of the Holy Land* (Jerusalem: Israel Universities Press, 1968).

[2] E.g., Onkelos ad loc.; S. R. Driver, *The Book of Leviticus* (New York: Dodd, Mead, 1898), p. 89; D. Hoffman, *Das Buch Leviticus*, vol. 2 (Berlin: Poppelauer, 1906), pp. 251–54; J. R. Porter, *Leviticus* (Cambridge: Cambridge University Press, 1976), pp. 156–57; J. H. Hertz, *The Pentateuch and Haftorahs* (London: Soncino, 1961 [1935]), p. 503; and Martin Noth, *Leviticus*, rev. ed. (Philadelphia: Westminster Press, 1977), p. 143.

[3] Porter, *Leviticus*, p. 157

[4] Hertz, following Dillman, *Pentateuch*, p. 503; Gordon J. Wenham, *The Book of Leviticus* (Grand Rapids: William B. Eerdmans, 1979), p. 271.

[5] JPS, *The Torah* (Philadelphia: Jewish Publication Society, 1962), p. 217; Herbert G. May and Bruce Metzger, eds. *The New Oxford Annotated Bible*, Revised Standard Version (New York: Oxford University Press, 1971), p. 147; Hertz, *Pentateuch*, p. 503; Porter, *Leviticus*, p. 156.

[6] E.g., dates, figs, olives, grapes, pomegranates, almonds; see Deut. 8:8, Num. 13:23, Judg. 9:10–13.

[7] Wilson Popenoe, *The Date Palm* (Miami: Field Research Projects, 1920), p. 212; Thomas H. Everett, *The New York Botanical Garden Illustrated Encyclopedia of Horticulture*, vol. 3 (New York:

Garland Publishing, 1981), p. 1016; Horticultural Crops Group, *Date Production and Protection: With Special Reference to North Africa and the Near East* (Rome: Food and Agricultural Organization of the United Nations, 1982), p. 35.

[8] William H. Chandler, *Evergreen Orchards* (Philadelphia: Lea and Febiger, 1950), p. 368.

[9] Jules Janick and James N. Moore, *Advances in Fruit Breeding* (West Lafayette: Purdue University Press, 1975), p. 576; Ira J. Condit, *The Fig* (Waltham, MA: Chronica Botanica, 1947), p. 24.

[10] Alan E. Simmons, *Growing Unusual Fruit* (New York: Walker, 1972), p. 284.

[11] Janick and Moore, *Advances*, pp. 138, 396.

[12] Popenoe, *Date Palm*, p. 7; Wenham, *Leviticus*, p. 271.

[13] George A. Buttrick, ed., *The Interpreter's Bible*, vol. 2 (New York: Abingdon, 1953), pp. 298–99.

[14] Victor R. Gardner, F. C. Bradford, and H. D. Hooder, *Fundamentals of Fruit Production* (New York: McGraw Hill, 1952), p. 564.

[15] Popenoe, *Date Palm*, p. 211.

[16] Simmons, *Growing*, p. 127.

[17] Philo, *Questions and Answers on Genesis*, tr. Ralph Marcus (Cambridge: Harvard University Press, 1971), 3:50, p. 251.

[18] The sages were also alive to the way in which animals served as metaphorical human beings in Israelite literature. In this respect, the rabbis were less alienated from the symbolic language of Israelite religion than are its modern interpreters.

[19] I am following John Bright's translation, which interprets *belahemo* as "in its sap." *Jeremiah, The Anchor Bible Commentary* (Garden City, NY: Doubleday, 1965), p. 84.

[20] On the importance of metaphor in structuring conceptual domains, see George Lakoff and Mark Johnson, *Metaphors We Live By* (Chicago: University of Chicago Press, 1980).

[21] Goor and Nurock, *Fruits.*

Part III

Mishnah and Gemara on Tu B'Shvat

[1] B. *Rosh Hashanah* 15b, Moed IV, p. 56, I. Epstein, et al., ed. and trans., *The Babylonian Talmud* (London: Soncino Press, 1935–1952).

Hayim Nachman Bailik and Yehoshua Ravnitzky, Midrash from *The Book of Legends, Sefer Aggadah*

[1] The usual word for "tree" is *etz*. Hence *siah*, used instead, is construed in a dual sense: "tree" and "converse, provide fellowship."

[2] Hayim Nahman Bialik and Yehoshua Hana Ravnitzky, eds., *The Book of Legends (Sefer Ha-Aggadah). Legends from the Talmud and Midrash*, trans. William G. Braude (New York: Schocken Books, 1992 [1908–1911]), p. 11.

[3] Ibid., p. 586.

[4] Ibid., p. 586.

[5] Ibid., pp. 594–95.

[6] Ibid., p. 773.

[7] Ibid., p. 773.

[8] Ibid., p. 773.

Joyce Galaski, "Shemonah Esrei for the New Year of the Trees"

[1] This poem was discovered in the Geniza manuscripts by the scholar Menahem Zulay, who published it in the article *"Rav Yehuda Halevi she-ayno Rav Yehuda Halevi"* in *Eretz Yisrael*, vol. 4, (Jerusalem: *Hachevra L'chakira Eretz Yisrael V'atikutecha*, 1956), pp. 138–144. The manuscript is at Oxford (Heb.e.33/Catalogue Cowley-Neubauer no. 2737B).

[2] See Menahem Zulay, *"Rav Yehuda,"* p. 138.

[3] Although it is still called *Shemonah Esrei*, meaning "Eighteen," the weekday *Amidah* we use today has nineteen sections. It is based on the liturgy developed by the Babylonian community. The weekday *Amidah* used in *Eretz Yisrael* in the tenth and eleventh centuries had eighteen sections. The difference is that the fourteenth and fifteenth sections in the Babylonian rite were a single section in the Palestine rite.

[4] In the manuscript, the words *Rosh shanah la-ilan* do not constitute a separate line but are written to the right of the poem, preceding its third line.

[5] The one exception is the ninth verse which begins with the word *tif*, meaning "drop of water," which in this context I have translated as "rain."

[6] I would like to thank Jeremy Schwartz, Ari Elon, and Dr. Joel Hecker for their assistance with the translation. I also made extensive use of the notes on the poem by Menahem Zulay in his article in *Eretz Yisrael* (see above) and of the notes by Yom Tov Levinsky in *Sefer ha-moadim*, vol. 5 (Tel Aviv: Dvir Co., Ltd., 1966), p. 328.

[7] The citations for the biblical quotations that comprise the fifth line of each stanza are as follows, listed in order by the number of the stanza: (1) Ps. 84:12, (2) Prov. 8:35, (3) Isa. 12:6, (4) Prov. 2:6, (5) Jer. 33:11, (6) Jer. 50:20, (7) Jer. 31:11, (8) Jer. 30:17, (9) Ps. 37:22, (10) Zech. 10:8, (11) Isa. 33:22, (12) Ps. 37:20, (13) Isa. 60:9, (14) Ps. 102:17, (15) Ps. 69:34, (16) Ps. 149:4, (17) Ps. 147:1, (18) Jer. 14:13.

[8] *Sharah may-rosin Amanah* ("the one who gazes from the peak of Amanah") is a reference to the woman in Song of Songs. (See Song of Songs 4:8.) Since in the rabbinic interpretation of Song of Songs she represents Israel, this phrase is a metaphor for the people of Israel. The use of the word *hader* at the beginning of this line may be a play on words; in Hebrew, it means "adorn," but it is very close to the Aramaic word meaning "return," which, of course, is the theme of this stanza.

[9] The Hebrew phrase *mi manah* is also a biblical phrase used to represent Israel. It literally means "who can count," but I translated it as "the seed of Jacob" since it refers to Numbers 23:10, *"Mi manah afar Yaakov?"* "Who can count the dust of Jacob?" (i.e., the seed of Jacob).

Eilon Schwartz, "Is the Tree Human?"

[1] Although the term "rabbinic" has a more generic usage, in the context of this paper it refers to the individuals who wrote and codified the *Mishnah* and *Talmud*. The *Mishnah* is the name of the earliest major rabbinic work, first appearing toward the turn of the third century C.E. It is the core document of the talmudic tradition, composed in very terse language and arranged topic by topic over a wide range of subjects. The Talmud primarily refers to the *Mishnah* combined with its later rabbinic commentaries, the *Gemara*. The earliest one is the Jerusalem, or Palestinian Talmud, dating from the first half of the fifth century. Some two centuries later the Babylonian Talmud was compiled. All talmudic references in this paper are to the Babylonian Talmud.

2 For a survey of the contemporary debate on the relationship of Judaism to the environment, and the theological/moral issues which are at the root of such a relationship, see Eilon Schwartz, "Judaism and Nature: Theological and Moral Issues to Consider While Renegotiating a Jewish Relationship to Nature," *Judaism*, 44 (Fall 1995), pp. 437–447.

3 The *halacha* is the set of rules, often known as "Jewish law," that governs Jewish life. The *halacha*, however, contains far more than what is usually suggested by the term "law," as is demonstrated in the paper.

4 The author would like to thank most deeply Ms. Michal Smart, with whom he originally explored these texts.

5 R. Solomon b. Isaac [RaShI] (1040–1150). Perhaps the most influential biblical and talmudic exegete. France.

6 Shmuel ben Meir, commentary on Deut. 20:19, in *Torat Chaim* (Jerusalem: Hotzaat Mosad HaRav Kook, 1993). Rashi's grandson. One of the *Tosafists, halachic* commentators on the Talmud in twelfth- to fourteenth-century France and Germany.

7 Nahmanides, commentary on Deut. 20:19, in *Torat Chaim*. Spanish.

8 Ibid.

9 All quotes from the *Mishnah* and the Talmud are taken from the Soncino translation, unless otherwise cited.

10 I have here changed parts of the Soncino translation, translating similar to Adin Steinsaltz in his Hebrew translation of the Talmud.

11 *Tannaim* refer to the generation of rabbis who were the authors of the *Mishnah; Amoraim* to the subsequent generations who authored the *Gemara*, the commentary on the *Mishnah*. Together they make up the Talmud.

12 Moses Maimonides, *Judges, Mishnah Torah* [Hebrew] (Jerusalem: Hotzat Mossad HaRav Kook, 1962), Laws of Kings 6:10. Perhaps the most influential Jewish philosopher ever.

13 Moses Maimonides, *Judges, Mishnah Torah*, Laws of Mourning 14:24.

14 Maimonides, *Mishnah Torah*, "The Book of Judges," Kings 6:8–10.

15 Scholars whose efforts were concentrated on determining the *halacha* in practice.

16 Tosefot Baba Metzia 32b.

17 Judah he-Hasid? *Sefer Ha Chasidim* (Jerusalem: Aharon Block, 1992), no. 339.

18 Ovadiah Yosef, *Yabiah Omer* (Jerusalem, 1993), part 4, *Even HaEzer*, no. 9. Former Sephardi Chief Rabbi of Israel.

19 Ovadiah Yosef, *Yabiah Omer*, part 3, *Yoreh Deah*, no. 18.

20 Shabbat 105b.

21 Abraham Isaac HaCohen Kook, *Mishpat Cohen* (Jerusalem: HaAguda L'Hotzaat Sifrei HaRav Kook, 1937), no. 21. Zionist leader. First Askenazi Chief Rabbi of Palestine.

22 Moses Maimonides, *Responsa* (Hebrew), trans. Jehoshua Blau (Jerusalem: Mekize Nirdamim, 1958), no. 112.

23 Judah B. Samuel Rosannes, *Mishneh la-Melekh*, commentary on Maimonides, *Mishnah Torah*, Isurei Mizbeah, 7:3 as it appears in *Baal Tashchit, Encyclopedia Talmudit* (Jerusalem: Hotzaat Encyclopedia Talmudit, 1973). Turkish Rabbi.

24 Baruch Baandit Wiesel, Makor Baruch as cited in Meir Ayele, *The Fear of Chopping Down Fruit Trees in the Responsa Literature in Tura: Studies in Jewish Thought* (Tel Aviv: Kibbutz HaMeuchad, 1989), p. 138.

[25] Naphtali Zevi Judah Berlin, *Meshiv Davar* (Jerusalem, 1993), Chap. 2, no. 56.

[26] Yaakov Tzvi from Kalenburg, *HaKatav v'HaKabalah* (Nuremburg, 1924), Deut. 20:19.

[27] Jonah ben Abraham Gerondi, *Sefer Sha'arei Teshuva* (Jerusalem, 1960), Chap. 3, no. 82. Spanish rabbi and moralist.

[28] Menahem Azariah Da Fano, Responsa, 129 as quoted in Meir Zichal, *Environmental Protection in Jewish Sources* [Hebrew] (Ramat Gan: The Responsa Project, 1989), p. 31. Italian rabbi and kabbalist.

[29] Ephraim Weinberger, *Yad Ephraim* (Tel Aviv: HaVaad HaTziburi LiHotzaat Kitvei HaRav Weinberger, 1976), no. 14. Member of Tel Aviv rabbinic council.

[30] Jacob Reischer, *Shevut Yaakov* (Jerusalem, 1972), part 3, no. 71.

[31] Shneur Zalman of Lyady, "Laws of Protecting the Body and the Spirit and Bal Tashchit," *Shulhan Arukh of the Rav* (New York: Kehot Publication Society, 1975), 31:b. Founder of Habad Hasidism.

[32] *Sefer Hachinuch: The Book of Education* (New York: Feldheim Publishers, 1989), no. 529.

[33] Zevi Ashkenazi, Haham Zevi, as quoted in Zichal, Environmental Protection in Jewish Sources, p. 9.

[34] Jacob Reischer, *Shevut Yaakov* (Jerusalem, 1972), part 1, no. 159.

[35] Jair Hayyim Bacharach, *Havvot Yair* (Jerusalem, 1968), no. 195. German talmudic scholar.

[36] Jacob Ettlinger, *Binyan Zion* (Jerusalem: Davar Jerusalem, 1989), no. 61.

[37] Moses Sofer, *Responsa of Hatam Sofer* [Hebrew] (Jerusalem: Hotzaat Hod, 1972), *Yoreh Deah*, no. 102.

[38] Ovadia Yosef, *Yabia Omer* (Jerusalem, 1969), vol. 5, *Yoreh Deah*, no. 12.

[39] Pinhas Hai Anu from Ferrara, *Givat Pinhas*, part 8, no. 2 as it appears in Meir Ayele, *"Givat Pinhas": The Responsa of R. Pinhas Hai ben Menahem Anau of Ferrara* in *Tarbitz*, 53, no. 2 (January–March, 1984). Northern Italian rabbi.

[40] Yaakov ben Rabbi Shmuel from Tzoyemer, *Beit Yaakov* (Diehernport, 1696), no. 140.

[41] Naphtali Zevi Judah Berlin, *Meshiv Davar* (Jerusalem, 1993), Chap. 2, no. 56.

[42] Tosefot on Pesachim 50b.

[43] Greenwald, *Keren LeDavid* (Satmar, 1928), *Orech Chaim*, no. 30. Hungarian rabbi.

[44] Joseph Karo, *Avatak Rochel* (Leipzig, 1859), no. 18. Author of the *Shulkhan Arukh*, the authoritative code of Jewish law.

[45] Abraham Isaac Kook, *Daat Kohen* (Jerusalem: Mossad Harav Kook, 1969), *Yoreh Deah*, no. 122.

[46] Tzvi Pesach Frank, *Har Tzvi* (Jerusalem: Machon Harav Frank, 1973), *Orech Chaim* 2, no. 102; *Noda Yehuda, Yoreh Deah*, no. 10.

[47] Lev. 25:23.

[48] It is quite significant that trees are a central metaphor in Judaism. As one example, the Torah, those parts of the Bible traditionally revealed directly to Moses on Mount Sinai, is called "a tree of life." Trees played a central role in the economic life in the ancient land of Israel and were thus proper metaphors for bridging between the socioeconomic life and the theological-moral one.

[49] Michael Rosenak, *"Roads to the Palace": Jewish Texts and Teaching* (Providence: Berghahn Books, 1995), p. 5.

[50] Moshe Silberg, "Laws and Morals in Jewish Jurisprudence," in *Harvard Law Review* 75 (1961–1962), pp. 306–31.

[51] Mary Midgeley, "The Mixed Community" in Eugene Hargrove, *The Animal Rights/Environmental Ethics Debate* (Albany: The State University of New York Press, 1992), pp. 211–225.

[52] J. Baird Callicott, "Animal Liberation and Environmental Ethics: Back Together Again," in Callicott, *In Defense of the Land Ethic: Essays in Environmental Philosophy* (Albany: State University of New York Press, 1989), pp. 49–51.

[53] Paralleling the discussion of *bal tashchit* is the rabbinic precept of *tzaar baalei chaim,* describing duties toward prevention of animal suffering.

[54] See Avner de-Shalit, *Why Posterity Matters: Environmental Policies and Future Generations* (London: Routledge, 1995).

[55] This is perhaps the major point of Max Oelschlaeger, *Caring for Creation: An Ecumenical Approach to the Environmental Crisis* (New Haven: Yale University Press, 1994).

Norman Lamm, "Thou Shalt Not Destroy"

[1] Sefer Ha-hinnukh, No. 529.

[2] R. Yaakov Zvi Meklenburg, *Ha-Ketav Ve'ha-Kabbalah* to Deut. 20:19. He interprets the phrase *ki ha-adam etz ha-sadeh,* etc., not as above ("For is the tree of the field man that it should be besieged of thee?"), but as: "For as man, so is the tree of the field when it is besieged of thee," i.e., just as the enemy who has surrendered and is willing to pay tribute must not be destroyed, so the fruit tree which gives you tribute (fruit) must not be cut down.

[3] See Rashi *ad loc.*

[4] Commentary to the Mishnah, Introd. to *Seder Zera'im.*

[5] *B.B.* 26a; *B.K.* 96b; *Mak.* 22a; Maimonides, *Hil. Malakhim* 6:8.

[6] *Loc. cit., 9.*

[7] Commentary to *B.K.* 91b.

[8] Commentary on the Torah, to Deut. 20:20; supplement to Commentary on Maimonides' *Sefer Ha-mitzvot,* Pos. Com. no. 6.

[9] Indeed, Nahmanides (ibid.) appears to permit this, too, considering it necessary destruction and hence justifiable, the prohibition is limited to unnecessary and pointless devastation.

[10] Maimonides, *loc. cit.*

[11] Maimonides, *loc. cit.,* Apparently this passage implies that destruction of material other than fruit trees entails a rabbinic violation, and so did most commentators read Maimonides. Earlier, however, in his *Sefer ha-Mitzvot,* Maimonides held that other objects were equally included in the biblical proscription. Others, too, hold that all objects are included in the biblical commandment, so *SeMaG, Sefer Yere'im,* and apparently *Sefer Ha-hinnukh. Minhat Hinnukh,* however, reads this passage in Maimonides to mean that *all* objects are covered by the biblical prohibition, but whereas the destruction of fruit trees takes flogging as a biblically prescribed penalty, because it is explicit, the ruining of other objects is forbidden by biblical law, but no punishment declared for it. Such punishment (flogging) is, however, ordained by rabbinic decree.

[12] S.v. *ve'lo yashkeh; Sh. A. Harav, Hil. Shemirat Guf Va'nefesh* 14.

[13] Maimonides, *loc. cit.*

[14] Tzemach Tzeddek, cited in Pahad Yitzhak on Bal Tashhit.

[15] Turei Zahav to SH.A.Y.D. 116:6.

[16] Responsa *Havot Yair,* no. 195.

[17] The reason given is not the usual one, namely, that danger to life cancels out most other obligations. Such a rationale would limit the dispensation to severe illness entailing danger to life. Rather, the Talmud reasons that *bal tashhit* applies to one's body as well as to one's possessions, indeed more so, and, therefore, it is preferable to harm a tree than one's health. This reasoning is not limited to critical illness.

[18] *SeMaG,* Neg. Com. 229.

[19] *Supra,* n. 16.

[20] *Ibid.* The source for this is *B.B.* 25b. Cf. Maimonides, *loc. cit.* 6:9.

[21] *Supra,* n. 28.

[22] Hazon Ish to Maimonides, Hil. Melakhim 6:8.

[23] *Sh. A. Harav, loc. cit.* However, a problem is posed by the commentary of R. Asher to *Middot* 1:2 (and *Tamid,* chap. I, end) who says that destruction of property countenanced by the law for disciplinary purposes is not in violation of *bal tashhit* because of the principle that the courts declare such property ownerless *(hefker bet din hefker).* This implies the reverse of the ruling of *Sh. A. Harav.* But see Responsa *Noda Bi'Yehudah,* II, *Y.D.* 10; and appendix to Responsa *Devar Avraham,* Part I.

[24] *Supra,* n.21.

[25] *Sefer Hasidim, Tzavaot R. Yehudah Ne-hasid,* 45, and gloss of R. Reuven Margoliot.

Part IV

Gershom Scholem, "The Trees of Eden in the Kabbalah"

*Excerpted from *The Messianic Idea in Judaism* (Schocken Books).

[1] On this subject, cf. G. G. Scholem, *Von der mystischen Gestalt der Gottheit* (Zurich, 1962), chpt. 2: "Gut und Böse in der Kabbala."

[2] Tractate *Avot* VI, 2.

[3] Cf. the passages dealing with Israel at Sinai and with the first tablets in *Be'ikvot Mashiah,* pp. 93 and 100.

[4] Magen Abraham, pp. 134–35.

[5] The ideas are stressed in *Zemir Aritzim* and in other of Nathan's writings, especially in the *Sefer ha-Beriya* and in the *Drush Raza de-Malka.* Cf. also Scholem, *Sabbatai Zevi,* II, 695.

Aryeh Wineman, "The House of the World"

[1] Or Lamp of Darkness. On this term, see Moses De Leon, Elliot Wolfson, ed., *Book of the Pomegranate* (Atlanta: Scholars Press, 1987), 81, no. 29; Daniel Matt, *Zohar: The Book of Enlightenment* (New York: Paulist Press, 1983), pp. 207–8, 297; and Yehuda Leibes, *Perakim be-millon sefer hazohar,* Ph.D. dissertation, Hebrew University, 1977, pp. 146–51; 161–64; 327–31. In an ultimate sense, only this Supernal Spark exists; the existence of everything below it, including the *Sefirot,* is dependent on this Spark.

[2] One million.

[3] Based on the identification of Satan with both the evil inclination and the Angel of Death; *Baba Batra* 16a.

[4] Zohar 2:103a, 186b; Tishby, *Mishnat hazohar (The Wisdom of the Zohar),* trans. David Goldstein (Oxford: Oxford University Press, published for the Littman Library, 1989) vol. 2, p. 521.

[5] Mircea Eliade, *Myths, Rites, Symbols: A Mircea Eliade Reader*. ed. Wendell C. Beane and William G. Doty, 2 vols. (New York: Harper and Row, 1976), vol. 2, p. 381.

[6] Heinrich Zimmer, *Myths and Symbols in Indian Art and Civilization* (Princeton: Princeton University Press, 1946), p. 35.

[7] Ibid., p. 45.

[8] Juan Eduardo Cirlot, *A Dictionary of Symbols* (London: Routledge and Kegan Paul, 1962), p. 328.

[9] Ibid.

[10] Ibid., p. 331.

[11] Eugene Goblet, *The Migration of Symbols* (New York: University Books, 1956), pp. 140–54.

[12] Ibid., p. 155.

[13] Ibid. p. 169.

[14] Ibid., p. 171.

[15] *Sefer habahir*, ed. Reuben Margaliot (Jerusalem, 1951), p. 119.

[16] Ibid., p. 23.

[17] See also Margaliot, *Sefer habahir*, p. 6.

[18] Ibid., p. 22.

[19] Ibid., pp. 95 and 119; note also the analogy from English literature cited in Northrop Frye, *Anatomy of Criticism* (Princeton: Princeton University Press, 1957), p. 144.

[20] Gershom Scholem, *Major Trends in Jewish Mysticism* (New York: Schocken, 1946), p. 124.

[21] Echoing Margoliot, *Sefer habahir*, pp. 95 and 98.

[22] For a detailed survey of the tree as kabbalistic symbol, see Leibes, *Perakim bemillon sefer hazohar*, pp. 107–33.

Pinchas Giller, "The World Trees in the Zohar"

* For Ronni. My thanks to Naomi Gold and Jennifer Sylvor for their suggestions. All references to the Zohar literature refer to the Jerusalem editions edited by Reuven Margaliot (Mossad HaRav Kook, 1978); the abbreviations Z I, II, III refer to the main section of the Zohar. Other sections of the Zohar include the later compositions *Tiqqunei ha-Zohar* and *Ra'aya Meheimna,* as well as *Zohar Hadash,* an anthology of early compositions.

[1] William James, *The Varieties of Religious Experience* (New York: Modern Library, 1985), p. 400.

[2] See, in particular, Maimonides' *Guide for the Perplexed,* 1:46–70.

[3] Ḥemdat Yamim (Istanbul, 1735) 2: 108d-109a.

[4] *Zohar* I 220b, III 24a.

[5] *Zohar* II 108b.

[6] *Zohar* II 15b–16a, III 216a.

[7] *Zohar* I 264b, II 223b; *Tiqqunei ha-Zohar* 102b.

[8] *Zohar* I 15b–16a, II 186b, III 24a; *Tiqqunei ha-Zohar* 60a.

[9] *Zohar* III 202a.

[10] Tiqqunei ha-Zohar 82b.

[11] Ra'aya Meheimna III, 252a.

[12] *Tiqqunei ha-Zohar* 87a; cf. *Avot* 3:22.

[13] Jacob Zvi Yellish, *Kehillat Ya'aquov* (Lemburg, 1870), 26a–b.

[14] Two broad assessments of the phenomenon of the world tree are Gerhart B. Ladner, "Medieval and Modern Understanding of Symbolism: A Comparison" *Speculum* 54: 223–57; and David Bynum, *The Daemon in the Wood* (Cambridge: Harvard Press, 1978).

[15] Zohar I 35a, *Tiqqunei Zohar Hadash* 106c.

[16] See Pinchas Giller, *The Enlightened Will Shine: Symbolization and Theurgy in the Later Strata of the Zohar* (Albany: State University of New York Press, 1993), pp. 40–43.

[17] *Zohar* I 35a, III 239a-b.

[18] *Tiqqunei ha-Zohar* 34b, 87b, 98a.

[19] Zohar I 193a; *Tiqqunei ha-Zohar* 87b, 141b; Ra'aya Meheimna III 274b; 255a.

[20] *Tiqqunei Zohar Hadash* 106c; *Ra'aya Meheimna* III 124b.

[21] *Zohar* I 35a; *Ra'aya Meheimna* III 124b.

[22] Zohar I (*Tiqqunei ha-Zohar*) 27a, 36a, III 283a.

[23] *Zohar* I 35a; *Tiqqunei ha-Zohar* 27b, 93a, 94a, 97b.

[24] *Tiqqunei ha-Zohar* 87b, 93b, 98a, 141b, *Tiqqunei Zohar Hadash* 107a; *Ra'aya Meheimna* III 247a.

[25] *Zohar* I 33a.

[26] Tiqqunei ha-Zohar 97a.

[27] See in particular *Zohar* I (*Tiqqunei ha-Zohar*) 26b; *Ra'aya Meheimmna* II 118b-119a, III 98a–b, 124a–125a, 153a, 252b–253a, 255a; *Tiqqunei Zohar Hadash* 106c, 107a. See also Gershom Scholem, *On the Kabbalah and Its Symbolism* (New York: Schocken Books, 1996), pp. 79, 109; *Sabbatai Sevi*, pp. 11, 809, 811, 818; Amos Goldreich, "Iberian Dialect in an Unknown Fragment from the Author of *Tiqqunei ha-Zohar*" (Hebrew) in *The Zohar and Its Generation: Jerusalem Studies in Jewish Thought* 8, ed. Joseph Dan, (Jerusalem: Magnes, 1989), 96n.

[28] Ra'aya Meheimna 98a–b.

[29] Tiqqunei ha-Zohar 141b.

[30] Yellish, Kehillat Ya'aqov, 26b.

[31] Zohar I (Tiqqunei ha-Zohar) 26a, Tiqqunei ha-Zohar 141b.

[32] *Ra'aya Meheimna* III 124b, 153b; *Tiqqunei ha-Zohar* 128b. See Yehudah Liebes, *Some Chapters in a Zohar Lexicon* (Hebrew) (Ph.D. dissertation, Hebrew University, 1976 (Jerusalem: Hebrew University, 1982), p. 118; Giller, *The Enlightened Will Shine*, pp. 26–27.

"Peri Eitz Hadar," translated by Miles Krassen

[1] The section on Tu B'Shvat appears in *Ḥemdat Yamim*, part 2, *Rosh Hodesh Shovavim*, chap. 3; Tu B'Shvat. Some of the more important differences involve *kavvanot* and the number of cups of wine.

[2] For a discussion of authorship, dating, and sources of the *Ḥemdat Yamim*, see Isaiah Tishby's Hebrew articles, reprinted in *Paths of Faith and Heresy* (Jerusalem, 1982).

[3] See, for example, the reference to a fuller explanation of the thirty-two teeth and the name *Elohim* which the author claims to have presented in the previous chapter on *tikkun ha-se'udah*. Neither the explanation nor this *tikkun* appears in the previous chapter of *Ḥemdat Yamim*.

[4] See Friedberg, *Beyt 'Eqed Sefarim*, vol. 3, p. 851, no. 777.

[5] See the volume in the series *Sefarim Qedoshim, Seder Hamishah Asar be-Shevet ve Hamishah Asar be-Av* (Brooklyn, 1990). This anthology contains material on Tu B'Shvat, which has been gathered from seventy works, many of which are hasidic. It also contains the full text

of the *Peri 'Eitz Hadar*, despite the fact that it is not mentioned in any of the Eastern European sources.

[6] Only two cups are mentioned in the *Peri Eitz Hadar* text.

[7] The modern reader, unfamiliar with the Zohar and its outlook, is referred to Daniel Matt's introduction and translation: *Zohar: The Book of Enlightenment* (Paulist Press: New York, 1983).

[8] For an interesting discussion of the differences between such traditional and modern conceptions of nature, see Seyyed Hossein Nasr, *Man and Nature: The Spiritual Crisis in Modern Man* (London: 1988). Much of Nasr's account of Christian and Islamic cosmology applies to the view of nature that is found in the Zohar.

[9] For an account of the Lurianic theory of evil, see Isaiah Tishby's Hebrew work, *The Doctrine of Evil and the 'Kelippah' in Lurianic Kabbalism* (Jerusalem: 1984). The English reader should see Joseph Dan's article, "'No Evil Descends from Heaven: Sixteenth-Century Jewish Concepts of Evil," in Bernard Dov Cooperman, ed., *Jewish Thought in the Sixteenth Century* (Cambridge: Harvard University Press, 1983).

[10] The tenth *sefirah* is typically characterized as a female divine aspect.

[11] The examples found in medieval kabbalistic texts are decidedly anthropocentric. However, a more contemporary expression of kabbalistic symbolism might be extended to view all natural phenomena that threaten the ecosystem as symbols of the forces of evil, whereas those that maintain the ecosystem might be equated with holiness.

[12] This notion of the *kelippot* as *shomer* (guardian) is discussed in detail by Isaiah Horowitz in his classic work, *Sheney Luhot ha-Berit* (Amsterdam: 1648). See my *Isaiah Horowitz: Toledot Adam (The Generations of Adam)* in the Classics of Western Spirituality Series (Mahwah, NJ: Paulist Press, 1996).

[13] While a comprehensive study of *kavvanot* remains to be written, a useful introduction to the subject is provided by Daniel Matt's article, "The Mystic and the *Mizwot*," in Arthur Green, ed., *Jewish Spirituality: From the Bible through the Middle Ages* (New York: pub 1986). A detailed presentation of Lurianic *kavvanot* can be found the several volumes of Yehiel Abraham Barlev's *Sefer Yedid Nefesh* (New York: Crossroads Publishing Company, 1988).

[14] For a discussion of the Lurianic creation myth and its implications for spiritual practice, see Lawrence Fine's, "The Contemplative Practice of *Yihudim* in Lurianic Kabbalah," in Arthur Green, ed., *Jewish Spirituality: From the Sixteenth-Century Revival to the Present* (New York: Crossroads Publishing Company, 1987)

[15] See Louis Jacobs' articles, "The Uplifting of Sparks in Later Jewish Mysticism," in Green, ed., op. cit., and "Eating as an Act of Worship in Hasidic Thought," in *Studies in Jewish Intellectual History: Presented to Alexander Altmann on the Occasion of his Seventieth Birthday* (Alabama: University of Alabama Press, 1979).

[16] On the importance of the *sefirah Yesod* as divine phallus in Kabbalah, see Elliot R. Wolfson, *Through a Speculum That Shines* (Princeton: Princeton University Press, 1994).

[17] The period consists of the six weeks during which the first six portions of the book of Exodus are read in the synagogue.

[18] The six weeks during which the first six portions of the book of Exodus are read are considered a period of repentance. This is suggested by the fact that the first letter of the Hebrew name for each of these six portions spells *shovavim*, "wayward," which alludes to the verse, "Return wayward children." (Jer. 3:14).

[19] According to Zoharic Kabbalah, earthly acts that are performed with theurgic intention may positively affect the ten inner aspects of the Godhead called *sefirot*. In this case, the re-

ligious acts concerning fruit that are performed on the 15th of Shvat are said to effect the ninth *sefirah, Yesod,* or "foundation." The *sefirah* represents the male generative principle within the divine world called *Tzaddik,* or "righteous one." This *sefirah* is often anthropomorphically represented as a phallus.

20 Zohar, v. 1, 33a. Also see Zohar, v. 3, p. 87a. The meaning is that the production of fruit depends on the union of both male and female elements. Although the female tree bears the fruit, it depends on the male for fertilization.

21 Gen. 1:11

22 I.e., the tenth *sefirah, Malkhut,* which is female.

23 I.e., the ninth *sefirah, Yesod,* the male.

24 *Tamim* in Hebrew.

25 The term *tikkun* has two primary connotations. First, it refers to an act of rectification in which some aspect of the damaged cosmos is restored to its desired state. However, it may also mean an act of preparation in which specific cosmic aspect is made ready for some subsequent development or process. In either case, the implication here is that the custom of celebrating the Fifteenth of Shvat through eating and praising fruit has a powerful theurgic effect. The male and female *sefirot, Yesod and Malkhut,* that are responsible for releasing divine abundance into the world are positively effected. The ultimate desired result is the production of fine *etrogim,* the *peri eitz hadar,* which are required for the observance of Sukkot, during the following fall.

26 It rectifies and energizes *Yesod* above and results in abundance in nature below.

27 *J. Kiddushin,* 48b. The text in *Peri Eitz Hadar* is garbled here.

28 Ps. 34:3.

29 Each year a special blessing is said whenever a fruit is eaten for the first time.

30 See *B. Berakhot* 35b.

31 I.e., Rabbi Hanina bar Papa in the passage from *Berakhot* 35b associates enjoying something from this world without a blessing with robbing one's father and mother.

32 The mystical or theurgic intention that is contemplated when one utters the blessing.

33 Jer. 51:44.

34 Job 20:15.

35 In the teaching cited from *B. Berakhot* 35b, the father is identified as the Blessed Holy One and the mother is the Community of Israel. Thus the kabbalistic meaning would seem to allude to sparks pertaining to *Tiferet* and *Malkhut* or to the *partzufim, Ze'ir 'Anpin* and *Nuqba.*

36 Pro. 28:24.

37 Deut. 8:3.

38 The blessing prevents the divine sparks in the food from being appropriated by the evil forces and recycles them to the forces of holiness.

39 The divine name *Elohim* appears thirty-two times in the first section of Genesis that details the stages of Creation. The thirty-two teeth which chew the food that has been blessed and return the divine sparks to holiness correspond to these thirty-two divine names. Thus they are alluded to by the "mouth of the Lord," mentioned in Deut. 8:3.

40 This is not found in the previous chapter of *Ḥemdat Yamim.* Location of this *tikkun* would aid in identifying the source of *Peri Eitz Hadar.*

41 Eccle. 7:14.

[42] I.e., their nature alludes to some characteristic of the divine world of the *sefirot*.

[43] Or, "were all compounded in one compounding."

[44] Zohar, *Shemot*, 15b.

[45] I.e., the *sefirot*.

[46] Song of Songs, 6:11.

[47] The tenth *sefirah*, *Malkhut*. It is often called *Shekhinah*, the divine presence.

[48] The chariot is described in Ezekiel's vision. It is located under the tenth *sefirah*.

[49] Zohar, ibid.

[50] Literally, "impurity." Here, the meaning is "forces of evil," represented by the *kelippot* (shells).

[51] The cosmology assumed by the author consists of four worlds that are hierarchically arranged between the divine source, which is completely holy, and the forces of evil, which are completely impure. The thirty species of fruit have their roots in the second, third, and fourth worlds, called Creation, Formation, and Making. They are classified according to the nature of their shells, which symbolize the type of protection required, due to the extent that evil is present in that world. The fruit, which correspond to the World of Creation, have no shells because their roots are so far from the force of evil that no protection is required.

[52] They may be eaten in their entirety. There is no shell or kernel to discard.

[53] Or *uzerad*, a kind of crabapple, mentioned in the Mishnah, *Demai* 1:1.

[54] The World of Making is bordered by the realm of evil forces that is characterized by lust or pleasures entirely separated from holiness.

[55] The spiritual battle that must be waged between good and evil, or holiness and impurity, is confronted directly in the World of Making. Consequently, the fruit that correspond to that world require a hard outer shell. The fruit that symbolize the World of Formation have only a hard inner kernel, because that world is not directly assailable by the forces of evil, but may only be penetrated by evil/impurity.

[56] The human soul potentially contains a series of grade or parts that hierarchically correspond to the series of worlds. The lowest grade, *nefesh*, like the World of Making, is directly assailable by the forces of evil.

[57] Literally, "of all refuse."

[58] It bears no edible fruit. Thus it contains no divine sparks.

[59] I.e., the forces of evil.

[60] Eccle. 5:7.

[61] I.e., they were alluding to the *sefirah*, *Tiferet*, which is symbolized by the "Tree of Life."

[62] The letters that spell *ilan* have the numerical value of 91. This equals the value of the sum of the two divine names, *YHVH* and *ADoNaY*. The combination of these two names, *YAHD-VNHY* represents the union of the *sefirot*, *Tiferet*, and *Malkhut*, respectively, i.e., the sacred union of the male and female principle within the Godhead.

[63] Zohar, v. 3, 58a.

[64] When *ilan* is spelled *ALP YVD LMD NVN*, it equals 311 plus one for the word itself, total 312. Twelve permutations of *YHVH* equal 312.

[65] Zohar, vol. 2, 66b.

[66] Exod. 15:27.

[67] Zohar, vol. 2, 62b.

68 Ps. 90:17.

69 A pun on Eccle. 1:15: "That which is crooked cannot be made straight (*me'uvat* lo *yukhal litkon*)."

70 Although various forms of male sexual incontinence may be alluded to here, it is possible that the author has masturbation specifically in mind. The Zohar views ejaculation that does not occur during "normal" intercourse with women as an especially serious sin that cannot be rectified. If this is indeed the meaning, *Peri Eitz Hadar* would have to be considered an earlier *tikkun* for *shikvat zera le-vatalah* than the *Tikkun ha-Kelali* of Rabbi Naḥman of Bratzlav. See Yehuda Lieves, "*Ha-Tikkun Ha-Kelali* of R. Nahman of Bratslav and Its Sabbatian Links," in *Studies in Jewish Myth and Jewish Messianism* (SUNY, 1993), pp. 115–50.

71 Literally, "his wound."

72 See above, page 12. Sexual irregularities, the "flaw of the covenant," have a negative effect on the ninth *sefirah, Yesod*, the *Tzaddik*, which represents the divine phallus. Since the 15th of Shvat *tikkun* affects this *sefirah* and deals with supernal potency, it can also correct the damage caused in that region by aberrant sexuality. It is interesting to note the implied magical relationship between human sexuality and fecundity of nature. Male irregularities in this area damage the divine quality that is ultimately responsible for the quality of the year's fruit.

73 See note 18.

74 Ps. 104:24.

75 Paraphrase of Ps. 107:37.

76 Gen. 1:11.

77 Ps. 104:13.

78 Paraphrase of Jer. 2:7.

79 Hosea 14:9.

80 Ezek. 47:12.

81 Song of Songs 8:11.

82 Gen. 1:11.

83 Gen. 2:9.

84 Mal. 3:11.

85 Ps. 21:7.

86 Lev. 26:4.

87 Ps. 133:3.

88 Gen. 49:24.

89 Ps. 5:13.

90 Job 20:15.

91 Isa. 55:13.

92 Ps. 72:16.

93 Ps. 96:12.

94 Deut. 26:2.

95 Isa. 35:1-2.

96 Ps. 90:17.

97 The twelve permutations of *YHVH* serve as *kavvanot* for the first twelve fruits that are blessed.

[98] I.e., the Name, *YHVH,* spelled *YVD HY VYV HY,* which equals 72. This Name is associated with the World of Emanation.

[99] The *Ḥemdat Yamim* claims that the secret to which figs allude is not to be found in the *Zohar.* However, it associates the fig with both *Malkhut* and *Binah.* It also observes that the Hebrew for fig, *te'enah* equals three spellings of the Name, *EHYH,* plus one for the word itself. The three spellings (*milu'im*) are *ALF HY YVD HY* (161), *ALF HH YVD HH* (151), *ALF HA YVD HA* (143). For a fuller explanation of the implications, see Ya'qov Zevi Yolles, *Qehilat Ya'aqov,* q.v. *te'enah.*

[100] The name of 63 is *YHVH* spelled *YVD HY VAV HY.* This Name is associated with the World of Creation.

[101] Here the *kavvanah* is the last letters of *ha-motzi'leheM miN,* which equal 91, the sum of the two Names *YHVH* and *ADNY.*

[102] The Name of 45 is *YHVH* spelled *YVD HA VAV HA.* This Name is associated with the World of Formation.

[103] The fruit's name in Hebrew is *uzerad,* a type of crabapple.

[104] The Name of 52 is *YHVH* spelled *YVD HH VV HH.* This Name is associated with the World of Making.

Tzvi Elimelekh Shapira and Hayyim Elazar Shpira, "Conceiving the World"

[1] More apt to the dating might be to say that forty days before the Creation, God decreed the joining of God's Own Self to the Universe. Thus Tu B'Av celebrated the very first covenant of all, and that is why we have the covenantings of that day.

Part V

Tsili Doleve-Gandelman, "Zionist Ideology and the Space of *Eretz Yisrael*"

[1] J. Weitz, *"Anu Not'im"* (We Plant). *Shorashim* (1936)1:22–28.

[2] A. Minkovitch, "Early Childhood Education in Israel," in *History and Theory of Early Childhood Education,* eds., S. J. Braun and E. P. Edwards (Worthington, Ohio: C.nA. Jones, 1972), pp. 132–45.

[3] N. Shargadovska, *"Al Erech Ganei ha-Yeladim"* (The Value of the Kindergarten), *Netiveinyu* (1931)1:24–27.

[4] Ts. Katinka, *"Ha-Hafifa ba-Gan"* (Festivals in the Kindergarten), *Hedha,* 1935.

[5] Sh. Tchernichovsky, *"Al Kupat Meir ba'al ha-Ness"* (The Meir Ba'al haNess Charity Box), in *Kinus kofsatot ha-KKL* (Varsovie: KKL Edition, 1930).

[6] H. Verbah, *"Ra'ayon ha-Geula be-Gan ha-Yeladim"* (The Idea of Redemption in the Kindergarten), *Hed ha-Gan* (1940)5:42–45.

[7] A. J. Heschel, *The Sabbath: Its Meaning for Modern Man* (New York: Farrar, Straus and Young, 1951).

[8] L. Dumont, "The Modern Conception of the Individual: Notes on Its Genesis and That of Concomitant Institutions," *Contributions to Indian Sociology* (1965) 8:13–61.

[9] Ts. Doleve-Gandelman, *Identité Sociale et Ceremonie d'Anniversaire dans les Jardins d'enfants Israeliens,* Ph.D. diss., Paris, École des Hautes Étude en Science Sociales, 1982.

[10] T. Haskina, *"Yom-Huledet ba-Gan"* (Birthday Party in the Kindergarten), *Hed ha-Gan* (1940) 5:34–37.

[11] S. Fayens-Glick, *"Kene Gananot: KKL be-Gan ha-Yeladim"* (Congress of Kindergarten Teachers: the KKL in the Kindergarten), *Hed ha-Gan* (1942) 9:11–17.

[12] N. Alterman, *"Yom Huledet"* (Birthday), in *Ma Aaper la-Yeled!* (What shall I tell the child?), ed., Y. Gurevitch (Tel Aviv, 1946).

[13] Sh. Zbodanski-Rodanski, *"Yovel KKL ba-Gan"* (The KKL Jubilee in the Kindergarten), (1947)13:41–42.

[14] Ts. Katsiri, *"Yom Huledet la KKL be-Tel Aviv"* (The Birthday of the KKL in Tel Aviv) (1931).

[15] A. Glazer, *"Stair la-KKL"* (Song for the KKL), *Hed ha-Gan* (1942)7:57.

[16] See Deut. 8:7–8.

[17] See Gen. 43:11; Jer. 1:11.

[18] L. Kipnis, *"Yom Huledet Ha-Shkediya"* (The Almond Tree's Birthday), 1919.

[19] L. Gorton, *"Yom Huledet shel ha-Shkediah"* (The Almond Tree's Birthday), *Hed ha-Gan* (1943)9:69–71.

Yael Zerubavel, "The Forest as a National Icon: Literature, Politics, and the Archaeology of Memory"

* An earlier version of this article was written during a year of fellowship at the Center for Judaic Studies at the University of Pennsylvania. I would like to thank the Center and its Director, David Ruderman, for providing an excellent environment for pursuing academic research and to thank my colleagues in that year's seminar on history and memory for their helpful comments. I am particularly grateful for comments by Eviatar Zerubavel, Berel Lang, Omer Bartov, Elchanan Reiner, Israel Bartal, Ian Lustick, and Zali Gurevitch on an earlier version of this paper.

[1] The analogy between trees and children is a central theme in a short story, *"Yom Huledet Ha-Shkediya"* (The Almond Tree's Birthday), written by the famous writer of children's literature, Levin Kipnis. First published in *Gilyonot* 1 (1930), pp. 25–27, this story was often reprinted in Tu B'Shvat anthologies or textbooks for early grades. See, for example, *Mikraot Yisrael* for the second grade, eds., Z. Ariel, M. Blich, and N. Persky (Tel Aviv, 1960), pp. 231-32. See also "HaTe'omot" [The Twins], *ibid.*, pp. 237-38. For a fuller discussion of the children-trees analogy, see Tsili Doleve-Gandelman, "The Symbolic Inscription of Zionist Ideology in the Space of Eretz Yisrael: Why the Native Israeli Is Called Tsabar," in *Judaism Viewed from Within and Without*, ed., Harvey E. Goldberg (Albany, NY, 1987), pp. 257–84.

[2] The quote is taken from the first brochure issued by the Association of Jewish Foresters in Palestine [*Agudat haYa'ar be'Eretz Yisrael*], which was founded in 1945, marking twenty-five years of afforestation efforts (Yosef Weitz, ed., *Ha-Ya'ar* [The Forest], 1947, 12). The participants noted the emergence of afforestation as a Jewish profession as a significant historical change in its own right (*ibid.*, 41).

[3] The Jewish National Fund was founded by the Fifth Congress of the World Zionist Organization in 1901 and gradually assumed the tasks of purchasing land in Palestine, improving the terrain for settlement purposes and advancing afforestation projects. On the concept of "redemption" as alluding to national revival through land purchase, see Shmuel Almog, "HaGe'ula ba'Retorika haTsiyonit" [Redemption in Zionist Rhetoric], in *Ge'ulat haKaka be'Eretz Yisrael* [Redemption of the Land in Eretz Israel], ed., Ruth Kark (Jerusalem, 1990), pp. 13–32.

[4] On other rituals connecting schools and the JNF, see Doleve-Gandelman, "The Symbolic Inscription of Zionist Ideology," pp. 260, 265–77. It is important to note that the JNF created a

teachers' committee and played a significant role in sponsoring children's literature that was educational in its thrust. In some cases the JNF commissioned the writing of literature that highlighted its activities. See, for example, the correspondence with Anda Pinkerfeld, who was commissioned to write a play on the JNF's afforestation efforts for Tu Bishvat (Nov. 11, 1936, and Dec. 20, 1936; The Central Zionist Archives, file KKLs/7622, the *Tu Bishvat* Project).

[5] This popular image of the country's forested landscape during antiquity obviously supports Zionist collective memory and ideology but may not be as well grounded in historical evidence. Similarly, the claim that all modern afforestion efforts are the product of Zionist activity ignores other factors, such as the afforestation policy of the British Mandatory authorities. See Yehuda Felix, "Al ha'Etz ve'haYa'ar be'Nofa haKadum shel ha'Aretz" [On the Tree and on the Ancient Landscape of the Country], *Teva Va'Aretz* 8 (1966), 71–74; Nurit Kliot, "Idiologia ve'Yi'ur be'Yisrael: Ya'ar Ma'ase Adam be'Emstsa'ut haKeren haKayemet le'Yisrael" [Ideology and Afforestation in Israel: Man-Made Forests of the JNF], *Mehkarim be'Ge'ographia shel Eretz Yisrael* [Studies in the Geography of Israel], *a festschrift for Professor Dov Nir* (The Society for the Exploration of Eretz Israel and Its Antiquities, 1992), pp. 88, 91; and Nili Lifshitz and Gideon Bigar, "Mediniyut haYi'ur shel haMimshal ha Briti be'Eretz Yisrael," *Ofakim be'Ge'ografia* [Horizons in Geography], no. 40–41 (1994), pp. 5–16.

[6] Trees were a sign that a land was indeed in use. Ottoman law concerning land ownership even recognized the entitlement over trees that were planted on someone else's property, if the owner did not interfere for three years (Shaul Ephraim Cohen, *The Politics of Planting: Israeli-Palestinian Competition for Control of Land in the Jerusalem Periphery* [Chicago, 1993], pp. 36–37.) On the range of Zionist goals of the JNF afforestation project, see Avraham Granott, "Mediniyut haYi'ur be'Eretz Yisrael" [Jewish Afforestation Policy in Palestine], in his Bi'Sedot haBinyan [in the Building Field] (Jerusalem, 1951), pp. 162–78, and Kliot *"Idiologia ve'Yi'ur be'Yisrael,"* pp. 88–100.

[7] See Yosef Haim Yerushalmi, *Zakhor: Jewish History and Jewish Memory* (Seattle, 1982).

[8] For a more extensive discussion of the Zionist collective memory, see Yael Zerubavel, *Recovered Roots: Collective Memory and the Making of Israeli National Tradition* (Chicago, 1995), pp. 13–36.

[9] The practice of naming forests after important historical figures associated with the Zionist revival began soon after the JNF began planting trees in Palestine. For example, "Herzl Forest" was established following Herzl's death, and the planting of "Balfour Forest" began in 1928. *HaEntsiklopedia haIvrit* [The Hebrew Encyclopedia] (Jerusalem, 1978), vol. 30, 265; Weitz, "Ya'ar Balfour—Ben Esrim Shana [Balfour Forest Twenty Years Old], in *HaYa'ar*, p. 43.

[10] On the commemoration of the Holocaust within the national framework, see James Young, "When a Day Remembers: A Performative History of Yom HaShoah," in *History and Memory*, 2(3) (1990): 54–75; Zerubavel, *Recovered Roots*, pp. 70–76, 192–95. Ruth Firer, Sokhinim shel haHinuch haTsiyoni [The Agents of Zionist Education] (Tel Aviv, 1985), p. 101.

[11] Quoted in *Mesihot le'Arvei Shabat u'Mo'ed le'Batei Sefer ve'Hevrot No'ar* [Youth's Parties on Sabbath Eve and Holidays for Schools and Youth Movements] eds., Nahum Vermel and Baruch Ben-Yehuda (Tel Aviv, 1957), p. 140. Interestingly, the "Forest of Martyred Children" is presented there, not only as a living memorial for the dead children, but also for the European forest that had tried to protect them and then died with them (Anda Amir Pinkerfeld, *Be'Sod Hasdei haYa'ar* [The Secret of the Forest's Grace], *ibid.*, p. 142).

[12] See also my analysis of the Tel-Hai myth as a paradigmatic text of the pioneering narrative and its representation of "the end" in line with this emphasis on the success of the Zionist settlement. On the centrality of the theme of struggle against all odds, see also Nurit Gertz,

Shevuya ba'haloma: Mitosim ba'Tarbut haYisra'elit [Captive of a Dream: National Myths in Israeli Culture] (Tel Aviv, 1995), pp. 13–34.

[13] Gershon Shaked, "Livnot u'Lehibanot Ba: Al Roman ha Hityashvut" [To Build and to Be Rebuilt in It: On the Settlement Novel], in *The Proceedings of the Sixth World Congress for Jewish Studies* (1973), pp. 517–27.

[14] *Anshei Be'reshit* was originally published by Shtibel (Warsaw) in 1933; it has had successive editions and printings in Hebrew and has been translated into several languages. References to the Hebrew text draw on Murray Roston's translation, *Frontiersmen of Israel* (Tel Aviv, 1964), although I chose to use the more current English translation of the title, *The Founders*, as suggested by the 1973 Am Oved edition. Quotes and page numbers refer to the above English edition, except where an important nuance of the original Hebrew was lost and therefore required some alteration. In those cases, I note "modified translation" and provide page references to both Hebrew and English versions.

[15] A. B.Yehoshua's *Mul haYe'arot* [Facing the Forests] was written in 1963 and published in a volume of the same title by HaKibbutz HaMeuchad (1968). Page references for the Hebrew text refer to Yehoshua's anthology *Ad Horef* 1974 [Until Winter 1974] (Jerusalem, 1975), pp. 92–122. References to the English translation by Miriam Arad relate to the English anthology of Yehoshua's stories, *The Continuing Silence of a Poet* (London, 1988), pp. 203–36.

[16] *The Founders* was well received by the Hebrew youth as well as critics. See the reviews by Nahum Ish Gamznu in *Ba'Ma'ale*, February 24, 1933, p. 7; Y. Ori in *Bustenai*, April 26: Y. Burla in *Moznaim* 4:33 (1933) p. 12; Sh.RP. in *Ketubim* 7:13 (1933), 3; Avraham Breudes in *Davar*, 26 Adar 1933, p. 4; Uriya Feldman in *Ha'Aretz*, Feb. 24, 1933, p. 5; Ezra Reichert in *Do'ar haYom*, Feb. 3, 1933, p. 4. Outstanding within this context is Raznitsky's critique of the lack of any psychological depth in Smolly's portrayal of characters and the inappropriateness of the Robinson Crusoe model for the pioneers; *HaPoel haTsair* 26:21 (1933),13–14. Smolly received the Bialik Prize for Children's Literature for *The Founders* in 1936 and was awarded the Israel Prize for Literature in 1957. On the impact of the book on generations of Hebrew youth, see a special issue devoted to Smolly, *Sifrut Yeladim va'no'ar* II:4 (1976); and Uriel Offek, *Sifrut haYeladim haIvrit* 1900–1948 vol. 2 [Hebrew Children's Literature, 1900–48] (Tel Aviv, 1988), p. 467. As Offek points out, *"anshei be'reshit"* has become so popular as a term that it appears as a concept in Even-Shoshan's *HaMilon beHadash* vol. 3 [The New Dictionary] (Tel Aviv, 1988), p. 1243.

[17] Baruch Kurzweil refers to Yehoshua as "the authentic representative of the young generation"; *Hipus haSifrut haIvrit* [In Search of Hebrew Literature](Ramat-Gan, 1982), 307. *Facing the Forests* has received much critical consideration. For examples, see Gershon Shaked, *Gal Hadash ba'Siporet haIvrit* [New Wave in Hebrew Literature], 2nd ed. (Tel Aviv, 1974); Yosef Ofir,"HaYa'ar ve'haEtsim."

[18] For more critical reviews of *Facing the Forests*, see Mordekhai Shalev, "HaAravim ke'Fitaron Sifruti" [The Arabs as a Literary Solution]in *Ha'Aretz*, Sept. 30, 1970, pp. 50–51; B. Y. Michali in "Alegoria Kefuya be'Mul haYe'arot" [Forced Allegory in *Facing the Forests*], *Moznaim* 46:5–6 (1978), 382–93; Moshe Steiner, "HaKivun HaNihilisti ba'Siporet haYisra'elit [The Nihilistic Orientation in Hebrew Fiction], in *HaTehiya haLe'umit be'Sifrutenu* [National Revivial in Our Literature] (Cherikover, 1982), pp. 141–52.

[19] The only comparison between these two works that I have found is suggested by Yedida Itzhaki, *HaPesukim haSemuyim min haAyin: Al Yetsirat A. B. Yehoshua* [The Concealed Verses: Source Material in the Works of A. B. Yehoshua](Ramat-Gan, 1992), pp. 101–105.

[20] *The Founders* borrows heavily from Alexander Zeid's settlement experience but is ultimately presented as a work of fiction. (Sifrut Yeladim va'No'ar II:4 [1976], 8, 18) Alexander

Zeid was hired by the JNF to guard the forests of Sheikh Abreik and built his own farm there. In 1929 the Zeid family refused to leave its home and all their crops were burned down by Arabs. In spite of this setback, they refused to join one of the nearby settleements and remained in Sheikh Abreik. Zeid was later killed by Arabs in 1938 (Yaacov Shorer and Uri Shefer, eds., *Givat Alonim Tivon: Nof va'Adamm* [Tivon, the Hill of Oaks: Landscape and People] [Jerusalem: Ministry of Education and Culture, 1990], pp. 116–20). Smolly also translated and edited Zeid's diaries and published a book based on these entries *(Mi'Hayei Rishonim [From The Founders' Lives]* (Tel Aviv, 1941), as well as a book devoted to Zeid's "legend," *Shomer Yisrael* [The Guard of Israel] (Tel Aviv, 1970).

21 Generations of Israeli students read *The Founders* during the Yushuv and the early state periods, and it was still included in the Ministry of Education's list of recommended reading in the 1960s *(Davar,* Jan. 1, 1966, 24). A special conference for eighth graders devoted to *The Founders* was held in 1965 *(Hed haHinukh,* Feb. 18, 1965), and a special issue devoted to Smolly in *Sifrut Yaladim va'No'ar* also includes guidelines for teaching the novel (II:4 [1976], 28–31).

22 The guard of *Facing the Forests* enters the forest alone; although Smolly's protagonist settles down in the forest with his wife and three children, their characters are underdeveloped. When other characters are introduced into these narratives, they remain marginal, represented only in relation to the guards and the settlement process.

23 On natural forests in the Carmel region, see *Madrikh Yisrael* [A Guide to Israel], ed., Arye Yitzhaki, (Jerusalem, 1978), the volume on the Carmel and the Northern Valleys. In an interview in 1978, Smolly recalled: "When I came to the country, I walked from Jaffa to Jerusalem and I didn't see on the way anything but barren land, rocks, and stones, and occasionally a single old tree near some sheikh's grave." He contrasts this with the possibility of being lost in the forests today (Naomi Gotkind, *Eretz Ye'arot Avotim: Siha im haSofer Eliezer Smolly* [The Land of Dense Forests: A Conversation with the Writer Eliezer Smolly], *HaTsofe,* Jan. 20, 1978, p. 4). It is interesting also to compare the Smolly's literary depiction of Hermoni's excitement at the sight of the hills and the forest and does not reveal his own feelings at the moment (Smolly, *Mi'Hayei Rishonmim,* p. 210).

24 On Smolly's love for nature that was instilled during his childhhood in the Ukraine, see *Sifrut va'No'ar* II:4 (1976), 8; see also Gotkind, *Eretz Ye'arot Avotim.* On the impact of European landscape imagery on Hebrew writers who grew up in villages, see Benjamin Harshav, *Language in Time of Revolution* (Berkeley, CA, 1993), p. 65.

25 When Galili, an old friend of Hermoni, urges him to leave the isolated frontier farm, he argues: "It is a desert [*midbar*] here and you'll have to be on your guard for many years to come" (p. 57). At another point, some other Jewish visitors comment: "A queer place and queer people; who could settle in such a desert [*midbar shemama]"* (Heb. 184, modified trans.). The interchangeability of "forest" and "desert" is also expressed in the references to Hermoni as both a "desert dweller" (Heb. 148 /Eng. 170) and a "forest dweller" (Heb. 166/Eng. 191).

26 That settlement implies the introduction of social order into nature becomes clear when the Hermoni family plants trees for the first time: Hermoni, who supervises this ceremonial planting, takes particular care to ascertain that the new trees will form a straight line (123).

27 This idea is a familiar theme in the literature and popular culture of the early pioneering period. See Zerubavel, *Recovered Roots,* pp. 24–29, and passim.

28 Hermoni remembers that in his childhood he conformed to the image of the exilic Jew and was the object of repeated teasing by Gentiles for being a "Jewish coward" [*yehudon pahdan*] (58). This may also explain Hermoni's harsh response to his own son, Eitan, when the boy

showed signs of fear while being attacked by barking dogs. Eitan's fear violated the expectations from a "native Hebrew" and may have been alarmingly too close to Hermoni's own behavior as a child in exile.

[29] The wish of HaShomer members and other Second Aliya settlers to become "Jewish Bedouin" is clearly manifested in posed photos of the period. See also Itamar Even Zohar, *"HaTsemiha ve'haHitgabshut shel Tarbut Ivrit mekomit ve'Yelidit be Eretz Yisrael, 1882–1948"* [The Emergence of Native Hebrew Culture in Palestine], *Cathedra* 16 (July 1980), 165–204; Pesach Bar-Adon, *"Be'Oholei Midbar: Mi'Reshimotav shel Ro'e Tson Ivri Bein Shivtei haBedu'im"* [*In Desert Tents: Notes of a Hebrew Shepherd Among the Beduin*], first published by Shtibl (Warsaw, 1934), and reissued by Kryat Sefer (Tel Aviv, 1981).

[30] Finding ancient relics during preparations for construction or while working in the fields is part of reality in Israel, but it is also used as a Zionist literary trope. It is interesting to note here that Alexander Zeid's son mentions the discovery of relics as an example of Smolly's embellishment of his family stories (relics were indeed found after the publication of the novel). See Giora Zeid, "Eliezer Smolly—haMoreh ve'haYadid" [Eliezer Smolly, Teacher and Friend], in *Sifrut Yeladim va'No'ar* II:4 (1976), 18. Meyer Levin's movie *My Father's House,* based on his novel of the same name, ends with the same trope while the foundations of a new Zionist settlement are being laid.

[31] The rising tensions between Jews and Arabs indeed led to Zeid's assassination in 1938, but this happened a few years after the publication of *The Founders.*

[32] Earlier in the novel, Hermoni rejects Abu Naomi's offer to share the revenues from the exploitation of the forest and defines his refusal in moral terms: "It is a sin to watch them destroy the forest and keep quiet, *because trees are like human beings."* (Heb. 48, my trans; emphasis added).

[33] Given the allusion to the ancient forest as "the shiny, green temple" (Heb. 99), the devastation the fire caused to it is reminiscent of the destruction of the Temple in Jerusalem, thus emphasizing the significance attached to the forest as a sacred site.

[34] See my discussion of the Tel-Hai commemorative narrative and its strategies of highlighting the battle and Trumpeldor's heroic death while obscuring the settlers' withdrawal from the settlement at the end of that day (*Recovered Roots*, pp. 161–63, 222–27). Nurit Gertz notes that the settlement literature of the 1930s often ends with the settler's death and that this ending ultimately serves to highlight the values for which the settler has sacrificed his life (Gertz, *Shevuya be'Haloma*, pp. 24–26).

[35] See Shalev's interpretation of *Facing the Forests* as an Oedipal struggle embodying the figure of the Jewish Father (Shalev, *"HaAravim ke'Fitaron Sifruti"*).

[36] On the guard's desire for the fire as a product of his inner state of confusion, see Nili Sadan-Loebenstein, *A. B. Yehoshua,* (Tel Aviv, 1981), pp. 175–88. On the student's lack of moral sensitivity, or real cooperation with the Arab, see also Hanan Hever, "Minority Discourse of a National Majority: Israeli Fiction of the Early Sixties," *Prooftexts* 10 (1990), 133. It would be interesting to compare Yehoshua's portrayal of the guard's fantasy about fire with Binyamin Tamuz's story *"HaPardes"* [The Orchard] and its depiction of the Jewish brother's fantasy to burn the orchard.

[37] I disagree with those critics who see the guard as being transformed as a result of the fire experience, highlighting his memory gain (Ofir, *"HaYa'ar ve'haEtsim,"* 54–55; Gila Ramras-Rauch, *The Arab in Israeli Literature,* [Bloomington, IN, 1989], pp. 130, 138–39). The guard already displays a historical memory in the forest prior to the fire, as his stories to the Arab about the Crusades demonstrate (229).

38 For the argument that Yehoshua gave the Arab a central role in his fiction, see Michali, "Alegoria Kefuya be'Mul haYe'arot," pp. 386–91. Other critics point out that the Arab's character is not fully developed but, rather, is introduced into the story to mirror some aspects of the Israeli Jew's identity. See Shalev, *"HaAravim ke'Fitaron Sifruti"*; Simon Levi, *"Shevuyim be'Vidayon,"* Mosnaim, 57:5–6 (1983), 73; and Ehud Ben-Ezer, *Be'Moledet haGa'agu'im haMenugadim: Haravi ba'Sifrut haIvrit* [The Arab in Israeli Fiction: An Anthology](Tel Aviv, 1992), p. 33.

39 Quoted in Ramras-Rauch, *The Arab in Israeli Fiction,* p. 140.

40 A. B. Yehoshua, *Bizechrut HaNormaliyut* [Between Right and Right] (Tel Aviv, 1980), p. 75.

41 For a more elaborate discussion of the fictional representation of a minority's view, see Hever, "Minority Discourse of a National Majority." Hever sees the arson as well as the shedding of words (i.e., Hebrew), as aggressive acts of deterritorialization of Zionist ideology and politics. Yehoshua himself explained the aggressive nature of his fiction as manifestations of repressed guilt toward the Palestinians. See Shabtai Tevet, *"Tehushat haAshma Poretset be'a-gresiviyut"* [Guilt Feelings Expressed though Aggression], *Ha'Aretz* (24 May 1968), 18, 23. See also Mordekhai Shilgi, *"HaAravi hallem ve'haStudent haAlim ke'Hasrei Pitaron"* [The Mute Arab and the Violent Student without a Solution], *Gazit* 30:5–8 (1973), 19.

42 The symbolic association of the fate of the Israeli trees with the suffering of Jews in exile is also manifested in the description of the first tree burning as "a tree wrapped in prayer . . . going through its hour of judgment and surrendering its spirit" (231), thus recreating it in the traditional image of an exilic Jewish martyr.

43 In contrast to the scene of destroyed trees, the guard fantasizes that the [word missing] "had never burnt down but had simply pulled up its roots and gone off on a journey, far off on a journey, far off to the sea . . ." (232). This fantasy does not even allow the forest to have a monument within the landscape; it creates an analogy between it and the medieval Crusaders, who came and then went away on a long journey overseas.

44 Gertz, *Hirbat Hizma,* 92. Gertz also provides other examples of circular temporal ordering of the narrative in Yehoshua's and Amos Oz's fiction.

45 A JNF circular states that 54,000 trees were destroyed in JNF forests during 1936 (circular no. 20/97, Dec. 15, 1936, file KKL5/7622, the *Tu-Bishvat* Project, in the Central Zionist Archives). See also Weitz, *HaYa'ar,* p. 593.

46 Yosef Weitz, *"Ya'ar Balfour—Ben Esrim Shana"* [Balfour Forest Is Twenty Years Old], in *HaYa'ar,* p. 43.

47 For the announcement on the death of the trees in the Balfour Forest, see *Tu-Bishvat,* ed., Nehemia Aloni (Jerusalem, 1937), p. 17 (The Aviezer Yellin Archives of Jewish Education in Israel and the Diaspora, Tel Aviv University). On the Israeli patterns of anonymous or numerical commemorations, see Zerubavel, *Recovered Roots,* p. 45.

48 Cohen, The *Politics of Planting,* p. 11.

49 In the "tree wars" between Israelis and Palestinians, Palestinian Human Rights Information Center of Jerusalem quotes 92,000 uprooted trees between December 8, 1987, and September 30, 1990 (a flyer entitled "Israeli Violations of Palestinian Rights," n.d.). A study quoted by *Ha'Aretz* estimates the number of trees uprooted by Israelis in the West Bank to be around 170,000 from the outbreak of the Intifada in December 1987 until December 1994. In the Galilee, 5,000 of the JNF's eucalyptus saplings planted on land in dispute between the JNF and Kfar Kanna were uprooted during one night. The uprooting of about 3,000 olive trees that once belonged to the village of Ktannah (many of them replanted in other sites) made Ktannah emerge as a Palestinian symbol for Israeli destruction of Palestinian trees (Cohen, *The Politics of Planting,* pp. 122–29).

[50] See *Yediot Ahronot*, June 12, 1988, 1, 13; Nurit Kliot and Gideon Kedar, *"Srefot Ya'ar ve'Hatsatot ve'Gormeihen haEnoshiyim be'Yisrael"* [Forest Fires and Their Human Factors in Israel], *Ofakim be'Ge'ografia* [Horizons in Geography], nos. 35–36 (1992), pp. 29–30. An Israeli paper announced that arson was one of the tests of candidates for Palestinian "terrorist organizations" (*Ha'Aretz*, July 21, 1988, p. 3). See also Cohen, *The Politics of Planting*, pp. 5, 123–26.

[51] Moshe Rivlin of the JNF was quoted in *HaDo'ar*, June 17, 1988, p. 3. For the JNF campaign, see its public announcements in *Ha'Aretz*, January 18, 1989, p. 7, and *Davar*, January 20, 1989, p. 3.

[52] See *"Shomrei haYemarot"* [The Forest Guards], *Davar*, January 19, 1989, p. 10. Cohen notes that this campaign revived earlier patterns of the Yishuv period to increase afforestation efforts in response to the deliberate destruction of forests by Arabs. The campaign resulted also in an increase in donations to the JNF (*The Politics of Planting*, pp. 123–125).

[53] *Yediot Ahronot*, September 21, 1989, pp. 1–6; Heda Boshes, *"Mul haYe'arot"* [Facing the Forests], *Ha'Aretz*, September 26, 1989, p. 13. The campaign to rehabilitate the Carmel Forests was called the "Carmel Fund" (*Davar*, September 24, 1989, pp. 1–2). It was reported to have collected 6 million Israeli shekels (*Yediot Ahronot*, May 24, 1990, pp. 24–25).

[54] Cohen gives the example of arson fires in lands belonging to the village of Anabta in the West Bank, where settlers prevented firefighters from putting the fire out (*The Politics of Planting*, pp. 123, 126).

[55] Amos Carmel, *"HaYeladim ve'haYa'ar"* [The Children and the Forest], *Yediot Ahronot*, September 25, 1989, p. 19.

[56] Yaron London, *"Adam—ve'Lo Etz haSade"* [A Person and Not a Tree], *Yediot Ahronot*, September 25, 1989, p. 19.

[57] Ron Ben-Yshai, *"Hatsatot: Shita Yedu'a u'Mukeret ba'Aretz Me'az Reshit haHityashvat haYehudit be'EretzYsrael"* [Arson: A Known and Familiar Method Since the Beginning of Jewish Settlement in Palestine], *Yediot Ahronot*, June 13, 1988, p. 2.

[58] Boshes, *"Mul haYe'arot,"* p. 13.

[59] Michael Handelsatz, *Orekh Yarkhon Aravi le'Din al'I'haGashat Sipur le'Tsenzura"* [Editor of an Arabic Magazine Sued for Failing to Submit a Children's Story to the Censor] *H'Aretz*, July 13, 1992. The State later dropped this charge (*Ha'Aretz*, November 30, 1992). I would like to thank Michael Handelsaltz for these references.

[60] Tom Segev, *"Ma'ase be'Aravi she'Lo Anas Yalda"* [The Story of an Arab Who Did Not Rape a Girl], *Ha'Aretz*, December 11, 1992.

[61] The scar, the result of the "searing burn in the guts of the land" that the fire creates, also appears in Zali Gurevitch's poem No. 2 in *Yabasha* [Land] (Tel Aviv, 1989), pp. 11–12. The following excerpt has been translated by Gabriel Levin:

> *The JNF*
> *will replant saplings*
> *will grow hair*
> *a new forest will rise*
> *on the scar*
> *a new forest will cover*
> *the baldness of the scorched land*
> *consumed by fire . . .*

[62] It is interesting to quote at this juncture Azmi Bishara's statement about the issue of memory: "The [Israeli Palestinian] villages that are no longer in existence were pushed out of the

domain of public space, out of the signs of memory. They received new names of Hebrew settlements, yet they have left some traces in these settlements such as cactus plants or stone-fences, or bricks of ruined houses. . . . The Arab villages have no monuments or memorials. There will be no equality and no historical compromise until they will receive a tombstone" (*"Bein Makom le'Merhav"* [Between Place and Space], Studio 37 [1992], p. 6). See also Jonathan Boyarin's article, *"Horvot ba'aliya li'Yerushalayim"* [Ruins, Mounting toward Jerusalem] in the same issue.

Shaul Cohen, "A Tree for a Tree"

* This work draws significantly on the author's work, *The Politics of Planting: Israeli-Palestinian Competition for Control of Land in the Jerusalem Periphery* (Chicago: University of Chicago Press, 1993).

[1] Mark Twain, *The Innocents Abroad; or, The New Pilgrims' Progress* (New York: Heritage Press, 1962 [original publication, 1869]).

[2] Yosef [Joseph] Weitz, *Forest and Afforestation in Israel* (Israel: Massada, 1970 [Hebrew]), p. 93.

[3] Henry Kendall, *Jerusalem the City Plan 1948: Preservation and Development during the British Mandate 1918–1948* (London: His Majesty's Stationery Office, 1948); Shaul Cohen, *The Politics of Planting: Israeli-Palestinian Competition for Control of Land in the Jerusalm Periphery* (Chicago: University of Chicago Press, 1993).

[4] Weitz, *Forest,* p. 386.

[5] Ibid.

[6] Cohen, *Politics.*

[7] Ibid.

Poems by Zelda and Malka Heifetz Tussman, trans. by Marcia Falk

* From *The Book of Blessings: A Re-Creation of Jewish Prayer,* copyright © 1998 by Marcia Lee Falk, and *With Teeth in the Earth: Selected Poems of Malka Heifetz Tussman,* trans., ed., and introduced by Marcia Falk (Detroit: Wayne State University Press, 1992).

Part VI

Ismar Schorsch, "Trees for Life"

[1] *State of the World 1991* (New York & London), p. 3.

[2] Quoted from *The Gay Science* by Walter Kaufmann, Nietzsche: Philosopher, Psychologist, Antichrist (Meridian Books, 1990), p. 81.

[3] Andrew Revkin, *The Burning Season. The Murder of Chico Mendes and the Fight for the Amazon Rain Forest* (New York, 1990). p. 38.

[4] Lecture by Dr. Anne Whyte at conference for Joint Appeal in Religion and Science in New York, June 3, 1991.

Howard M. Solomon, "Nebuchadnezzar, Naḥman's Cripple," and Groundhog Day: A Meditation on Tu B'Shvat"

[1] Pirke de-rabbi Eliezer 34. Hayim Nahman Bailik and Yehoshuattana Ravitzky, eds., *The Book of Legends (Sefer Ha-Aggadah),* trans. by William G. Brande (New York: Schocken Books, 1992 [1908–1911]), p. 773.

David Seidenberg, "The Human, the Tree, and the Image of God"

[1] All translations of the Bahir were done by the author of this essay. Note that the Hebrew pronoun that refers to the cosmic tree can be translated as either "he" or "it." In most of the passages where the image of the tree is highly personified, the translation "he" is preferred.

[2] For a very basic discussion of fractals, see James Gleick's *Chaos: Making a New Science* (New York: Viking Penguin, 1987).

[3] David Abram, *The Spell of the Sensuous* (New York: Vintage Books, 1996), p. 46.

[4] The following discussion is indebted to Irene Diamond's *Fertile Ground : Women, Earth and the Limits of Control* (Boston: Beacon Press, 1994) and to a paper which she wrote jointly with me on Jewish ecofeminism.

[5] See Elliot Wolfson's detailed scholarly analysis in "The Tree That Is All," in *Along the Path: Studies in Kabbalistic Myth, Symbolism, and Hermeneutics* (Albany: SUNY Press, 1995), or Jeremy Cohen's more accessible summary in *Be Fruitful and Increase, Fill the Earth and Master It: The Ancient and Medieval Career of a Biblical Text* (Ithaca, NY: Cornell University Press, 1989), pp. 199–205.

[6] Zohar III: 269a–b, trans. in Roy Rosenberg, *The Anatomy of God* (New York: Ktav Publishing, 1973), pp. 177–79.

[7] Elliot R. Wolfson, *The Circle in the Square: Studies in the Use of Gender in Kabbalistic Symbolism* (Albany: SUNY Press, 1995), pp. 108–9.

[8] Luce Irigaray, *The Sex Which Is Not One* (Ithaca, NY: Cornell University Press, 1985), p. 28.

[9] Maurice Merleau-Ponty, *The Phenomenology of Perception* (London: Routledge Press, 1992).

[10] Abram, *Spell*, p. 62.

Ari Elon, "Through Tu B'Shvat to Yah B'shvat"

[1] *Dubi*, in Hebrew, is a children's name for a little bear, either living or stuffed, as a teddy bear. [Translator]

[2] In my opinion one must place the expression "*peshat*/plain meaning" in quotation marks, since it has no place in the postmodern era, in which even the most "plain" word has much more than a single meaning. As long as Modernism reigned, scholars allowed themselves to divide their two-dimensional world into "*peshat*/plain meaning" and "*derash*/interpretation." Now, in contrast, in the post-*peshat* era, everyone faces no less than "seventy faces of Torah."

[3] *Gematria:* the Hebrew correspondence of numbers and letters. [Translator]

[4] The common translation of YHWH as "The Lord" disguises the fact that YHWH is, in fact, a proper name for God. [Translator]

[5] It is worth noting that in Hebrew, "humankind" is, literally, "the Enoshic kind." [Translator]

[6] Many commentators have noted the seeming relationship between existence, *hawayah*, and the divine name, YHWH, and some authors have even written "existence" as a substitute for the divine name, YHWH, out of the traditional reluctance to spell the latter out. [Translator]

[7] *Terumah* (plural: *terumot*): originally free-will offerings brought to the Temple in Jerusalem. [Translator]

[8] The chief prophet and promoter of Shabbetai Zevi. [Translator]

[9] This is the context, also, of the need to publish this anthology. In the seventies, when the editors of the Jewish Publication Society decided to publish a series of anthologies on the Jewish holidays, Tu B'Shvat wasn't included. Only lately, because of the growth in awareness

about this special day in the Jewish world, in particular among American Jews, was it decided to add Tu B'Shvat to the official list of Jewish holidays.

[10] The somewhat archaic word "outland," which means a foreign country, or foreign countries collectively (approximately synonymous with "abroad"), is an almost literal translation of the Hebrew term for places outside the Land of Israel. [Translator]

[11] Landofisrael: I am following the author's spelling, which is sometimes used today in Israel, in which the words are put together as one word. [Translator]

[12] *Halakhot:* Whatever you consider Halakhah to be—binding or outmoded Jewish law, a way of life, etc.—halakhot (singular = halakhah, lower case 'h') are the individual bits that make up the Halakhah. [Translator]

[13] Maimonides' introduction to his Commentary on the Mishnah.

[14] On this topic, see, for example, the extensive material on the subject in this anthology; specifically, the article by Eilon Schwartz.

[15] Yom To Levinski, ed., *Sefer Ha-mo'adim* (Tel Aviv: Duir, 1956). Sefer *Ha-mo'adim* (The Book of Festivals) is not available in English.

[16] In an interview in *Yehadut Hofshit : Free Judaism: Quarterly of the Israeli Secular Movement for Humanistic Judaism.*

[17] The wording in the prayer book is "The Jews had . . . [*Layehudim haytah. . . .*]"

[18] Levinski, ed., *Sefer Ha-Moadim* (Tel Aviv: Dvir, 1956), pp. 187–188.

[19] "Holiday activists": I chose to use this literal translation of the Hebrew phrase, rather than something less strange sounding to American (or young Israeli) ears, like "those who plan holiday activities," because the notion of "holiday activists" conveys something of the Jewish intensity and social(ist) deliberateness that have existed in Israel and particularly on kibbutz. [Translator].

[20] Azaryah Alon, "Who Needs Tu B'Shvat," in the *Inter-Kibbutz Festival Commission Anthology,* ed. Aryeh Ben Gurion, (Inter-Kibbutz Festival Commission, 1968), p. 77.

[21] Ibid.

[22] In Hebrew, the phrases *kitzutz haneti'ot,* "rooting out the plantings," and *tikkun,* "healing," express the central opposition of Kabbalah. The primal metaphysical shattering of the universe, associated with the sin of Adam, is referred to as *kitzutz haneti'ot,* while the task of metaphysical healing from that event is *tikkun.* [Translator]

[23] Azaryah Alon, "Who Needs Tu B'Shvat," p. 77.

[24] "A kosher and joyous holiday" is the traditional Hebrew greeting for Passover. [Translator]

[25] See Levinski, *Sefer Ha-mo'adim,* p. 473, concerning Avraham Shimoni's calling the day a New Year of Nature.

[26] The Hebrew original fits the rhythm of the last line of the song and means, literally, "On Tu Tu Tu Tu the Arabs will die." I've translated it to give the original feeling of a sick children's rhyme.

[27] See, for example, the words of Rabbi Avraham Ya'akov of Sadigorah that appear in the *Inter-kibbutz Festival Commission Anthology,* ed. Aryeh Ben Gurion (Inter-Kibbutz Festival Commission, 1968), p. 68, as well as the words of the Seer of Lublin that are quoted on the same page.

[28] An early collection of midrashim.

[29] Their cattle was spared, since they heeded the warning of Moses (Exodus 9:20).

[30] The traditional halakhah understands the Hebrew word *ger* to refer to a convert to Judaism, although this makes no sense in the context of the verse being quoted.

[31] *Pilpul*: argumentation in the intricate/convoluted style of the Talmud.

[32] *Batei midrash* (singular: *bet midrash*): houses of study, seminaries.

[33] See the detailed explanation of this in the important work of Miles Krassen, included in this anthology.

[34] Meretz and Moledet are, respectively, left-wing and right-wing political parties.

[35] Arkia is Israel's domestic airline.

[36] *Ḥevruta*: the traditional system of paired text-study.

[37] Ari Elon, *From Jerusalem to the Edge of Heaven*, trans. by Tikva Frymer-Kensky (Philadelphia: The Jewish Publication Society, 1996), 93.

[38] Ibid., pp. 95–96.

[39] Ibid., pp. 96–97.

[40] Ibid., p. 97.

[41] In the Hebrew, the verbs in these suggestions, "minted," "established" and "fixed," are all the same word, *tiken*, from which the verbal noun *tikkun* comes.

[42] The author is playing on the similarity in Hebrew of *asiyah*—"action"—and *Esav,* as well as on the indicated connection of Esau with the practical Romans.

[43] In light of the above explanation about "word" and "thing," the English reader may want to consider the effect on the meaning of substituting the equally admissible "word" where I have chosen "thing" and vice versa.

[44] The quotation marks around "Hebrew" are due to the fact that the "Hebrew" translation *taratz* is actually an Aramaic loan-word.

Part VII

Ellen Bernstein with Hannah Ashley, "Cooking Up a Tu B'Shvat Seder"

[1] Ayreh Kaplan

[2] Ayreh Kaplan

[3] Rabbi Nachman of Bratzlav

[4] David Rains Wallace, *The Klamath Knot.*

[5] Adapted from Wendell Berry, *The Gift of the Good Land.*

[6] Aryeh Kaplan, *The Waters of Eden.*

[7] Lao Tzu, *Tao Te Ching.*

[8] Peter Warshall, *The Whole Earth Catalog.*

[9] Shlomo Carlebach.

[10] *Peri Eitz Hadar.*

[11] Lyall Watson, *The Wind.*

[12] Lao Tzu, *Tao Te Ching.*

[13] Ranier Maria Rilke (1899), trans. Robert Bly, *Book for the Hours of Prayer.*

[14] Rav Kook.

[15] Emily Dickinson.

[16] Annie Dillard, *Pilgrim at Tinker Creek.*

[17] Rumi, *Open Secret.*

[18] Rabbi Nachman of Bratzlav.

[19] These blessings are feminist alternatives.

Elisheva Kaufman, "Caring for a Tree of Life"

[1] Martin Buber, *Tales of the Hasidim: Later Masters* (New York: Schocken Books, 1948), p. 220.

Michal Fox Smart, "Getting to the Root of the Tree of Life—Outdoors"

[1] Encyclopedia Judaica, *s.v.* "Animals of the Bible and Talmud."

[2] Steve Copeland, "From Outer Form to Inner Meaning and Back Again: the Metaphoric Imagination in Jewish Learning," in *Studies in Jewish Education,* 4 (1989), p. 83.

Everett Gendler, "Ever Since Eden"

[1] John Pedersen, *Israel: Its Life and Culture,* III–IV, p. 510.

[2] Ibid., III–IV, p. 507.

[3] *Midrash Hagadol,* cited in M. M. Kasher, *Torah Shlemah* (New York: American Biblical Encyclopedia Society, 1944), vol. 4, p. 592, [Hebrew]

[4] Cited in F. Brown, S. R. Driver, C. A. Briggs, *A Hebrew and English Lexicon of the Old Testament,* based on the lexicon of William Gesenius (London: Oxford University Press, 1962), p. 18; ascribed to B. Stade, *Geschichte des Volkes Israel,* p. 455.

[5] Morton Smith, "The Image of God"—Notes on the Hellenization of Judaism, with especial reference to Goodenough's work on Jewish symbols in *Bulletin of the John Rylands Library* (Manchester, England) vol. 40, no. 2, p. 473–512, March 1958.

[6] *Peri Eitz Hadar,* I, 102b.

[7] *Peri Eitz Hadar,* 3a, Livorno edition.

[8] Cedric Wright, *Words of the Earth* (San Francisco, Sierra Club, 1960), pp. 38, 40.

[9] Yehoash, trans. Marie Syrkin in N. and M. Ausubel, *A Treasury of Jewish Poetry* (New York: Crown Publishers, 1957), p. 234.

[10] *Peri Eitz Hadar,* 12a.

[11] Ibid., 2b.

[12] Ibid., 2a.

[13] R. M. Rilke, *"Sonnets to Orpheus"* Part I, Sonnet XIII, in R. M. Rilke, *Selected Works,* Vol II, Poetry, trans. J. B. Leishman (New York: New Directions, 1960).

[14] *Peri Eitz Hadar,* 2a.

[15] Edith Sitwell, *"Harvest and Eurydice."* in Edith Sitwell, *The Collected Poems of Edith Sitwell* (New York: The Vanguard Press, 1954).

CONTRIBUTORS

Ellen Allard and her husband **Peter Allard** are children's performers, songwriters, educators, and recording artists, who live in Worcester, Massachusetts. "The Fifteenth of Shevat" comes from their first Jewish recording, *Sing Shalom: Songs for the Jewish Holidays*.

Gilda Angel, author of *Sephardic Holiday Cooking*, was the food columnist for the New York *Jewish Week* for ten years. She lectures extensively and has published numerous articles on Sephardic culture and cuisine. Mrs. Angel and her husband, Marc, rabbi of the Spanish and Portuguese Synagogue in New York, have three married children.

Hannah Ashley reconstructed Judaism for herself in college through a study group called LENTL (Lesbians Eating-N-Torah Learning). Since then, wherever she resides she has been an active member of a havurah or shul, currently Congregation Mishkan Shalom in Philadelphia. She is the co-author of the memoir *Eight Bullets*.

Fran Avni's recordings for children, CBC *Sesame Street* compositions, and twenty-six cassettes for Tal Selais Hebrew Language Arts curriculum have become standards in schools across North America. With several adult Israeli recording albums to her credit, she presents concerts and workshops internationally.

Ellen Bernstein founded Shomrei Adamah/Keepers of the Earth, the first Jewish environmental organization, and is the editor of *Ecology and the Jewish Spirit*.

Hayim Nachman Bialik (d. 1934) was one of the leading Hebrew poets of the twentieth century. Born in the Ukraine, he moved to Odessa in 1891, where he was drawn to the circle of Ahad Ha'am. In 1921, he left Soviet Russia for Berlin and emigrated to the land of Israel in 1924.

Martin Buber (d. 1965) studied philosophy and art at the universities of Vienna, Zurich, and Berlin. While in his twenties he helped organize the Zionist movement. Buber is best known for his I-Thou philosophy, which emerged from his reinterpretation of Hasidism. From 1938 to 1951, Buber taught philosophy at Hebrew University.

485

Shaul Cohen holds a Ph.D. in geography from the University of Chicago and now works in the geography department at the University of Oregon. He is the author of *The Politics of Planting: Israeli-Palestinian Competition for Control of Land in the Jerusalem Periphery* and researches the politics of land use.

Tsili Doleve-Gandelman is researcher for the NCJW Institute for Innovation in Education at Hebrew University and lecturer at Technion in Haifa, Israel.

Rabbi Howard Eilberg-Schwartz is the author of *The Savage in Judaism*, winner of the 1991 American Academy of Religion Award for Excellence, and other books.

Ari Elon was born in Jerusalem in 1950. For sixteen years, he taught Talmud and Midrash at various institutions throughout Israel. He has been the director of the Rabbinic Texts Program at the Reconstructionist Rabbinical College and is the author of *From Jerusalem to the Edge of Heaven*.

Marcia Falk, poet, translator, and Judaic scholar, is the author of *The Book of Blessings: New Jewish Prayers for Daily Life, the Sabbath, and the New Moon Festival*. She also wrote *The Song of Songs: A New Translation and Interpretation*.

Rabbi Joyce Galaski is a 1998 graduate of the Reconstructionist Rabbinical College and rabbi of Congregation Am Haskalah in Allentown, Pennsylvania. She is a student of medieval Hebrew poetry, a human rights activist, and the mother of three children.

Rabbi Everett Gendler was born in Iowa and served congregations in Mexico, Brazil, and Princeton, New Jersey, before spending nearly twenty-five years as the rabbi at Temple Emanuel, in Lowell, Massachusetts, and nearly twenty years as chaplain and instructor at Phillips Academy, in Andover, Massachussetts. He is an organic gardener and an avid proponent for nonviolence, social justice, peace, and the environment.

Pinchas Giller is a member of the faculty of Washington University, St. Louis.

Rabbi Shefa Gold is a teacher of spiritual leadership and Jewish meditation and a composer and performer of spiritual music. She is a graduate of the Reconstructionist Rabbinical College, has received smicha from Rabbi Zalman Schachter-Shalomi, and is a Pathfinder of ALEPH: Alliance for Jewish Renewal.

A. D. Gordon (d. 1922) was a Zionist philosopher and Hebrew writer and spiritual mentor to the segment of the Zionist labor movement that emphasized settlement on the land as a path toward self-realization.

Joel Lurie Grishaver is a teacher, storyteller, writer, editor, family educator, cartoonist, and itinerant preacher. He has served as a counselor, youth advisor, teacher, camp director, principal, consultant, and professor. He co-owns two publishing companies, Torah Aura Publications and the Alef Design Group, and has written more than sixty books.

Judith Hankin is a printmaker and graphic artist living in Eugene, Oregon. A member of the American Guild of Judaic Art and the Accredited Synagogue Artists of the Union of American Hebrew Congregations, she has exhibited for more than twenty years in numerous solo and group shows across the country.

Rabbi Yosef Hayyim of Baghdad (d. 1909) known by the name of his most famous work, *Ben Ish Hai*, authored more than twenty-four published works on halakhah and Kabbalah. Although he was the recognized leader of the Jewish community of Baghdad, he refused all official titles or positions.

Rabbi Yitzhak Husbands-Hankin serves Temple Beth Israel in Eugene, Oregon. He is a composer and performer of Jewish music, a cellist, guitarist, and vocalist.

Naomi Mara Hyman is the editor of *Biblical Women in the Midrash* and a student in the Professional Development (Smicha) Program of ALEPH: Alliance for Jewish Renewal.

Ivan Ickovits, a child of Holocaust survivors, was born in Hungary and grew up in Israel, Canada, and Los Angeles. He has worked as a physicist and aerospace engineer. He studied with Rabbi Zalman Schachter-Shalomi and Rabbi Jonathan Omer-man and teaches classes and seminars in meditation, Hasidut, and Kabbalah.

Elisheva Kaufman works in Israel facilitating ecological agriculture, sustainable food systems, and Jewish renewal. She teaches composting in Jerusalem with the Society for the Preservation of Nature in Israel (SPNI) and at the Jerusalem Ecology Farm, an urban farm center for composting, organic gardening, and ecological action.

Rabbi Miles Krassen is associate professor of religion and director of the Jewish Studies Program at Oberlin College. His publications include *Isaiah Horowitz: The Generations of Adam* and *Uniter of Heaven and Earth: Rabbi Meshullam Feibush of Zbarazh and the Origins of Hasidism in Eastern Galicia.*

Rabbi Norman Lamm is president of Yeshiva University, New York. He was born in Brooklyn, New York, and was ordained by the Rabbi Isaac Elchanan Theological Seminary. He founded and was first editor of *Tradition,* a journal of Orthodox Jewish thought, and he is a prolific writer, interpreting Orthodox thought on contemporary problems.

Rabbi Gil Marks, a chef, writer, and historian, is a leading expert in the field of Jewish cookery. The founding editor of *Kosher Gourmet* magazine, Marks lectures frequently on Jewish cooking. He lives in New York City.

Rabbi Nachman of Bratslav (d. 1811) was a hasidic tzaddik in Podolia and the Ukraine and at the center of a theological and social storm throughout most of his life. On his mother's side he was the great-grandson of Israel b. Eliezer, the Ba'al Shem Tov.

Jackie Olenick, a Judaic artist specializing in paper collage, creates a spirited collection of Judaic illuminations and bright, upbeat Jewish and feminist T-shirts. She is inspired by Torah text and her four grandchildren. She lives in Miami with her husband, Leon.

Marge Piercy is the author of more than a dozen novels, including *Woman on the Edge of Time, Gone to Soldiers,* and *He, She and It,* and more than a dozen collections of poetry, including *Mars and Her Children, The Moon Is Always Female,* and *Available Light.*

Alix Pirani, M.A., practices humanistic and transpersonal psychotherapy in Great Britain and conducts workshops and seminars exploring spiritual mythology and creative process. She has published extensively, and her many theoretical and imaginative works include *The Absent Father: Crisis and Creativity* and *The Absent Mother: Restoring the Goddess to Judaism and Christianity.*

Rabbi G. Rayzel Raphael is a graduate of the Rabbinical College and also studied at Indiana University and the Hebrew University. She is Rabbi of Leyv Ha-Ir Reconstructionist Congregation in Philadelphia. A songwriter/liturgist, she sings with MIRAJ, an acappella trio. *Bible Babes A-beltin'* is her latest recording.

Yehoshua Hana Ravnitsky (d. 1944) was a pioneer of modern Hebrew journalism and publishing. A native of Odessa, he became Bialik's closest collaborator. Together they founded the publishing house of Moriah, which brought forth the first edition of *Sefer Ha-Aggadah* in 1908–1911. Ravnitzky settled in Tel Aviv in 1921, where he and Bialik founded the Dvir Publishing House.

Rabbi Zalman Schachter-Shalomi was ordained as a Lubavitch-trained rabbi and has received his M.A. in psychology from Boston University and a Ph.D. from Hebrew Union College. He holds the Chair of World Wisdom at Naropa Institute, is a Pathfinder for ALEPH: Alliance for Jewish Renewal, and has published more than 175 articles, translations, and books.

Gershom Scholem (d. 1982) was the leading authority in the field of Kabbalah and Jewish mysticism. His works in English include *Major Trends in Jewish Mysticism* and *The Messianic Idea in Judaism*.

Rabbi Ismar Schorsch is chancellor of the Jewish Theological Seminary.

Eilon Schwartz directs the Heschel Center for Environmental Learning and Leadership, dedicated to the fostering of an emerging social-environmental vision for Israeli society. He also teaches at the Melton Centre for Jewish Education of the Hebrew University and writes on the philosophy of environmental and Jewish education.

Howard Schwartz is professor of English at the University of Missouri-St. Louis. He has published several books of poetry and fiction and edited many volumes of Jewish folktales, including *Miriam's Tambourine: Jewish Folktales from Around the World; Lilith's Cave: Jewish Tales of the Supernatural;* and *Gabriel's Palace: Jewish Mystical Tales*.

Rabbi Jeremy Schwartz, a graduate of the Reconstructionist Rabbinical College, is assistant director of Kolel: A Centre for Liberal Jewish Learning. His broad areas of teaching include liturgy, Hebrew poetry, and the search for Jewish economics. Rabbi Schwartz lives in Toronto with his wife, Merle Potchinsky, and their daughter Arielle.

Richard H. Schwartz, Ph.D., is a professor of mathematics at the College of Staten Island. He is the author of the books *Judaism and Vegetarianism, Judaism and Global Survival,* and *Mathematics and*

Global Survival. He frequently speaks and writes on the connections between Judaism, the environment, and dietary issues.

Rabbi David Mevorach Seidenberg is rabbi of Congregation Emanu-El in Victoria, British Columbia, and is a graduate of Jewish Theological Seminary, where he is completing his Ph.D. He is the founder of hasidic egalitarian minyanim in Los Angeles and New York and past president of the Alliance for Judaism and Social Justice in New York.

Rabbi Hayyim Elazar Shapira (d. 1937) was rabbi of Munkacs, Hungary, from 1913 until his death in 1937 and was a hasidic tzaddik. He succeeded in combining talmudic dialectics with the ability to reach halakhic decisions and had a wide knowledge of Kabbalah and hasidic learning.

Rabbi Tzvi Elimelekh Shapira (d. 1841) was a hasidic tzaddik in Dynow, Galicia, often known for his major work, *B'nei Yissachar* (Zolkiew, 1850). He was devoted to Kabbalah as the essence of Judaism.

Rabbi Rami M. Shapiro serves the Miami congregation Beth Or. He is also president of Simply Jewish.com, a consulting firm for Jewish leaders (www.simplyjewish.com), and director of the Virtual Yeshiva, an on-line resource for Jewish spirituality at www.rasheit.org. His most recent book is *Minyan, 10 Principles for Living Life with Integrity*.

Tova Shimon is the director of curriculum development for The Jewish Education Council of Federation CJA.

Cantor David Shneyer directs Am Kolel, a Jewish resource and renewal center based in Rockville, Maryland. An educator and a social and environmental activist for more than twenty-five years, David edited the first makhzor printed on 100-percent recycled paper. His band, the Fabrangen Fiddlers, is known for original and traditional folk music.

Hanna Tiferet Siegel is a singer/songwriter and spiritual guide whose soul music of earth and heaven is sung in homes and communities around the world.

Susan Goldstein Singer, M.Ed., is a holistic psychotherapist and dream analyst in private practice in Philadelphia. As a cancer survivor, she finds new richness in Jewish ritual practices, the healing potential of dreams, and her work as a para-chaplain. Susan frequently lectures on dreams, healing, and Judaism.

Michal Smart pioneered Jewish environmental education, serving as COEJL's Director of Education, chair of the CAJE Environmental Education Network, and executive director of Camp Isabella Freedman. A Fulbright scholar in Jewish thought, Michal received her B.A. from Princeton University and an M.S. in Natural Resources from Cornell University as a Wexner Fellow.

Howard M. Solomon is professor of History at Tufts University.

Rabbi Margot Stein is a musician/liturgist who directs New Legends, a nonprofit organization dedicated to Jewish education through the arts. Her award-winning musical, *Guarding the Garden*, toured North America and was seen by some 25,000 people. She also sings and records with the a cappella trio, MIRAJ.

Naomi Steinberg has served since 1995 as student rabbi for B'nai Ha-Aretz in rural northern California, where she organized Tu B'Shvat in the Redwoods in 1997. A storyteller, folksinger, and songwriter, Naomi has performed with Noah's Dove and the Jewish Wedding Band.

Malka Heifetz Tussman (d. 1987), a Yiddish-American writer, published six volumes of poetry during her lifetime.

Rabbi Arthur Waskow is a Pathfinder of ALEPH: Alliance for Jewish Renewal, director of The Shalom Center, and author of *Down-to-Earth Judaism, Godwrestling—Round 2*, and *Seasons of Our Joy*, and co-author of *Tales of Tikkun: New Jewish Stories to Heal the Wounded World*.

Rabbi Aryeh Wineman is a literary scholar, author, and rabbi of Temple Beth El in Troy, New York. He is a graduate of Washington University and of the Jewish Theological Seminary. He holds a Ph.D. in Hebrew Literature from the University of California at Los Angeles.

Jonathan Wolf is director of the West Side Center for Jewish Life in New York and was founding president of the Jewish Vegetarians of North America. One of the leaders in the revival of the Tu B'Shvat seder, he has conducted seders for twenty-three years in homes, synagogues, and campuses.

Rabbi David Wolfe-Blank (d. 1998) received Lubavitch ordination, sat in a Zen center, worked with body-based therapists, and received an M.A. in Somatic Psychology. He is the creator of the *Meta-Siddur* and the *Meta-Parshiot*. His goal was to improve Jewish spiritual life through experimentation in davenen to deepen our soul connection with Torah.

Zelda (d. 1984) was an Israeli poet, born in Chernigov, Ukraine. Her poems, rooted in the traditional Jewish world, bore a completely modern sensibility. She was the recipient of a number of literary prizes, including the Bialik Prize for Literature in 1978.

Yael Zerubavel is professor of history and director of The Center for the Study of Jewish Life at Rutgers: The State University of New Jersey.